POVERTY IN AMERICA

Chandler Publications in

POLITICAL SCIENCE

VICTOR JONES, *Editor*

POVERTY IN AMERICA

Proceedings of a national conference held at the University of California, Berkeley, February 26–28, 1965

Edited by MARGARET S. GORDON

Published for the Institute of Industrial Relations
University of California, Berkeley

CHANDLER PUBLISHING COMPANY
124 Spear Street, San Francisco, California 94105

LIBRARY OF CONGRESS CATALOG CARD NO. 65–23477

PRINTED IN THE UNITED STATES OF AMERICA

Contents

List of Contributors

William L. Batt, Jr.
  Administrator, Area Redevelopment Administration, U. S. Department of Commerce, Washington, D. C.

Edgar S. Cahn
  Office of Economic Opportunity, Washington, D. C.

Jean Camper Cahn
  Consultant on Law and Poverty to the Office of Economic Opportunity, Washington, D. C.

Nathan E. Cohen
  Professor of Social Welfare, University of California, Los Angeles

Kingsley Davis
  Professor of Sociology, University of California, Berkeley

Frank L. Fernbach
  Research Economist, American Federation of Labor and Congress of Industrial Organizations, Washington, D. C.

Marion B. Folsom
  Director, Eastman Kodak Company, Rochester, New York

Varden Fuller
  Professor of Agricultural Economics, University of California, Berkeley

Nathan Glazer
  Professor of Sociology, University of California, Berkeley

Margaret S. Gordon
  Associate Director, Institute of Industrial Relations, University of California, Berkeley

R. A. Gordon
  Professor of Economics, University of California, Berkeley

WILLIAM HABER
Dean, College of Literature, Science, and the Arts, University of Michigan, Ann Arbor

A. H. HALSEY
Director, Department of Sociology and Administrative Studies, Oxford University, England

FREDERICK HARBISON
Director, Industrial Relations Section, Princeton University

MICHAEL HARRINGTON
National Chairman, League for Industrial Democracy

PHILIP M. HAUSER
Professor of Sociology, University of Chicago

RAYMOND M. HILLIARD
Director, Department of Public Aid, Cook County, Illinois

PAUL JACOBS
The Fund for the Republic, Inc.

FRANCIS KEPPEL
Commissioner of Education, U. S. Department of Health, Education, and Welfare, Washington, D. C.

JOSEPH A. KERSHAW
Provost, Williams College, Williamstown, Massachusetts

ROBERT J. LAMPMAN
Professor of Economics, University of Wisconsin

SAR A. LEVITAN
Consultant, The W. E. Upjohn Institute for Employment Research, Washington, D. C.

BERNARD E. LOSHBOUGH
Executive Director, ACTION Housing, Inc., Pittsburgh

FRITZ MACHLUP
Professor of Economics, Princeton University, and President-Elect, American Economics Association

Herman P. Miller
Research Economist, Institute of Government and Public Affairs, University of California, Los Angeles, and U. S. Bureau of the Census, Washington, D. C.

Hyman P. Minsky
Associate Professor of Economics, University of California, Berkeley

Daniel P. Moynihan
Assistant Secretary, U. S. Department of Labor, Washington, D. C.

Gunnar Myrdal
Director, Institute of International Economic Studies, Stockholm, Sweden

Gösta Rehn
Director for Manpower and Social Affairs, Organization for Economic Cooperation and Development, Paris

Frank Riessman
Mental Health Services, Albert Einstein College of Medicine, Yeshiva University, New York

Charles I. Schottland
Dean, School of Social Welfare, Brandeis University

Herman M. Somers
Professor of Politics and Public Affairs, Princeton University

Neil V. Sullivan
Superintendent of Schools, Berkeley, California

Lloyd Ulman
Director, Institute of Industrial Relations, University of California, Berkeley

Robert C. Weaver
Administrator, U. S. Housing and Home Finance Agency, Washington, D. C.

Mary B. Wirth
Social Work Consultant

Preface

In editing the papers in the present volume, no attempt has been made to take account of legislative enactments and other developments since the conference was held on the Berkeley campus at the end of February, 1965. Congress has acted on a number of important measures discussed by the contributors, and no doubt will act on others before the end of the present session. But any attempt to take account of all these developments would have interfered with prompt publication of the volume, which seemed highly desirable in view of its potential usefulness to scholars and to policy-makers at the federal, state, and local levels.

I should like to express my very great gratitude to my secretary, Mrs. Barbara Palmer, who has lived with the poverty conference since the plans were first initiated in February, 1964, and who has been responsible for the final typing of all the papers.

MARGARET S. GORDON

Berkeley, California
July, 1965

Foreword

LLOYD ULMAN

This volume is a collection of essays which were prepared for a Conference on Poverty in America held on the Berkeley campus of the University of California. The primary purpose of the conference was to discuss the effectiveness of a variety of proposed and existing policies for the reduction of poverty. The participants were accordingly drawn from federal, state, and local government and other nonacademic areas as well as from assorted campuses; and they included economists, sociologists, social workers, psychologists, political scientists, part-time journalists, and full-time radical critics of contemporary society. These papers reflect the diversity of backgrounds and points of view represented at the conference, and they also reflect agreement on the need to employ an arsenal of diverse weapons in the war against poverty. This agreement is not the outcome of sociable log rolling nor of perfunctory caution on the part of the experts involved. On the contrary, it reflects dissatisfaction with the present state of most of the institutions and arts which came under scrutiny. And it also resulted from analysis of the complex nature of the problem itself, together with constraints imposed on the employment or modification of policy instruments by pre-existing policy objectives or traditional national values.

One highly relevant characteristic of the American poverty problem is the magnitude of the problem and its direction of change. According to data cited by Miller, about 34.5 million people, or 18 per cent of the total population, were in families "with incomes insufficient to purchase an adequate budget" in 1963. The amount by which the income of these people falls short of $3,000 per family (what Lampman terms the "poverty gap") totals $12 billion. Now these magnitudes are not unimpressive; but neither are they daunting. The $12 billion figure is less than the annual average increase in gross national product in the postwar period (about $16 billion in 1964 prices); it represents about 2 per cent of GNP; and it is far less than the gap between potential and actual GNP ($27 billion in 1964). Moreover, the gap, whether measured in dollars or as a proportion of the population, has been shrinking over the years, even when allowance is made for a secular rise in the "poverty line."

These findings bear at least two implications for public policy. In the first place, they have been widely—but not unanimously—interpreted as indicating that the winds of history are favorable; and nothing is more important to reformers—from Karl Marx to Everett McKinley Dirksen—than the conviction that the odds strongly favor success. There has been much speculation, in these pages and elsewhere, as to why the wealthiest of nations has apparently elected to concentrate much of its political energy on the problem of poverty; one reason is simply that most of us believe that, for the first time, the prospects for success are favorable, while the problem remains large and ugly enough to arouse a significant portion of the body politic and to challenge the remainder.

The second policy implication is, on superficial inspection, paradoxical. One might expect that the reduction of poverty to politically manageable size would militate in favor of the adoption of a single policy line, perhaps after spirited competition among rival claimants—to the monopoly position. An analogy might be found in the more exuberant manifestations of the recent controversy between the proponents of the "aggregate demand" and the "structuralist" theories of unemployment. But a similar situation is not likely to arise in connection with the evolution of anti-poverty policies. For one thing, poverty appears to be a phenomenon whose economic heterogeneity varies inversely with its magnitude. Thus the Council of Economic Advisers, in its January 1964 Report, noted that, as the incidence of poverty (defined as family income under $3,000 in 1962 prices) declined in the postwar period, the proportion of poor families with the following characteristics rose: family head 65 years of age and over, female family head, no wage earners, nonwhite. To be sure, this effect is reduced if we allow for a rising poverty line; according to Miller, "As the poverty line is moved closer to the middle of the distribution, there is a greater tendency to include average families rather than those with special characteristics." But if it is true that the poverty line does not rise as rapidly as national income, then the poverty group will become increasingly heterogeneous. It will consist to an increasing degree of families outside the labor market and of families with very high birth rates. As R. A. Gordon—a leading exponent of the aggregate demand approach to the unemployment problem—puts it, "Today's poverty problem is largely structural in character. It is the kind of poverty that feeds on itself."

This implies that, if we wish to speed up the rate of reduction in poverty, we will have to accelerate the rate of economic growth by present methods or we will have to rely to an increasing degree on developing or improving other policy instruments. Among those under current discussion only subsidy could be generally applicable (and, as Machlup points out, only cash subsidy could also be restricted to the benefit of the poor). In fact subsidy is in principle more general in scope than policies designed to promote general economic growth. The other major policy categories—income maintenance, training and education, and geographic development—are all limited in scope. Thus, granting the improvements in the social insurances urged in these pages—e.g., increased levels and duration of benefits, wider coverage, higher tax bases, and even Margaret Gordon's qualified suggestion for contributions out of general revenues—would not transform their historic and primary missions of relating eligibility to labor force participation and benefit payments directly (although not proportionately) to past wage income. Similarly, even a reorientation of fiscal policy, as proposed by Minsky, to provide "tight full employment" and concentrate on public spending directly on jobs for which the unskilled poor would be suitable would be of uncertain benefit to the 40 per cent of the poor families without a head in the labor market.

Of course, the structural aspects of the poverty problem do not imply that benefits derived from efficient application of well designed policies to particular subsets of the poor will be restricted to the areas of injection or, to generalize the point, that the effectiveness of a given policy will not depend on the existence and effectiveness of other policies. The dependence of vocational education, manpower training, and rehabilitation of welfare recipients on full employment furnishes an obvious example; first, because an unemployed trainee's diploma must be a job offer (R. A. Gordon), second, because training is most effective when the trainee is already employed and free from economic insecurity (Rehn), and again because employment status itself enhances the employability of the individual (Batt). Similarly, Keppel and Hilliard underscore the dependence of adult training programs on general education (to eliminate illiteracy). And effective education of impoverished children (who comprise a shockingly high percentage of the young) requires not only provision of in-school subsidies in kind (Sullivan) but also help to adults in order to induce them more effectively to limit the numbers of children born to the poor (Davis).

These are but a few examples of the interdependence among different policy instruments which are suggested to the reader of this volume, but I should like to refer to one additional example, because it concerns an area of policy which has proved troublesome to lawmakers and academics alike. The problem concerns the role of minimum wages, and the old controversy is reflected in two of the essays: Fernbach urges that they be raised to provide above-poverty incomes to low-wage employees, while Machlup claims that they should be abolished in order to provide more jobs for the poor who are unemployed. The latter feels that the effectiveness of collective bargaining (and unilateral employer wage policies) in raising the wages of the more highly paid employees has, by sealing off employment opportunities in the high-wage industries, made it more imperative to remove the floor to wages in the low-wage industries. One might agree with this analysis of the wage structure but argue that the existence of private constraints calls for a policy aimed at narrowing the spread rather than further increasing it. Thus Minsky would join Fernbach in raising the minimum wage, but only if a policy of full employment failed to result in greater increases in low wages (above minimum levels) than in high wages. In other words, if a minimum-wage policy is combined with a vigorous aggregate demand policy, the dilemma of benefitting some poor by hurting other poor is largely avoided. The adverse effects presumably appear in the form of price inflation, which is borne by the entire community, including workers working at minimum wages and workers working at building trades wages.

As suggested above, our choice of anti-poverty policies is influenced by other national objectives and values as well as by the nature of the phenomenon itself. In some instances, such influence has been stimulating; in others, it has assumed the form of constraint. The discussions of urban renewal (Weaver, Hauser and Wirth) afford a good example of how national policy in a different area not only stimulated public concern over poverty ("urban renewal lifted the edge of the rug"), but became partially transformed itself in the process.

Some of the Kennedy-Johnson Administration's successes and frustrations in the area of broad national economic policy furnished a stimulus to the drive against poverty and at the same time constrained the program in its employment of policy instruments. The Administration succeeded brilliantly in devising an expansionary fiscal-monetary policy in the face of ingrained economic superstition among the citizenry at large and the business and financial communities in particular, and of an adverse balance of payments. The trick was turned by tax cuts in which corporations and individuals in the higher income brackets shared generously as well as by liberalized depreciation allowances. The upswing (which began early in 1961) was nourished and sustained by these measures; and the poor shared in the general prosperity, for, as the Council of Economic Advisers noted in its 1965 Annual Report, the number of families below the $3,000 poverty line declined by 300,000 in 1963 alone. On the other hand, the "interim" unemployment target of four per cent (excessively modest by international standards) was not attained. Under these political and economic circumstances, the liberal economists in the Administration were happy to urge the adoption of a broad program which would be designed to benefit the poor directly; and a Council which stoutly defended the virtues of broad fiscal policy in reducing unemployment against structuralist skeptics dwelled upon the limitations as well as the efficacy of "growth" in alleviating poverty. But whether the Administration will accord the antipoverty objective equal status with its other objectives—strengthening the goal of full employment and operating as a constraint on balance-of-payments and possibly price stability policies—remains to be seen.

The program was also stimulated and shaped by the traditional national aversion to the implications and practice of poor relief. Reaction by liberal opinion had been decisive in the adoption of unemployment and old-age insurance in the 1930's, whereas distrust by conservatives of local "giveaway" programs reached a postwar peak only a few years ago. This probably means that recourse to education and training measures will be increasingly encouraged as "investment in human capital" designed to pay off in increased opportunity to the poor individual, whom the American community now believes and insists will be assimilated into its mainstream as successfully as past generations of immigrants. (The essays of Kershaw, Glazer, and Halsey are particularly relevant to this issue.)

By the same token definite limitations will be set on the scope of any subsidy system, which does belong to the "assistance family" and whose putative adverse effects on work incentives, while probably not of great magnitude, assume increased importance in the context of an effort to motivate and train the poor. In addition, the concept of a variable as opposed to a fixed standard of poverty income derives support from the general refusal to regard the poor as intrinsically or potentially inferior to or different from the successful majority and hence to regard poverty as necessarily a permanent phenomenon. Given this assumption, a rising standard of poverty may be justified not on grounds of compassion alone but as a necessary condition for the success of the investment approach. The argument was not new in this century; it was well put by Alfred Marshall who wrote that

> . . . the income of any class in the ranks of industry is below its *necessary* level when any increase in their income would in the course of time produce a more than proportionate increase in their efficiency. . . .
>
> In addition, perhaps, some consumption of alcohol and tobacco, and some indulgence in fashionable dress are in many places so habitual, that they may be said to be conventionally necessary, since in order to obtain them the average man and woman will sacrifice some things which are necessary for efficiency. Their wages are therefore less than are practically necessary for efficiency, unless they provide not only for what is strictly necessary consumption, but include also a certain amount of conventional necessaries.

Fear of automation has been cited as an anti-poverty stimulant in a number of these essays; according to Moynihan, "it is at least possible that some of the things that have been producing prosperity have also been producing poverty." It is understandable why this apprehension should arouse public interest in a program to eliminate poverty, for it suggests that the forces making for a declining trend will be—or indeed have been—overwhelmed by forces designed to throw many more Americans into poverty unless strong governmental action is taken. The specific policy implications are literally radical, as Harrington maintains: neither measures designed to promote economic growth through fiscal-monetary policy, nor improvement of the social insurances which are primarily designed to maintain income earned in the labor markets, nor education and training designed to increase labor efficiency can be regarded as specifics against poverty in an economy in which human labor has ceased to be an economic resource, with one possible exception. The exception would appear to be a program of cash subsidies to the poor, for this instrument is indeed a mechanism for divorcing personal income from labor. This desideratum, incidentally, is shared with many traditional economists who oppose any schemes of income supplementation which would tamper with market prices; it is interesting that the negative income tax is strongly championed by Professor Milton Friedman, who regards himself as a "radical liberal."

However, Harrington and his fellow Triple Revolutionaries insist on a genuinely radical approach to work and leisure. If their analysis and prognosis are correct, then the view that the community can "afford" to tackle poverty—in the sense that the cost will be low, not only in terms of reallocation of material resources, but also in terms of the dislocation of preexisting social policies and institutions—is wrong. The underlying economic argument has received some support from economists associated with the "structuralist" side in the controversy over contemporary unemployment. However, most economists would hold that the possibility mentioned by Moynihan—of the rate of increase in productivity outrunning the rate of increase in the development of new wants (which furnishes justification for a moving poverty standard)—is not a probability. The prevailing view is stated in Myrdal's essay, in which he also notes that automation has been a boon rather than a bugbear in Europe and no obstacle to the achievement of full employment. This interpretation of the impact of automation, incidentally, is consistent with his optimistic assessment on the potentialities for enlisting the cooperation of "big business"—an assessment in which Folsom's interesting remarks on the pre-depression evolution in big business thinking would lead him to concur. In 1952 it was said that Harry Truman ran out of poor people; in 1965 Lyndon Johnson is running after them, hopefully accompanied by a great consensus among the fortunate majorities.

The relationship between anti-poverty policy and the Civil Rights Movement has naturally been commented on by many of the contributors to this volume. The relationship is characterized by a high degree of mutual dependence. If it is true that poverty has been reduced in scale to politically feasible proportions, by the same token the problem is in danger of generating insufficient political thrust. The Civil Rights Movement supplies political thrust, and, as this movement increasingly involves itself with economic concerns, it will lend increasingly strong support to the anti-poverty program. In the process it will also influence the nature of the community action programs established under the Economic Opportunity Act. Provision for these programs is consistent with the law's Declaration of Purpose which finds it desirable that "every individual (have) the opportunity to contribute to the full extent of his capabilities and to participate in the workings of our society."

Various contributors present different reasons for participation by the poor in local antipoverty programs: to provide information concerning their own needs (E. S. Cahn); to overcome the inertia of local welfare bureaucracies (Glazer); to exert pressure on local political administrations (Loshbough); to develop native and unspoiled leadership (Riessman); to overcome political inertia, reduce the danger of creating a dependent and apathetic "under class," and thereafter to encourage the "challenging of existing institutions" (Cohen, Riessman, Jacobs).

Fuller, on the other hand, points to the failure of attempts to institutionalize challenge to the power structure under the Farm Security Administration and Local Land Use Planning in the New Deal period; and Moynihan warns against overreliance on an approach which relies on impetus from an isolated outgroup. This point of view will, I suspect, be validated by the future experience of the Civil Rights Movement which, in order to develop maximum political effectiveness, will reach out from the enclaves of black poverty for support by and cooperation with other groups in the community. The support by the NAACP of the trade-union-sponsored amendment to the Taft-Hartley Act which would nullify state "right-to-work" laws is an interesting example of widening political horizons at the national level, especially in view of frequent instances of friction and criticism by Negro groups of restrictive union policies at the local level. For more effective cooperation between the trade union movement and civil rights groups at the local level—especially in the area of work training—more vigorous full employment policies are probably required. These, in turn, would require close political cooperation between the national movements.

* * * *

The diversity of backgrounds and points of view represented

in this book was also reflected in planning for the Berkeley Conference on Poverty in America out of which it arose. The conference was sponsored by the Center for the Study of Law and Society, Department of Economics, Department of Political Science, Institute of Governmental Studies, Institute of Industrial Relations, School of Law, School of Social Welfare, and University Extension. Included on the Planning Committee were Milton Chernin, Dean, School of Social Welfare; Varden Fuller, Professor of Agricultural Economics; Margaret Gordon, Associate Director, Institute of Industrial Relations; Morton Gordon, Director, University Extension; Eugene Lee, Vice President-Executive Assistant; Davis McEntire, Professor of Social Welfare; Dwight Waldo, Director, Institute of Governmental Studies; Harold L. Wilensky, Professor of Sociology; and this writer. The latter can testify to the industry and devotion of his colleagues. He speaks for them in acknowledging with gratitude the exceptionally effective contributions made by Grant Barnes of University Extension and John K. Hislop of the Institute of Industrial Relations to the planning and running of the conference. Finally, it is the consensus of our small society that the major element in the success of the enterprise consisted of the effort, imagination, and leadership imparted by the editor of this volume.

POVERTY IN AMERICA

PART ONE

POVERTY IN THE UNITED STATES

1. An Economist's View of Poverty

R. A. GORDON

I think it is fair to say that the outstanding fact about the problem of poverty in the United States today is our increased sensitivity to it. There is nothing new about poverty; it has always been with us. And by almost any criterion, there is less of it now than there was 25 or 50 or 100 years ago. But, as it has been well put in an article that appeared only last month:

> A revolution of expectations has taken place in this country as well as abroad. . . . The legacy of poverty awaiting many of our children is the same that has been handed down to their parents, but in a time when the boon of prosperity is more general the taste of poverty is more bitter.[1]

Poverty in the midst of affluence—it is the growing sharpness of this contrast that disturbs us. With an eloquence that I can only envy, Michael Harrington, one of the participants in this morning's program, made us newly aware of this contrast in his moving descriptions of *The Other America.* And another distinguished guest at this conference, Gunnar Myrdal, has also recently challenged the conscience of our affluent society and pled with us to remove the poverty, discrimination, and lack of opportunity still in our midst.[2]

This challenge has been taken up by the federal administration, by the Congress, and, with varying degrees of enthusiasm, by the American people. And this, in essence, is why we are here.

---

[1] Mollie Orshansky, "Counting the Poor: Another Look at the Poverty Profile," *Social Security Bulletin,* XXVIII (January, 1965), p. 3.

[2] Gunnar Myrdal, *Challenge to Affluence* (New York: Pantheon Books, 1963).

WHAT IS POVERTY?

It is usually a good idea to begin at the beginning. The beginning in this case involves knowing what we are talking about. What, then, do we mean by poverty?

What we have meant by poverty seems to have changed over the decades. It is fair to say that, as income per capita has risen through the nineteenth and twentieth centuries, our estimate of the level of income which divides poverty from nonpoverty has also risen. The figure of $3,000 per year for family income ($1,500 for a single individual) has had wide currency in the last year or two, in part because it was used by the Council of Economic Advisers in the January, 1964, *Economic Report of the President.* But not so long ago, at the beginning of the 1950's, a "poverty line" of $2,000 was being used. In terms of the 1962 prices used by the Council of Economic Advisers, this would amount to an income of $2,300–$2,500 a year, depending on the particular year from which we chose to measure the rise in prices which has occurred. Thus, just during the last dozen years or so, we seem to have raised the "poverty line" by some 20 to 30 per cent, after allowance for the rise in the cost of living during this period.

This process of raising our sights did not begin with the end of World War II. It has been going on for a long time—probably as long as we have been aware that the lot of the average man was improving, as long, that is, as income per capita has been rising.

It is hopeless to try to trace back into the nineteenth century this gradual raising of our sights as to what constitutes poverty. The relevant evidence diminishes with distressing rapidity as we move back into the early decades of this century. Much of the relevant information that is readily available has been brought together by Dr. Herman Miller in his excellent paper for this conference.

We can begin with Robert Hunter's book, *Poverty* (a starkly simple title), which was first published in 1904. Hunter rejects various suggestions which, around the turn of the century, would have drawn the poverty line somewhere in the range of $520–

$750 per year for working-class families in Eastern cities. Instead Hunter used a figure of $460 for an average family with three children. Prices have approximately trebled since he wrote, and, in terms of comparable purchasing power, Hunter's "poverty line" would come to something like $1,400 today—less than half the $3,000 figure currently being used. With appropriate adjustment for the rise in prices, it would have amounted to a bit more than half the $2,000 figure being used at the beginning of the 1950's.

Dr. Miller cites some further interesting estimates taken from studies by Ruth Mack and Eugene Smolensky. While the figures are obviously quite rough, they suggest a rise in the "poverty line" of perhaps from 40 to 75 per cent between 1935 and 1960. In the same quarter century, real disposable income per capita increased by about 85 per cent.

It is clear that we are steadily raising our sights as to the minimum income needed to keep a family from sinking into poverty. But to say this is not to give us a definition of poverty. The Council of Economic Advisers offers the following definition: "By the poor we mean those who are not now maintaining a decent standard of living—those whose basic needs exceed their means to satisfy them." [3] The Council goes on to recognize that these "basic needs" depend on many factors and are not the same for all families, although the Council winds up using the single standard of $3,000 per family. The Department of Health, Education, and Welfare has just published a more flexible standard which takes account of some of the more obvious differences in need—for example, depending on size of family, location, and sex of the head of the family. These minimum family budgets range from a little over $1,100 for a farm family of two, aged 65 and over, to about $5,000 for a nonfarm family of seven or more persons.[4]

What is particularly striking is that this flexible poverty line yields substantially the same estimate of the number of needy persons in 1963 (34.6 million) as did the single standard ap-

---

[3] *Economic Report of the President,* January, 1964, p. 57.

[4] See Orshansky, *op. cit.,* pp. 3–29. The specific poverty income criteria for different types of families are listed on p. 28.

plied by the Council of Economic Advisers (33.4 million). But there are significant differences in the composition of the poverty group according to the two estimates. In particular, the flexible standard gives lower estimates of the number of rural and aged poor and substantially increases the estimated number of children in the poverty group.

Whichever of these methods of estimation we use, we come up with the bald fact that nearly a fifth of the American population is poverty stricken by the standards that we are inclined to use today, however much higher these standards may be than those which our parents or grandparents might have used.[5] It is today's standards that lead to action today—whether the action is holding such a conference as this or the successful drive to secure the passage of the Economic Opportunity Act.

How Much Has Poverty Declined?

It is clear that the extent, or incidence, of poverty in the United States has declined since, say, the 1920's. But it is not easy to say just how much improvement there has been. Not surprisingly, the answers we get depend on the yardstick that we use.

First of all, do we use a fixed poverty line, that does not vary over the years (except to allow for changes in the cost of living), or do we let the poverty line rise with our rising standards? If incomes generally are rising, obviously we shall get a larger decline in the incidence of poverty if we use an invariant poverty line than if we let the poverty standard itself rise. Ruth Mack's figures are extremely interesting in this connection.[6] Using her "average poverty line" and letting this line rise over the years, we find that the incidence of poverty among families is almost cut in half between 1929 and 1960 (with most of the improvement coming before 1950). If we keep the poverty

[5] For a further discussion of where to draw the poverty line, and a higher estimate of the number under this line than those cited here, see the appendix in Michael Harrington, *The Other America: Poverty in the United States* (New York: Macmillan, 1963).

[6] As yet unpublished. Cited in Herman Miller's paper for this conference.

line fixed at its 1960 level, the decline in the percentage of families in the poverty group is much greater—a decline of about 70 per cent compared to a bit less than half with a rising poverty line.

The answers we get when we try to measure the decline in poverty also depend on how high or low we set the poverty line. If we set a low poverty line, even if we then let it rise as incomes generally increase, we tend to get a larger decline in the incidence of poverty than if we use a relatively high (and rising) poverty line. Thus, using Mrs. Mack's low poverty line (which rises to a family income of only $2,400 in 1960), we find that the percentage of families below this line fell from 26 per cent in 1929 to 10 per cent in 1960. This represents more than a 60-per-cent reduction in the incidence of poverty. If we use a higher poverty line (rising to about $3,800 in 1960), the percentage of the families below this line falls from 40 to 21 per cent over the same period. Here the decline in the incidence of poverty is a little less than 50 per cent.

This result is largely due to the fact that as incomes generally rise, our standard of a bare minimum of existence is likely to rise less rapidly than our standard of, say, a minimum of decency. Thus the higher of the two poverty lines just cited (which came to $3,800 in 1960) rose by about 50 per cent between 1929 and 1960, while the lower line rose only about half as fast.[7] Hence, as incomes generally rose—among the lowest as well as among the higher income groups—it was easier to rise above the lower poverty line than to move above the more rapidly rising higher line.

In other words, there is no single answer to the question: How much has poverty been reduced—since 1947 or since some earlier date. The available evidence suggests that, after an obvious and tragic widening of the circle of poverty in the early years of the Great Depression, poverty rapidly diminished from the mid-thirties to the end of the war. This was the period during which we made our most rapid gains. The inci-

[7] The war seems to have disturbed this relationship. According to Mrs. Mack's figures, the lower line rose relatively more rapidly than the higher one between 1941 and 1950.

dence of poverty continued to decline during the postwar years. If we use the fixed standard of the Council of Economic Advisers, the incidence of poverty dropped from 32 per cent in 1947 to a little under 20 per cent today. If we use a rising standard as to what constitutes poverty, the improvement has not, of course, been as large as these figures suggest.

Who Are the Poor?

In a very general way, the answer to this question is well known. But a detailed, precise, and unequivocal answer is very difficult. Here again the question of definition arises. If we use the inflexible dividing line of $3,000 per family (and $1,500 for unrelated individuals) regardless of size of family, location, or age, we get one answer. If we use the flexible standard suggested by the Social Security Administration, by which the poverty line for a rural aged couple is much less than for an urban family with 4 or 5 children under 18, we get a somewhat different answer. Until convinced otherwise, I am inclined to think the flexible standard is more useful, although this does not mean that I might not argue with one or another of the minimum budgets currently used in this standard.

Using this flexible standard, the incidence of poverty is heaviest among nonwhites, families with a very young head, the aged, broken families, very large families, families without a breadwinner, the unemployed, and families headed by farmers or unskilled laborers.[8] To these we must add unrelated individuals living alone, regardless of age, sex, or color. No less than 44 per cent of all such individuals living alone were classified below the poverty line in 1963.[9]

Tomorrow's Poor

These are today's poor. Will they also be tomorrow's poor if the trends evident since the last World War continue unchanged?

---

[8] This listing is based on Table 2 in Orshansky, *op. cit.* I have listed all of her groups in which the incidence of poverty was as high as 25 per cent, except that I have added families with a head aged 65 and over (with an incidence of 24 per cent).

[9] *Ibid.*, Table 3.

This, obviously, is not an easy question to answer. For one thing, how far into the future do we want to go for our "tomorrow"? And as we move toward that (hopefully) ever more affluent tomorrow, by how much shall we want to raise our standards as to the dividing line between poverty and non-poverty? And how are we to interpret recent trends when we come to project them into the future?

My crystal ball is no better than the next man's. But the following interpretation and projection of recent experience may be of some interest to this audience.

Let me pose the following question. Without allowing for a further rise in the poverty line, among what groups will poverty be concentrated 10 or 15 years from now? In the absence of further government action, and assuming that income per capita rises at roughly the same rate as during the past decade, in what respects will the identity of the poor be different in 1975 from what it is in 1965?

The answer I arrive at is the same one that a good many others have reached. Poverty, which is already predominantly an urban phenomenon, will become increasingly so. And within the urban population, poverty is likely to become increasingly concentrated among the groups in which the incidence of poverty is already highest. The over-all incidence of poverty should continue to decline, but the improvement will be least marked among those urban groups which now have the highest poverty rates.

This has been our experience since the war, and I think that it will take stronger action than anything thus far begun to alter this trend. Let me cite a few facts by way of illustration.

Last year's *Economic Report of the President,* using its $3,000 poverty line, classified poor families in 1947 and 1962 according to a number of different characteristics. If we take the groups with the *highest* incidence of poverty in 1947 (excluding the South and farm families), we find that without exception the incidence of poverty in these groups declined *less* to 1962 than in the population as a whole. Further, in all but two of these groups the absolute number of poor families actually rose between 1947 and 1962, despite a decline of 22 per cent in the total number of poor families. And the decline in the number of poor families in the other two groups—farm families and families in the South—was less than 10 per cent. As a result, these high-poverty groups accounted for a considerably larger proportion of the total poor in 1962 than in 1947. And so far as I can see, this trend is likely to continue.

It is hardly necessary to list these high-poverty groups: families without a breadwinner or whose head is unemployed, families with a very young head, the aged, families headed by women, and nonwhites. I should mention also families with three or more children under 18. The incidence of poverty among such families is not above average and fell substantially after 1947, but the postwar rise in the total number of families with three or more children has been so great that the number of poor families in this group has risen. In this connection, let me cite the following without elaborative comment: While something like one-fifth of the total population is poor by today's standards, "some 17 to 23 million youngsters, or from a fourth to a third of all our children, are growing up in the gray shadow of poverty." [10]

A word about rural poverty. The incidence of poverty on the farm is diminishing less rapidly than in the cities, but the rapid decline in the farm population means that the rural poor make up a steadily declining fraction of the total number of poor families. Similar considerations hold for the South, with its very high rate of poverty. The South's population has been growing less rapidly than in the nation as a whole.

Meeting the Challenge

Until not so long ago, it could be fairly said that the chief causes of poverty in the United States were low wages and unemployment, accentuated by our unwillingness (before the New Deal) to develop an adequate social insurance and welfare program. This is no longer true, although we would do well to remember that the incidence of poverty is still appallingly

[10] Mollie Orshansky, "Children and Youth," in Committee on Education and Labor, House of Representatives, *Poverty in the United States* (Washington: 1964), p. 63.

high among families whose chief breadwinner is an unskilled laborer, a farmer or farm worker, or a domestic or other unskilled service worker. Today's poverty problem, as it has been frequently put, is largely "structural" in character. It is the kind of poverty that feeds on itself. It does not automatically disappear as the favored majority becomes steadily more affluent.[11]

We are reaching the hard core of the underprivileged and the unfortunate. The time has clearly come for strong measures aimed directly at the specific and particular problems of the poor. The general directions in which we need to move are clear, and we have made a beginning. Presumably, much of this conference will be concerned with spelling out the specific further steps we need to take.

In concluding, let me make one thing unequivocally clear. We must now, as I have suggested, attack directly the structural aspects of poverty. But in doing so, we must not forget one essential condition. Structural reform will do no good if we do not maintain a rapidly expanding, stable economy. It will do no good to educate and train the children of poor parents, and the parents themselves, if there is not a rapidly expanding job market to absorb their new skills and training. Here, as in meeting the general problem of structural unemployment, particular measures and programs are required, but they will not accomplish their purpose if we do not first of all maintain, by appropriate fiscal and monetary measures, a prosperous and continuously expanding economy.

---

[11] See the interesting article by W. H. L. Anderson, "Trickling Down: The Relationship Between Economic Growth and the Extent of Poverty Among American Families," *Quarterly Journal of Economics,* LXXVII (November, 1964) pp. 511–524.

2. A Sociologist's View of Poverty

NATHAN GLAZER

It is, I believe, symbolic of the position of sociology in society generally that this sociologist, today, is placed between an economist and, as the program describes him, a reformer. Sociologists—at any rate, this sociologist—lack the massive volume of hard data which economists today dispose of with such fluency. And on the other hand, sociologists—and again, certainly this one—find it difficult to maintain for long the direct passion of the reformer in response to the problem of poverty. It is also in the nature of our discipline that it dissolves, or attempts to dissolve, both hard data and hard passions; that it attempts to complicate the analyses of the economists and the solutions of the reformers. And it is understandable that the problem of poverty in the richest nation in the world should arouse such responses.

Poverty in the richest country in the world is of course only the first paradox with which we are confronted. Economists and reformers have set the income line for poverty at a figure that spells comfort in the countries of northwestern Europe. On the one hand this tempts critics to interpret poverty in this country not as absolute deprivation, but in relative terms. Our poor, we are told, would be the upper middle class of India or the respectable working class of Sweden, and thus we deal with a statistical artifact when we speak of poverty in the United States. This argument—which is extreme—is nevertheless given a certain plausibility by the unqualified insistence of some economists and reformers that all the poor, by the standard of the income test, are poor. But then the critic—whether Irving Kristol or Dwight Macdonald—will note that one quarter of the poor, even in the figures of economists and reformers, own cars, and even more of them own their own homes, and writing from the rather special perspective of New York City, where even well-paid critics do not own cars or their own homes, they will find some reason for their skepticism.

We cannot easily resolve the question of why an income that would spell comfort in some countries is actually poverty in America, but there is no question that it is. We know that some eight million people can demonstrate to the satisfaction of hard pressed and often unsympathetic departments of public welfare that they are truly impoverished, and incapable of providing themselves with food or shelter without public funds. We know too that the food and shelter they receive under these limited public allotments is not markedly superior to the food and shelter that the poor enjoyed in this and other industrial countries fifty years ago. If the paupers of Edwardian England lived on tea and bread and margarine and scraps of meat, then the poor of our country are doing only a little better. If the poor fifty years ago lived in crowded and crumbling rooms, with inadequate plumbing and heating, then we find the same living conditions for a large part of our poor population today. There have been gains—the automobiles that have bemused some writers on poverty, the television sets that are almost universal, the clothing that is cheaper and better than that of fifty years ago, the public health services. But it is odd to note the extent to which the improvements in the living conditions of the poor, which are undoubtedly reflected in the income level we now draw to mark the line of poverty, have gone to peripheral improvements—television sets replacing the stoop for conversation and the automobile replacing cheap public transportation.

We certainly have to accept some skepticism at the figure of 40,000,000 poor. On the other hand, the eight million on relief are certainly only a part of the problem. Somewhere in between we have a large population that is without the means to maintain a modest standard of living.

The second large paradox we have to deal with is the sudden rise of public concern and political action over this question in the United States in the past few years. The problem itself has not changed in character. Professor Gordon, for example, has shown that there have been no major changes in the relative impact of unemployment on youth and nonwhites in recent years, as is widely believed, while unemployment itself as well as poverty has declined somewhat. The numbers on the public assistance rolls show a remarkable stability. It is true there is a steady increase in the Aid to Families with Dependent Children category, but this is not much greater than the increase in the population under eighteen.

SOME BRITISH COMPARISONS

Let me suggest something even more surprising. In England, with all its wide array of welfare institutions—its extensive programs of national health, social insurance, family allowances—the number that becomes dependent on National Assistance—their equivalent of our public welfare—is a little larger than it is here in proportion to population; that is, about 6 per cent of the population of Great Britain to about 4½ per cent here. Obviously one should not make too much of the fact that the figures are so close—they have more old people on national assistance, fewer children, and there are very large differences in the systems of social insurance and social welfare in the two countries. It is nevertheless enlightening for us to ask: why is there no outcry in England over the problem of poverty when, with all the wealth of social insurance schemes, three million people a year are dependent on weekly grants for direst need from the National Assistance Board?

It was revealing to me to leaf through the past six or seven months of an English weekly devoted specifically to problems of social welfare and social change, *New Society,* in search of articles on poverty in England, which these statistics had suggested to me was as much of a problem as poverty in America. The only article I came upon was a report on President Johnson's war on poverty in the United States.

I would ask further: to the extent that this problem is discussed there, why is it that it is seen as one requiring various adjustments in the social security system, perhaps some new approaches in social work for the worst cases, and the like; while here we see the poverty problem as demanding much more than tinkering with benefits and eligibilities? Here radicals, liberals, and even some conservatives call for a social and psychological revolution, requiring us to develop a completely different attitude to the casualties of industrial society, an attitude capable of remaking them rather than providing simply better care.

Let me try to explain the failure of other countries to see some of their problems as problems of poverty. England is still afflicted with a housing shortage and slums; Sweden still has a severe housing shortage; but this is no longer seen primarily as a problem of poverty. It is seen as a problem of allocation of resources. Since housing is in such large measure in these countries a public utility, the question becomes, who gets it, rather than, why don't people have enough money to pay for it? The questions then are questions of small administrative or larger social decisions—do we favor the young married couple over the aged couple or individual, do we provide housing for the divorced woman, or must she move in with her parents, and so on. This is true of other elements of income too. They depend on laws and regulations and their interpretation. Obviously our situation is very different. Our goods—housing or medical care are prominent examples—are to a much larger degree allocated by the free market. And even if the distribution of income is not much more unequal here than there, its differential impact on the standard of living of those at the lower end of the scale must consequently be much larger.

I would suggest then that one of the reasons for the difference of response to the problem of poverty in England as in the other countries of northwestern Europe is that a floor of services has been built, a standard floor for the entire nation, beneath which theoretically no one may fall. This floor is by definition designed to provide adequacy. Somewhat less effectively, there is also a floor of minimum income, as well as minimum services. The mechanisms by which it is provided consist of a variety of elements, such as old age pensions, unemployment insurance, family allowances, national health insurance and the like, and it turns out, as we have seen, that despite the artful construction, people do slip below the floor.

And the proportions that slip below in England are statistically not less than those that here find themselves in such desperate straits that they must apply for public aid. Yet because of the existence and acceptance of these national floors, the common reaction to poverty appears to be, repair the floor, adjust the mechanisms so they eliminate the problem of people slipping below. National assistance is thus viewed, at least officially, as an adaptation to some bad fitting planks in the national floor, rather than a sign of failure and inadequacy and moral defect, as it is here. With the passage of time, it takes steady and hard carpentry work in the welfare state to keep the floor in good shape. Inflation makes old age pensions inadequate; charges are reintroduced for some elements of health care and some people cannot afford them; much of the regular social insurance is related to regular work, and those who have not worked regularly do not qualify for it; many people do not know their rights and legal benefits—as many here do not—and some will not take advantage of them.

Our Emphasis on Individualism

But we must explore these differences in reaction to poverty a bit further. Why is it that our system of social insurance and public assistance form a much more jagged and uncertain floor than does that in England? Is it only a matter of the uncompleted revolution of the New Deal? This is one way of looking at it, but why did the revolution remain so partial? Daniel P. Moynihan has pointed out that we in this country find the idea of a high minimum for all much less attractive than the opportunity of high income for some—and that some by now includes very substantial parts of the working class. We do have a lower floor than in Europe, or rather a more irregular floor, with some parts of it—as in New York, Michigan, and Illinois, quite high, and other parts, as in the South, falling deep into the cellar—but we also have higher plateaus, on which very substantial numbers are located.

I would like to explore some concrete manifestations of this important generalization. If we look at the history of the past few years, when we find Democratic administrations in control nationally, we are surprised to discover that there has been relatively little interest in raising the floor, in completing and filling out our patchy system of social insurance and welfare. This lack of interest is almost as evident in liberal opinion as in conservative opinion. Conservatives prefer people to work and support themselves rather than to become dependent on public means, on a high floor. Oddly enough liberals seem to think the same way. There is little pressure for an increase in the very low social security payments, which would rapidly eliminate a good share of the poverty in the United States. There seems to be much more interest in work training programs, of all kinds, among liberals as well as conservatives—even though the liberals will also add that work training without jobs is insufficient. It is interesting to note that, whereas England is far ahead of us in so many spheres, our work training and retraining programs, under MDTA, the Economic Opportunity Act, and other acts, are considerably in advance of what we find in England. Of course, one reason for this is that our unemployment rates in general are higher, our youth unemployment is much higher, our fear of job loss through technological change considerably greater.

And yet one additional explanation is to be found in our greater interest in protecting the plateaus and opening more routes to them rather than raising the floor. Another example of our concern for the plateaus is the labor unions' insistence on a high minimum wage for youths employed on community work projects which are designed to train them. The unions will not accept the idea that the minimum wage—which is oddly enough one of the supports of the plateaus in our peculiar system, because so much work is done at less than the minimum wage—may be given up even briefly for training. It is even less likely that they would accept the idea of a lower minimum wage for young and presumably less experienced and less responsible workers in general. The auto insurance companies insist on charging the driver under 25 a good deal more, to make up for his irresponsibility, but the unions will not let the employer pay him less, which the same characteristics might justify. And now the labor movement announces it will open a drive for a $2.00 minimum wage, which can only exacerbate the problems of youth unemployment. The problem is an old one. Helen Bosanquet, in her report of the work of the Poor Law Commission in England in the 1900's, did not have to worry about youth unemployment, but she was concerned about unemployment among the older workers, and she made the sensible point that "the remedy lies partly with the trade unions, which should make universal their occasional practice of allowing older men to earn a lower wage than the younger. . ."

Obviously the unions have many good arguments against weakening the line that holds the minimum wage for some work. But we are less interested in the specific content of the arguments here than in what we learn from them about the American style of response in such matters. We might sum up the style in a single word, individualism, and I am willing to use that difficult sponge term because I think I can demonstrate that it does characterize our distinctive inability to build a high floor. For example: unions will argue that no exception can be made to the minimum wage because every wage must be a living wage. But do we need a living wage for every *individual* or do we need a living income for every *family?* It is because we think of the individual worker alone rather than the family that we find it easy to accept as a public policy that 16-year-old dropouts without experience should be paid the same wages as heads of families—which is the policy of our youth employment programs. What is this but a surprising excess of individualism? It is because once again we seem incapable of thinking in family terms that in our Youth Conservation Camps, we will make it possible and easy for all the income (and it is substantial) to be given to the youth himself. It is interesting to reflect on the social change implicit in the departure from the practice of the New Deal's CCC camps, where in contrast almost all the money went to the boy's family, and the program was considered valuable primarily for its contribution to family income and for its conservation work, not for its education in work habits. It is even more sobering to consider whether an incentive to work—so as to improve the country and aid one's family at home—was not perhaps more effective in teaching better work habits—though this was not part of the explicit program of the CCC—than the direct effort to teach good work attitudes and work skills on which we are now engaged.

Alvin Schorr, one of our most subtle analysts of social policy, points out how our programs have again and again begun with the individual, and only as an afterthought have been forced to realize that most individuals are still parts of families: "For example, the Social Security Act was enacted in 1935 and family benefits were added in 1939; disabled workers were covered in 1956, and their dependents in 1958. In the aid to dependent children program, federal participation was at first available only for the children in a family home; participation in aid to mothers was added fifteen years later. Fathers in need because of unemployment [were added only in 1962]"—and we might add only after the evidence that the ADC program that excluded fathers was effectively breaking up homes.

Our jagged floor represents our virtues as well as our defects—if, that is, we are to consider, as I do, that a concern for the individual as an individual, freed from the restraints of the family as well as of other traditional organizations and institutions, is in some measure a virtue. One of the reasons why the unions insist on a living wage for young working people without responsibilities and one of the reasons the government is willing to grant it is that we do expect our young people to move out of their homes young, to support themselves in an independent establishment rather than help support their younger brothers and sisters, to marry young. But then we must also be aware that our systems of wage reward and public assistance also erode more rapidly whatever remains of family and kin loyalty. It is this, we must realize, that makes it possible for impoverished countries, far far poorer than our own, to manage with almost no system of public welfare at all.

Our jagged floor also reflects another mixture of virtues and vices—the degree of autonomy possessed by states and communities in this country, an autonomy which permits some to attain high levels of social concern and social practice, others to fall far short of them. We are well aware of the potential and actual faults of this system of local autonomy: the fact, for example, that some states and countries are too poor to carry out their responsibilities to the poor properly, and that others, even though they may have the funds, will not. The degree of this variation from state to state is, from the point of view of the unified and homogeneous nations of Europe, almost fantastic. New York and Illinois provide an average of more than $200 a month for families with dependent children; Mississippi and Alabama an average of less than $50. In the North and West, aid to families with dependent children is given on the assumption that women with young children should not work but should care for them. In large parts of the South, where Negro women with young children and without male supporters have worked since the days of slavery, they still work.

The Racial Problem

I now come to the most distinctive dimension of American life, which gives a unique coloring to our poverty problem and which is undoubtedly the chief reason why poverty has become a major issue in this country. This is the race problem—and I would place this within the larger context of the ethnic and racial composition of the American people. The chief reason why our impoverished population forms a major social problem, and England's does not, is because of who they are. There they are the bottom stratum of almost randomly defined unfortunates, with no common social definition larger than that of casualties of the welfare state. Here the bottom stratum is a group defined by more than bottomness. It is true that the statistics show that only one quarter of the poor, as defined by the $3,000 income line, are Negroes. But this larger estimate of the poor, as I have pointed out, is in part a statistical artifact. The poorest, as defined by the public assistance rolls, are in much larger proportion Negro, Mexican American, and Puerto Rican. In many of our great cities, the majority of those who seek public assistance are Negroes. It is the civil rights revolution that makes poverty a great issue in America, not merely poverty. And in other developed countries, it is the absence of a great social division coinciding roughly with the line of poverty that keeps poverty from becoming a great issue.

It is true that those seeking national assistance in England are probably disproportionately colored, perhaps disproportionately Irish immigrants. But these groups are not yet significant forces in English politics.

Nor can we separate the cluster of issues we have summed up under the ideas of individualism and state and local autonomy from the fact of racial division and ethnic complexity. We cannot in this country set the kinds of standards that a more homogeneous country can—and our efforts to do so bring us far more perplexities. Let me again refer to the debates around the Poor Law Commission of 1909 to indicate a contrast. Sidney and Beatrice Webb at that time analyzed the problems of poverty in industrial society in terms that we can scarcely improve upon today. They defined its causes—in age, illness, poor education, unemployment—very much the way we do today. Their proposed programs were also similar to those which advanced social workers and labor market economists would suggest today. They emphasized the over-all principle of prevention, and they associated with it three other principles—the principle of Universal Provision, or floor-building, the principle of Curative Treatment, or nonpunitive and truly helpful aid, and finally, the principle of Compulsion. At that point, we may notice the difference. Compulsion meant that if parents could not raise their children properly, they would be taken away. If men would not prepare themselves for useful labor, they would be required to do so. The principle of Compulsion reflects the fact that all Englishmen may potentially agree on what is a proper way to live and what measures a government may adopt to require it. And we see the same principle at work in the advanced countries of northwestern Europe today, where those who will not live properly in public housing may be put under the care of social workers who will teach them how to arrange their lives and to raise and discipline their children.

Recently I have read an account—again by Alvin Schorr—of French social workers. The French system of social security places great emphasis on the care and protection of the family. The social workers themselves are trained primarily in two areas—in nursing, and in the various laws and regulations. They work with single families, and are responsible for getting their families the various kinds of aid the law provides. One gets an image of these self-confident and energetic women—they are all women—confident of the quality of their training and the virtues of the law, arranging matters for these families, in a way in which our social workers would never dare—because ours are aware, as Americans must be, of the vast difference in the attitudes of different families, in their structures, in their ways of life. The sophisticated among us may take this into account—but we all know it is an incredibly complex problem to decide just how to take this into account. Are we turning our poor into middle-class Protestants? Do they want to be so turned? Is this the only way to solve their problems? Is there another route? But these are the questions of the sophisticated. Most of our social workers, we must realize, react with distaste to different standards, norms, values, and behaviors, the same distaste that the self-assured French social worker would probably feel when confronted with the incomprehensible foreigner.

Of course when I speak of social workers I have in mind too the vast numbers of other personnel—counsellors, teachers, testers, policemen, probation officers, vocational experts, and the others that the well administered welfare state requires. They, of course, reflect the great variety of cultures, behaviors, standards, that exist in this country—and they react with varying degrees of uncertainty, competence, and emotion to the different varieties of behavior and standards that they meet among those they are supposed to help. And of course, for many, distaste is erected into a rigid and formalized reaction, which condemns whole races to treatment less than fully human.

We cannot adopt, to the same degree that other nations can, the principles of compulsion and national uniformity, because the standards which we would make uniform do not as a matter of fact evoke the same general degree of acceptance and commitment that they do in other nations, with a narrower ethnic and racial base. In this country, all these groups have met a remarkable degree of official indifference to the pursuit of their own ways, the creation of their own social institutions, their own schools, their own political movements. The standards of the white Protestants, if they become law and practice, are inhumane or inadequate or ineffective for large parts of our population. And yet practice and law must assume something.

Are children to be held responsible for their parents? Are men to be held responsible for their children? Should effort be rewarded? Must men be motivated to work by the threat of poverty? I would argue that however we answer these questions, on one side or the other, they are much easier to answer in Sweden or Germany or England than in the United States simply because of the greater cultural and ethnic uniformity in those countries.

THE PROBLEM OF BUREAUCRACIES

I would raise finally another dimension which distinguishes us from the other developed nations. I think we must consider seriously the nature of American bureaucracies. Again, one key fact will suggest to us how significant this problem is. One of the most characteristic programs we have seen proposed in the Community Action Programs to fight poverty consists of efforts to increase pressure on government bureaucracies. We are all acquainted with such programs; they organize the impoverished community to press its demands upon the schools, the housing inspection services, the police, and so on. The assumptions behind such programs, developed by sociologists and social workers, are also clear. Government services respond to pressure. They are better in middle-class areas than working-class areas in part because the pressure there is greater. They can be made responsive to the poor and their needs and demands if the poor organize and put pressure on them. I would now like to suggest, again from the perspective of northwestern Europe, how astonishing such programs are. There, it is assumed that if one wishes to improve education, or the organization of the labor market, or police work, one does something political or legislative or administrative which leads to new forms of organization and new and expanded programs. We do this too, of course, but our more sophisticated social workers and sociologists see little gain from such efforts. They suggest that government funds should go to set up organizations that counterattack other major government efforts, that the best way to improve services is by attack from the outside, rather than by reform from the inside. When local government protests that federal money is used to attack it and its services, the federal administrator will have to explain, but that is the only way to get you to do your job.

I am not sure just how successful this new combative approach will be. I think in the end the art of using government funds for what we may call controlled revolution will turn out to be too demanding for both federal administrators and local community action organizers. But leaving aside the effectiveness of this technique, what do we learn from the fact that it is so popular here, and almost unknown, as far as I know, in the welfare states of Europe? We may conclude that our bureaucracies are more difficult to adapt to new needs than those in Europe, and that reformers, progressive administrators, and clients alike despair of making any great impact upon them, and so prefer to set up competing organizations, or to attack them to force them into change. This is true even where much of the power is in the hands of the reformers, the liberal administrators, and the client population—as it is in New York City. We may speculate upon the causes of this presumed rigidity and inadequacy. I would suggest that one of the underlying causes is the ethnic and racial difference that inevitably develops between bureaucracies and client groups in a nation characterized by a history of waves of immigration into our large cities, each of which takes over the jobs of the bureaucracy at different times. The older group, confronting the newer group, is unable to effectively understand and respond to their problems.

On occasion we do become one nation—in wartime, when there is need for everyone's labor, and we perform wonders that even advanced welfare states come to study. But the pressure on us is rarely that great. We do not run a tight ship. We are not short of labor. We must not compete with dangerous competitors for overseas markets to live. And in the absence of such pressures, and in the presence of ethnic and racial diversity, we find it difficult to draw forth from our government servants and social workers the degree of human effort and empathy and compassion that is necessary to really transform and change people. This is why the simple elaboration of bureaucracies with more funds evokes such little enthusiasm from sociologists and social critics. Economists, I believe, must assume that the reallocation of resources to certain services will improve them. While those who administer these services can never admit it, they are not so sure that the provision of more personnel and resources will improve results.

I believe we must take the measure of our strengths and weaknesses more adequately than we have done, and adapt our efforts to them.

CONCLUSIONS

I have tried to suggest some of the major questions we must look into as we try to improve our poverty programs, and have argued that we cannot probably do as much through centrally administered state social services as Europe has done. But I think we can do other things better. Much more of our achievement has come from private, group, voluntary, and nonstate effort—whether in the form of private business for profit or voluntary efforts for social ends. We are remarkably efficient—as Eric Hoffer and others have pointed out—in organizing work. The WPA in the Great Depression and the war effort in the Second World War both stand as examples of the rapid employment in efficient work of millions of workers with relatively little investment in special work education, counselling, social services, and the like. Our entrepreneurs are efficient and ingenious in the development of new kinds of services. Private groups of all kinds—religious, political, trade union, charitable—have been ingenious in designing programs to help their own members and others. The returns from such efforts, where they can be counted, are often as surprising as the weakness of official and governmental efforts is depressing.

For example, of all the new types of social programs that

have been started in recent years, volunteer tutoring programs show perhaps the highest degree of success in relation to effort. For another example, consider the Freedom Schools and Community Centers that are being planted in the Deep South. I cannot conceive of official governmental efforts that could be anywhere as effective. The really creative part of our consideration of the problem of poverty must be to learn how to stimulate such efforts, how to support them, how to put government funds into them without blighting them. And since the problem of poverty is so largely concentrated in our Negro population, I am convinced that much of the effort and manpower involved in overcoming it must come from the Negro community, even if the funds that power it come from the Federal government. It is axiomatic to me that Negro organizations—whether they educate, train, advise, employ, organize, or what not—can potentially do far, far more with Negro clients than can governmental organizations. It is in the stimulation of individual and group effort—whether motivated by profit, charity, by group pride, or by the desire for individual fulfillment or salvation, that I see the most productive courses we can follow to overcome poverty.

3. A Social Reformer's View of Poverty

MICHAEL HARRINGTON

Although this is a scholarly conference, there are some very specific, practical issues in the war against poverty. As Paul Jacobs remarked to me just yesterday: "The war against poverty is not simply against an abstraction called poverty. There are actually some people on the other side." We meet in a state which has the most invisible poor, the most curious invisible poor, in the country. They are called growers. We meet in a state which through its senators and its governor has taken a pauper's oath and is now declaring that this state and its agriculture can survive only by importing and exploiting foreign labor and not paying American labor a decent wage. Support of the excellent stand which the Secretary of Labor has taken on this issue so far might eventually make a greater contribution to ending poverty than all of our discussions at this conference.

What I want to do today in terms of analysis is to try to relate two of our current fashionable themes, the war against poverty and the great society. In addition, I want to make the following assumption and then let it rest—that we have made a tremendous advance in having a war against poverty and that that is enormously to the credit of Presidents John F. Kennedy and Lyndon B. Johnson. But I intend to concern myself mainly with ideas that go beyond our present program and premises. In attempting to do this, I should like to relate the war against poverty and the great society in three different ways: (1) to consider the growth potential of poverty in the United States, which I think is considerable; (2) to make a few remarks about government programs that we now have and attitudes that we should have; and (3) to discuss some of the new concepts, the radical departures, that it seems to me are necessary if we are either to end poverty in the United States or establish a great society.

The Growth Potential of Poverty

In its latest Economic Report, the Council of Economic Advisers has taken into account the more sophisticated recent statistics relating poverty to family size, and, as a result, has increased the number of large families which are defined as poor. The new data show that 15 million American children, one out of every four American children, are poor. Professor Gordon has cited some statistics which suggest that the figure is even higher—that perhaps as many as 23 million children, one out of every three, are poor. So we have, therefore, by official definition, a higher incidence of poverty among young people than in the population as a whole. We know that this high incidence of poverty among young people represents a growth potential for poverty, because all of the evidence now points to the fact that one of the best ways to be poor is to be born into a poor family.

Further evidence from the Department of Labor study of Selective Service rejectees indicates that there is developing in this society a kind of hereditary poverty. An extraordinary number of these young people—one out of every four young Americans that took the Selective Service exam—failed because of lack of enough education and training to qualify as a private in the Army of the United States. We also know that a large number of these young people are the children of the poor. We have come to realize more and more that the dropout cycle is not a willful and wrong decision by a young person at 16 to quit school, but something with more basic roots than that.

Clearly a process of retardation often takes place in the slum and in the slum family. Young people from the slums frequently arrive at school already two years behind. In the first three grades they are not taught how to read, write, and count, because we have inferior schools in the slums. Thus by the age of nine, these children learn how to hide the fact that they don't understand what is going on, and, at the age of 16, they have the good sense to leave because they realize they have learned nothing for the past five or six years.

Now that we have a better understanding of this process, we realize that if approximately a fourth to a third of our young people are in poor families, it means these young people have an extraordinarily good prospect of becoming poor themselves, and raising poor families. In this decade, characterized by a tremendous flow of young people entering the labor market, we know that about a third of these new entrants are going to have less than a high school education, and about ten per cent of them less than a grade school education. What kinds of jobs are they going to get?

In terms of a study just completed by two staff members of the Bureau of Labor Statistics, Sophia Cooper and Dennis Johnston, we now have a labor force of 77 million. On the basis of conservative assumptions which do not allow for productivity increases or any reduction in unemployment, they estimate that by 1970 we will have a labor force of 86 million, and, by 1980, 101.4 million people. This means that we must over the period between now and 1980 create a million and a half new jobs a year.

Now I have two questions about this prospect in terms of the problem of poverty. Will we succeed in creating these jobs and do we care what kinds of jobs we create if we do? There is first the purely quantitative question of whether there is going to be something for these young people to do, and secondly, there is, if you will, the great society question, of whether that something is going to be worthwhile? I think that under our present assumptions and programs, we haven't begun to face up to these issues.

Let me, finally, in terms of posing this problem of the growth potential of poverty, consider the way in which it relates to our manpower revolution. Our poverty today, I am convinced, is new. Our wisdom about poverty—the great American wisdom of the immigrant groups—is becoming day by day more useless, because those groups were the adventurous poor who came to an expanding economy that needed blue-collar workers and had communities and religions and languages. The poor today have none of those characteristics and, above all, they face automation.

Between 1962 and 1963, we produced 1,100,000 new jobs, but 70,000 of those new jobs were for production workers in manufacturing, and 295,000 of them were in education. Young people are entering an economy in which there are more than four times as many new jobs for people in education as in factories—in which there is a greater demand for school teachers than for mill hands. What do we do with them? What do we do when we consider statistics showing that, in January 1965, despite a sizable increase in the number of production workers, there were seven per cent fewer production workers than in August 1953? We are moving into a radically different type of society, which is not being created by social reformers, but by our technology. We have an enormous population of the young poor who are not prepared to meet that society, and we have not yet developed a program to deal with this tremendous gap between these young people, their skills, and the society they face.

Existing Government Programs

In discussing existing programs, I would like to call attention to the testimony of Professor Galbraith before the Joint Committee on the Economic Report the other day. He spoke of new criteria distinguishing between liberals and conservatives, pointing out that the old rules do not apply any more and that we are now getting something which he called reactionary Keynesianism. We have reached the point at which it is so obvious to everybody, including the most conservative businessmen, that we must increase demand in the economy to buy the products of the automated machines, that Ebenezer Scrooge would today be a neo-Keynesian, and Barry Goldwater came out for successive tax cuts. Galbraith makes the charge that tax reductions are stimulating individual consumption, not social consumption. We cannot substitute tax cuts for social spending, he argues, and then elaborates his point in somewhat bitter words:

I am not quite sure what the advantage is in having a few more dollars to spend if the air is too dirty to breath, the water too polluted to drink, the commuters are losing out in the struggle to get in and out of the city, the streets are filthy, and the schools so bad that the young perhaps wisely stay away, and hoodlums roll citizens for some of the dollars they saved in the tax.

SOME NEW CONCEPTS

In line with Galbraith's thesis, what I am suggesting is that, if we are to solve the problem of these young people faced with a manpower revolution, we are going to have to commit ourselves to some massive social investments and social spending. For example, we are putting a tremendous amount of money into a second educational system. The Secretary of Labor is now an educator, the Council of Economic Advisers is an educator, the Secretary of Defense is an educator, and just about everybody has an education program to accomplish at ages 16 and 17 what we did not accomplish at six and seven.

Despite all this, we know something. We know that slums are a more powerful educator than schools. As yet, nobody has proposed the obvious idea in the war against poverty of abolishing slums. We are well behind what the late Senator Robert Taft said we should be doing in the field of housing. In 1949, Taft projected a housing goal for 1953 that we are going to reach in 1968. Given the need for jobs and the tremendous educational influence of the slum on precisely the young people whom we want to help, this is obviously a way in which we could create jobs and abolish poverty.

As a matter of fact, I would suggest as a simplified slogan in the war against poverty the notion "let us hire the poor to abolish poverty." Let us make a commitment to housing, to schools, to hospitals, to transportation systems. Let us make a commitment to the great society, if you will, which is so strong that it will enable us to put everybody who is unemployed and underemployed in the United States to work building a decent kind of a society. To those who will ask where the money is to come from, I would reply that there are a whole series of answers. One answer has been given by Leon Keyserling, who has computed that, if we had had full employment between 1953 and 1964, tax revenues would have increased by $135 billion.

Secondly, it is important in discussing these massive social investments to emphasize the point that they *are* investments. Milton Friedman, as Barry Goldwater's economic advisor, computed that in 1961 the tax cost of poverty was $33 billion. Mayor Robert Wagner pointed out last spring that the City of New York spends, at a minimum, a quarter of its budget for the problems of the poor. Poverty is an extremely expensive item, and the abolition of poverty is not simply a matter of giving a few dollars to a panhandler. The abolition of poverty is a social investment and should be thought of in those terms.

The GI Bill of Rights was a good example of the kind of investment I mean. Under that program, from which I am sure many people in this room benefited, we paid people to go to school, but is there anyone so shortsighted as to think that that was money given away? I am sure everybody realizes that by paying these veterans to go to school, this society gained in any calculus we want to use.

We now have a proposed second round in the poverty program which will involve spending slightly less than the profits of General Motors last year. That is not enough. We can afford a little more than that to deal with the problem of poverty. And, more specifically, I think that some of the ideas developed by the Senate Subcommittee on Manpower and Employment under the chairmanship of Senator Clark begin to address themselves to meeting the need. Senator Clark has introduced a bill which would enact the Full Employment Bill we should have adopted in 1945. That was the bill that finally emerged as the Employment Act of 1946. Congress could not bring itself to put a subversive word like "full" in front of "employment." If Clark's new measure is adopted, we will finally catch up with French businessmen and British Tories by accepting the idea that the gross national product is too important to leave to the mercies of economic fluctuations. Clark maintains that, if next year's GNP will result in unemployment of over three per cent, then we must increase GNP enough to bring unemployment down below three per cent. This kind of policy is what we need, plus Clark's proposal that we spend an additional five billion dollars every year for worthwhile social programs. An increase of five billion dollars every year over a three-year period would mean a total increase of $30 billion. Without spending of this magnitude, all of the community action in the world is not going to accomplish much in the direction of abolishing poverty.

Finally, let me speak of how this relates to the great society, in a very social reformer mood, or, more specifically, a social utopian mood. And I should like to begin with a caviat. I commend the President of the United States for beginning to speak of something called a great society, but I think that he has made some optimistic assumptions in his talk about the great society. Perhaps he has been reading Daniel Bell and Raymond Aron, because he is now saying that our economy is becoming so abundant that the claim of every group can be satisfied by compromise. Therefore, there is no more need for struggle and conflict as the motive force of politics. Consensus is the way to achieve the great society. You might say that he is calling for the capitalist road to socialism, or that he is proposing a revolution which will take place without the inconvenience of changing any basic institutions in the society. I believe he is right in saying that we are facing a new type of economy and a radical challenge, but wrong in thinking that we can achieve this transition without a little conflict and a little argument.

We must begin to redefine what we mean by work in the United States. Our present definitions of work and rewards are not adequate for our technology, or for the situation facing the quarter to a third of our young people who are utterly unprepared for the society they are entering. For example, we should now be able to say that the most unproductive thing a young person can do is to work and the most productive thing he can do is to go to school. And this is not simply true in terms of the individual, but in terms of society. From society's point of view the most unproductive thing for a 16-year-old to do is to go to work, because, if the 16-year-old goes to work today, it means that he will be a drag on society tomorrow, in addition to harming himself grievously. Therefore, I believe that we should begin to think of education as productive work, as something that is worth paying people for. But I am not proposing to pay young people to go to present slum schools. That would amount to a proposal to bribe them for staying off the streets and behaving, as well as a proposal to turn teachers into cops.

Secondly, it seems clear that we are in the process of redefining the working life of people. The leisure problem which we occasionally talk about is becoming a basic problem. People are going to enter the labor force later and leave earlier. The idea of the sabbatical, I hope, will extend to every job in the United States. But that will call for other changes in our old ways of thinking. The steelworkers, as you know, have a 13-week sabbatical in their contract. I talked to some men from *Look* magazine who went out to discover what the steelworkers did with their 13 weeks, and they found out that what they did was just what they had been doing previously with their two or three weeks of vacation, i.e., they did nothing new on the whole. They had a particular problem in that the first steelworker they interviewed had previously used his two or three weeks to drink, and was now using his 13 weeks to drink. Even so, the problem of what are we going to do with increased leisure can be attacked. I suggest that work can be provided for people catering to the leisure-time needs of others. Even the problem of Appalachia might be related to it, for example. One of the things that might be done in Appalachia is to create a gigantic area for leisure.

Thirdly, I think we have to invent new jobs. We have done it for middle-class people. We have invented the job category of the Peace Corps. That is excellent. It is also excellent that the president of Yale has proposed that the Peace Corps be given the same status in universities and colleges as the ROTC. It is a new kind of job—Peace Corps. We are now going to have a new job called Vista Volunteer. We have a new kind of job called graduate student, which develops in the affluent society, in which young people can consider studying for a whole decade between their twentieth and thirtieth birthdays. We have another new type of job from which I have benefited. It is called foundation consultant and involves getting paid for sitting around a table and talking.

In other words, we have been very resourceful in inventing new jobs for middle-class people. We have been unresourceful in inventing new jobs for poor people. But I think that there are new jobs to invent for poor people and that we are beginning now to understand this. We can, for example, simplify jobs right here and now, without waiting for the great society. We have done it with metermaids and auxiliary policewomen. That is to say, a metermaid is part of a policeman who doesn't have to have all of the attributes of a policeman, because all she has to do is collect the coins from the meters and give out parking tickets. And an auxiliary policewoman standing outside a school, helping the children across the street, is also part of a policeman. In Chicago, Travelers Aid has hired women from Appalachia to help attend the desk in the bus depot, working with social workers. These women from Appalachia have very little education, but they have one important attribute—they can talk to people from Appalachia.

One of the most fashionable phrases in a lot of the community action programs this year is "indigenous work." That is good. We are now getting the idea of turning poor people into social workers. In Washington, D. C., under the federal poverty program, they are training some slum dwellers to be social workers, because they can communicate. They can probably find out more than many a professional social worker. One difficulty, however, is that when you hire, let us say, a gang leader to be a consultant to the Ford Foundation, the gang becomes suspicious of him.

But I have not exhausted my suggestions for inventing new work. Let me give you another example, the job of teacher's aide. You can hire women who have no degrees whatsoever, who have less than an eighth grade education, to come into school rooms to blow noses and take youngsters to the bathroom. This will be an enormous gain for the teacher and a gain for the woman. In fact, if we apply ourselves to the problem of inventing work, we can develop very useful kinds of work which can be performed by many of the poor people. But we must also make certain that the new kinds of work we invent will improve the quality of the society. And that is the link, it seems to me, between the war against poverty and the great society—between the quantity problem and the quality problem.

Much of this relates, if you will, to what Aristotle said about automation. In Aristotle's *Politics,* there is a defense of slavery in the course of which he says that there is one circumstance in which masters would not need slaves and managers would not even need subordinates. That one circumstance would exist if inanimate objects would, by intelligent anticipation, do things, i.e., if the statues of Daedalus could come to life. The statues of Daedalus were created by the cunning craftsmen of the Greek legend of Daedalus, and of them it was said that once they were sculpted they danced of their own motion. What I suggest now is that the statues of Daedalus are beginning to dance among us. We call it automation and cybernation. Therefore, this incredible Aristotelian dream of a society in which there need be no relation of master and slave or even of manager and subordinate is becoming not a possibility, but a practical necessity. That is because, in this kind of work, we can move in two ways. On the one hand, we can create a society which will be split between the engineers and the janitors. We might even provide floors of welfare for the janitors, for the unemployed, for the under-classes, as Gunnar Myrdal has called them, but it would be a miserable society. And on the other hand, the same technology can progressively free this society, including the poor people in it, from repetitive and miserable jobs and create the possibility of doing something really useful and positive.

Conclusion

It may be somewhat "far-out," but it seems to me that in both the war against poverty and the fight for the great society what perhaps we are talking about is a concept of a new Athens. In the old Athens, there were human slaves who did the dirty work, and there were the Greek citizens who would only bother themselves with specifically human activities, including sports, the intellect, and the arts. And it seems to me that in creating jobs for the poor people today, we might adopt this radical and way-out concept of the new Athens and say that we now have the possibility, both in abolishing poverty and in trying to create a great society, of progressively freeing people from all the routine and inhuman tasks and of providing work which is really human—things like sports, the intellect, and the arts.

PART TWO

SOME VIEWS ON ANTI-POVERTY PROGRAMS

4. Three Problems in Combatting Poverty

DANIEL P. MOYNIHAN

The war on poverty is the newest initiative in an ancient struggle. It involves new ideas, new men, and is evolving new institutions. Just as the problem of poverty itself commands our attention, so does our effort to get rid of it once and for all deserve some similar scrutiny.

Of all the events of the recent period in American domestic affairs, there has been none, I feel, which more exactly fits Nathan Glazer's description of the professionalization of reform in modern society.

The war on poverty did not come about because the nation was struck by economic disaster. On the contrary, it was begun at a moment of unprecedented prosperity. In legislative terms, it was enacted within weeks almost of the Revenue Act of 1964, unquestionably the moment in the history of political economy when the United States finally learned how to make an industrial economy work. The war on poverty began, in other words, at a moment when the prospects for an immense expansion in national wealth had never been better.

Nor did the war on poverty come about because of any great surge of popular demand. The civil rights movement, while much involved with problems of poverty, was nonetheless at that time primarily directed to problems of civil rights as such. If anything, the most distinctive political movement of that time was the ultraconservative stirring on the right, which led to the nomination of Senator Goldwater.

The origins of this effort simply cannot be explained in deterministic terms. It was more a rational than a political event. Men at the center of the government perceived the fact, to use the terms by which the *Economist* described the origins of

President Johnson's message on conservation, "that ugliness, like poverty, is all around them and that the powers of government might eliminate it."

The 1960 Democratic platform had been explicit about the persistence of poverty in the United States, and the idea had begun to develop early in the Kennedy Administration. Secretary of Labor W. Willard Wirtz from the beginning of his tenure was pressing for a national effort to eliminate poverty and ignorance. In the summer of 1963, Walter Heller, then Chairman of the Council of Economic Advisers, devoted a large portion of an address to the Communications Workers to the problem of poverty. And during this time, of course, men such as Michael Harrington, Gunnar Myrdal, and Robert Lampman were publishing immensely influential tracts on the subject, and even before that, Senators Paul H. Douglas and John J. Sparkman had pursued the matter in Congressional inquiries.

Inevitably some specifically political events did contribute to the course of events. Following his confrontation with the steel industry, President Kennedy found that his domestic program came almost to a halt in Congress. This stalemate was in turn broken by his assassination. President Johnson then had an opportunity to move forward, which he seized with skill and energy—and strongly-held convictions about what needed doing in this country. His decision to define the issue in terms of a *war* on poverty was decisive. It turned out, as the President perceived, to be a conception that brought men together at what Erik Erikson has called a higher unity: men, for example, who could not agree about civil rights, or trade unions, or fiscal policies, could come together with clearly shared convictions on the subject of an effort to abolish poverty.

But from the outset this has been most characteristically an effort that reflects the growing capacity of modern government to respond on its own to new information and new circumstances. Government too, alas, has become a machine that thinks. Whether this is a development that will ultimately diminish the role of the citizen by rendering his relatively unskilled services obsolete, or whether it will lead to a new and richer age of public affairs, characterized by an enhancement of the quality of public life comparable to the flood of private riches we are promised by industrial automation, remains to be seen.

For the moment it is to be noted, again in the pattern Glazer has described, that a distinctive characteristic of the anti-poverty program is the degree to which it was developed by research and experimentation. Most of the program items, far the greater part in terms of budget allocations, consisted of activities that had been operated either in large scale or in prototype at some point in the past, as for example, the youth employment programs; or which had direct analogues in ongoing programs, such as VISTA and the Peace Corps. Far the most distinctive of these, in terms of a new departure in public policy and program, is the Community Action Program, provided by Title II of the bill.

A history of the idea of community action has not been written, but it should be. It is an idea that is likely to have considerable effect on American society. It is an amalgam, clearly, of certain theories of social action and social psychology that developed in the universities over the past several decades. There is clearly some carry-over from the idea of community development worked out through the Foreign Aid Program and in various international agencies. Live experiments, as it were, were financed by one of the great foundations in the 1950's. In 1961 the Juvenile Delinquency and Youth Offenses Control Act provided some $15 million to pursue the subject further. An interdepartmental committee headed by the Attorney General sponsored projects in a number of cities, the best known of which is Mobilization for Youth on the lower East Side of New York. Community action was a powerful idea and was supported. When the time came to put together a poverty program, the initial impulse within the second echelon of the government was simply to launch a greatly expanded community action program, following the models already in action. Other considerations led to the establishment of a more diverse program, but community action remains at the center of the present program.

That the war on poverty was an idea whose time has come

was surely indicated by the response in Congress, and among the public at large to the President's proposal. The lead time, again to borrow a term from the world of technology, between the conception of this effort and its actual commencement was less than a year—surely a record in itself, and a measure of the vitality of the idea.

For that very reason, it seems to me, those of us in government have a responsibility to be candid with the public where we feel there are gaps in our knowledge, or weaknesses in our argument. Possibly this is only taking the professionalization of reform to the next stage of the internalization of critique, but that is a risk, or a temptation, we must accept.

I would like to take up three more or less related aspects of the problem of poverty, which I feel we have not yet faced up to. Obviously I speak for myself alone, as a sometime professor, at a university conference. I hope it will be taken as a measure of my respect for all of the persons now at work in the anti-poverty program, that I do not hesitate to speak of shortcomings, or of things we don't know or don't understand—because neither do they.

The Persistence of Poverty

The first point I would make is that the war on poverty began on the basis of the undisputed persistence of poverty in the United States, but without any agreed upon explanation for this fact. Clearly the poor were still with us. The gross national product had increased exactly tenfold from the time President Roosevelt took office to the time President Johnson took office—but the cities and countryside of America swarmed with impoverished communities, the likes of which are simply no longer to be seen in Western Europe. Yet we had no view as to why this was so, nor even a good working hypothesis.

The point here is that it is at least possible that some of the things that have been producing prosperity have also been producing poverty—possible, in other words, that the relation between poverty and affluence in the United States is not paradoxical, but in some aspects causal. I do not have an opinion on this point, I simply think it important to explore it. The relation to technology is obvious: Appalachia is the site of an industrial work force, the soft coal miners, which has been impoverished by an advancing and shifting technology that has nonetheless brought great prosperity to the nation as a whole. The relation to social justice is equally clear. I think it entirely possible that the phenomenally cheap food and fiber available to the American consumer is at least in part a result of the phenomenal indifference we have shown to the welfare of agricultural labor, both when employed at Iron Age wages or when replaced altogether.

I would like to accept with great appreciation, on his behalf, the kind words that have been said here about Secretary Wirtz and his handling of the problems of agricultural labor in recent weeks. However, he would not want anyone to suppose that for every *bracero* who does not enter the United States a regular job is going to be created for an American. The machines have destroyed those equations long ago, as we have had occasion to watch as the supply of *braceros* was steadily cut over the past four years.

It would be convenient if the connection between poverty and prosperity, assuming it does exist, could simply be blamed on automation, and let go at that. But to be an American, as Henry James observed, is a complex fate, and simple answers rarely do.

To touch on a point I have made elsewhere, it seems to me that at least part of the singular dynamism of the American economy and the society that produces it, can be ascribed to the unprecedented mixtures of ethnic and religious groups that make up our population. I suggest you can feel this at a campus such as this one here at Berkeley, in contrast to those campuses which are more unitary in class or ethnic or religious composition. This has led, however, to discontinuities in the American social structure and social conscience that not only acquiesce in the persistence of poverty amidst affluence, but even help perpetuate it.

The situation of the Negro American is only the most obvious instance. Michael Harrington spoke yesterday of the absurdity of setting up peripheral education systems designed to teach persons to read properly at age 18 when it is well enough known that this can be done most efficiently at age six. What he was saying is that, with the exception of Canada and West Germany, the United States is surely the only industrial democracy in the world that does not have a system of national assistance to elementary and secondary education, a fact which is abundantly evident in the wide disparities of the abilities of young persons entering the labor force, disparities that are particularly harmful to the children of the poor. This is not the case because we haven't tried, but because we haven't been able to break down or circumvent the ethnic and religious barriers to a national consensus on the subject of education. That we may be doing so at this moment in Washington is not the least sign that new things are at hand in the United States, but for the moment, the barriers remain, and the effects are felt.

As an example of the quite different economic situations of different ethnic groups in the United States, I would cite the male unemployment rates revealed in the 1960 census. In that year the rate for all white males was 4.7 per cent. By contrast, the rates for the various groups lumped together in our monthly statistics as "nonwhite" ranged from half to almost four times the white rate: 2.4 per cent for Japanese, 3.8 per cent for Chinese, 6.3 per cent for Filipinos, 8.9 per cent for Negroes, and 16.2 per cent for Indians. Noting the diversity within the nonwhite group, we can almost assume a similar pattern would be found in the white group were it analyzed in these terms.

I would suggest that a "high and sustained level of economic growth," the necessity for which must preface all discussions of this subject, may perhaps improve things and may not: according to what growth and which group is in question. I suggest it is high time we began differentiating between benign growth and other kinds. Surely there is a "mix" in the increments to the gross national product that is susceptible to analysis from the point of view of whether on balance it improves or worsens the situation of working people.

Similarly, community action on behalf of the poor, and even on the part of the poor, is likely to turn out to be a more difficult matter than supposed.

It is fair, I think, to point out that the concept of community action involves the effort to change the poor who are produced by the system, rather than to change the system that produces the poor. That is all right with me: I am in all things a man of the center; I think we have produced the best social system the world has so far seen, despite the obvious fact that it can be improved. However, it is not going to do us any good to pretend that this will not involve in most cases an effort by middle-class persons who will usually be of quite a different ethnic and religious background, to persuade lower-class persons of another background to be different from what God, or the social system, or the climate, or whatever, made them.

A powerful lot of presumption goes into this kind of effort, and with the best of intentions it shows through. Only a middle-class American could have thought up the term "indigenous disadvantaged." The British would have called them "natives." I believe the term among Belgian colonial administrators was *indigènes*. It might prove counter productive, as they say in the State Department, to equip all of our community action workers with a copy of *The Revolutionist's Handbook and Pocket Companion,* but perhaps somewhere in the briefing papers for community action workers we could include Shaw's maxim, "Do not do unto others as you would they should do unto you: their tastes may not be the same."

POVERTY AND THE FAMILY

The second general point I would like to make is that it is very clear that after only a year of general discussion the question of poverty is leading us to a major reassessment of the effect upon family structure of the way we do things in this country.

Several things emerge. First it becomes more obvious that the primary function of community welfare programs is to provide surrogate family services. The logic of this relationship has taken us well beyond the original provision of food and clothing and money, to far more complex matters of providing proper attitudes towards work, reasonable expectations of success, and so forth. Obviously these are matters which for most persons are handled within the family system, and most of us would risk the speculation that the traditional family arrangement is probably the more efficient one.

It also emerges, however, that in general our arrangements do not pay much heed to this fact. In this respect we are different from most of the industrial democracies with which we otherwise share many characteristics. We are, as Nathan Glazer noted, implacably individualistic. We stand for God and Country, even for Yale. But to stand for family as well is a matter for newly migrated Italians or middle-class Irish Catholics whom the dictates of conscience have burdened with nine children and left, therefore, with no alternative.

The shortsightedness of this view is, as I suggest, becoming more and more clear, thanks in particular to Robert Lampman and the Council of Economic Advisers who began by defining poverty in terms of families, rather than individuals, below the poverty line, and more recently to the brilliant work of Miss Orshansky of the Social Security Administration in showing the heavy incidence of poverty among larger families.

The Department of Labor has been working on the data, such as they are, and I would expect before long that some important further facts will emerge. We may eventually startle the world with a statistical demonstration of the fact that the poor get children—or perhaps that people who get children get poor as well. What is emerging is the fact that not only is the American wage system not geared to providing any extra income for persons with extra family responsibilities, but further, the larger the family in the United States, the poorer it is. For both urban and rural families, median income rises until there are, as it were, three children—after which it drops off precipitously. This is how it is possible that a third of the children living in poor families have family heads that work all year round.

We are finding that unemployment strikes differentially at large families below certain income levels. Unemployed family heads in March 1964 had slightly fewer children under 18, on average, than did employed family heads. For those with family incomes under $3,000, however, the reverse was true—unemployed family heads had substantially more children than did employed ones, on the average: 1.88 to 1.27. One-third of the poor families with unemployed heads had three or more children, compared to less than one-fourth of the poor families with employed heads.

We are beginning to see something of the relation of unemployment to family structure. We are learning what you might expect to learn, but it is still a matter it would appear the nation as a whole does not understand. It may be that this line of inquiry will enable us to redefine the problem of unemployment—so easily viewed as a matter of economic waste, and therefore of relatively marginal importance in an age of economic abundance—and cast it in terms of the problem of delinquency and crime and welfare dependence and such, which by and large are problems the nation knows it has and would like to see dealt with.

In any event, I would think it is becoming clear that the discussion of poverty is leading us steadily towards a much more realistic view of the importance of maintaining a stable family structure at all levels of the society—and, most importantly, of the ease with which well-meaning or unthinking social policies can work against that objective. Here I would simply cite the policy of our Aid to Dependent Children program, which for a quarter-century *required* that fathers not be present in order for children to receive welfare assistance.

The next great social issue raised in America ought to be the question of how to insure a decent family income and a decent family setting for the working people of America, as we have already done—and as a result of no inconsiderable intervention of the federal government—for middle-class Americans.

INVOLVING THE POOR

There is a third, and concluding point I would like to make. If it is a somewhat unruly one, I plead the influence of environment.

I am a little suspicious of those who are too much enamored of the poor. There is a long tradition in Western humanitarianism of imputing to suffering but inanimate creatures—or social classes—a delicacy of feeling, a heightened sensibility that unfailingly commends itself to the solicitude of other, more fortunate, persons who also share those qualities. I believe this is what Bertrand Russell had in mind when he pointed out that the British parliament enacted legislation on behalf of mine ponies generations before doing anything for mine workers—a group known for their rowdy, intemperate, and leveling ways.

I very much fear there is a theme running through much of the academic literature on community action, for example, which indulges this temptation to some considerable length. The prospectus for the Mobilization for Youth project, for example, contained this passage under the heading of "Organizing the Unaffiliated":

> Most efforts to organize lower-class people attract individuals on their way up the social-class ladder. Persons who are relatively responsible about participation, articulate, and successful at managing organizational "forms" are identified as lower-class leaders, rather than individuals who actually reflect the values of lower-class groups. Ordinarily the slum's network of informal group associations is not reached.
>
> This project proposes to remedy this situation by means of a "Starter Program," through which indigenous community organizers will be recruited and trained . . .

Note what is to be remedied: instead of getting hold of local people who are "relatively responsible about participation, articulate, and successful at managing organizational 'forms'," Mobilization for Youth is going to get hold of a lower level of true and genuine leaders who are—what?—inarticulate, irresponsible, and relatively unsuccessful? I am sorry, but I suspect that proposition. I was raised on the West Side of New York, and I must report that those are not the principles on which Tammany Hall, the International Longshoremen's Association, or the New York Yankees recruited indigenous leadership.

I will be blunt. Midge Dechter has suggested that the idea of The Proletariat is very much evident in this type of thinking, and to the extent that it is, it is doomed to disappointment. Sargent Shriver has clearly indicated his own concern on this point. Whatever the American poor may be, they are not modeled on a European prototype, and will break the hearts of those who set out to do something for them on that assumption. (It is interesting to note that at the last election, the greatest Democratic sweep in history, the citizens of Harlan County, Kentucky, or the surrounding district, elected a Republican Congressman, as is their ancient practice. I have no doubt this gentleman will be a fine legislator—this is his first term—but I question whether he will be a particularly radical one.)

I raise all this not to be negative, but rather to make a serious point. I do not think it is in any way possible for the problems of the American poor to be solved in isolation. We have got to build a Great Society that rests on the provision of reasonable expectations for everyone, not just the poor, but for all of the nonprofessional, nonmanagerial wage workers of the nation.

This requires first of all that we get on with a great deal of unfinished business. Our social insurance system is unfinished. Our wage system is unbalanced and incomplete. Our employment nexus is frighteningly inadequate. These are fundamental political issues, and there does not yet exist a consensus that they should be resolved. Trying to cure poverty without attending to these matters is treating symptoms.

The only force in American society—or any other industrial democratic society that I know of—that is capable of providing the mass citizen support for solving these fundamental problems, and for sustaining such efforts over long periods of time, is the trade union movement.

The trade union movement was the original anti-poverty movement in this nation, and it remains incomparably the most significant one. The trade union movement was the original organization of the "indigenous disadvantaged," and it remains incomparably the most effective and established model for organizing working men and women to look after their economic and social interests. The trade union movement was the original mass force pressing for improved education and living standards for all Americans, and it remains one of the most important ones.

The problem is that the American trade union movement

is incomplete. It has not reached that point of membership and program and influence whereby it can provide the mass support that is needed to bring about solutions to the fundamental problems of which I speak. It is necessary, however, to ask why the trade union movement is incomplete. The reasons are twofold. First, trade unions are human institutions, and therefore unsatisfactory, if not grossly imperfect. That is the life that is given us on this earth. But there is another reason. The American trade union movement is incomplete because it has been relentlessly attacked and harassed and impeded by other forces in American life. For the longest while, and still today, these forces have come from the Right. But in our time the attacks have been coming from the Left as well, and have probably done as much harm.

The attacks from the Right are easy enough to understand. The twin ideals of American Democracy are Liberty and Equality. But over the years Liberty has acquired vastly the greater prestige. Equality, although an ideal at least as old in Western political thought, has never been fully accepted in some circles of American life. And the trade unions have been rightly seen as the principal force pressing for equality in an industrial society. Nor have they presented themselves as anonymous and gratefully poor. They have been the same limited, exasperating, demanding human beings we all are. The trade unions have therefore been seen as threatening the interests of property, which is understandable. But in our time, they have suffered the fiercest attacks from the Left, not because they were doing terrible things, but because they were *not* doing them, or at least not doing them the way they were supposed to. That, I submit is helping not at all.

There is a strong temptation among some groups to suppose that the war on poverty can be won by welfare work. It cannot. There is a mighty presumption by some others that the political base from which to attack our fundamental problems can be built with well-intentioned and socially-minded persons, most of whom have long since decided the trade union movement was not interesting enough, or radical enough to merit their support. It cannot. The war on poverty will not be won unless the American nation learns genuinely to accept and value the role of the trade unions as the representatives of the interests of the working people, and until the trade union movement, responding to that acceptance, comes more completely to warrant it.

5. The Attack on Poverty

JOSEPH A. KERSHAW

At the outset I believe I should make my role quite clear. I do not speak to you as a representative of the Office of Economic Opportunity, but as a private and interested economist who in a weak moment pledged fifteen months of his life, beginning in June, to the war on poverty.[1] But that stint has not yet begun, so I bring no "red-hot inside dope" fresh from the bureaucratic inner councils, nor has my manuscript been cleared by the bureaucracy. As I look over the list of participants at this impressive conference I confess that I feel quite overwhelmed. Since I have neither the practical nor the research experience of most of those here on the poverty problem, I expect to take rather than to give, and perhaps to test out a few ideas that have occurred to me as I have contemplated my future assignment.

What I would like to do this evening is to throw out a few notions that seem to me relevant to what OEO can do, tell you a little about the particular job I shall be attempting, and suggest a few of the many problems I see ahead in that job.

The Impact of Aggregate Demand

In the first place, OEO is very much at the mercy of the over-all economic and fiscal policies of the government. Since OEO's clients are the first to lose their jobs when unemployment rises and demand falls, the maintenance of aggregate outlay is surely a necessary if not sufficient condition of success in the war on poverty. There are familiar imperfections in the

[1] Editor's note: At the time of the conference, Mr. Kershaw's appointment as Assistant Director, U. S. Office of Economic Opportunity, effective June 1965, had been announced.

market that keep high and growing aggregate demand from being immediately translated into more jobs, particularly semi-skilled and unskilled jobs. But it is well to remind ourselves that in 1940 there were many million hard-core unemployed, and we all assumed they were unemployable, having been out of work for many years. Yet three years later we had only 700,000 unemployed in the entire country, not much over a one-per-cent unemployment rate.

I don't recommend a return to Professor Galbraith's disequilibrium system—i.e., our wartime system of excess aggregate demand, combined with price controls and rationing—to get our unemployed back to work.[2]

But this experience does indicate the power of aggregate outlay when it is great enough to permeate the bottlenecks of immobility. And there is another appropriate lesson to be learned from tightness in an economy. I refer to what happened in the United Kingdom as unemployment fell below three and then below two per cent during the postwar period. Employers began looking for geographical areas with surplus labor to which they could subcontract parts of their orders, and depressed areas began to feel the impact of economic activity once more.

In our country we have had great skill, or great good fortune, in fashioning the 1964 tax cut. Its results, as were predicted, have been successful and have had wide support. All of us can rejoice with the Council of Economic Advisers in this outcome. It's a little sobering, though, to recall that it took fourteen months to get the bill through Congress, and would have taken longer had it not been for the tragic assassination of a President. But perhaps the measure's success will make it easier to get similar action in the future. No one should hope so quite as vigorously as OEO personnel. The centrality of the aggregate demand variable to the poverty problem can hardly

---

[2] Editor's note: The reference is to an article written by Professor Galbraith shortly after the war, in which he took the position that wartime controls were removed too quickly. See J. K. Galbraith, "The Disequilibrium System," *American Economic Review,* XXXVII (June, 1947), pp. 287–302.

be questioned—serious errors in managing this can negate much of what OEO can do.

INCOME REDISTRIBUTION

Of course, the poverty problem is not only a job problem. Indeed, one of the many disturbing facts about the 35 million people in poverty is that something like 40 per cent are in families whose head is not in the labor market. More jobs will help most of these people only indirectly and only after the passage of considerable time. And this brings me to the next principal question I want to pose: just what leverage does the government have? There are, it seems to me, two ways to go about the job of combatting poverty. One is to bring about a further redistribution of income, away from the rich and toward the poor. This largely means increasing welfare payments of one sort or another—something which is very much needed. Too many of the poor are outside the welfare and social security systems and are destitute because of it. Furthermore, I should like to point out that much redistribution of this sort has basic and long-range as well as short-range effects. Frequently it is the factor that will permit a child to stay in school, or a mother to work or become literate, and hence will have a payoff in increased productivity of labor.

With the important exception suggested in the previous sentence, most income transfers simply result in different ways of slicing the income pie. Incidentally, it is an indication that the problem is no longer so overwhelming as it once was that some $12 billion given to the poor would raise them all to the poverty line as presently defined by the Council of Economic Advisers. This is only a third or so of our annual growth in gross national product. Such an income transfer, of course, even if politically feasible, would not represent a long-run solution to the problem, and no one would propose it. What we need in the longer run are ways to increase the productivity of the poor, ways to make them valuable in jobs, and ways of getting them from where they are to where the jobs are. Measures that do this increase the size of the pie, not just the way it is sliced.

RAISING PRODUCTIVITY

Many of the poor have essentially zero productivity now. They lack skills, education, motivation, and sometimes even literacy. This is why there is so much emphasis on training and education in OEO programs, and this is why there is so much concern with youth. An elderly unemployed or retired person can usually be helped only by some form of income transfer; a dead-end 18-year-old high school dropout can become a charge on society and a probable crime statistic, or he can become a productive citizen for half a century. For society as well as for the individual, the option is incredibly important. Here lies the tremendous appeal of the Job Corps and the other job training parts of the program, for their success will mean, not only turning young men and women into better adjusted people, but a real and continuing increase in the size of the GNP. The poor will be generating themselves the resources which will help eliminate poverty, not only this year but for all those years to come.

There is, of course, a critical assumption here. It is that there will be jobs available for these newly trained workers to take, jobs that were not already filled by others who became displaced and unemployed. In other words, placing these newly trained young people must result in a net increase in the number of job holders. I believe this assumption can be made at unemployment rates near or below our present one, though it would become invalid if the rate went much above its current level. On February 1, the President issued a statement calling attention to the paradox that, with four million unemployed, many job vacancies exist, and that among other indicators of this "we have been admitting almost 200,000 foreign workers annually because American workers were not considered available." At present there are jobs, I am convinced, if we can get workers trained and motivated so that they can perform in the required ways.

The conclusion, I believe, is that there *is* real leverage available if we can find the right handles. Raising the productivity of a substantial part of the labor force can have a very real impact on the future size of national income. On various assumptions this can be easily enough calculated, and no doubt will be.

EVALUATION OF THE RESULTS

Someone is going to have to watch the many parts of the anti-poverty program and see whether these fine results are in fact achieved. This brings me to the point at which I want to discuss briefly some of the evaluation problems I will face in June, and on which people in my office in OEO are already working. In a nutshell, the question is whether the government is getting its money's worth in the anti-poverty programs. I suppose a basic first query is whether we are really having any impact on poverty at all. As incomes have risen, poverty has been declining over the years, at a rate of about one per cent a year on the basis of the generally accepted definition, and this will no doubt continue. OEO will spend some $780 million this fiscal year, and the President has asked for $1.5 billion for fiscal 1966. With expenditures of this magnitude, we ought to get an acceleration of the decline in poverty, unless we are to assume that the rate of decline would have slowed in the absence of the expenditure. I expect to be asked to demonstrate that the impact of our expenditures is in fact producting these results.

Perhaps more interesting, how do we measure the relative effectiveness of resources spent one way rather than another? If the Job Corps costs four times as much per poor person served as the nonresidential youth centers, does it buy four times as much, or more or less? These are classic cost-benefit types of problems, with the usual difficulty introduced by a system output that is difficult to specify, let alone quantify. Progress in conceptualizing and solving this sort of problem has been made in the national security field and to a lesser extent in education. I do not know of much similar work concerned with social factors, as ours will be, except perhaps for the case of water resource developments and the excellent about-to-be-published Brookings Institution study on the problems of evaluating urban renewal projects by Jerome Rothenberg.

Systems analysts frequently find that their most valuable contributions take the form of inventing new systems, sometimes as a by-product of the analysis and comparison of existing systems. My hope is that this will also occur in our case; as I understand my charter, it will encourage us to do just this.

As in so many evaluative studies, we will have our problems with criteria. It isn't enough for Job Corps graduates to have a fine employment record if they are simply replacing high school graduates in jobs. Or, to take another example, recently Kermit Gordon, Director of the Bureau of the Budget, called attention to the weaknesses in our agricultural subsidy program, for which he ought to get a medal. Suppose we were to reorient those subsidies more toward the poor farmer. I would argue that it would not help much if the subsidies tended to keep inefficient farmers on the farm, even though their incomes might rise. The proper way to use such funds is to encourage the adjustments needed to bring about increased efficiency, which probably means, in the case of agriculture, training and moving allowances.

These examples suggest, I believe, that it would be all too easy for us to adopt too proximate a criterion and thus measure our achievement against the wrong objective. As a former colleague of mine would state it, this would put us in the position of committing a brilliant error.

Such is a brief statement of the nature of the job as I see it. To accomplish these objectives, we will have a staff of some 35 or so in Washington, including economists, comptroller-type analysts, and others, all of whom I hope will be imaginative and inventive. But we also have money for supporting external research projects, and my earlier experience with this kind of research encourages me to emphasize it in connection with evaluation of the poverty program. I have several different sorts of things in mind.

First, I hope to interest a number of economists, and perhaps others, in becoming consultants. These experts would prepare occasional papers on aspects of the poverty problem in which they were interested, attend meetings from time to time, help us recruit, and maintain a general interest in our program.

Second, I hope to get several projects going at universities which would involve people in several disciplines. Mixed research teams would be asked to make careful studies of the impact of the poverty program in their particular localities. We would like to analyze the relationships between our activities and social variables such as level of income, extent of unemployment, high school dropout rates, and perhaps eventually such phenomena as drug addiction, divorce rates, church attendance, and so on. I would hope that we could find groups of professionals who would initiate and carry out such studies in different areas. Moreover, duplication in such research is devoutly to be desired, at least in the beginning. Clearly, designing such evaluative studies will require great skill and imagination, but it seems equally clear that payoffs should be correspondingly high.

Finally, we are thinking about the possible establishment of a research institute dedicated to research on poverty—a RAND Corporation for poverty, if you will. I'm not sure that this idea makes sense, but we do feel the need for facilities where some of the longer range problems could be studied at leisure, and where a high quality staff would be concerned with our problems in a basic, as opposed to an operational, sense.

This brings me to the problem of the time dimension. My view is that a meaningful portion of our research funds ought to be spent in connection with projects in which payoffs come only after a considerable period of time or may actually be problematical. A number of parts of the poverty program are of this nature. OEO is launching a program this summer known as Project Headstart, which will give intensive training to several hundred thousand pre-school children to prepare them for the rigors of first grade. An effective means of measuring the impact of this training on these children will yield results only after the passage of a considerable period of years.

I want to conclude these wandering remarks on a hopeful note. The task of speeding up the retreat of poverty is going to be a difficult one, without simple solutions. But I am convinced that the federal government does have substantial leverage if it uses its resources wisely. And what encourages me most is a very strong determination, on the part of the director of the program as well as his lieutenants, to test it every step of the way to be sure the resources *are* being spent wisely, and to search for alternatives which may work better. To economists, whose central concern is always with efficiency defined in our own private way, this is indeed gratifying. It is slightly frightening as well, because it means that we are going to have to come up with answers to questions that will be mighty difficult.

6. Measures to Reduce Poverty

MARION B. FOLSOM

When I saw the program for this conference, with so many academic people from the social sciences, I naturally hesitated to appear as the only businessman on the list. But I consented because during the past forty years I have been dealing with programs to protect the individual employee against the major economic hazards of life—ill health and disability, unemployment, premature death, dependent old age.

In the middle 1920's there were exceedingly few employee benefit plans. I recall that when the Kodak Company, in 1928, adopted a retirement annuity, disability benefit, and life insurance plan, with a substantial payment on the accrued liability, it created quite a sensation in business and insurance circles. We were about the first large company to adopt an actuarially sound plan, underwritten by an insurance company. In 1929, I contributed an article to the *Atlantic Monthly* on the need for industrial pension plans, which concluded as follows:

> Good, humane management will not permit employees of long service to be discharged if they have not adequate means of sustenance. Yet good management cannot keep employees on the force when they are no longer productive. The solution is the inauguration of a sound and adequate pension plan. The longer the solution is delayed by business organizations, the more expensive it becomes.

This view has over the years become well recognized.

As one of the five employer members of the Advisory Council which helped draft the original Social Security Act in 1934, I recall that the principal problem as to dependency in old age was whether we should adopt a contributory social insurance system or rely on the assistance-relief method. Fortunately for the country, the decision was made for social insurance. The principal problems in unemployment compensation were whether the system should be on a federal or a state basis and whether there should be experience-rating or not. I was a strong advocate of experience-rating; because of our experience in stabilizing employment at Kodak, I felt that the variation in rates would result in increased efforts to reduce fluctuations in employment. In spite of the opposition of most of the academic people, the option was granted to the states to have experience-rating provisions.

At that time, social insurance was something new in this country, although such plans had been in operation for years in other industrial countries. It was probably natural that a great majority of businessmen and many others were opposed to these two plans. The objections generally raised were that a governmental system would interfere with the incentive of an individual to provide for himself; that the benefits would get entirely out of line; and that the plan could not be administered efficiently.

None of these predictions has been borne out and the two plans are now generally accepted with little opposition. With the constructive attitude of the two congressional committees and the assistance of advisory councils, the old age insurance system has been kept up-to-date on a sound basis and broadened to include survivorship protection and total disability. In addition, coverage has been extended to practically all employed groups. The system is being well run, with an administrative cost of only two per cent. It has greatly stimulated a rapid expansion of supplementary private plans, and there has been a great increase in all forms of individual savings.

Compulsory health insurance was on the agenda of the original council, but President Roosevelt, with most of the advisers agreeing, felt that unemployment insurance and old age insurance would be enough for the country to absorb at that time and that we should not get into the complexities of health insurance.

In the late 1930's and early 1940's there was a growth of voluntary prepaid hospital insurance plans, while after the war there was very rapid growth of Blue Cross-Blue Shield plans.

This growth was the principal factor in the defeat of efforts during this period to enact a compulsory governmental health insurance plan.

Present Situation

Through governmental plans, basic protection is now provided to practically all employed persons against the hazards of industrial accidents, dependent old age, total disability, temporary unemployment, and loss of the family breadwinner.

In the last 40 years, there has also been a broad expansion in other voluntary company benefit plans. About 25 million workers, or about half the nonfarm work force, are covered under supplemental company pension plans, and about 2,500,000 are receiving benefits. The reserves are growing rapidly, now amounting to over 75 billion. A high percentage of employees has life insurance, temporary disability protection, and some type of health insurance.

The protection under the voluntary plans varies widely, with those who need it most having little. In effect, from the standpoint of amount of protection, we have three distinct groups of wage-earners:

1. Employees of large or progressive companies, with wages well above the average, and liberal employee benefits. The employers generally pay a large part of the cost of these plans and sometimes all.
2. Employees of smaller concerns—manufacturing, trade, and service—and casual workers; wages are generally lower; few concerns have supplementary pension plans; sickness benefit and health insurance plans are inadequate.
3. The poverty group, including the poorly educated and unskilled, with low wages when employed, and often unemployed. Although this group represents a small percentage of the work force, it is still the sizable group about which we are now concerned.

No accurate estimate can be made of the proportion of workers in each of these groups. There is a steady shift from Group 2 to Group 1 and, as education improves, many are moving out of the poverty group. On the other hand, slippage occurs from the lower scale of the second group into the poverty group, because of heavy expenses resulting from severe illness in the family or other misfortunes. There is also a slippage, especially in the older ages, caused by technological changes. Although those in the poverty group will decline in periods of prosperity, there will still be a hard core of unemployed among the unskilled. In 1951–1953, with the unemployment rate down to 2.7 per cent for all groups, the rate for nonfarm laborers was 5.8 per cent.

CAUSES OF POVERTY

General measures—fiscal and monetary policies, urban renewal, reduction of race discrimination—which affect the whole economy are important in reducing poverty, but I will confine my discussion to those measures which have a direct effect upon the poverty groups. Of course, one of the basic causes is the lack of motivation and other personal defects, but these defects are often the result of the other factors I will discuss.

It seems to me that the principal causes affecting the individual are: (1) lack of adequate education and training; (2) ill health and disability; (3) inadequate social insurance measures; (4) inadequate welfare measures and methods; (5) failure of many employers to provide adequate protection for their employees against economic hazards and the failure to provide adequate training and retraining measures; and (6) slowness of the general public to adjust its attitudes to the rapid change from a rural to a highly industrialized urban society.

EDUCATION

Many studies have indicated the close correlation between high unemployment and low income on the one hand and inadequate education on the other. For example, in 1961 low-income families (those with a cash income less than $3,000) represented 47 per cent of the families whose head had less than eight years of schooling, but only 12 per cent of those who had completed high school. In 1962, unemployment among white males with one or more years of college was two per cent, but among white males with less than eight years of schooling it was over eight per cent. Unemployment among nonwhite males of less than eight years schooling was 14 per cent. A study by Herman P. Miller, in 1964, showed that, on the average, men with less than eight years of schooling earned $143,000 (at 1960 rates) during their lifetimes, while those with high-school education earned $247,000 and those with four years of college, $385,000.

A subcommittee of CED has been studying the unemployment problems arising out of technological changes for two years. In December 1963, I presented to the Senate Subcommittee on Unemployment our findings to that point, which have been confirmed by our subsequent study. Based upon this and other studies, I feel that while personal traits, lack of motivation, ill health, discrimination, and compulsory wage levels are contributing factors, probably the most important cause of unemployment, as far as the individual is concerned, is the lack of education and training at all levels, from pre-kindergarten through college, and training within industry.

I suggested to the Senate committee that it was necessary to devote more resources to schools in areas with a high percentage of low-income families. Schools in such areas should have smaller classes because there is likely to be a greater discipline problem and more need for individual attention. To reduce dropouts, students need more and better guidance and counseling, in part because their parents are unable to provide it, and remedial courses. There should be a great expansion of nursery and kindergarten schools, and more practical vocational programs. There should be more rapid expansion of community colleges, in both career and academic programs, and expansion of evening courses in universities to enable people to keep up to date in their trade or profession. Industry could expand its in-plant training and retraining programs.

Proposed legislation

The legislation recently proposed by President Johnson would provide federal funds to the states to meet these same objectives as far as schools are concerned, and it is intended primarily to improve education and training of children and adults in low-income families.

I am convinced that additional funds devoted to pre-schools and schools in these low-income areas are sound investments and will result in increased employment and productivity and reduced welfare expenditures. I supported the bill in testifying before the Senate committee earlier this month. To provide more funds I suggested one major change—that the grants to the states should be put on a matching basis, with the matching terms varied to favor the low per capita income states.

Another provision of the bill I strongly favored is an increase in funds for research in education. Total expenditures for research into new methods and techniques of teaching from all sources now amount to only $72 million—1/5 of 1 per cent of total educational expenditures—very small indeed when compared with the amount of research in other fields. There is great need for research and demonstration projects to determine the best methods to motivate and teach children in nursery, kindergarten, and lower grades in schools in low-income areas.

I have also favored, and still do, a program of general federal aid for all schools, especially to assist the states with low per capita income. But many efforts in recent years to obtain legislation of this type have failed, and we shall have to rely on grants for specific purposes, which have proved so successful in the National Defense Education Act and which are now being proposed in this current bill. But the problem of aiding those low-income states which already spend a higher percentage of their income on education than the wealthy states, but much less per student, still remains and there are many low-income families in these states.

ILL HEALTH

Great progress has been made in recent years in medical science and practice. Average life expectancy at birth has increased from 50 years in 1900 to 70 years at present. Most of the progress has been in the practical elimination of contagious and other diseases affecting the younger age groups.

Our medical research problem now relates primarily to the

diseases of middle and older ages—heart, cancer, and stroke, which account for 70 per cent of deaths. Much knowledge has been obtained from the research in these diseases—as to early detection, prevention, rehabilitation, and cure—but as the President's Commission has recently stated, the problem now is to apply this knowledge. In fact, this is the chief problem with many other diseases. It is more difficult to put this knowledge of the latest advances and practices into effective use among the lower income groups—even for those diseases the incidence of which has been greatly reduced among the rest of the population.

Dr. George James, Health Commissioner of New York City, has recently pointed out that, with the same health service available for all the people in the City, the number of reported tuberculosis cases was 226 per 100,000 population in central Harlem, 183 in the lower East Side, and 20 in Flushing. The infant mortality rate was 38 per 1,000 in Harlem and 14 in Flushing.

A study by the Department of Health, Education, and Welfare showed that only one-third of all children in families with annual incomes of under $2,000 have ever been to a dentist, but in families with incomes of $7,000 or more, more than 90 per cent have been. It also showed that persons in families with incomes below $2,000 are almost five times as likely to have disabling heart conditions as those with incomes above $7,000, and nine times more likely to have a visual impairment.

As to protection against the cost of medical care, the study indicated that, in June 1963, over 87 per cent of families with incomes above $7,000 had some kind of health insurance, as compared with 52 per cent with incomes from $2,000 to $4,000 and only a third of families with incomes below $2,000. It was also shown that the insurance carried by the poorer people covered a smaller part of the cost of medical care.

The higher incidence of illness and disability among these lower income families, the lack of preventive care, the lack of proper home or hospital care when sick, the failure to use rehabilitation services, and the general home situation all have manifold effects on the individual and society. The increased lost time, the increase in severity of illness due to lack of early attention, and the larger hospital bills result in reduced income and savings. The chain of events either keeps the individual in the poverty group or causes him to slip into it. The final result is apt to be long-term institutional care in many cases, with heavy relief costs.

To meet this situation, the local public health service should provide comprehensive family care clinics in neighborhoods with a high concentration of low-income families. The clinics should bring about improvement in preventive and early care, maternal and child care, rehabilitation, and a reduction in stay at hospitals and long-term care facilities. The increased costs would probably be offset by the savings in welfare costs, to say nothing about human values.

Community planning

One important factor in the sharply increasing cost of hospital and medical care is the haphazard planning of hospitals and lack of coordination of local hospitals and health facilities and services. As a result, in most communities there is an excess of beds in the acute general hospital—the most expensive type—and a shortage of long-term care facilities, extended care, self-care units, which can be built and operated at a lower cost, and of organized home-care programs. These other facilities are often better suited to the health needs of the patient. There is also an unnecessary duplication of expensive facilities and services which often results in inferior quality of care. Some communities, such as Rochester, have found that a strong council, to plan and coordinate hospitals and other health facilities and services, can bring about better health care on a more economical basis.

Such councils should direct special efforts to the needs of the low-income groups. State and regional councils should also be established with some authority to bring about such planning and coordination. The National Commission on Community Health Services is now engaged in a four-year program to stimulate better community planning and action.

Hospital insurance for the aged

Illness among the aged is one of the principal causes of poverty. With the high cost of medical care, especially hospitalization, the higher incidence of illness, the lower income and inadequate insurance, the aged often have to exhaust their savings to meet these costs and many are forced to go on relief.

The pending federal legislation should be enacted to provide care in general hospitals and extended-care facilities and organized home care for persons over 65 in age—to be financed through the contributory social insurance mechanism and administered, as far as possible, by local private agencies. This plan is better than the relief system for the same reasons, both humane and fiscal, which underlay the decision in 1934 to finance old age pensions through contributory social insurance. There would be opportunity for private agencies to insure all other medical costs.

State legislation

Probably two-thirds or three-fourths of the work force now receive some sickness benefits when ill, but many of those in the low-income group who need this protection most do not have it. Legislation should be enacted by the states to make it compulsory for employers to cover their employees on a contributory basis for a reasonable number of weeks of temporary disability benefits, either on an insured or self-insured basis. New York, California, New Jersey, and Rhode Island now have such laws.

The state legislation for compulsory temporary disability benefits should also include a provision for compulsory coverage on a contributory basis for a reasonable number of days in a hospital or extended-care facility and at home under an organized home-care program. The coverage would be provided through a Blue Cross agency or insurance company. While a substantial majority of workers now have this protection, many of those in the low-income groups do not, and for those who do, frequently the protection is inadequate protection and the employer does not participate in the cost. It is very unlikely that these groups can be adequately covered except by compulsory legislation. A bill along this line has been introduced in the New York State Legislature.

SOCIAL INSURANCE

Unemployment insurance

Since 1937, when the unemployment insurance system became effective, there have been five recessions, with resulting increases in layoffs. The $35 billion paid out in benefits during this period have enabled many workers to get along during their unemployment without having to exhaust their savings, and many others have been prevented from going on relief. In addition to meeting human and social needs, the billions of dollars paid out currently by these and the other social insurance systems have helped to stabilize the economy and prevent recessions from becoming more severe.

Certain improvements should be made in the federal-state system especially to help those workers in the lower income levels.

The principal defect in coverage is that the federal law now applies only to employers with four or more workers. Thus, the many low-income workers employed by very small concerns are deprived of this protection. Many states, including New York, have covered employees of one or more for several years and no serious administrative problems have been encountered. There is no logical reason why the federal law should not be changed to this basis, as recommended by Presidents Eisenhower and Kennedy.

Changes should also be made in the benefit structure in most states because the level of benefits has not kept up with rising wage levels. It was the objective of the system that benefits should be set at 50 per cent of normal earnings. Because of low maxima and the increase in wages, few beneficiaries actually receive 50 per cent of their earnings. The average weekly benefits in 1963 were only 34.6 per cent of the average weekly wages. To meet this type of situation, President Eisenhower recommended that the benefits should be improved in the state systems so that a majority of the workers would receive one-half of regular earnings for 26 weeks or more. Good progress has been made in reaching the duration goal but few states have acted on reaching the benefit goal.

In the 1958 and 1961 recessions, temporary Federal legislation was enacted to provide extended benefits, with the cost to be borne by the states. In recent years, we have been faced with a certain amount of longer periods of unemployment, due to technological and industrial changes. I feel that federal legislation should be enacted to make available at all times 13 weeks of extended benefits to workers with a long attachment to the labor market, such benefits to be financed by the federal government. The beneficiary should be required to take training courses, if feasible, to fit him for new occupations. State laws should also provide that regular benefits be paid to workers enrolled in vocational training courses.

Old-age insurance

Under the Old-Age, Survivors, and Disability Insurance Plan, almost 20 million persons are currently receiving monthly benefits, of whom 15.5 million are aged. Total monthly benefits amount to over $1.3 billion.

To accomplish the objective of the system—to prevent dependency in old age—the benefits must be kept in line with the current level of wages and prices. The Federal Advisory Council has recently recommended that benefits should be increased to take into account the increases in wages and prices since the last general increase in 1958. It also recommended that the period for computing benefits for men should be based, as is now the case for women, on the period to age 62 instead of age 65—which would give larger benefits to those retiring earlier. It also felt that the Social Security program should pay the costs of rehabilitation for disability beneficiaries likely to be returned to gainful work through such help. These changes would all be helpful to those in the lower income level.

WELFARE

Dependent families

Despite the increasing prosperity of recent years, expenditures for relief and public assistance have continued to increase. Total payments (federal, state, and local) amounted to $4.6 billion in 1963, compared with $3.25 billion in 1958. The largest items in 1963 were Old-Age Assistance of $2.4 billion and Aid to Dependent Children of $1.4 billion. The latter amount shows the fastest growth, having doubled in six years.

Many demonstration projects have shown that a considerable number of families receiving this assistance can be put on a self-supporting basis by the use of competent, experienced case workers. There are good examples here in California. Some progress has been made in recent years because of the change in federal legislation, regulations, and increased efforts, but much more can be accomplished. It will require more trained social workers and higher salaries to attract competent persons and greatly increased effort by local and state welfare officials.

Rehabilitation

It is estimated that there are over two million adults in the country suffering from physical disabilities, who are unable to support themselves but could be made self-supporting. About 120,000 disabled people are now being rehabilitated annually under the Federal-State Vocational Rehabilitation program, but the number could be substantially increased if the funds and rehabilitation personnel were available. Federal grants are provided to the states on a matching basis, but only nine states in 1963 put up enough to receive their full federal allotment. This is one program in which it can be clearly demonstrated that the tax collections from those returned to gainful employment will greatly exceed the cost of rehabilitation, not to mention the human values from the program.

Another promising field for rehabilitation is in the inmates of penitentiaries. A computer analysis of the inmates of the

Rochester penitentiary showed that almost three-fourths of them were alcoholics and about three-fourths were repeats. During their stay, practically nothing is done in the way of rehabilitation, which accounts for many of the repeats. Specialists estimate that an appreciable number of these inmates can be rehabilitated and returned to gainful employment.

Private agencies

In recent years there has been a great increase in the number of voluntary health and welfare agencies at both the national and the local levels. There is a question as to whether their programs are being adjusted to meet changing needs and whether some of them should not be combined or terminated.

Little is being done in the way of evaluating the services rendered by these agencies. Little information is available about the cost of rendering each service so that the board members can judge whether the funds are being spent most wisely and effectively, and the community can determine how its voluntary funds should be allocated. To provide this basic information, the Community Chest agencies of Rochester recently adopted a system of functional cost accounting and budgeting similar to that employed in business and industry.

Because of the need in both the public and the private agencies for more trained social workers, the schools of social work should be expanded.

EMPLOYEE BENEFITS

A study of 1,150 companies in 1963 by the United States Chamber of Commerce showed that employee benefits represented an average of 25.6 per cent of the payroll and 20 per cent if the legally required payments are excluded. There is a wide variation between the companies, with those described in Group 1 above being well above those in Group 2. For example, employee benefits of the Kodak Company in 1963 amounted to 36.7 per cent, exclusive of legally required payments.

Pensions

Pension costs are the largest single benefit item. Since inauguration of the Social Security plan, there has been a rapid growth in supplementary pension plans, especially since World War II. Many of these plans are not on a sound financial basis and will require larger annual payments by the companies. The number of smaller companies setting up pension plans is steadily increasing as they are finding out their value.

It will be many years, however, before these supplementary pension plans will be providing benefits to many of those in the low-income groups, as they are likely to have been with companies without pension plans or have shifted employment constantly without accumulating pension rights.

One defect, from the social point of view, in most supplementary pension plans is the long period before vesting becomes effective—20 or 25 years in many cases—while some plans have no vesting. Many companies, however, have reduced the vesting period to fifteen years. If the vesting to be required in the future by Canada—ten years after age 45—were in effect, it would be particularly helpful to those older workers who are laid off due to technological changes in finding new employment. To prevent a sudden increase in cost, the aim should be a gradual approach to this shorter vesting period.

Sickness benefits

The payment of sickness benefits is one area which needs improvement. For example, the average for all the companies surveyed represented only 0.7 per cent of payroll, compared with 2.4 per cent for Kodak. A recent study by the Department of Health, Education, and Welfare shows that group protection against income loss due to temporary disability represented only 16.7 per cent of income in the states without compulsory laws. Improvement in these plans would be of distinct benefit to workers at the lower wage levels.

Likewise, there is need for more employer participation in the payment of Blue Cross-Blue Shield or other types of health insurance plans. This is especially true with many smaller concerns. Many larger companies are now covering their employees on a contributory basis for major medical insurance, with high maximum limits, but there has been little progress in the companies included in Group 2 above. It is also becoming more and more the practice of larger, progressive companies to continue to cover their retirees for health insurance. The federal insurance plan for the aged would, of course, cover the retirees for the hospital insurance part.

Training and retraining

A large amount of training is now being done by industry. A Department of Labor survey in 1962 showed that about three million workers in nonagricultural industries were enrolled in training programs, mostly in the larger establishments. There needs to be more attention given to retraining workers in declining occupations to fill jobs in expanding occupations. Larger companies are in a better position to do this, but to be effective they will have to do systematic advance planning for future personnel requirements.

Many concerns are too small to do much in the way of training or retraining and larger concerns cannot be expected to do all of it for their workers. Much dependence will have to be put on the educational system, the technical institutes, the community colleges, the current college evening courses, and all the other programs for continuing education. The employer should, as many now do, pay part or all of the tuition costs.

PUBLIC ATTITUDE TO FEDERAL PROGRAMS

This last subject is one with which you people from the universities should be particularly concerned—that is, the slowness of the general public and public opinion to adjust to the shift from a rural to a highly industrialized, urban society. This is natural when you consider the rapidity with which the change has taken place. For instance, in 1890, 77 per cent of the population was rural; in 1900, 60 per cent; in 1960, only 30 per cent was rural and 70 per cent was urban.

In my work in recent years in the fields of health, education, and welfare, I have been impressed with the opposition which develops toward almost any program involving the federal government. I get the impression that one of the difficulties is that many people do not realize the effects of the change which has taken place in our economy and that the federal government is the logical and often the only source of revenue available to meet new national needs.

Just think of the change in the educational system from 1900, when only four per cent of the college-age population went to college. Although over 100 years ago large grants of land were made to colleges, it is only very recently that the federal government has put any appreciable money into higher education, and opposition still prevents the federal government from making general grants to elementary and secondary schools.

Much of this trouble is attributable to the fact that the people do not have enough information, and you people in the universities should supply the facts. For example, people are very much concerned about so-called Big Government, or the Welfare State. However, analysis would show that the cost of running the regular departments of the government—excluding defense and defense-related items and interest on debt, due mostly to wars, represents only 10 per cent of the gross national product, and the percentage has been declining. Many people are very much worried about the federal debt and the burden we are supposed to be passing on to our grandchildren. Yet, as a percentage of the gross national product, the federal debt has declined from about 130 per cent in 1945 to about 50 per cent at present. These people don't seem to realize that we are also passing on many permanent assets which have all been paid for.

They are also worried about the federal deficit, although it amounts to less than one per cent of total expenditures. And if the budget were constructed in the way that practically all state, local, and foreign governments' budgets are—with capital items not being included in the regular operating budget—it would show a sizable surplus. I am not advocating a capital budget because of the danger of abuses, but I certainly think these factors should be brought to the attention of the public.

With the great needs which will be developing in the fields of education, health, and housing, expenditures will have to increase at all levels of government. The rising gross national product will permit large increases, but we might have to increase some items more than that. The difficulty is that the needs are greatest in the states or areas where the income is lowest, and aid from the federal government is necessary. Expenditures in these areas are sound investments for the country as a whole.

A recent development in the federal government, which has proved to be very helpful to various agencies, has been the increased use of advisory councils, composed of informed persons from the general public, to assist the particular agency in developing its programs. There are 272 of these advisory councils in the Health, Education, and Welfare Department alone. But in the most important task facing the federal government—the allocation of resources to various needs—there is no advisory council. The whole budget process, as far as major decisions are concerned, is now more or less hit-or-miss—much depending upon the judgment and inclinations of a few key people. Would it not be wise to have a small advisory group, composed of the ablest persons, to make an objective study of the broad needs of the economy and give advice periodically to the President and Congress regarding the allocations of our resources? With its perspective, such a council could be of great assistance to the Executive Department, to Congress, and to the general public.

In conclusion, I have indicated several practical measures for reducing poverty which can, without additional study or experimentation, be adopted by the particular agency concerned—the federal government, state or local government, voluntary agency or business establishment. The expenditures involved would be largely offset by the more effective use of manpower and reduced welfare expenditures. Any additional expenditures required would be a sound investment from both the humanitarian and the economic points of view.

PART THREE

INCOME DISTRIBUTION POLICIES

7. Changes in the Number and Composition of the Poor

HERMAN P. MILLER

The inclusion of a paper on counting up the poor in a session devoted to income redistribution policies can only mean that we wish to take a backward glance at the dimensions of poverty as we move forward in the search for new solutions to this ancient problem. It is fortunate that our policies in this and other areas do not await the perfection of statistics. If they did, we might find ourselves suffering intolerable evils for want of a proper measure. At the same time we must recognize that blind action, unaccompanied by a solid factual base, can be equally dangerous. It is important, therefore, that, as we forge new programs designed to alleviate poverty, we re-examine our concepts and our statistical measures to make certain that we can properly appraise the results of our efforts.

In this paper I do not intend to focus on the shortcomings of statistics on the distribution of income, because they are widely known. Many authors have written about the problems associated with the inaccuracies in the data, the use of a money income concept, the use of a single year's income, the changes in family composition, the failure to account properly for the increased tendency of the young and the old to live alone, etc. I do feel compelled to say, however, that, although the status of our knowledge in this area is better than it was 30 years ago when we first started collecting income data systematically, it is still deplorable. Only six months ago T. W. Schultz wrote, "Our President is now focusing attention on poverty in the United States. But unfortunately we are ill prepared to act because we have been out of touch. . . . All we have is a handful of crude data, mostly on family incomes, and they tell us very little." [1] Similar statements were made years ago by Dorothy Brady, Simon Kuznets, and other leaders in the field.

Although the problems have been known for a long time, the solutions have not been forthcoming. The Census Bureau, for example, is still compiling income statistics according to the same procedures and definitions that were used twenty years ago when the annual income survey was introduced as an experimental innovation. After nearly a quarter of a century of experience, it is time to move on to more sophisticated statistical approaches to the problem and to new data that are more specifically oriented to the problem as it is viewed today.

Revised Estimates of Poverty

Figures recently published by the federal government provide the best measure of the number and characteristics of the poor that has been available since the onset of the current debate on poverty. When the Council of Economic Advisers made its study of poverty several years ago, it used a cash income of less than $3,000 in 1962 as the poverty line for families of two or more persons and income of less than $1,500 for unrelated individuals (persons living alone or with nonrelatives). The failure to take various factors like size of family, the age of family head, and farm residence into account was recognized as a serious shortcoming that had to be tolerated because of the lack of more refined estimates. Early this year, however, the Department of Health, Education, and Welfare retabulated the Census Bureau's sample statistics for 1963, using a flexible poverty line which eliminates many of the shortcomings cited above.

The basic procedure employed in preparing the revised estimates involves the use of an economy budget, developed by the Department of Agriculture, which specifies in great detail the weekly quantities of foods needed by men, women, and children in various age groups in order to maintain nutritional adequacy. According to the HEW report, this budget, which is "adapted to the food patterns of families in the lowest third

[1] Theodore W. Schultz, "Our Welfare State and the Welfare of Farm People," *The Social Service Review,* XXXVIII (June, 1964), pp. 123–129.

of the income range, has for many years been used by welfare agencies as a basis for food allotments for needy families." [2] Using the quantities specified in the budget and food prices published by the Department of Agriculture, annual estimates of food costs needed to maintain nutritional adequacy were prepared for 124 different types of families classified by farm and nonfarm residence, age and sex of head, and number of children. These annual food costs were converted to incomes on the basis of assumed relationships between food expenditures and total income.

Families of three or more persons were assumed to be in poverty if their income was less than 33 per cent of the cost of the economy food budget. The poverty line for these families was obtained by multiplying the cost of the food budget by a factor of three. Data recently available from the 1960 Survey of Consumer Expenditures suggest that this is a reasonable relationship between income and food expenditures for low-income families.[3] A ratio of 27 per cent was used for two-person families, while unrelated individuals were assumed to need 80 per cent of the requirement for a couple, "on the premise that the lower the income the more difficult it would be for one person to cut expenses such as housing and utilities below the minimum for a couple." [4] The estimates for farm families are based on the assumption that they would need 40 per cent less cash income than nonfarm families of the same size and type, since many farmers receive part of their food and most of their housing without cash payment.

A summary of the dollar values used as the poverty line for selected types of families is shown in Table 1. The poverty line of $3,130 for a nonfarm family of four assumes that a daily expenditure of 70 cents per person will provide an adequate diet and that an additional $1.40 per person will provide

---

[2] Mollie Orshansky, "Counting the Poor: Another Look at the Poverty Profile," *Social Security Bulletin,* XXVIII (January, 1965), pp. 3–29.

[3] Helen H. Lamale, "Expenditure Patterns of Low Consumption Families," paper presented at the December 1964 meeting of the American Statistical Association.

[4] Orshansky, *op. cit.*

TABLE 1. SELECTED POVERTY INCOME CRITERIA FOR FAMILIES, BY SIZE, SEX OF HEAD, AND RESIDENCE, UNITED STATES, 1963

Number of persons in family	*Income on nonfarm residence*		*Income on farm residence*	
	Male head	*Female head*	*Male head*	*Female head*
1 (under age 65)	$1,650	$1,525	$ 990	$ 920
1 (aged 65 and over)	1,480	1,465	890	880
2 (under age 65)	2,065	1,875	1,240	1,180
2 (aged 65 and over)	1,855	1,845	1,110	1,120
3	2,455	2,350	1,410	1,395
4	3,130	3,115	1,925	1,865
5	3,685	3,660	2,210	2,220
6	4,135	4,110	2,495	2,530
7 or more	5,100	5,000	3,065	2,985

Source: Mollie Orshansky, "Counting the Poor: Another Look at the Poverty Profile," *Social Security Bulletin*, XXVIII (January, 1965), Table E.

for all other needs—housing, clothing, medical care, transportation, etc. The poverty lines for other family types are designed to provide equivalent levels of living. Using these dollar values, retabulations were made of the income data from the March 1964 Current Population Survey, comparing the income reported for each family with the income "required" by that family. If the reported income was below the required amount for that family type, the family was classified as poor. Families identified as poor on this basis were then retabulated according to various characteristics.

An examination of the revised estimates of poverty shows that, in 1963, about 34.5 million persons were in families with incomes insufficient to purchase an adequate budget. They constituted slightly less than one-fifth (18 per cent) of all persons in the United States. About 5 million lived alone or with nonrelatives and 30 million were members of family groups. One-half of the 30 million were children, the great majority of whom were living with both parents (Table 2).

A comparison of the economy budget estimates with those that would have been obtained by the application of the cruder standards used by the Council of Economic Advisers shows a remarkable similarity in the over-all totals. The CEA standards

TABLE 2. PERSONS IN POVERTY STATUS IN 1963, BY ALTERNATIVE DEFINITIONS (NUMBER IN MILLIONS)

Type of unit	*Total U. S. population*	*Below the economy budget*[a]		*Below the CEA definition*[b]	
		Number	*Per cent of total*	*Number*	*Per cent of total*
All persons	187.2	34.6	18	33.4	18
Farm	12.6	3.2	25	4.9	39
Nonfarm	174.6	31.4	18	28.5	16
Unrelated individuals	11.2	4.9	44	4.9	44
Members of families	176.0	29.7	17	28.5	16
Children under 18	68.8	15.0	22	10.8	16

[a] Economy level of the poverty index developed by the Social Security Administration by family size and farm-nonfarm residence, centering around $3,100 for four persons.

[b] Interim measure used by Council of Economic Advisors—under $3,000 for families and under $1,500 for unrelated individuals.

Source: Mollie Orshansky, "Counting the Poor: Another Look at the Poverty Profile," *Social Security Bulletin,* XXVIII (January, 1965), Table 1.

would have produced about 33.5 million persons in poverty, or approximately one million less than the number based on the economy budget. The CEA standard would also have produced an additional 1.5 million impoverished farm residents (because of the failure to take noncash income into account), and, most significantly, 4 million fewer impoverished children (because no adjustment was made for size of family).

Leading characteristics of families with incomes below the economy budget are shown in Table 3. Attention is called here to some of the more significant highlights:

(a) About 7 million families and 5 million unrelated individuals were in poverty in 1963. Their aggregate income was $11.5 billion below their estimated minimum requirements.[5] This amount might be regarded as a rough estimate of the cost of raising the incomes of all families and individuals above the poverty line as that term is now defined.

(b) Although the 2 million families with a female head accounted for about one-fourth of the poor families, they accounted for nearly one-half of the income gap between actual receipts

[5] *Ibid.,* Table 4.

TABLE 3. SELECTED CHARACTERISTICS OF FAMILIES IN POVERTY STATUS IN 1963, BY ALTERNATIVE DEFINITIONS (NUMBER IN MILLIONS)

Selected characteristics	*Total number of families*	*Families below economy budget*		*Families with incomes under $3,000*	
		Number	*Per cent of total*	*Number*	*Per cent of total*
All families	47.4	7.2	15	8.8	19
Residence					
Farm	3.1	0.7	23	1.3	43
Nonfarm	44.3	6.5	15	7.5	17
Color					
White	42.7	5.2	12	6.8	16
Nonwhite	4.7	2.0	42	2.0	43
Age of Head					
14 to 24 years	2.7	0.7	26	0.8	30
25 to 64 years	38.0	5.0	13	4.9	13
65 years and over	6.7	1.5	24	3.1	45
Type of Family					
Male head	42.5	5.2	12	6.5	15
Female head	4.9	2.0	40	2.3	47
Size of Family					
2 persons	15.3	2.5	16	4.6	30
3–5 persons	25.5	2.9	11	3.2	13
6 or more persons	6.6	1.8	27	1.0	15
Employment Status of Head					
Not in labor force	8.8	3.0	34	4.3	49
Unemployed	1.4	0.4	28	0.4	28
Employed	37.2	3.7	10	4.1	11
Work Experience of Head in 1963					
Worked in 1963	40.7	4.6	11	5.1	13
Worked at full-time jobs	37.9	3.6	10	3.8	10
50–52 weeks	30.7	2.0	7	2.1	7
Worked at part-time jobs	2.8	1.0	36	1.4	50
Did not work	6.7	2.6	38	3.7	55

Source: Mollie Orshansky, "Counting the Poor: Another Look at the Poverty Profile," *Social Security Bulletin*, XXVIII (January, 1965), Table 2.

and minimum requirements. At a cost of about $5 billion all families with a female head could be provided with incomes sufficient to meet minimum requirements as that term is currently defined.

(c) About 2 million families (about a fourth of all the poor families) were headed by a person who worked full-time throughout the year. Increases in aggregate demand and a full-employment economy probably would not benefit these families, except perhaps by providing work for wives and children.[6] Although the heads of this large segment of poor families were fully employed, their incomes were insufficient to raise their families above the poverty line. As an incidental fact, it may be noted that, if the families with a female or a nonwhite head are subtracted from the total, we find 1.3 million poor families (about 20 per cent of the total) headed by a white man who was fully employed throughout the year.[7] These figures dramatize the fact that low wages are still a major cause of poverty in the United States.

(d) About 1.5 million family heads worked at full-time jobs, but did not work throughout the year. The poverty of these families was attributable to a combination of low wage rates and periods of idleness associated largely with unemployment or illness. Although today's poor are frequently presented as psychologically or spiritually handicapped, the fact is that about 50 per cent of them are headed by a full-time worker whose wages are simply too low to support a family.

(e) The 2 million nonwhite families constituted about one-fourth of the poor families. About 40 per cent of these families were headed by women, few of whom had year-round full-time employment. A very large proportion of nonwhite poor live in the South; only about one-fourth live in large metropolitan areas in the North or West.

(f) The 1.5 million families with an aged head constitute about one-fifth of the poor families. The aged are a far smaller fraction of the poor when the economy budget rather than a flat $3,000 is used as the poverty line.

---

[6] If aggregate demand were increased to the point at which there was an extreme shortage of unskilled labor, there might be a tendency for the wages of the unskilled to rise more rapidly than the wages of skilled workers, as was the case during World War II. Such a situation is highly unlikely today, and, even if it existed, it would be accompanied by severe inflationary pressures.

[7] Orshansky, *op. cit.*

Is Poverty Being Reduced Fast Enough?

The chapter on poverty in the *Economic Report of the President* for 1964 begins with a call to action. It states that we have "been erasing mass poverty in America. But the process is far too slow. It is high time to redouble and to concentrate our efforts to eliminate poverty." [8] The reason for haste, presumably, is that poverty, in the eyes of the Council of Economic Advisers, has become an anachronism in our society. We tolerated it in an earlier era because we had no choice. Now, however, we have it within our means to raise the floor below which we will not let people fall. Since poverty can now be eliminated, the report argues, it should be.

There is an implication in the Economic Report that there has been a slowdown in recent years in the rate at which poverty is being reduced. The report states that "from 1957 through 1962, when total growth was slower and unemployment substantially higher (than in 1947–1956) the number of families in poverty fell less rapidly." [9] The statement is carefully phrased in terms of the *number* rather than the *proportion* of families below the poverty line. The latter, however, is the more critical relationship since the number of families is constantly rising over time.

An examination of the basic figures used by the CEA shows that between 1947 and 1963 the proportion of families with incomes below $3,000 (in terms of 1962 purchasing power) dropped from 32 per cent to 19 per cent (Table 4). In other words, during this 16-year period we moved 40 per cent of the way toward the complete eradication of poverty as that term is now defined. Between 1947 and 1956 the proportion of families with incomes under $3,000 dropped from 32 per cent to 23 per cent or at the rate of one percentage point per year. There was no change between 1956 and 1958. Since that time the proportion of families below the $3,000 poverty line dropped once again from 23 per cent to 19 per cent or just under one percentage point per year.

---

[8] *Economic Report of the President,* January, 1964, p. 55.
[9] *Ibid.,* p. 60.

TABLE 4. PER CENT OF FAMILIES WITH MONEY INCOME LESS THAN $3,000, 1947–1963 (1962 DOLLARS)

Year	*Per cent of families*
1947	32
1950	32
1951	29
1952	28
1953	26
1954	28
1955	25
1956	23
1957	23
1958	23
1959	22
1960	21
1961	21
1962	20
1963	19

Source: Figures for 1947 to 1962 from *Economic Report of the President,* 1964, p. 57; estimate for 1963 derived from U. S. Bureau of the Census, *Current Population Reports—Consumer Income,* Series P–60, No. 43.

In other words, the experience in the reduction of poverty from 1958 to 1963 was not appreciably different from the experience during the decade immediately following the Second World War. Even if the reduction in the incidence of poverty during recent years had been less rapid, the slower progress would not necessarily have been attributable to a slowdown in the rate of economic growth as alleged by the Council. In the first place, as the numerical base diminishes it becomes increasingly difficult to achieve the same absolute rate of reduction in the incidence of poverty. It was much easier to reduce the incidence of poverty by one percentage point when one-third of the families were below the poverty line than it is at present when fewer than one-fifth are at that level. Moreover, we must remember that, as we get closer to the very bottom of the income distribution, we are dealing increasingly with the hard-core poor whose incomes in a large proportion of the cases arise outside of the labor market and are not necessarily responsive to economic growth.

Although economic growth tends to reduce poverty by pushing

families above the poverty line, it also tends to increase poverty in a statistical sense by making it possible for the young and the old to maintain their own residences, thereby creating large numbers of low-income families that might not otherwise exist as independent units. The available statistics suggest that the observed reductions in poverty during the 1950's were not appreciably affected by these kinds of statistical aberrations. If we examine, for example, changes in the incidence of poverty among urban families headed by a person 35 to 44 years of age (Table 5), we find trends that closely parallel those noted for

TABLE 5. PER CENT OF URBAN FAMILIES WITH HEAD 35–44 YEARS OF AGE WITH INCOMES UNDER $3,000, 1947–1960 (1959 DOLLARS)

Year	*Per cent of urban families*
1947	20
1948	20
1949	21
1951	17
1952	16
1953	15
1954	14
1955	11
1956	10
1957	12
1958	11
1959	11
1960	11

Source: Data for 1947–1960 from Herman P. Miller, *Trends in the Income of Families and Persons in the United States: 1947 to 1960*, U. S. Bureau of the Census, Technical Paper No. 8, Table 3.

the entire population. Since this group of families is not likely to be affected by the process of fractionalization described above, it can be inferred that the change in the incidence of poverty among them reflects the impact of economic forces.

In general, it appears that the conclusions based on data for all families do not require significant alteration when changes in the living arrangements and in the urban-rural distribution of the population are taken into account. A more sensitive test of this thesis can be made by the application of a standardization procedure to the data. The actual percentage distributions for families by residence and age of head are available for each year since 1947. If a constant set of population weights is applied to these data, estimates can be made of the change in the proportion of families below the poverty line, independent of changes in the residence or age distribution of the population. The application of this standardization procedure to the data produced results that did not differ appreciably from the unadjusted data shown in Table 4.

IS THE COMPOSITION OF THE POOR CHANGING?

This is an important question, and it is one that we should be able to answer on the basis of available data; yet it turns out to be quite complex. If $3,000 (in terms of 1962 purchasing power) is used as the poverty line, we can agree unequivocally with the Council of Economic Advisers that "certain handicapping characteristics, notably old age, or absence of an earner or of a male head, have become increasingly prominent in the poor population."[10] We find that in 1963, 35 per cent of the families with incomes under $3,000 were aged as compared with only 26 per cent in 1951 (Table 6). Similarly the proportion of broken families among the poor increased from 19 per cent to 26 per cent, and the proportion of nonwhite

TABLE 6. SELECTED CHARACTERISTICS OF "POOR" FAMILIES, 1951 AND 1963

Family income for selected year	*Per cent of families with family head characteristics*		
	65 years and over	*Female*	*Nonwhite*
1951			
Under $2,000 (current dollars)	32	23	21
Under $3,000 (1962 dollars)	26	19	20
1963			
Under $3,000 (1962 dollars)	35	26	23

Source: Derived from U. S. Bureau of the Census, *Current Population Reports—Consumer Income,* Series P-60, Nos. 12 and 43.

[10] *Ibid.,* p. 72.

families increased from 20 per cent to 23 per cent. All of these changes support the conclusion of the Council.

However, is $3,000 the appropriate poverty line for 1951? The congressional study of low-income families that was conducted in 1949 used $2,000 as the poverty line for that year. Evidently the contemporary conception of poverty that prevailed in the United States shortly after the Second World War called for a poverty line of about $2,000. Are we justified in changing our conception of poverty for this earlier period and imposing a new and higher poverty line merely because our current standards have changed? I think not. If we examine the composition of the poor using a $2,000 poverty line for 1951 (in current dollars) and a $3,000 poverty line for 1963 (also in current dollars) we find very much smaller changes in the composition of the poor than those cited above. The aged, for example, represented 32 per cent of the poor in 1951, using the $2,000 poverty line for that year, and 35 per cent of the poor in 1963, using the $3,000 poverty line. Similarly, broken families constituted 23 per cent of the poor in 1951 and 26 per cent in 1963.

Thus, the use of contemporary definitions of poverty suggests that there has been very little change in the composition of the poor, whereas the use of a fixed poverty line suggests that there has been a great deal of change. The reason for the difference is obvious when the underlying statistics are considered. The magnitude of poverty and the characteristics of the poor depend to a large extent on the location of the poverty line. The aged, broken families, and similar disadvantaged groups will be prominent among the poor if a low poverty line is used. As the poverty line is moved closer to the middle of the distribution there is a greater tendency to include average families rather than those with special characteristics. In 1951, an income of $3,000 (in 1962 purchasing power) represented the lowest third of the income distribution, whereas in 1963 the same income represented the lowest fifth. Since the $3,000 poverty line in 1951 was much closer to the middle of the distribution, the aged and broken families represented far smaller fractions of the poor.

The question of the appropriate poverty line that should be used for historical analysis is only now receiving mature consideration. The historical analysis of the change in the number and composition of the poor in the *Economic Report of the President* for 1964 is in terms of a fixed poverty line of $3,000. All references in that report to the elimination of poverty must be construed as the elevation of families above the $3,000 mark measured in terms of 1962 purchasing power.

This static view of the poverty line was more specifically stated in a recent article by Robert Lampman in which he said, "the precise income level selected to mark off poverty from nonpoverty is not critical, *so long as it is unchanged over time,* except for necessary adjustments relative to the prevailing price level." [11] This position may represent sound strategy for a short-term viewpoint; however, it is fraught with peril for historical analysis. Moreover, it represents economically unsound thinking for a dynamic society and is at variance with the way in which we have actually gone about measuring poverty at different points in time.

The essential weakness of this position can perhaps best be seen by re-examining some of the observations made about the poverty line in 1904 by Robert Hunter who made one of the first quantitative studies of poverty in the United States. In this study, which is most sympathetic to the plight of the poor, Hunter states, "However desirable and socially valuable an income of $754 a year for each family would be, it is unquestionably too high for a fair estimate of the minimum necessary one. . . . To estimate in the most conservative way possible, let us take more or less arbitrarily $460 a year as essential to defray the expenses of an average family—a father, a mother, and three children—in the cities and industrial communities. . . . In the South, about $300 a year would probably cover the cost of like necessities." [12] Even if we allow for a tripling of prices since 1900, it is apparent that at the turn of the century Hunter could not conceive of a poverty line as high as $2,000

[11] Robert J. Lampman, "One-fifth of a Nation," *Challenge,* XII (April, 1964), p. 12.

[12] Robert Hunter, *Poverty* (New York: MacMillan, 1907), p. 52.

(in current dollars) for a family of five living in a metropolitan area.

We can see what a disservice Hunter would have done to the cause of the poor if he had been willing to settle for a fixed poverty line based on the experience of his time.

There is ample evidence of a relatively sharp upward movement in the poverty line even during the short period since the end of World War II. As previously noted, when the Joint Economic Committee made the first congressional investigation of low-income families in 1949 the poverty line was set at $2,000 for a family of two or more persons. Price increases since that time should have raised the level to about $2,500 in 1962; but the poverty line actually used in 1962 was $3,000, an increase of about 20 per cent in 13 years, or roughly 1.5 per cent per year. Further evidence of this tendency is provided by BLS data which show that the cost of a "modest but adequate" level of living (excluding taxes) for a working-class family of four persons in New York City was about $4,000 in 1947 and about $5,200 in 1959 (both figures in terms of 1961 purchasing power). In other words, the modest but adequate level of living rose by 28 per cent in New York City in this 12-year period—a growth rate of about 2 per cent per year.

The essential fallacy of a fixed poverty line is that it fails to recognize the relative nature of "needs." The poor will not be satisfied with a given level of living year after year when the levels of those around them are going up at the rate of about 2.5 per cent per year. Old-timers may harken back to the "good old days" when people were happy without electricity, flush toilets, automobiles, and television sets; but they must also realize that, once it becomes possible for all to have these "luxuries," they will be demanded and will quickly assume the status of "needs." For these reasons, it is unrealistic in an expanding economy to think in terms of a fixed poverty line.

Recently, T. W. Schultz has attempted to use the elasticity concept borrowed from the theory of demand to explain the relationship between the rise in per capita income and the rise in the poverty line. He notes that the rise in the poverty line over time "represents an increase in the demand for welfare services for the poor, that this increase in demand as it is revealed by the social-political process is a function of the rise in per capita income which can be treated as income elasticity." [13] Schultz goes on to state that "the underlying behavior here is consistent with an income elasticity somewhat less than unity. During the period since the mid-thirties real income per family virtually doubled and the poverty line, measured in constant dollars, appears to have risen by 75 per cent." [14]

This formulation of the problem treats the poverty line in a way that is analogous to the treatment of other economic variables. For example, on the basis of empirical evidence we know that the relationship between aggregate income and saving behaves in a more or less predictable way over fairly long periods of time. Despite the persistent annual growth in per capita income during the past 15 years the per cent of income saved has ranged between 6 and 8 per cent. This evidence suggests that as incomes have risen during the postwar period consumers have decided to devote a more or less constant proportion of that rise to savings. Analogously, we might find upon investigation, that there is a similar relationship between the level of income and the poverty line. If it is true, as Schultz alleges, that the percentage change in the poverty line is not as great as the percentage change in income, then we might expect on that account alone to find a decrease in the incidence of poverty over time in a growing society. It was not too many years ago that Dorothy Brady stated before a congressional committee that "the attempts of investigators for more than half a century have apparently led to about the same answer to the question, 'what proportion of the population does not have a minimum standard of living?' " [15] We now seem to be coming up with a different

[13] Theodore W. Schultz, "Investing in Poor People: An Economist's View," paper presented at the December 1964 meeting of the American Economic Association.

[14] This estimate is based on an unpublished study by Eugene Smolensky, "The Past and Present Poor," prepared by the U. S. Chamber of Commerce, quoted in Schultz, cited above.

[15] Statement of Dorothy Brady at *Hearings Before the Subcommittee on Low-Income Families,* Joint Committee on the Economic Report, 81st Cong., 1st sess., p. 475.

answer to this question. Here certainly is a problem that deserves more attention than it has received.

LONG-RUN CHANGES IN THE INCIDENCE OF POVERTY

Although the evidence is scanty, there seems to be general agreement that there has been an appreciable reduction in the incidence of poverty even when contemporary (rather than present) definitions of poverty are used. In reporting on changes during the postwar period, Oscar Ornati has used three different poverty lines: minimum subsistence defined as less than $2,500 per year in 1960; minimum adequacy which is less than $3,500; and minimum comfort, less than $5,500.[16] Using these concepts, with adjustments for changes in prices and standards over time, Ornati concludes that

> the proportion of the poor living below levels of minimum adequacy and minimum comfort has not changed very much. Indeed in 1947, by 1947 standards, 27.5 per cent of the people (that is of individuals living in households) lived below minimum adequacy levels and in 1960, by 1960 standards, 26 per cent were in this class. The proportion living below minimum comfort was 39 per cent in 1947, while in 1960 it was 40 per cent. The story is different when abject poverty is considered. Here, when the proportion living at or below minimum subsistence in 1947 is compared with the per cent barely subsisting in 1960, we find that the proportion decreased from 15 per cent to 11 per cent.[17]

These findings suggest that during the postwar period, at least, the rise in the "adequacy" line has kept pace with the rise in average income. Since there was no change in income distribution during this period, the proportion of families living below the level of adequacy remained fairly constant. It appears, however, that the "poverty" line did not rise as rapidly as average income. Consequently, there was a drop in the proportion of families with incomes below the poverty line.

---

[16] Oscar Ornati, "Affluence and the Risk of Poverty," *Social Research,* XXXI (Autumn, 1964), p. 334.

[17] *Ibid.* Details underlying these estimates are not given in the report cited. The report notes, however, that details will appear in a forthcoming publication of The Twentieth Century Fund by Oscar Ornati, *Poverty in the Affluent Society.*

In an unpublished manuscript, Ruth Mack has attempted to extend our knowledge in this area back to 1929.[18] She uses three different poverty lines: A "low" poverty line based on budgets prepared by the New York Department of Welfare since 1934; a "high" poverty line based on the "modest but adequate" Heller budgets since 1920; and an "average" poverty line based on a variety of budgets that represent low, medium, and high poverty lines. For each year, the various poverty lines were compared with the income distributions for families of two or more persons prepared by the Office of Business Economics.

Dr. Mack's figures suggest that the incidence of poverty in the United States has been sharply reduced regardless of the poverty level that is used (Table 7). The most marked reduction appears to have taken place for those groups nearest the bottom of the income distribution. Even during the prosperous 1920's, it appears that about one-fourth of the families had incomes below what we might call a "subsistence" budget. That proportion increased somewhat during the depression, was sharply reduced by the outbreak of the second World War, and has been dropping ever since. In 1960, only about one-tenth of the families had incomes below this "subsistence" budget. It is interesting that the sharpest reductions in "abject" poverty appear to have taken place between the depths of the depression and the outbreak of World War II. This period also coincides with a great rise in per capita income and the institution of various income maintenance measures introduced by the Roosevelt Administration. Both factors contributed to the very significant reduction in abject poverty during this period.

The proportion of families with incomes below the high poverty line, which some have called "deprivation," has also been reduced, but not as sharply as the proportion living in "abject" poverty. It appears that about one-half of the families were "in deprivation" prior to World War II as compared with about one-third of the families during the postwar period. In view of

[18] Dr. Mack has generously given me permission to use the data cited here. These figures should be used with caution since I have omitted some of the qualifying conditions and the more detailed descriptions of the adjustment procedures contained in the original manuscript.

TABLE 7. PER CENT OF FAMILIES WITH INCOMES BELOW VARIOUS POVERTY LINES, BASED ON CONTEMPORARY DEFINITIONS OF POVERTY, 1929–1960

Year	*Poverty line (1960 dollars)*[a]			*Per cent of families with incomes below each poverty line*		
	Low	*Average*	*High*	*Low*	*Average*	*High*
1929	$1,960[b]	$2,531	$2,938	26	40	50
1935–36	1,741	2,735	3,787	28	48	65[c]
1941	1,613	2,638	3,707	17	33	48
1950	2,213	3,334	4,352	13	27	36
1960	2,422	3,827	5,104	10	21	35

[a] These figures have been adjusted for comparability with respect to changes in average size of family. Average family size was 4.0 in 1929; 3.9 in 1935–36; 3.7 in 1941; 3.5 in 1950; and 3.3 in 1960. On the basis of these averages, the poverty levels for each year were multiplied by the factors shown below. The factors used to convert *current dollars* to 1960 prices are also shown below:

Year	*Adjustment factors*	
	Size of family	*Price changes*
1929	1.00	58.0
1935–36	1.00	46.4
1941	.96	49.7
1950	.93	81.2
1960	.91	100.0

[b] This estimate is based on the budget compiled by the Community Service Society whereas the "low" poverty line for later years is based on the New York Welfare Department budgets. For this reason, the apparent decrease in the "low" poverty line between 1929 and 1935–36 may be spurious.

[c] Dr. Mack notes that this figure is out of line. The Heller budget on which it is based was revised in 1935 and sharply increased.

Source: Based on unpublished data provided by Dr. Ruth Mack, Institute of Public Administration, New York, New York.

the stability of income distribution since the early 1940's, it appears that the rise in the deprivation line has more closely approximated the rise in average incomes than has been the case for the subsistence poverty line.

The reduction in the incidence of poverty appears to be far greater than that shown above if the 1960 poverty lines are used for the earlier years. Table 8 shows that during the depression nearly one-half of the families had incomes below the "subsistence" budget. This proportion dropped to about one-

TABLE 8. PER CENT OF FAMILIES WITH INCOMES BELOW VARIOUS POVERTY LINES, BASED ON 1960 DEFINITIONS OF POVERTY, 1929–1960

Year	*Families with incomes below poverty lines (%)*		
	Low	*Average*	*High*
1929	36	70	80
1935–36	47	70	83
1941	31	53	70
1950	26	34	55
1960	10	22	35

Source: Unpublished data provided by Dr. Ruth Mack, Institute of Public Administration, New York, New York.

third at the outbreak of the second World War; it dropped further to about one-fourth by the end of the war; and in 1960 only one-tenth of the families were in "abject" poverty. The reduction in poverty during the 1950's appears to be far greater if the 1960 proverty lines rather than contemporary poverty lines are used. This fact suggests that there was a relatively small rise in the "low" poverty line relative to the rise in income during this period.

Eugene Smolensky, using data and estimating procedures that are different from those used by Ruth Mack, provides a somewhat different picture of the reduction in the incidence of poverty since the depression.[19] Smolensky attempts to establish a relationship between the "real minimum-comfort per capita" budget and real GNP per capita for different points in time. The results are shown in Table 9. The budgets are defined simply as those "that have been prepared at various times for New York City workers." On the basis of this evidence, Smolensky concludes that "the minimum-comfort budgets per capita have generally been around one-half of real gross national product per capita." [20]

Smolensky then assumes that the minimum-comfort estimates shown in the above table for New York City "accurately reflect the relative rise in welfare levels demanded by some national

[19] Smolensky, *op. cit.*
[20] *Ibid.*, p. 8.

TABLE 9. SELECTED NEW YORK CITY BUDGETS AND REAL GROSS NATIONAL PRODUCT, 1903–1959 (1954 DOLLARS)

Year	*(1)* *Real minimum-comfort per capita*	*(2)* *Real GNP per capita*	*Ratio (1):(2)*
1903–05	$ 527	$ 924	.57
1914	358	1,026	.35
1918	587	1,109	.53
1935	776	1,166	.67
1947	919	1,865	.49
1951	1,006	2,102	.48
1954	1,057	2,125	.50
1959	1,022	2,421	.42

Source: Unpublished study by Eugene Smolensky, "The Past and Present Poor," prepared by the U. S. Chamber of Commerce.

consensus, except for the 1935–1936 budget, which will be arbitrarily scaled down to fifty per cent of gross national product per capita in these years, on the grounds that the other budgets surrounding it tend to point to that ratio."[21] He then suggests that if $3,000 in 1959 is used as the contemporary definition of poverty, "a poverty measure for each of the years 1935 and 1947 can be constructed on the assumption that the ratio of the 1935 and 1947 poverty limits for the nation as a whole should be the same as the ratio of these years to 1959, evidenced in the New York City budgets."[22] The results are shown in

TABLE 10. PER CENT OF FAMILIES WITH INCOMES BELOW THE POVERTY LINE, 1935, 1947, AND 1959 (ESTIMATES ARE IN 1959 DOLLARS)[a]

Year	*Poverty line*	*Per cent of families below poverty line*
1935	$1,710	32
1947	2,697	27
1959	3,000	23

[a] The estimates are based on a variable poverty line centered around a $3,000 value for 1959.

Source: Unpublished study by Eugene Smolensky, "The Past and Present Poor," prepared by the U. S. Chamber of Commerce.

[21] *Ibid.*, p. 33.

[22] *Loc. cit.*

Table 10. These figures suggest that about one-third of the families were in poverty in 1935 and about one-fifth were in poverty in 1959 using a variable poverty line centered around a $3,000 value for 1959. The estimates prepared by Ruth Mack suggest a much sharper reduction in poverty during the past 30 years than those prepared by Smolensky.

8. Income Distribution and Poverty

ROBERT J. LAMPMAN

Currently the lowest fifth of consumer units in the United States in terms of income, with personal income under $2,900, receive only 4.6 per cent of total family personal income. At the same time, 9 million families with less than $3,000 of total money income and 5 million unrelated individuals with less than $1,500 of total money income—or a total of almost 35 million persons—are classified as "poor."

What is the difference between these two statements? Do they refer to the same people? Is concern with inequality of the size distribution of income the same as that with poverty? Do similar policy considerations come to the fore regardless of which set of facts one examines? Is the anti-poverty emphasis of the Johnson Administration either based upon or entangled with the inequality issue?

In approaching these questions, I suggest that we first take a look at the process by which income is distributed and redistributed in the economy; second, that we ask whether inequality has been changing; and third, that we consider the way in which poverty has been changing and can be changed and how that change relates to income distribution.

How "Income" Is Distributed and Redistributed

The gross national product of the American economy, currently running at the rate of $640 billion, is divided among consumers, governments, and business firms on the basis of 65, 20, and 15 per cent for each, respectively. The division is effected by purchases, which are made out of the incomes of households and business firms and the tax revenues of governments. These incomes and tax revenues, in turn, are paid out by governments, business firms, and households, thus creating a circular flow.

Incomes take the form of labor income, property income, and transfer payments (payments made on a basis other than for current production). Of income payments for current production, about 75 per cent are for labor and 25 per cent are for use of property. About six per cent of total income is transferred by governments from one set of businesses and households to another. Further transfers are accomplished privately. The most notable institution making such transfers is the family, which combines and transmutes producer-contribution incomes into consumer incomes for or on behalf of individuals. However, other institutions can perform this "transfer" function; employing firms or insurance companies, as two examples, can be used to modify the conversion of producer income to consumer income. Finally, governments and employers serve as collective consumers or transferors of goods and services, some of which add directly to individual consumer welfare and hence may be considered as alternative to money income.

This highly simplified account of the income distribution process is depicted in Figure 1. Figure 2 shows the same process

FIGURE 1

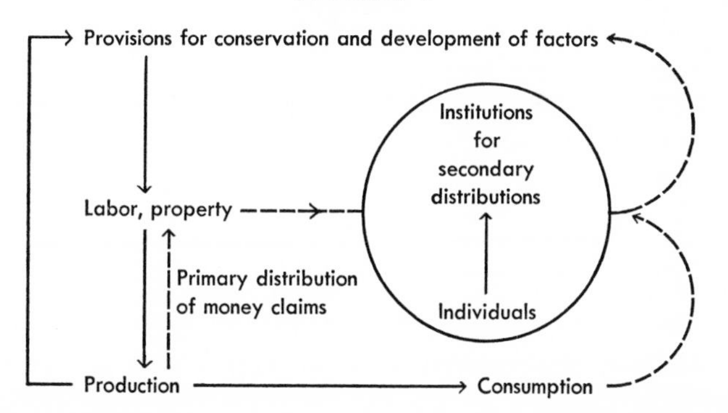

with the family at the center and emphasizes that an individual, if he is to survive, must either earn income or tie into a public or private transferring institution. It is a corollary of this that an individual may have a low income if he or another member

FIGURE 2

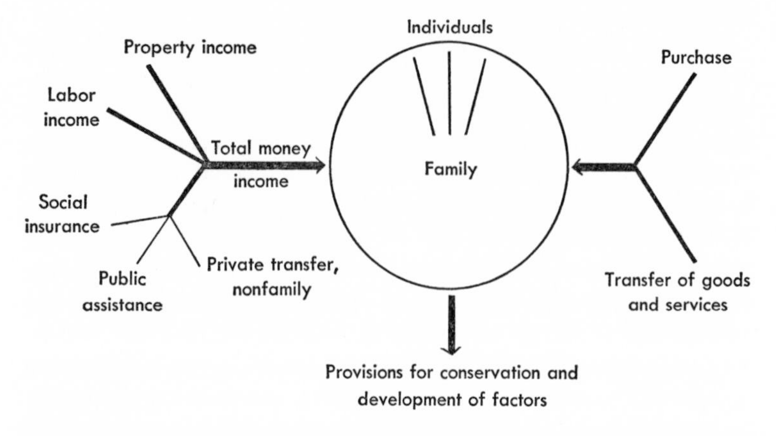

of his family supplies little saleable labor or property service and if he has only a limited claim on the secondary distribution.

Has Inequality Been Increasing?

Over time the lines on these charts that have been increasing in relative importance are the labor income and public transfer lines. These changes have been associated with changes in the structure of the economy and in the scope of the family redistribution. It can be argued that increased reliance upon labor income and the breakdown of the extended family have given rise to new problems of income insecurity and irregularity which have called forth new arrangements for secondary redistribution. The problems of income management also, no doubt, influence decisions about family formation, relative responsibility, labor force participation, savings, insurance, and provision for extraordinary needs at various stages in the life cycle. Hence it may be that intra-family distribution and redistribution of income over time are changing in such a way as to offset the apparent meaning of the rise in public transfers. But the general impression one gets is that the functional income shares have moved to accommodate a decline in the inequality of the size distribution of income, that is, in the distribution of the total of all functional income types among consumer units of all types.

Size distribution data are hard to compare over time because what is comprehended in the key definitions of income, income period, and income-receiving unit changes over time. Careful working and reworking of all available data by numerous scholars have produced a consensus that there was indeed a lessening of inequality in the 1938–1948 period and no clear trend one way or another since 1948. The lessening of inequality seems to be confined to those groups within the top half of the income distribution, with no great change in the income share of, and no change in inequality within, the bottom half. The lowest one-fifth of the consumer units (families and unattached individuals) got 4.1 per cent of the total family personal income in 1935, 5.0 per cent in 1947, and 4.6 per cent in 1962.

Over the period from the prewar to the postwar years, so many variables have been in the picture that one needs to be cautious about any easy generalization on changes in income inequality. For example, size of family moved into closer positive association with level of income (there was undoubling of middle and lower income families, earlier marriage, and a rise in number of children for upper income families), thus suggesting that the decline in inequality is understated by a simple consumer-unit distribution. On the other hand, home-produced services fell in importance and capital gains and expense-account living increased, suggesting that the decline in inequality is overstated.

If one were trying to find an explanation or justification for the current interest in poverty from sharp changes in the overall size distribution, I'm afraid he would be disappointed. I suppose it is possible that there is some significance for the lowest fifth in the compression of the distribution within the top half, but it seems rather remote. However, there are a few straws in the wind which suggest that 1949–1950 was a turning point toward more economic inequality among persons. These straws include the following:

(1) In my study of top wealth-holders, I found that the share of wealth held by the top two per cent of families fell steadily from 1929 to 1949, but then rose between 1949 and 1956. This finding is confirmed and extended by data from the Survey of Consumer Finances which show that, between 1953 and 1962, the share of net worth of the top decile of wealth-holders rose from 58 to 61 per cent, and that of the bottom fifth of income receivers fell from 11 to 7 per cent.

(2) The narrowing trend in the Negro-white differential was halted and reversed about 1950, in spite of a continued closing of the education difference between the two groups.

(3) There seems to be an increasing association between extremely large families and very low incomes.

(4) Fringe benefits won by organized and highly paid workers have not been extended to lower-income workers.

(5) Earnings of young men aged 20–24 years were more unequal in distribution in 1961 than they were in 1951 or 1941, according to an unpublished study by Dorothy S. Brady and F. G. Adams. However, this is not reflected in over-all income for the younger age groups as reported by Herman Miller.[1]

(6) Increasing numbers of highly educated married women are adding to middle or higher incomes of their husbands.

(7) Early retirement of low-income men seems to be increasing.

(8) It may be that inequality in the distribution of skill and of educational attainment is increasing.

(9) Progressivity of federal, state, and local taxes combined has been decreased.

I would emphasize that these facts and surmises about facts are only straws which have not yet been reflected in income data—and may not be. I would conclude that we have not had and are not currently experiencing an increase in income inequality. However, concern over the halting of the narrowing of inequality and over the possibility that inequality may in-

---

[1] Herman P. Miller, *Trends in the Income of Families and Persons in the United States: 1947 to 1960,* U. S. Bureau of the Census, Technical Paper No. 8, Table 3.

crease again may have contributed to thinking about poverty issues. It is also possible that increased knowledge about changes in the composition of the lowest fifth of consumer units may have aroused sympathy. Between 1947 and 1960, the unattached individuals, the aged, the female heads, and the heads who were out of the labor force increased in relative importance in this bottom group. This led some to observe that low income was not so much the product of class or economic problems as a sign of social or political failure. The fact that the low-income group included so many who were without influence or even without families and who were out of the mainstream of the economy made the inequality seem different, even if it wasn't quantitatively very different.

Has Poverty Been Increasing?

Here we can leave the change in inequality and turn to the matter of poverty. Size distribution data of the standard kind do not tell us who the poor are, primarily because they do not show income in relation to need. Family size and composition and other variables need to be taken into account. The consumer units in the bottom fifth of the size distribution are not, in all cases, the ones in the poverty group if we use a $3,000-per-family and $1,500-per-unattached-individual income cutoff. This is even more markedly the case if the income cutoffs are given further variation for family size and composition and residence. I think it is fair to say that the human interest in income distribution progressively rises as we shift attention from functional shares to size distribution to the poverty-line and level-of-living distinctions. This is the shift from concern with Ricardian factors of production and Marxian abstract masses in the grip of abstract forces to concern with ordinary people in trouble. At least a third of these people in trouble are children; almost half of the family heads are not in the labor force, and two-thirds of them have only an elementary education. Most of them are involuntarily poor because of events, social barriers, or personal limitations.

It is plausible to conclude from the poverty information that we are approaching a time when further reduction in the per-cent of the population in poverty will be harder to achieve. But that is not to say that poverty is increasing. The percentage of poor has been falling at about one point per year and is now at 19 per cent. The poverty income gap (the amount by which the total income of the poor falls short of $3,000 per family) is now $12 billion and is declining. Instead of getting worse, as some have alleged, poverty is getting "less worse," particularly in relation to our national resources for dealing with it.

The Process of Change in Poverty

Reduction of poverty and the filling of the poverty-income gap have been proceeding in recent years at the same time as, and partly because of, the fulfillment of other economic and social goals. Further, the rate of advance out of poverty can be sustained only if other rates of increase are sustained, e.g., the rate of economic growth, the rate of increase in educational attainment by the poor, and the rate of increase of social welfare expenditures in behalf of the poor. While assisting people to get out of the lowest fifth of the income distribution would be a never-ending proposition, it is conceivable that, by helping some to rise above a fixed, constant dollar poverty income line and, at the same time, helping others to stay above the line, we could achieve the end of involuntary poverty in the nation.

It is, I think, helpful to consider the process by which the number of poor families is changed from year to year. Some of this year's poor families will rise out of poverty, some will be dissolved by death or otherwise, and some new families and families who were not previously impoverished will start out in or retreat into poverty. So long as the exits from poverty exceed the entrances into poverty, the total poverty population will diminish. Thus, ways to speed the movement out of and to slow the movement into poverty should be sought. (One point deserving emphasis here is that there will soon be a great increase in the rate of family formation, and the poverty rate of these new families will be influential in determining the over-all poverty rate.) But neither should it be overlooked that filling the poverty income gap, and thus perhaps raising the median income of the poor (now $1,800), is of value in itself, even though it is not, in all cases, a way to stimulate further reduction of the poverty rate.

The range of ways to achieve the goals of the anti-poverty movement is to a degree implicit in Figure 2. Public and private resources can help the poor to develop their earning power and more nearly to realize their potential. This can be done either for adults or for children. Where that strategy is not feasible, it may be both possible and desirable to fill part of the poverty income gap by public transfers from the nonpoor to the poor. But it should be pointed out that $12 billion of transfers per year would not be sufficient to fill the gap if such payments induced a reduction of other income to the poor. An income of $3,000 for nine million families would be $27 billion per year, and that might not be enough if those above the $3,000 mark elected to take a grant rather than earn income. Hence, to fill the poverty income gap with anything short of such massive outlays doubtless requires some care. One program which I would favor as a partial step in this direction is a family allowance system extending out of the income tax, building upon the tax exemptions and deductions for families which are not available to all families except the poor. Hopefully, low marginal rates of reduction in allowances against extra earned income would make this a workable idea for filling some of the poverty income gap.

SHARING THE COST OF POVERTY AND ANTI-POVERTY EFFORTS

Any and all of these programs are going to cost somebody something, and this takes us back to the income distribution question again. First, however, we should note that it costs us something to have poverty. The poor part of the population contributes very little to the national output. At the same time they consume very little. They produce about three per cent of the total (three per cent of wages and salaries, five per cent of capital income), but they consume about five per cent of the total product. The difference between three and five is largely explained by the fact that the lowest fifth gets 30 per cent of the total of transfer payments, which includes social security, unemployment compensation, public welfare, veterans' benefits, and other transfers.[2]

The total income of the lowest fifth is about $25 billion including $10 billion of transfers ($4 billion of which is public assistance). Only four per cent of families and unrelated individuals (or one-fifth of the poor) receive any public assistance payments. One-half of the poor families receive no transfer payments of any kind.[3]

The "cost of poverty" to the nation is the low productivity of the poor as measured by their earnings and capital income. By definition, poverty would not exist if such incomes were high enough to place all families above the $3,000 line. However, in the short run at least, poverty could be only partially solved by adding to productivity, since a third of poor families do not even have a single earner. If, say, six million poor families and three million poor unrelated individuals were to add enough to their wages and salaries to take them just above the poverty-line, about $7 billion would be added to their incomes. This gives what might be called a minimum estimate of the cost of poverty. The figure would need to be somewhat larger, say, $10 billion, to take them out of poverty at the same time that public assistance payments to families with earners were being reduced.

It is plausible to argue that increasing wages and salaries by $7–10 billion dollars is not the end of the story. Wages are 70 per cent of national income; $10 billion divided by 70 per cent equals $14 billion. This adjustment seems necessary, since improving the quality of labor will increase the productivity of capital and land, and hence will raise interest, rent, and profits as well as wages. Moreover, more capital might be formed if taxes were lowered. This approach yields what might be called the high estimate of the cost of poverty.

---

[2] George Katona, Charles A. Lininger, and Richard F. Kosobud, *1962 Survey of Consumer Finances* (Ann Arbor: University of Michigan, Survey Research Center, Monograph No. 32, 1963).

[3] James Morgan *et al., Income and Welfare in the United States* (New York: McGraw Hill, 1962), pp. 216, 314.

A proper accounting would adjust the *gross* gain or cost to show the *net* gain, by deducting the cost to the nation of improving the productivity of the poor workers (through increased expenditures on education and health, for example). If such additional expenditures amounted to $1 billion per year, the gross gain of $7–14 billion would represent a net gain of $6–13 billion. A full measure of the "investment" would account for the added effort and foregone income by the poor themselves in improving their productivity.

To the extent that the present poor can raise their incomes by more productive effort, less transfer income will be required to alleviate poverty. Hence, a burden can be taken off the nonpoor population. Note, however, that this burden or cost is already accounted for in the estimate of cost in terms of $7–14 billion dollars of added national income. Hence, it would be double-counting to add the savings in transfers to the increase in production. The poor would lose the transfers which the rich save.

One crude estimate of the transfer involved is the total of public assistance payments—$4 billion per year. This $4 billion does not, however, take account of redistributive elements in social insurance, nor does it include the value of public services which are provided free of charge to poor persons but on which the subsidy is reduced or withdrawn as persons become nonpoor. Examples of this are hospital and medical care, public housing, and family counseling services. Health care is quantitatively most important. Perhaps as much as $1 billion of public funds are involved in this general category of free services. Again, what the nonpoor gain, the poor lose through this conversion of free to nonfree services. Hence, there is no net national gain.

There is another point concerning the burden which the poor place upon the nonpoor, namely, the cost of "nuisance abatement." Presumably the need for police, fire, and public health protection (which presently cost $8 billion per year) would be somewhat reduced by the rise in well-being of the poor. Perhaps the nonpoor could save as much as $1 billion. This would represent a gain to the nation since it would free resources for other uses.

There is still another point concerning the gain to the nonpoor from reducing poverty. As the poor earn higher incomes, they will be able to pay a larger share of the total tax burden, thereby sharing more fully in the support of governmental services. (This point should not be confused by the fact that the tax burden on the poor is now quite substantial as a share of income that goes to taxes. If we include all taxes of federal, state, and local governments, the poor pay directly and indirectly over 20 per cent of their income in taxes. The over-all tax system is roughly proportional to income through the lowest three-fifths of the income range.) The present poor who would be lifted out of poverty in the future would also be able to carry a larger share of the community's nontax responsibilities. For example, they would contribute more nearly their share of military draftees.

Finally, there would be a qualitative gain to the nonpoor from elimination of poverty, in the form of more complete integration of the population. Rather than having to live in a divided community of poor and nonpoor worlds, they would find themselves in a more open community where all would participate, compete, and cooperate. Everyone (with some exceptions) would benefit from the development of the talents and sense of responsibilities of the submerged poor.

We have been reviewing the question of the cost of poverty and the gain from its elimination. Now, let's turn the question around and ask: what will it cost to reduce poverty? A subsidiary question is: what amount of poverty-reduction can we buy for each billion dollars? This question arises naturally enough out of the debate over the proposed government expenditures of more than a billion dollars for next year. Actually, of course, the total "investment" will be far more than this. It will include state and local as well as federal funds, private as well as public monies, and effort and foregone consumption by the poor as well as the nonpoor.

What will the nation get in return for this outlay? How will the return be divided between the poor and the nonpoor? I suggest in Table 1 a three-part framework for ordering answers to these questions and offer some very rough estimates for Parts

TABLE 1. A THREE-PART FRAMEWORK FOR ESTIMATING COSTS AND GAINS FROM THE ANTI-POVERTY PROGRAM (BILLIONS OF DOLLARS)

	Poor	*Nonpoor*	*All people*
PART I. OUTLAY OR INVESTMENT PER YEAR			
Federal funds	.1	.9	1.0
State and local funds	.1	.5	.6
Private funds	—	.1	.1
Foregone income	.2	.1	.3
Total	.4	1.6	2.0
PART II. GAIN TO NATION PER YEAR (AFTER PROGRAM HAS BEEN IN EFFECT FOR x YEARS)			
Added production resulting from higher quality labor and added capital	—	—	—
Added wages	—	—	—
Added property income	—	—	—
PART III. REDISTRIBUTION OF TAXES AND TRANSFERS PER YEAR			
Reduced public assistance cost	−1.0	+1.0	—
Reduced free services to poor	−1.0	+1.0	—
Reduced cost for abatement of "nuisances"	+0.1	+0.9	+1.0

I and III based on programs which invest in "productivity raising." The estimates would differ if we considered a transfer-payment approach, but the method is of general applicability. No estimates are offered for Part II. Such estimates should have high priority for research.

CONCLUSIONS

This paper opened with some questions about the difference between inequality and poverty. I hope we have conveyed the impression that both terms are "words of art," but that it is sensible to distinguish between them. Income inequality traditionally has referred to the sharing of arbitrarily defined "income" among arbitrarily defined "income receiving units." Poverty, on the other hand, may be defined by relating an absolute real income level to family size and other indications of need.

Inequality does not seem to have changed dramatically in recent years, or at least it does not seem to have worsened the income share of the bottom half of the income distribution. However, there are some straws in the wind that may presage a future worsening of that kind. Poverty, on the other hand, is retreating, both in terms of reduction of the per cent of people below a poverty-income line and in terms of a filling of the poverty-income gap. This process has gone on and can go on without notable changes in inequality of income distribution. However, new attempts to speed up the rate of poverty reduction or the filling of the poverty-income gap could, depending on what methods are followed, cause changes in the share of total income received by the nonpoor. The costs of poverty and the costs and gains of poverty reduction are shared by both poor and nonpoor.

The emphasis on poverty is a logical extension of social scientists' long concern with inequality. And it will, I hope, be a valuable part of a continuing effort to comprehend and improve the workings of the social and economic systems so that they better serve the needs and aspirations of people.

9. Policies Affecting Income Distribution

FRANK L. FERNBACH

Although we still await the perfection of statistical procedures by which to measure the level and distribution of income, to provide a precise definition and counting of the poor, and to reach an exact determination of all of the factors that account for poverty, surely enough is already known to guide policy makers effectively in their pursuit of the war on poverty.

According to the yardstick used by President Johnson a year ago—based upon Bureau of the Census findings on multi-person families with cash incomes of under $3,000 and single-person families with less than $1,500—almost 35 million Americans are poor.

A more sophisticated but equally rigorous yardstick recently developed by the Social Security Administration—which includes the important refinements of family size and the value of food raised and consumed on farms—similarly concludes that about 35 million are "among the undoubted poor." Using "a somewhat less conservative but by no means generous standard," the Social Security Administration concludes that "a total of 50 million persons—of whom 22 million are young children—live within the bleak circle of poverty or at least hover around its edge." [1]

Even short of the perfection of statistical measurement, it appears that between a fifth and a fourth of all Americans still are in want. Their incomes in cash and in kind are just too small to lift them out of poverty or beyond its fringe.

About 30 years ago, a view about income distribution goals was expressed by President Franklin Roosevelt which, if taken to heart over the intervening years, would have made a con-

[1] Mollie Orshansky, "Counting the Poor: Another Look at the Poverty Profile," *Social Security Bulletin,* XXVIII (January, 1965).

ference on poverty in 1965 superfluous. He said: "The test of our progress is not whether we add more to the abundance of those who have much: it is whether we provide enough for those who have too little."

Since the Great Depression, when one-third of the nation was considered "ill-housed, ill-clothed, and ill-fed"—and, surely, more than a third on the basis of today's concept of minimum family needs—millions have escaped from poverty status. This has happened not only because of over-all economic growth but, also, because of a conscious public and private effort. Nonetheless, the fact that today at least one-fifth of the populace remains impoverished, in the most productive nation of the world and in one whose citizens pride themselves on their humanitarianism, is a national scandal.

What is more, if our priority income distribution goal is, indeed, to "provide enough for those who have too little," our progress in raising the income share of the hard-core poor who comprise the most impoverished fifth of our families, has been scant.

In 1962, according to the latest findings of the Office of Business Economics of the United States Department of Commerce, the income share of the bottom 20 per cent of our families—a group with a top income of $2,790—was only 4.9 per cent of total multi- and single-person family income, after federal income tax.[2] It should be noted that the OBE "income" concept includes both money and nonmoney income: cash as well as wages received in kind, fuel, and food produced and consumed on farms, and the rental value of owner-occupied homes.

By way of contrast, the income share of the most fortunate top five per cent of all families, with incomes of over $15,240 in 1962—after payment of federal tax—was 17.7 per cent of the total. The $67 billion of net income received by this top five per cent exceeded the total income in cash and in kind of the bottom 40 per cent of all our families. The neediest 20 per cent at the bottom received less than $19 billion of the total of $377 billion of family income.[3]

Besides informing us about current family income distribu-

---

[2] Orshansky, *op. cit.*, Table 1.

[3] *Survey of Current Business*, XLIV (April, 1964).

tion, OBE studies tell us about the change in the family income share of the lowest fifth, after federal tax, back to 1941. Since then, the rise has been slow indeed, from 4.3 per cent in 1941 to 4.9 per cent in 1962 (Table 1).

Most significant, all of this gain occurred during the first half of the period and, in fact, the share of the poorest fifth reached a peak of 5.4 per cent during the Korean War year, 1951. Since then, the income share of the lowest fifth actually has been going down.

Although it may be argued that this wrong-way income trend at the bottom over the last decade reflects, in part, the rapid growth of single-person families—among both the young and the old—as national income has increased, two counterbalancing factors suggest the probability of an overstatement of the income share reported for the lowest fifth. First, the OBE income concept excludes the sizable factor of realized capital gains and ex-

TABLE 1. FAMILY INCOME RECEIVED BY LOWEST 20 PER CENT OF FAMILIES,[a] 1941–1962 (AFTER FEDERAL INCOME TAX)[b]

Year[c]	*Per cent of family income*
1941	4.3
1950	5.1
1951	5.4
1952	5.3
1953	5.3
1954	5.2
1955	5.2
1956	5.2
1957	5.0
1958	5.0
1959	4.9
1960	4.9
1961	5.0
1962	4.9

Source: U. S. Department of Commerce, Office of Business Economics.

[a] Multi-person and single-person families. Income includes both money income (exclusive of realized capital gains) and nonmoney income (wages in kind, value of food and fuel produced and consumed on farms, and net imputed rental value of owner-occupied homes).

[b] If other federal taxes and state and local taxes also had been deducted, the share of the bottom 20 per cent of families would be less than here shown.

[c] Years are omitted when data are not available.

pense account living, substantial income benefits that the poor do not share but which are important to upper-income recipients. Second, the findings take no account of the impact of the regressive burden of state and local taxes, which proportionately fall heaviest on those who have the least.

The Impact of Policy Measures

Up to a decade ago the progress in lifting millions out of poverty and in raising the income share of the poorest fifth was by no means accidental. In large part, it resulted from sound public programs specifically intended to achieve these ends.

New Deal inspired social and economic measures—like the minimum wage, the 40-hour workweek, premium overtime pay, and social insurance and welfare aids for the aged, survivors, the unemployed, and the indigent—were designed, in large part, to raise the income of the neediest. The concurrent encouragement of collective bargaining also helped to increase the earnings of millions of the underpaid. Then, the impact of World War II and, later, the Korean War, in generating full employment—within a framework of wartime price controls and tax policies which effectively prevented a regressive income shift—further helped to make inroads on poverty and to lift the income share of those at the bottom.

The slower rate at which Americans have escaped from poverty over recent years and the downward trend of the income share of families in the lowest fifth reflects many adverse and complex factors. Two of them, however, require particular note if the war against want is to be won.

First, the persistent high level of unemployment and underemployment of recent years, plus the inadequate coverage and level of minimum wage protection, have perpetuated the poverty status of millions of families who have a member in the labor force.

Second, lagging benefits and coverage under federal and state social welfare programs—initially conceived to assure protection of family incomes against the worst economic hazards of modern life—have frozen several million families without breadwinners into a permanent poverty status.

It is true, on the other hand, that several vitally important programs, indispensable in the effort to banish want, have recently been enacted by the Congress or now are pending.

With adequate resources and effective leadership, the Manpower Development and Training Act, the Economic Opportunity Act, and President Johnson's proposed federal aids for education can immensely help the poor—and particularly the children of the poor—to acquire schooling, counselling, and skills essential to an escape from poverty.

Federal aid for community development and help for chronically distressed areas and whole regions can, in time, help create new opportunities for the poor.

Passage of the Civil Rights Act—and, now, its forceful implementation—holds promise of opening new opportunities for members of minority groups long locked by prejudice in the ranks of the very poor.

All of these undertakings—the so-called "structural" approach to the problems of want—were vigorously championed by organized labor, and are indispensable parts of an all-out effort to eradicate poverty. However, even if all of them are successfully pursued, failure to create adequate full-time jobs at decent pay for those who seek them and failure to provide sufficient family income under our social insurance system to support families without breadwinners above the level of want, will surely frustrate the great expectations generated by the war on poverty.

It is noteworthy that Bureau of the Census and Social Security Administration studies reveal that over half of all families of the poor are headed by a person who is a member of the labor force—employed, underemployed, or jobless.

In many cases the would-be breadwinner in the family is unemployed as a result of technological displacement, discrimination, lack of skill, or simply because no job is available. Characteristically, his unemployment is of long duration.

Often, the heads of families of the poor have a job, but are compelled involuntarily to work part-time, generally at low wages.

In most cases, however, the heads of families in want who are in the labor force actually are employed at full-time jobs. In fact, some 25 to 30 per cent of all American families are headed by a person who works full time year 'round for 50 weeks or more. These, indeed are the "working poor."

THE NEED FOR MORE VIGOROUS MEASURES

If the more than half of our impoverished families whose head is a member of the labor force are to be effectively aided, more than an increase in job training, improvement of labor mobility, and the end of discrimination—vital as these are—are now needed.

To help those seeking work but who can't find it or who can find only a part-time job, measures to end the persistently high rate of unemployment and underemployment must be more vigorously pursued. In the face of predictions that by the end of the year the unemployment rate may hardly show a significant decline—despite earlier forecasts that the tax cut would soon bring it down to four per cent—bold measures are overdue.

To raise employment quickly a substantially increased program of federally supported public works—which would utilize idle manpower and, at the same time, provide needed facilities of enduring worth such as schools, hospitals, mass transport, public housing, and slum clearance—should now be undertaken. To increase job opportunities in an age of advancing automation, a 35-hour week and double premium time for overtime should be enacted. To further stimulate full employment, improved fiscal and monetary policies are also needed.

Every measure that helps to create job opportunities for those seeking work must be viewed as an essential underpinning of the war against want.

To help lift out of poverty the more than two million families who are impoverished even though their heads are regularly employed full time, the federal minimum wage and its coverage must be increased substantially. The present $1.25 hourly minimum, which provides annual earnings of barely $2,600 even for the fully employed, is a poverty wage. About 15 million wage and nonsupervisory salary earners—largely employed in hotels, restaurants, laundries, hospitals, retail trade, agriculture, and agricultural processing enterprises where many of the poorest work—are not covered by the federal minimum wage.

The fact that millions of employed Americans actually receive less than $1.25 because they are not protected even by the substandard federal minimum, is a tragedy.

When the Congress passed the Fair Labor Standards Act more than a quarter of a century ago, it stated that one of its main objectives was "the maintenance of the minimum standard of living necessary for health, efficiency, and general well-being of workers." Even by 1965, this objective has not been fulfilled. A few sincere people—and some who are not so well-meaning—argue that a higher minimum wage and broader coverage are not advantageous to the poor. If this apprehension had prevailed back in the 1930's, however, even the $.25 minimum enacted then would have been rejected. Yet, it is the working poor who need an increased minimum wage and broader coverage and are benefited by them most of all. Surely, it now is timely to complete the job the New Deal began so many years ago.

Further to assist the working poor—who now are largely unorganized and thus exert little collective pressure to improve their own conditions—continuing public and private acts that impede the exercise of the right to join unions should finally be ended. The extension of the benefits of collective bargaining to low-paid workers who need them most is also an important aspect of the war on want.

The social insurance programs of the federal government and of the states are the basic mechanisms on which millions of our citizens without income from a job—because of old age, illness or accident, unemployment, or the death of the family head—must depend to help sustain themselves. For the families of the poorest, they are often the only income source.

Today, these programs transmit billions of dollars to Americans, most of whom need them badly in an effort to sustain a decent standard of life. But the fact that the system leaves so many of its beneficiaries still in poverty proves the inadequacy of the fulfillment of its goal. Although social insurance is one of the best weapons we have to ward off want, in some respects, especially with regard to benefit levels, these programs have actually regressed. What is more, millions of Americans are still outside the protection of these systems, with the single exception of the federal old-age, survivors, and disability insurance program.

This federal program covers nine out of every ten workers in gainful employment in the United States. But its benefits, which for many years have lagged tragically in relation to wage and salary loss, have also been lagging behind the rising cost of living since 1958.[4]

The very top benefits now paid under the social security system are hardly above the poverty level. In yearly terms, the maximum retirement benefit for a single worker is a little over $1,500; for an aged couple, under $2,300; for an entire family, not quite $3,050. Average benefits, of course, are much lower. In June 1964, the average retired worker received a benefit, computed on a weekly basis, of less than $18, about 60 per cent of the $1,500 per year poverty standard (Table 2). For an aged widow, the average weekly benefit was $15.67; for a disabled worker, $21.13; for an aged couple, $30.26; and for a widowed mother with two children, $45.09.

Although some recipients have supplementary income from property, savings, and private insurance, of course, it is the plight of the poor that they do not. Because benefit levels are so low, they are condemned to a permanent state of impoverishment.

Under the original state unemployment insurance laws, jobless

TABLE 2. AVERAGE SOCIAL INSURANCE BENEFITS ON A WEEKLY BASIS, JUNE, 1964

Program	*Amount*
Federal Old-Age, Survivors' and Disability Insurance	
Retired worker	$17.97
Aged widow	15.67
Disabled worker	21.13
Aged couple	30.26
Widowed mother and two children	45.09
State Unemployment Insurance	
Fully unemployed worker	35.27

Source: U. S. Department of Health, Education, and Welfare and U. S. Department of Labor.

[4] U. S. Advisory Council on Social Security, *The Status of the Social Security Program and Recommendations for Its Improvement* (Washington, D.C.: U. S. Government Printing Office, 1965).

workers could generally expect benefit payments of at least half their regular weekly wages. Today they average only one-third, and some get as little as one-fifth. Rising wages for the working population have not been matched by commensurate increases in unemployment benefits, mainly because state legislatures have retained obsolete maximums on benefit amounts (Table 3). In every state the maximum benefit today is a smaller proportion of average wages in the state than it was in 1939.

In June 1964, the average unemployment benefit for the United States was only $35.27—barely 35 per cent of average weekly wages in manufacturing. And the average maximum period of eligibility was only 24 weeks.

Those drawing benefits—inadequate as they are—can be counted among the more fortunate. Only about half of the jobless draw any benefits at all because of limitations of program coverage, disqualifications, and maximums on the length of time benefits can be paid. In fact, according to careful estimates by Professor Richard A. Lester, only about 20 per cent of all wage and salary losses caused by total unemployment are compensated by benefits under the state and railroad public unemployment insurance programs.[5]

TABLE 3. MAXIMUM BENEFITS UNDER STATE UNEMPLOYMENT COMPENSATION LAWS

Maximum benefit as per cent of each state's average weekly wage[a]	*Number of states*[b] *in given year*	
	1939	*1964*
70 and over	18	0
60–69	17	1
50–59	15	6
40–49	1	26
30–39	0	17
20–29	0	1

Source: U. S. Department of Labor, Bureau of Employment Security.
[a] In covered employment.
[b] Fifty states and the District of Columbia.

[5] Richard A. Lester, *The Economics of Unemployment Compensation* (Princeton, N. J.: Princeton University, Industrial Relations Section, Research Report Series No. 101, 1962).

Workmen's compensation laws—the oldest of the social insurances in this country—have similarly lagged behind in benefit levels. Originally, the intent was to compensate injured workers with benefits equal to about two-thirds of pay. At the time most of these laws were passed, half a century ago, the average wage was about $13 and the average benefit about $10. Today, the average state benefit for temporary total disability is around $35 to $45, but average wages of factory workers are over $100 a week. Because of obsolete benefit maximums, the top benefits now payable in more than half the states are less than 50 per cent of average weekly wages in the state.

Family income insurance during periods of illness now is limited to four states and the railroads, and social insurance to cover medical costs—except for the aged—still remains to be won. Yet, we know that illness is an important poverty cause, and, on the other hand, poverty contributes to illness.

With benefits and coverage under our social insurance systems still so inadequate, millions of the poor are forced to depend on public welfare. For example, of the nearly 35 million Americans who are most impoverished, four million adults and children receive family aid under the federal-state program of aid for families with dependent children. According to a special study conducted in 1961, the average AFDC family consists of four persons, with an average total income from all sources, including relief payments, of $1,680 in 1961—and the figures are still valid today. In even the richest state, the average did not reach $2,400.[6]

No war against want can succeed without adequate family-income protection for those who cannot be self-supporting, even under conditions of full employment. It was precisely to meet the income maintenance needs of these families—to keep them from impoverishment—that the concept of social security against the worst hazards of modern life was conceived. Unfortunately, expectations that our social insurance program would adequately meet this need have not been realized.

Clearly, social security benefits for retirees, survivors, and the disabled must be increased. Moreover, national health insurance

---

[6] Gerald Kahn and Ellen J. Perkins, "Families Receiving AFDC: What Do They Have to Live On?", *Welfare in Review,* II (October, 1964).

for all Americans should be a major goal. The benefit and coverage levels of all state social insurance and welfare programs should be brought up to date. Federal standards are needed to upgrade the unemployment insurance and archaic workmen's compensation systems of the states. Insurance for the families of breadwinners separated from payrolls by illness should be improved and extended nationally. Public assistance standards immediately should be raised.

Two further areas of great importance affecting poverty and public policy require at least mention in this brief résumé, because they are too often neglected.

In waging war on want, rural America must not be ignored. If the production of abundance automatically brought prosperity, those who produce our food and fibre surely would be most prosperous. Yet, poverty pervades the American countryside.

One of the proper objectives of federal farm policy is income maintenance aid for farm families who clearly need it. Yet, millions of tax dollars go to vast agro-business enterprises that, by this criterion, have no valid claim to them. Federal farm policy should be devoted entirely to helping those in agriculture who need the aid. At least, a ceiling should be placed on the amount of federal aid allowable to any farm.

What is more, the desperate plight of those who work on farms for wages no longer can be ignored. By any yardstick they are the most impoverished and exploited group in the labor force. They receive the lowest wage of all, an average of barely 90 cents an hour. Moreover, they are denied the benefit of virtually every federal and state social welfare and labor law enacted over a generation. They are excluded from protection of the federal and most state wage and hour laws, of state unemployment compensation laws, and of most state workmen's compensation laws—although they work in one of our most hazardous industries. The Congress has even denied the protection of the National Labor Relations Act to farm workers—who, more than any others, need it. Not content, until recently the Congress also subjected these underpaid and underemployed workers to the cruel competition of foreign workers under various labor import programs.

Not only is there much to be done to fight poverty in rural

America; the war also must be waged wherever tax laws—federal, state, and local—are being written.

While governments at all levels should be intensely concerned with ameliorating the plight of the poor by every means, their combined tax levies now extract about $1 billion annually from the 35 million Americans most in want. This is a conservative estimate by the U. S. Treasury; studies by others put the figure higher.

Despite the recent tax cut, the federal individual income tax, according to the Treasury, still takes $100 million annually from the very poor while federal excises draw another $200 million from their meager incomes. What is more, regressive state and local sales and property taxes impose more than twice as heavy a burden on their piteously small incomes. Moreover, the over-all trend is toward greater dependence on regressive taxes and less on progressive ones.

This mockery of the concept of taxation based upon ability to pay is unconscionable. Helping to end it must be viewed as a mandate by those committed to fighting want.

In the judgment of experts, only a gap of $11 billion to $15 billion is estimated to exist between the present aggregate income of the 35 million poorest and the sum needed by them to achieve a multi-person family income of $3,000 and $1,500 for single persons living alone. In terms of the allocation of dollars this surely is an achievable goal for an affluent nation that enjoyed a national income of $510 billion last year. In fact, last year alone, income received by individuals and business enterprises rose by over $31 billion. Over the last ten years, it rose by over $200 billion.

Yet, closing the poverty gap is a complex and many-faceted undertaking. Ending for all time the cycle of want must include improved general education and job training—particularly for the children of the poor—as well as family counseling and measures to increase the mobility of the labor force. Ending discrimination—for whatever cause—is vital to success. An all-out attack on chronic area distress, on rural poverty, on inequitable tax laws, and on the too frequently substandard housing of the poor and the slums in which they live, are all essential parts of the effort to eradicate want.

Most important, bold policies must be pursued that will achieve full employment at decent wages to underpin opportunity for the millions of impoverished in families whose heads are in the labor force. And concurrently, the American social insurance system—the life line to adequate family income maintenance for the additional millions without breadwinners who now exist in want—must be made worthy of this nation.

The greatest challenge we face is not lack of knowledge about what should be done to mount a war on poverty; it is whether Americans now have the will to wage this war and to win it.

PART FOUR

EDUCATION POLICIES

10. Vocational Education and Poverty

FRANCIS KEPPEL

Let me start off with the basic subject assigned—"General Education and Vocational Education." It is clearly a topic of large dimensions and possibilities, but I think we need to bring it into somewhat sharper focus. If we consider general education and vocational education as virtually one and the same within the educational structure, we are likely to speak with sense and purpose, but if we consider them as separate and distinct within the educational structure, we will fail to make sense.

I suggest that we recall what President Kennedy emphasized in his message on education which led to the Vocational Education Act of 1963, and what President Johnson reminded us of in his educational proposals for 1965. They repeatedly urged us to realize that all aspects of education are inter-related, that each aspect of education is a part of the whole, that no part of American education—whether by intent or by indifference—can be permitted to remain in a second-class status. This is particularly important in creating a new thrust for vocational education, which has far too long been regarded as the sub-basement or dumping ground of education by educators themselves.

With this thrust and parry, let us now turn to the subject which has called us to this conference. Throughout America, we are becoming aware of the paradox of poverty in a day of affluence, of our challenge to meet it, and specifically of the role of vocational education in what may well be the greatest educational challenge in our life as a nation.

In the same way that vocational education cannot be sensibly viewed as separate from general education, so must we recognize that the Vocational Education Act of the 88th Congress is kith and kin to a variety of other acts bearing on education during the past two years—to provisions for higher education for librarians, for teacher institutes, and for educational research, as well as such other legislation touching on education as the Civil Rights Act and the Economic Opportunities Act of the 88th Congress, and President Johnson's new education program now before the 89th Congress.

All these measures, directly and indirectly affecting education, are devoted to meeting our greatest national problem—and surely democracy's most notable flaw—the fact that we have grown affluent as a nation while hundreds of thousands among us have been victimized by unemployment, poverty, and discrimination. Some say the problem of unemployment and even of poverty is attributable to automation, to our advancing technology. But this oversimplifies the problem. There are many related factors—including our exploding population and a rapid shift from a rural to an urban society.

But, important as these factors are, the basic problem, to my mind, is our failure to grow up to our changing times. Change has been painful since man's first venture from darkness to the light.

Alfred North Whitehead once said—long before the advent of automation or electronics:

> It is a profoundly erroneous truism, repeated by all copy-books and by eminent people when they are making speeches, that we should cultivate the habit of thinking what we are doing. The precise opposite is the case. Civilization advances by extending the number of important operations which we can perform without thinking about them.

Whitehead was right, of course. We are now advancing precisely because we have replaced the slavery of humans by what the technologists neatly call slave mechanisms. And the often-quoted Whitehead, I think, would be much amazed at the beating that automation and technology have taken in recent years as the villain of the unemployment problem. I think it is time that we recognize that the real villain has not been swift-moving technology, but slow-moving education, and education's difficulty in adapting to change.

Among educators there has been far too much argument for far too long about whether general education or vocational education is more essential to our children. Such arguments are above and beyond the sensible grasp of hill country children in New England, or poor Negro children in the South, or deprived children of any race in any of our city slums.

The really important point about education, of course, is that it should supply options of many kinds to all children who attend our schools—options for concentrated academic study and professional careers, for business study and business careers, for vocational study and technical careers—at the highest level the individual can profitably use. Far too often, we have tended to get muddled and befuddled about the real purpose of basic education. Today we still see in the newspapers solemn warnings that our schools are actually cheating a vast majority of our students by requiring them to take basic academic subjects—so-called college preparatory subjects—when they do not plan to go on to college. They assume that because these subjects are necessary for college, they are unnecessary for anyone who does not go to college.

To assume that academic subjects are merely an obstacle course for college admission is to miss the whole point of liberal education. It is in the great tradition of our secondary schools that history and geography, literature, science, and mathematics be made available to all of our citizens. If their only value were to test the best and frustrate the rest, then we would wisely abandon them even for the college-bound and find some other basis for deciding college admissions.

The Role of Vocational Education

Fortunately, we are beginning to see vocational education as another option of education—based upon sound basic learning and leading to creative lives. With the recent Vocational Education Act, vocational education has been given a new, vital opportunity to contribute as an essential and first-rate part of the educational structure. It has been granted an opportunity to change, to make a real difference in the possibilities our schools offer our youth.

Part of this change is that vocational education can now be

offered at every level of education—from secondary school to university. But change is nonetheless painful when old ways are deeply rooted. And we have evidence to document the difficulty of change in vocational education.

In carrying out the intent of the Congress, the states and territories retain full control of their vocational and technical education programs. To qualify for federal funds, the states have submitted comprehensive plans to the Office of Education. These have been carefully reviewed in accord with the Act and its Regulations. The new Act has required the states to review their vocational programs and come up with a new design to modernize and strengthen vocational training to meet the needs of today, to prepare youth for jobs that are now seeking candidates, not jobs that are passing into obsolescence.

This, of course, has preoccupied the states and the Office of Education with paper work in seeking mutual and realistic patterns which can effect the necessary change in vocational training. For more than six months, the duplicating machines have been churning out plans and revisions of plans until one might get the impression that paper work, however necessary, becomes an objective in itself.

During this same period, members of state advisory committees—composed of persons of much the same high talent we find here today—have been doing real and creative thinking. These advisors have included scholars and public officials, businessmen and leaders of labor, and the general public and the educators from both inside and outside the vocational field. Bringing these talents together in reasonable harmony is no minor matter. Such broad involvement in vocational education has never been seen before.

It has now become apparent to most of us, as it should have been for years, that vocational education cannot do its job alone. Educators and the whole community must be concerned, and work together, if we would provide programs that are creative and realistic. Community social services, industry, and labor must play large and continuing roles—not merely in these planning days, but in the months and years ahead if vocational training is to offer usable options to those in poverty and in every upward stratum of affluence.

VOCATIONAL PROGRAMS IN ACTION

Let me cite a few examples of how good vocational programs, well-planned and well-conceived, are beginning to have an impact. First, we have growing evidence that vocational programs can serve as a magnet in our communities, drawing people up from poverty:

A 35-year-old man in Chicago is now enrolled in a basic reading class as part of a vocational training course. For the first time in his life, he has managed to read a complete sentence out loud. He was so overcome that he broke into tears before the class.

A young father in Arizona brought his small daughter to school with him one day because he didn't have money for a baby-sitter and he didn't want to miss a day of instruction.

A man in St. Louis showed up in his bare feet for an adult vocational education class. He will not be able to afford shoes until he gets his first training allowance check. But he hasn't missed a class.

A young man in Appalachia was recently graduated from a vocational education course, was placed in a good job—and became the first person in his family for three generations to hold a job.

Another man in St. Louis has been walking six miles to vocational class every day for a very good reason. He doesn't have the money, yet, for carfare.

A young Negro, previously an unemployed dropout, went to a new vocational school near Miami, Florida, and completed an auto body and fender repair course. He now tells the director of the school that he is earning between $165 and $245 a week, depending on overtime. His employer tells the school director that he would like to have ten more mechanics just like him. This boy's father never held a steady job or earned a steady weekly salary.

VOCATIONAL TRAINING AND THE POOR

Second, there is a new focus in vocational training to meet the needs of the poor—the people whom the sociologists rather over-elegantly call the "socioeconomically handicapped." Beneath these polysyllables are the children of parents of low incomes who exist in our affluent society but do not really live in it or share in its benefits.

There is, of course, no one magic formula to break the cycle of poverty or to give these children an even fighting chance to fulfill their human potential. But we are seeing in vocational training a new and almost untapped source of remedy.

In the past, vocational education, for all its old second-class status, has largely served the relatively *more* prosperous in society rather than the poorest, the *more* able rather than the least equipped, the *more* privileged rather than the deprived and disadvantaged.

Vocational education has also been saddled heavily by discrimination because of race, just as the labor market itself has so long been saddled. But now we are beginning to see that the old ways won't do and won't work. Like a bemired water spaniel, vocational education is at last coming out of the water—and shaking itself clean.

This new approach is becoming clear as a necessity to labor, which has not been entirely free of discrimination in the past. It is also becoming clear to business, which has not been entirely free of discrimination in the past either.

Last month in Buffalo, United States Chamber of Commerce President Walter F. Carey said:

> If poverty is to be eradicated, more than the temporary palliatives of relief and welfare measures are needed. New concepts of education and new approaches to vocational training are what the order of battle calls for . . . and these can best be supplied by those who know the lacks of education as we practice it today.

This call for change, we must report, has been sounded more often outside education than by education itself. But, however the clarion was sounded, vocational education is now beginning to reach those whom it should have been reaching for generations.

In several states, new vocational programs are meeting the challenge of poverty within depressed school districts. While the beginnings of these changes have taken place largely under the

Manpower Development and Training Act, they are rapidly being expanded under the new Vocational Education Act.

New Jersey, for example, is now matching federal funds with sizable funds and plans of its own to bring youth up from poverty to useful and self-sufficient lives. Next year it will provide a whole range of modern laboratories and shops to train youth and adults to serve new industries and bring new ones into the state.

In New York's Harlem, a new vocational facility has been established to bring back to society poor children who have already descended the ladder from poverty to delinquency.

To serve the District of Columbia, the federal city that has known poverty to its shame, a Youth Center has been established at Lorton, Virginia, for young delinquents. Two weeks ago, 25 of these young men were graduated from a vocational course organized and operated under the impact of new federal legislation. For the first time, young men returning to society from this correctional institution are being discharged with skills in such fields as radio and TV repair, auto mechanics, and food service. Two classes have been graduated so far. All the trainees are now employed and on their road back.

Finally, we are seeing a beginning of change in vocational education's long and unproud pattern of discrimination—a voluntary fulfillment of the Civil Rights Act that is more heartening than any compulsory fulfillment.

In a proud—and rightly proud—school community in one Southern county, integration has taken place quietly and magnificently. With the development of new industry in the county, a need developed for trained adults to work with new skills. Both whites and Negroes were enrolled in a vocational training program and subsequently hired to work side by side in the new plant. During their vocational training and work experience, they learned from both Negro and white teachers and supervisors.

This whole unprecedented break from discrimination has come about with no particular difficulty and in a matter-of-fact way—the best way there is. It didn't make news, but it was the best kind of news. Moreover, as a direct result of this success, came a decision by county school officials to integrate all public schools during the current school year.

In vocational education, and particularly in its potential against poverty, the great era of change has barely begun. It will not come to pass easily or all at once or with the same success in all places.

Many of us have long been impatient to see these changes take place. Many of us know that we, as educators, have neglected our clear duty for too long. But movement is underway. It will continue and gather force. It will do credit to the beliefs we have long preached but all too seldom practiced. And it will fuel the light of hope for generations yet to come.

11. Youth and Employment in Comparative Perspective

A. H. HALSEY

INTRODUCTION

Youth is a social as well as a biological concept. In societies with a simple culture the translation from childhood to adult status is marked by relatively short *rites de passage* at or near the stage of puberty. Societies with complex cultures separate the social from the biological. In them social maturation extends beyond biological puberty to produce the problems of youth and adolescence which are so peculiar to industrial countries. At the same time there is evidence that in recent times biological maturation has been speeded up, puberty occurs at an earlier age, and the social gap is widened.

The main concern of this conference is with poverty. It is in this context that I am asked to look at the passage of young people from school to work. In doing so I must begin with a general apology for the irrelevance of what I have to say about the non-American world. But the fault here lies as much with the facts as with my incompetence. First, America is both the richest and the most advanced industrial nation in the world. The recent and current publicity given to poverty in America is a shock to most Americans because in the last generation they have come to accept the norm of affluence. Poverty for the American belongs to a world which has been left behind. Poor people are survivals from an earlier stage of society. To be reminded of them is to be forced to turn our eyes from the main stream of American life. But of course to a foreigner the world of poverty is ubiquitous. Poor standards of living, ill health, and illiteracy are the common human lot. About two-thirds of the world's population live in about a hundred countries sharing a third of the world's income with no obvious or immediate prospect of more than marginal amelioration. Industrialism with its high productivity and its elevated standards of health and welfare touches only a quarter of the human race, and these mostly in Western Europe and in North America.

Over most of the world poverty is simple to understand, if massively difficult to abolish, as the product of crude material forces. In America such conditions are confined to minorities who have yet to join the main stream of modern American history. Most immigrant groups have mounted the escalator of prosperity and status which is provided by rising American standards of education and employment opportunities. Those, especially the Negroes, who have failed to do so make their demands more clamorous and insistent precisely because their failure is "un-American" and therefore deeply wounding to self-respect and a glaring contradiction to the *normal* expectations of American citizenship. The consequent challenge to social policy is urgent. It is a challenge to assimilate at a faster rate than ever before the groups which hitherto have been, for whatever reasons, least assimilated.

In Europe and still more in the poverty world of Asia and Africa these problems scarcely exist. The expectations are lower, are contained more firmly in traditional social and economic hierarchies, and are rising at a much slower pace.

The basis of an anti-poverty program is different in America not only in its social context but also in the history of ideas concerning the explanation of poverty and of social policy towards it. Professor Glazer argues elsewhere in these conference papers that social policy in America has a distinctive history because of two characteristics of the country—its ideological individualism and its cultural diversity. Individualism as a creed shared by policy makers and the ordinary American has always lent support to explanations of poverty in terms of deficiencies in individuals rather than faults in the social system. Cultural diversity at the same time reduces the level of sympathy between groups and the degree of self-confidence of those who attempt to devise or administer national solutions to problems of social welfare. These two forces combine to support the belief that individuals are primarily responsible for their own welfare—each must seek his own path to full and affluent American citizenship. At the end of the nineteenth century the most influential explanation of failure was that of individual genetic deficiency; later belief in low motivation came into prominence. Now the trouble with the poor man is characteristically identified with his lack of education. None of these individualistic theories is without foundation. Yet it seems to me to be especially relevant in America to remind ourselves of Bernard Shaw's aphorism that the trouble with the poor man is his poverty.

Such a view points first at the social system and only second at individual shortcomings. It puts education in its proper perspective in social policy. America after all has conspicuously failed in the postwar years to provide full employment for its working population. This and the continuance of gross inequalities of property and income must remain the starting point for any attack on poverty. Educational programs are important mainly for their potential impact on earning capacity and the differential value of the labor services of educated and uneducated people.

Again the problems of youth and employment are set in a totally different social context in America compared with most of the countries of the world. In poor countries the young are normally in or out of work. Only in affluent America are they to be thought of as in or out of school. In America the problems of youth employment are defined *educationally*. In Europe and still more in the underdeveloped world these problems are located in the work place. So here again, a comparative view is in effect a backward look at American history. If it has value this will lie in a reexamination of the desirable relationship between school and work experience.

Whatever this relationship may be, a general principle has emerged in social policy concerning the young. An advanced industrial country, partly out of concern for the efficiency of its economy and partly out of concern for the individual development of its citizens, will aim at defining both childhood and youth up to the age of full adult citizenship as a period in which everyone has the right to be educated as far as his capacities will allow and the right of access to experience and opportunity and to guidance which will enable him to embark on a working life as an adult, as suited as possible to his capacities and inclinations. This ideal implies a comprehensive system of educational and vocational guidance for all up to the age of, say, 21. No country yet has this and for the great majority of young people no such experience is on the remotest horizon.

The Demographic Background

The principal underlying factor in youth employment is that of world population growth. The population of the world is expected to double or more than double between now and the end of the century, when it may be expected to lie between six and seven billion, as a result of declining mortality and continuing high birth rates. As is clear from Table 1, the highest rates of growth tend to be concentrated in the low-income areas of the world, in Africa and Asia.

The population of young people aged fifteen to nineteen is growing at about the same rate as the total population in the world as a whole, but there are considerable variations between the continents. No less than 60 per cent of the world's young people are growing up in Asia and it is easy to overlook, from the vantage point of the industrial countries, that three-quarters

Table 1. RATES OF INCREASE IN POPULATION

Continent and region	*Average annual rate of increase 1958–1962 (per cent)*
World Total	2.0
Africa	2.3
North America	1.7
Asia	2.3
Europe	0.9
Oceania	2.2
U. S. S. R.	1.7

Source: United Nations, *Statistical Yearbook*, 1963, Table 3.

of the young seek to enter the adult world of employment in rural areas, with their associated conditions of poverty and ignorance and their narrow range of occupational choice. It is true that the 15- to 19-year-old age group is growing faster than the total population in the industrial countries of North America and Western Europe because of increased fertility since the Second World War. But this must not be allowed to obscure the fact that the world distribution of youth is heavily concentrated in the poor countries.

EMPLOYMENT RATES AMONG YOUNG PEOPLE

Given the demographic background, the rate of participation by young people in the labor force is determined by supply factors which include legislation on compulsory schooling, the structure of education and the development of educational opportunity beyond the statutory leaving age, and by demand factors varying with the nature of the economy and its general level of employment. The vast majority of young people enter employment at the age of 14 or 15, though in some countries there remains a problem of child labor, and children under 14 can in some cases constitute as much as 10 per cent of the total labor force. This problem has, however, been almost eliminated in the advanced industrial countries of North America, Western Europe, Australia, and New Zealand.

The percentage of 15- to 19-year-olds who are in the labor force is higher for boys than for girls, though there is some tendency towards a general evening up of participation rates between the sexes. It is clear from Table 2 that the poorer the country the higher the participation rate of young people and that there is a general trend towards lower rates of participation with economic growth and the expansion of educational systems. Nevertheless there are variations to be noted within the industrial world. The United Kingdom, for example, had a participation rate for boys of 83.9 per cent in 1951 compared with the Japanese rate of 48.1 per cent in 1956. The Indian rate, which is not included in the table, is possibly lower than that of Japan, but this is due not to the development of education but rather to lack of employment opportunities.

TABLE 2. LABOR FORCE PARTICIPATION RATES FOR YOUTH (AGES 15 TO 19 YEARS)

Country	*Year*	*Participation (percentage)*	
		Males	*Females*
Africa			
Egypt	1947	77.8	10.5
	1960	68.4	8.6
Union of South Africa			
White population	1951	52.5	42.0
Nonwhite population	1951	78.6	31.4
America			
Canada	1957	50.9	37.4
	1961	41.4	34.2
United States	1957	49.0[a]	30.3[a]
	1962	43.1[a]	28.7[a]
Brazil	1950	80.6	23.4
Asia			
Japan	1956	48.1[a]	44.8[a]
	1960	51.6	49.7
Philippines	1957	79.4	48.4
	1961	65.7	47.9
Europe			
Belgium	1947	66.8	41.8
France	1958	66.9	49.5
Germany (Federal Republic)	1950	84.7	77.5
	1961	81.6	78.6
Italy	1957	69.2[a]	41.3[a]
	1962	60.7[a]	41.3[a]
Netherlands	1947	66.0[a]	48.7[a]
	1960	63.1	59.4
Sweden	1950	74.4	54.3
	1960	52.8	46.6
Turkey	1950	87.6	73.3
	1960	78.9	66.2
United Kingdom	1951	83.9	87.7
Oceania			
Australia	1954	79.7	68.2

[a] 14 to 19 years.
Source: I.L.O., *Year Book of Labour Statistics*, 1963, Table 2.

It is also worth noting that the proportion of young workers in the total labor force of different sectors of the economy varies and in particular that the agricultural sector in both backward and advanced countries has generally a higher rate of participation by young people.

UNEMPLOYMENT

Young people generally are most prone to suffer the effects of unemployment, and in the advanced countries this is especially true for those with the least education. The unemployment rate for those under 20 in many countries is frequently double the general rate of unemployment. In the underdeveloped world, both unemployment and underemployment are heavy among young workers. For example, a sample survey in India in 1955 showed that 55 per cent of rural unemployment was made up of young men between the ages of 16 and 21, the equivalent figure in the urban areas being 40 per cent. Again in Cuba in 1956–1957 20 per cent of the unemployed were under the age of 21. In the industrial economies since World War II there have been better employment conditions than were typical in the interwar period though, as is shown in Table 3, there are considerable variations in the general rate of unemployment at the present time. A very high proportion of the unemployment of young workers in northwest Europe is of short duration and occurs at the stage of first job seeking.

In Britain since World War II there has been no serious

TABLE 3. INTERNATIONAL UNEMPLOYMENT RATES

Country	*Per cent of labor force unemployed, 1962*
Austria	2.7
Belgium	5.1
Canada	5.9
Germany (Federal Republic)	0.7
Ireland	5.7
Italy	3.0
Japan	0.9
Netherlands	0.8
Puerto Rico	12.3
Sweden	1.3
United Arab Republic	3.2[a]
United Kingdom	2.1
United States	5.6
Yugoslavia	6.8

[a] 1961.
Source: United Nations, *Statistical Yearbook*, 1963, Table 10.

problem of unemployment, which runs at a level of 1 or 2 per cent, though in many industries there is a problem of underemployment in the sense of three men doing two men's jobs. Moreover, there has been indication in the recent British statistics that the under-21-year olds have been more than proportionately affected by such unemployment as has existed. For example, in 1964, of the total of unemployed, which amounted to nearly 300,000, only 5.2 per cent were 18- to 20-year-olds.

Determinants of Demand

The dominant influence on the demand side of the juvenile labor market is the general employment situation. Here a contrast has to be drawn between the expanding economies of the Western industrial world and the relatively stagnant economies of the underdeveloped world. In many of the former in recent years there have been too few young people to fill the many new jobs which technical progress and the growth of new industries and services have created. In many underdeveloped countries there is chronic unemployment and underemployment, and it is in these countries that supply problems are also most difficult in that there are vast numbers of young people trying to enter the market. Under these circumstances it is almost impossible to speak realistically of occupational opportunity or choice. There is even a serious problem of unemployment among persons with general educational qualifications, in particular in Ceylon, India, and Pakistan where the administrative and public service and white-collar professions tend to be overcrowded and there is an insufficient supply of technically and professionally trained persons.

Apart from the general level of employment, there is the most important factor of a continually changing structure of occupations. The development of industrial countries creates new industries and causes shrinkage of employment opportunities in established ones. The shift is characteristically from primary and secondary into tertiary production. Agricultural jobs shrink proportionately as first industrial and second service occupations expand. There is a growth of new jobs in industries based on the new technology of nuclear physics and electronics and a growing specialization of jobs in all branches of the economy, including the distributive trades.

The shift towards the tertiary sector which is typical of industrial advance is also associated with rising qualifications for entry to a wide variety of occupations. The rising threshold of educational requirement is in part due to shifts in occupational structure but, also, and more importantly, to the raising of educational standards within established occupations. Thus the proportion of the total labor force in European countries which is classified as unskilled has typically fallen during the course of the present century from over a quarter to less than 10 per cent, and there has been a corresponding rise in white-collar employment and technical occupations. In the meantime traditional distinctions between manual and nonmanual, as well as between skilled and semiskilled, work, have become blurred. Automation plays its part in all this, cutting down the number of unskilled and semiskilled jobs and eliminating some skilled jobs such as accounting and bookkeeping, while simultaneously creating new types of specialized occupation.

These continuous and rapid changes in demand tend to outrun the response of educational and training institutions, giving a surplus of workers in some traditional fields and shortages of technically trained persons in engineering and science, as well as shortages and inefficiencies which arise from obsolete training for occupations which have changed their skill content.

YOUTH EMPLOYMENT SERVICES

Public policy in Europe and America towards youth employment is shaped by two considerations: first by moral judgments concerning the extent of the state's responsibility to provide education for each individual which will allow the fullest development of his capacities; and second by the need for an adequate and efficient labor supply. For an efficient economy it is necessary to make appropriate arrangements for an exact supply of qualified workers and, on the other hand, to give recognition to the idea of the rights of the individual. It is necessary that public policy should aim at equality of educational and employment opportunities so that everyone is launched into a working life which best fits his natural endowments. Clearly public action has to face complicated problems of economic forecasting and social engineering in order to achieve either the economic or the social aims of a modern policy for youth. Moreover, it cannot be assumed that the aim of economic efficiency and that of individual right necessarily coincide. In practice the youth employment services which have grown up all over the industrial world, especially since World War II, are devoted to adjusting and guiding individuals under conditions of supply and demand which are largely beyond the control of the youth employment officer or vocational guidance counsellor.

The growth of youth employment services in the industrial countries has its roots in reaction to the widespread social waste and individual unhappiness created by juvenile unemployment in the economic depressions of the interwar years. In more recent years conditions have markedly changed, and particularly the general rate of unemployment is much reduced. There is a shortage of labor, particularly skilled labor, and in general a widening horizon of economic opportunities for young people. Nevertheless, the problem of fitting supply to demand in individual cases has in the process become more complex and, what is most serious, there is a general tendency for educational qualifications to rise over a wide sector of employment and thereby to increase the difficulties of the educationally backward individual.

The youth employment services in general fall far short of the idea of a comprehensive guidance service. They often do not extend to those who most need them, especially in rural areas. They are frequently hampered by shortage of funds and qualified staff and, what is perhaps most important, only a tiny minority of young people are guided by follow-up inquiries as to their welfare and progress after the first job placement.

Research findings on the British youth employment service indicate that this agency is by no means the most important influence on vocational choice. The Department of Scientific and Industrial Research commissioned a detailed study of school-leavers in the city of Sheffield in 1959 and 1960, which shows that youth employment officers found jobs for 31 per cent of the boys and 23 per cent of the girls. "It appears that both children and employers tend to regard the service as a last resort—in the City of Sheffield, with over 5,000 young people leaving school each year, there were only nine youth employment officers."[1] An assessment which would command wide agreement is that:

> . . . although from the practical standpoint the service would seem to be working fairly well in many areas, there are several reasons why the situation is not so healthy as it might seem. In some areas the service is not the only connection between the schools and employment, and the heads of many schools, Secondary Modern as well as Grammar, prefer to make direct contact with the employers; schools are therefore sometimes in competition with each other in respect of the vacancies that exist. The Youth Employment Service has one foot in each of the camps of education and guidance on the one hand and industrial needs on the other, and this is typified by the way in which some youth employment offices are maintained by the local education authority, with a 75 per cent grant from the Ministry of Labour, whilst others are the direct responsibility of that Ministry. Many of the youth employment officers employed by local education authorities receive a low level of remuneration, less than that of a two-year-trained teacher on the lower scales, despite the fact that many of the advertised vacancies require education up to university standard. There is no national scheme for the training of youth employment officers. The Youth Employment Service would seem to be deprived in terms of both money and status at the present time; the fact that it still functions with comparative success in terms of present needs cannot be regarded as a guarantee that it is capable of meeting the developing needs of the future.[2]

EDUCATION AND THE SUPPLY OF LABOR

The organization of educational systems in industrial countries changes in response to changes in the structure of the economy. The need for skilled labor in an advanced economy

---

[1] William Taylor, *The Secondary Modern School* (London: Faber & Faber, 1963), pp. 75–76.

[2] *Ibid.*, pp. 76–77.

and the response to social and political demands for opportunity through education lead everywhere to educational expansion and the gradual establishment of universal common schooling in first the primary and later the secondary stages of education. Nevertheless these developments in each country are historically conditioned in ways which leave considerable international variation in the actual distribution of educational opportunity and attainment between different social strata.

In the U. S. S. R. since 1917 the organization of schooling has been closely geared to economic policy, planning the supply of skilled labor through selective technical education, and to social and political policy in fostering loyalty to Soviet society through polytechnic education fusing school and work experience and through political indoctrination. A most remarkable feature of the Russian plan, with its obvious relevance for the problems of familial and class barriers to realizing fully the goals of maximizing educability and equalizing educational opportunity, is the development of secondary boarding schools. By 1965 these schools will take in 4 per cent of the total number of pupils in the primary and secondary schools. By 1980 it is hoped to raise the percentage to 80.[3]

In Western Europe the organization of education still preserves its traditional form as a reflection of the educational demands of a class society. Secondary schooling is differentiated, with a minority of schools offering curricula which prepare pupils for entry to higher education. Outside the U. S. A., where secondary schooling largely derived from a movement to "Americanize" vast numbers of immigrants and to raise the

[3] Commission of Higher Education (Great Britain), *Report of the Committee Appointed by the Prime Minister,* under the chairmanship of Lord Robbins, 1961–1963 (hereafter referred to as the *Robbins Report*), Appendix 5, p. 192: "One reason for this policy is undoubtedly to make the augmentation of the labour force by married women that much easier. It has also been alleged that it is a conscious attempt to create an elite—although this is strenuously denied, and British observers have not found any occupational distinctions in the pattern of recruitment. It may well be that the aim is in line with that of the English boarding Public School—to assist in making education a moral as well as an academic process. Pupils in the boarding schools, as in the day schools, will still take part in productive work for two days of the week."

educational and social level of the masses,[4] educational organization typically has to face difficulty and opposition to the integration of extended compulsory schooling through elementary schools, with the class-linked academic type of school leading to the universities and to white-collar and professional occupations. The problem in Europe has been to produce a comprehensive type of school out of separate school organizations with different social prestige and traditions and historically designed for different social classes. Attempts in this direction have met with varying success, but there are strong comprehensive school movements especially in Scandinavia [5] and to a lesser extent in France [6] and Britain.[7] The European universities are elitist in conception and, though formally open to all secondary school graduates in many countries (with the notable exceptions of England and Russia), compared with America [8] they are highly restricted in both numbers and the social range from which they draw their students.

Nevertheless practically all these countries subscribe to the ideal of equality of educational opportunity: it is a challenge to establish a situation where inequalities are based solely on differences in innate capacity. But such an aim is peculiarly hard to realize. In reality the social circumstances of every child form the basis for his subsequent achievements, and even for the development of his intelligence quotient, which is commonly thought of as a measure of innate ability and which determines the kind of education for which he is later selected. Thus the ideal of educating everyone up to the limits of his

---

[4] See M. Trow, "The Second Transformation of American Secondary Education," *International Journal of Comparative Sociology,* II (September, 1961), pp. 144–166.

[5] T. Husen and S. Henrysson, editors, *Differentiation and Guidance in the Comprehensive School—Report on the Sigtuna Conference 1958, Stockholm* (Stockholm: Almquist & Wikoell, 1959). Also *Robbins Report,* Cmnd. 2154, Appendix 5.

[6] W. R. Fraser, *Education and Society in Modern France* (London: Routledge & Kegan Paul, 1963).

[7] R. Pedley, *The Comprehensive School* (Baltimore: Penguin Books, Inc., 1963).

[8] See M. Trow, "The Democratisation of Higher Education in America," *European Journal of Sociology,* III, 2 (1962), pp. 231–262.

capacity can mean very different things in practice, according to the degree to which social class enters into the process of defining capacity and educational performance.

In advanced industrial countries, prestige and status tend to be justified increasingly in terms of achievement, but in fact social, political, and economic opportunities and advantages are still largely ascribed rather than achieved. Professor Parsons has emphasized the role of the school in America as an agent for the indoctrination of achievement values,[9] but judging by the results of social selection and allocation in the system as a whole, the fundamental question would appear to be why, despite this role which Parsons analyzes convincingly in his treatment of the school class, there should continue to be such a close relation between filial and parental status.

In order to explain the relationship, i.e., to explain how it comes about that educational systems, though justified in terms of equality of opportunity, in fact act as the agents for the perpetuation of inequality, it is necessary to look at the social determinants of both opportunity and performance.

First, however, it must be remarked that there are significant departures from formal equality of opportunity in many systems of education, as in the case of the English public schools or the segregated Negro schools of the Southern United States or South Africa. Second, there are *de facto* departures from the ideal of equality of opportunity which allocate educational resources in favor of the higher strata of society. Residential segregation results in school segregation between whites and Negroes in many American communities. Urban and rural differences in many countries have similar effects. Third, differences of income and wealth between strata make the expensive forms of education more accessible to the rich than to the poor. Forces of this kind are obvious and unsubtle. The more subtle influences, which continue to operate within the framework of formal equality of opportunity, appear as cumulative determi-

[9] T. Parsons, "The School Class as a Social System: Some of its Functions in American Society," in A. H. Halsey, J. E. Floud, and C. A. Anderson, editors, *Education, Economy and Society* (New York: The Free Press of Glencoe, 1961), pp. 434–455.

nants of educability and include various cultural ingredients of the differences between social classes, such as the role of language in the development of capacity to use abstractions, the social distance between teacher and pupil, the level of educational aspiration, the definition of roles in the school, and the nature of peer groups in childhood and adolescence. These more subtle influences are a challenge to educational and vocational guidance in the modern world which is comparable to the place once occupied by poverty and sickness.

TRENDS IN CLASS CHANCES

Both the technological and political pressures to which I have referred have resulted in Europe in a slow expansion of educational provision from primary through secondary to higher education. Thus the expansion of secondary education in the first half of the twentieth century transformed the primary schools into common schools accessible to all social classes. After World War I in America and after World War II in Europe a similar movement began in the relation between secondary and higher education. Secondary schooling is now nearly universal in the U. S. A. In Europe the same process has begun but is still sharply modified by distinctions in the quality of provision between schools leading to university entrance and terminal schools within the secondary system as a whole.

In an inquiry into education and social selection in England in 1952,[10] it was appropriate to take entry to grammar as opposed to secondary modern schools as the crucial point of educational opportunity. Using entry to grammar schools as the measure of opportunity in the early 1950's, class chances descended from nearly one in one for the children of the professional and business owning and managing classes through one in two or three for the children of white-collar workers to one in six for skilled workers and one in ten for unskilled workers. During the subsequent decade, a slow modification of the English secondary system has taken place, with a slight in-

[10] J. E. Floud, A. H. Halsey, and F. M. Martin, *Social Class and Educational Opportunity* (London: William Heinemann Ltd., 1956).

crease in the provision of grammar school type courses, either in grammar schools or comprehensive schools, and through the extension of secondary modern school courses to enable children to take General Certificate of Education qualifications. Thus the proportion of the age group in school at age 17 rose from 6.6 per cent in 1950 to 7.9 per cent in 1954 and 12 per cent in 1962. The proportion attaining five or more "0" level passes in G. C. E. rose from 10.7 per cent in 1954 to 15.3 per cent in 1961. There are no data on recent changes in class chances in British secondary education, but in discussing this issue the authors of the Robbins Report have concluded that "if there were data on the educational attainment of school children in each social class in, say, 1950 and in 1960, this would probably not show a great narrowing of social class differences." [11]

Evidence relating to developments in France during the 1950's shows a somewhat different picture.[12] In 1953 a national survey showed that class chances of secondary education varied systematically with social status, from 87 per cent among the children of professional workers to 13 per cent among the children of agricultural laborers. The 1959 reform of the structure of secondary education included the development of long courses in *collèges d'enseignement général,* from which transfer can be made to the *lycées* at a later stage. If the G. C. E. courses are added to those at the traditional *lycées,* then it appears that between 1953 and 1962 the proportion of all children entering secondary courses (*entrée en sixième*) rose from 30 per cent [13] to 55 percent. The expansion was accompanied by marked reduction in differential class chances of secondary education. Thus, comparing the professional and unskilled groups, in 1953 the chances of children in the former group

---

[11] *Robbins Report,* Appendix I, Cmnd. 2154–I, p. 52.

[12] Alain Girard *et al.,* "Enquête Nationale Sur l'Entrée en Sixième et la Democratisation de l'Enseignement," *Population,* XVIII (January-March, 1963).

[12] Alain Girard *et al.,* "Enquete Nationale Sur l'Entrée en Sixieme the children attending the *Sixième* in public and private secondary schools. It is estimated that correction for these omissions would raise the figure for the whole age group to 35 per cent, but would not alter the distribution of class chances.

were four times better than in the latter, and in 1962 were only twice as good, though if only the *lycées* are considered there was an increase in the differential from four times to nearly five times.

In Britain, the trend in differential class chances of entry to full-time higher education in the period 1928–1960 again shows a static picture.[14] The proportion entering universities in the period 1928–1947 was 3.7 per cent and this had risen by 1960 to 5.8 per cent. The chances of entry for boys of all classes had roughly doubled, leaving the situation in 1960 as it was earlier, namely one in which the child of a nonmanual worker had six and a half times the chance of entry to university of that of a boy from the manual working class.

SCHOOLING AND VOCATIONAL CHOICE

The feature which most distinguishes European from American schooling is that the former is so organized as to demand that decisions which are critical for the vocational choice are made at the age of 11 or 12 when they can reflect only the largely class conditioned family environment of the child. There results a close association between type of schooling, length of school life, further education, and vocational choice. The majority of children in unselective schools leave at 15 and, in England for example, some three-fifths of the boys under 16 enter unspecified semiskilled and unskilled employment; about one-third enter apprenticeships or learnerships to skilled crafts and about one in twenty clerical employment.

In the European economies the most serious shortages are in the supply of persons capable of following the more skilled and responsible occupations and the educational system is the main source of rigidities here. It is true that, against the general background of full employment, shortages of juvenile labor have been created by the raising of the school leaving age and the expansion of further education. The resultant over-all shortage has tended to upgrade the range of opportunities formerly available to school leavers, and a special feature of recent years

[14] *Robbins Report,* Appendix I, Cmnd. 2154–I, p. 54.

has been the multiplication of apprenticeship and learnership schemes in many branches of industry with the aim of improving the conditions and prospects and therefore the attractiveness of a wide range of industrial openings for the young wage earner. However, selective systems of secondary education continue to set artificial limits to both the range of employment opportunities and the occupational aspirations of young people. Children are in effect graded "superior," "mediocre," or "poor" in intelligence and attainments at the age of 11, educated accordingly for a few more years, and turned over for guidance into employment as manual or nonmanual workers as their schooling dictates. Yet a knowledge of the real significance of the processes of educational selection, and their relationship to the family environment of children and the occupational structure which confronts them on leaving school, opens up the possibility of longer-term educational and vocational guidance policy directed towards improving the supply of trained labor at all levels to meet the growing demand for it.

Children in unselective schools are subjected to the inhibiting effects of rejection and their occupational aspirations are correspondingly lower than those of children in the grammar school, the *lycée* or the *gymnasium*. The limit of aspiration among these children seems to be the top of the manual working class from which in the majority of cases they originate. In one English study [15] it is reported that among secondary modern school leavers in Lancashire, office or clerical work was the kind of job most frequently rejected and half of those who rejected it did so because they considered themselves unqualified for it. In another study [16] it was found that fewer than 5 per cent of the pupils in a sample of secondary modern school children chose occupations unsuited to their educational standing. This author found the children "ambitious, but not excessively so," by which she meant that they tended to aim

[15] C. Jahoda, "Job Attitude and Job Choice among Secondary Modern School Leavers," *Occupational Psychology,* XXVII (April & October, 1952).

[16] M. D. Wilson, "The Vocational Preferences of Secondary Modern School Children," *British Journal of Educational Psychology,* XX (June & November, 1953).

at the highest levels available to the group to which they belonged. They showed, as she expressed it, "a healthy desire to climb to the top of the tree, but little yearning to move to another part of the forest where there are taller trees." She also produced evidence to show that selection at 11-plus produced a marked modification of vocational aspirations, the children directing their interests soon after their admission to secondary schools to the general field of occupations available to them—the modern school boys, for instance, turning realistically from occupational "fantasies" to skilled manual work. It has been noted by the American sociologist R. H. Turner that "fantasy choices" are much more common among American children. It would seem that the European systems of education have a general tendency to lower the occupational aspirations of the mass of the population and thereby to exchange the problem of frustrated ambition for the problem of an underdeveloped and rigid supply of labor.

School and Work

The emphasis in Russian education on integration between school and work experience has already been mentioned. Public policy elsewhere in Europe has begun to lay increasing stress on arrangements designed to link the transition more comprehensively than is possible through the youth employment service. In Sweden work experience has been introduced into the schools as part of vocational guidance. The Newsom Report in England [17] draws attention to the recent growth of similar schemes through local initiative; but these fall a long way short of the elaborate work experience programs in Sweden.

One of the most acute difficulties faced by these attempts to link school to work is the fact that school teachers typically have little knowledge and experience of industry and commerce. Vocational guidance services could do much more than they do in the way of organizing courses and conferences for teachers which would bring them into contact with representatives

[17] Ministry of Education, "Half our Future"—A Report of the Central Advisory Council for Education (England) (London: H.M.S.O., 1963), pp. 75–76.

from industry and further education in their area. There is room too for the development of courses introducing students to industry as part of formal teacher training.

Training for Skill

But the training of young people for skilled work in Europe is still centered, by contrast with America, on the work place. In many European countries, industrial training begins immediately after the end of ordinary schooling, usually with a trial period before the employer and the young worker completely commit themselves. The period of training is usually three years, a period which though it may not be necessary in terms of the theoretical and technical knowledge required for the skilled craft is widely held to be necessary in order to enable the adolescent to adapt himself to the life of the factory and to accustom himself to the physiological and emotional problems associated with this stage of life.

France and the United Kingdom have fixed periods of training but the other European countries recognize that there are different levels of skill attached to different trades and, accordingly, they vary the period of training. In some cases the period may be as short as one year; in others, for example in Germany, a distinction is made between apprenticeship which takes three years and learnership which takes less. Most countries have instituted a test of competence at the end of apprenticeship which is conducted by an independent authority and leads to a nationally recognized credential. This independent examining system makes it possible to undertake constant revision of the nature of the craft skill and consequently of the necessary curriculum. In this way obsolete methods can be eliminated from training and new skills introduced. At the same time those trades which are deskilled by technical innovation can be eliminated from apprenticeship and learnership schemes where necessary.

The recent tendency in Europe is for industrial training to be generalized beyond the confines of particular traditional skills so that the young worker is taught more than one trade and many different trades have a common basic training with specialization only towards the end of the apprenticeship period. In those countries where there are alternative methods of training for skill, i.e., either through apprenticeship on the job or by full-time training at an institution, it is possible to obtain a greater degree of flexibility in the system as a whole, both in relation to numbers and curriculum, and especially in relation to rapid changes in either the demand for skilled workers or the supply of young people. As long as apprentice training remains the responsibility of individual firms, production needs will tend to conflict with high standards of training. Small firms cannot provide a wide range of experience in the skilled crafts and often lack the resources for adequate supervision of apprentices and learners. They also tend to be reluctant to release young workers for part-time further education. The full-time schools in France, Sweden, Italy, and Switzerland, or the collective workshops which are found in Germany and Switzerland, have had considerable success in overcoming these difficulties. Moreover, where an independent examining body exists, it is possible to maintain a constant check on the adequacy of on-the-job training and to develop advisory services.

Finally, there is the difficult question of allocating the financial burden of industrial training as between firms, families, and the state. European countries have increased the level of state assistance in recent years in various ways. In some countries there are generous family allowances which help parents of apprentices to meet the cost of maintenance. Some states relieve the burden on the firm by direct grants paid for apprentices on a per capita basis and others have arrangements for remission of taxation, for example the *taxe d'apprentissage* in France or the reduction of heavy insurance contributions in Italy.

SUMMARY AND CONCLUSION

1. Poverty is ubiquitous, but American poverty is residual. Being confined to minorities and set in a norm of affluence, it represents an urgent challenge to public policy.

2. An ideal of public policy towards which all industrial countries have been moving in recent times has three principles:

(a) educational and vocational guidance for all up to age 21;
(b) equality of opportunity for individuals, whatever their social background;
(c) an efficient and flexible labor force.

3. Actual systems of educational and vocational guidance nowhere approach these ideals. Vocational guidance services are narrowly defined and most young people are untouched by them.

4. Equality of educational opportunity is prevented in practice by either formal inequalities or informal barriers arising from class or family background or the class conditioning of educational organization.

5. The organization of secondary schooling in Europe reflects and reinforces social stratification. This may reduce frustrated ambition, but it increases the rigidity of the labor supply and falls far short of the ideal of equality of opportunity.

6. America is contrasted with Europe in its extension of education to include vocational training for nearly all children up to the age of 18. In Europe industrial training is for the most part organized within industry from the age of 14 or 15. The trend is towards the American pattern, but there are many advantages to be gained from a flexible partnership between industrial and educational organization.

12. Approaches to the School Dropout Problem

NEIL V. SULLIVAN

Any school superintendent in America is eminently qualified to participate in a program on poverty. We have been operating in poverty for several hundred years, and now it is known by all concerned. From my varied experience—literally working from Maine to California—I can tell you that in the last five or ten years education has really changed in the public schools of America. The curriculum has been "beefed up." The attitudes of teachers have changed. There is a greater commitment. The state universities, in revising their courses of study, have started to see the light. Our teachers are really trying to do something with reading and advanced placement courses, accelerated courses, and foreign language courses. We are doing a much better job with the money we have available.

We are not, however, doing an improved job when it comes to solving the problem of school dropouts. Professor Halsey has indicated that the general subject of poverty is an ubiquitous one. It is not so ubiquitous when it comes to the school dropouts because we can count them. We know the situation. Some groups have worked with statistics in this field, and others have worked with definitions. The statisticians, going all the way back to the United States Office of Education and the National Education Office, tell us that Alabama, Georgia, Kentucky, Louisiana, North Carolina, South Carolina, Tennessee, and West Virginia still have an average dropout rate of over forty per cent. The national average is about thirty-three and one-third per cent.

And now for those who like to give definitions: You have heard of "kicked-outs" or "pushed-outs." The word "dropouts" can be used interchangeably here. Last spring I suggested to the National Citizens Committee that a new definition might be "forced-outs" or "locked-outs." Last year we had the "walk-outs."

The "forced outs" or "locked outs" were those youngsters I had met in Prince Edward County, Virginia. Virginia has a unique way of facing up to the dropout problem. It is not listed among the states having a critical problem, but it is actually the worst state in the union as far as dropouts are concerned. This state eliminates dropouts by eliminating the compulsory attendance law. There is no dropout problem because some children never get into school.

Virginia has been called "the mother of Presidents." Thomas Jefferson, one of the Presidents from Virginia, said many marvelous things. One of these was, "If we expect a nation to be ignorant and free, we expect what never was and never will be." Now, unfortunately, his descendents in that state are working hard trying to keep half of the population ignorant.

President Lyndon Johnson, on November 1, 1964, cogently pulled together the statistics on dropouts. He said, "Today forty-one million students are enrolled in our public schools. Four million more will enter by the end of this decade. . . . One student out of every three now in the fifth grade will drop out before finishing high school, if we let him. Almost a million people will quit school each year, if we let them. And over one hundred thousand of our smartest high school graduates each year will not go to college, if we do nothing." He concluded his statements with, "This cannot continue. It costs too much. We cannot afford it. The whole nation suffers when your youth is neglected."

All of our presidents from Franklin D. Roosevelt through John F. Kennedy have directed their attention to the problem. It was good to hear Lyndon Johnson say, "I plan to get on with the task." Speaking in Texas, close to his home, he indicated how he planned to do this. He prudently suggested that the nation's educators must come up with most of the answers.

The program called to our attention by President Johnson that day was a Job Corp training camp, the first to be announced, made possible by the Economic Opportunity Act of 1964. This program is designed to rehabilitate the dropout, the boy or girl between the ages of 16 and 21. The University of California probably will be involved with Litton Industries at Camp Parks. We are going to spend on these Job Corp training camps, on a per capita per annum basis, about $5,000 on each child. Now, this is a fine program.

What is disturbing to me is that some of the bureaucrats indicated to me on my last trip to Washington that they expect to do what we in education have failed to do. I want everyone to know why we have failed and why they may succeed. We have been spending somewhere in the neighborhood of $500 on each of these children. Those administering the Job Corps Program expect to spend ten times as much. They are going to put $30 in each boy's pocket, in each girl's pocket, to use as spending money. They are prepared to do a good job with these young people in terms of health, food, clothing, and almost a promise of a job.

THE RESPONSIBILITY OF THE PUBLIC SCHOOLS

However, I suggest to you that public schools must not abdicate their responsibilities in this area. It is fine for business to become involved, but I hope we do not remove ourselves too far from this field. I would like to think that the United States Office of Education could be coordinating these programs rather than the Department of Labor.

The problem for the public schools is to develop effective techniques to *prevent* dropouts. In order to do this, we must systematically identify, well in advance, just who these potential dropouts are. Once we identify the students, we have the responsibility of developing equally effective techniques for persuading these pupils that a high school education is necessary for survival in our society.

We must also come up with sophisticated skills and techniques for working with parents. The attitudes of parents significantly affect the decisions of young people to leave school early. The counselor must find the time and means of reaching parents. We are not doing this today.

When I think of poverty I think back to my first year of teaching. I made $80 a month then, and the community used to feed me. I would go to each home and eat with the families and the children. What a marvelous way to establish home-school rapport! I could counsel the children, I met the parents, and I got fat.

Our counselors must get into the homes, but at the same time the schools must not indicate that they have all the answers. We need to involve the church, every social organization, law enforcement groups, labor unions, and industry.

The harsh economic realities of everyday life frequently limit what the deprived parent can do for himself and his children. As a result, he forecloses not only on himself, but on his child's future. The parent is often faced with overwhelming economic problems at home, and, despite the fact that the child will invite second-class citizenship by dropping out of school, he still makes the calamitous decision. In cases like this, I recommend direct financial help to the parent for keeping the child in school. By this method, we can reassure the poor but able student that both his school and society value him highly.

A second direct approach is partial attendance at school. Students who are forced to work to supplement meager family income should be permitted to accept employment. The school should make arrangements at odd hours to accommodate the continuing educational needs of the student until he receives his high school diploma. The concept of the seven-day school and the twelve-month school should be fully explored, with flexible scheduling the order of the day. We cannot afford the luxury in our society of closing our schools such a high per cent of the time.

Third, a formal on-the-job training program should be provided with students receiving remuneration while dividing their school day between the office or factory and the school. This program should be carried out in every community, but especially in communities where a comprehensive high school or an area vocational high school does not exist.

According to James B. Conant, we only have about three or four truly comprehensive high schools in the entire country, so I am suggesting to you that on-the-job training programs are necessary in every community. Most studies on the dropout reveal that more concentrated efforts must be made by schools in small rural or large urban districts, where a low holding power exists. Those areas which lack adequate school facilities should fit more students into programs in every nook and corner of the community in direct on-the-job training programs—in the hospital, the telephone office, the library, the mill, the recreation department.

Fourth, the school should serve as a clearing house for job opportunities and as the placement office for its student body. Leadership must be taken by the school to find jobs for students during and after school hours, on weekends, and during vacation periods, especially in the summer months.

Fifth, the hidden costs must be eliminated. Our public schools are not really free. They are guilty of perpetuating practices which embarrass children, who are asked to bring money to pay for all sorts of things. I condemn particularly the practice in southern communities of not providing textbooks and supplies for the children in the Negro schools. It is true that they do in some cities, but typical procedure in the Negro schools in the South is to give the children nothing with which to work. The cupboard is literally bare. "Separate but equal" education makes effective universal education impossible for Negro children. When I went into school after school and asked to see the fourth grade arithmetic books, there would be three of them. How many spelling books? The answer would be five. This practice cannot be condoned in our society.

Sixth, clothing must be available in every school for every needy child. Innumerable dropouts occur because the child does not have the clothes, the simple undergarments, the shoes and stockings, to wear and is too proud to ask for help. Attendance in schools is poor in our large city urban districts and in the South. Researchers can easily discover the reason for poor attendance as far as clothing is concerned. It is true that children swap clothing to go to school. There may be four girls and only three dresses. There may be five boys and only four pairs of shoes. This is the kind of poverty that I am talking about. We must provide clothing for these children.

Seventh, proper care must be taken of the health of the

child. Some children are underfed and undernourished. We had children in Prince Edward County last year who would go to sleep about eleven o'clock. The Caucasians in the South said, "Oh, Dr. Sullivan, don't worry about those little Negro children going to sleep at eleven o'clock. They're lazy, you know, and are having a nap." Well, they didn't take a nap after we gave them breakfast at eight o'clock in the morning when they arrived at school. They were as lively a bunch of youngsters as I have ever seen. I suggest to you that we should feed these youngsters in the morning if they are not having breakfast at home.

Eighth, many dropouts occur because of sexual promiscuity, resulting in pregnancy and early marriage. The school permits the male to continue, but the female is banned. We must make the necessary arrangements to continue in school, under flexible scheduling, young mothers who are forced into the role of homemaker. Furthermore, we must address ourselves to the problem of including sex education and family living courses in our curriculum for all youngsters.

We have these girls in our schools two and three years before they have that first child, many of them as early as the age of fifteen, but our curriculum is structured so that they get home and family living courses in the eleventh or twelfth grade. I suggest to you that there is nothing wrong in beginning to teach home and family living to the child at eight or nine years of age. As a matter of fact, we are now moving mathematics and science down into the grade schools. It is obvious to me that we had better also pass down what is probably a more important subject to many of these children—home and family living courses.

The Roots of the Problem

The eight suggestions I have just made deal with a direct approach, administering to the immediate problem. These positive steps must be taken. However, we should attack the dropout problem long before it is imminent, and the time to do this is when the potential dropout is two or two-and-one-half years of age. Why do children leave school? For economic reasons?

For reasons of health? Because they have been embarrassed? Yes, partially, for all these reasons.

But the real reason in many cases is because they are failing, because they cannot compete academically with their peers, because they have failed from the very first year in school. Now, why do they fail? I think we all know the reason: because they lack the cultural and sophisticated backgrounds of their peers. Although they are the same chronological age, they have had to compete with peers possessing a two- to three-year advantage over them in areas the school and society consider most important. The minority child frequently is not privileged to have a parent who reads to him, a long summer vacation at a boy's camp, an aquarium and a terrarium, or a membership in the boy scouts or the cub scouts. Neither does he have a set of encyclopedias in his bedroom. Instead he has a stunted intellect that needs to be nurtured creatively.

I am sure that most of you are familiar with the work of Blum and of Breuner. Studies such as theirs suggest that IQ can be stimulated and stretched 20 points, 10 before the child is 6 and 10 more between the ages of 6 and 18.

At present, instead of using creative techniques, we often throw this child to the lions. The arena is the classroom, and the lion tamer is a teacher who has more lions than she can possibly train. So she spends her time with those who can respond to her middle-class techniques. She is given textbooks written on and about her middle-class children. She is underpaid and unhappy with the additional problems created by the slow learners. She rewards the successful with praise, but ignores the slow. The final *coup de grâce* comes at the end of each semester when the child is told over and over again that he has failed.

The only way to avoid failure in grade one is to enroll the minority child in school at the age of two-and-a-half or three and provide him with the enriching childhood experiences his middle-class brother is receiving. We must also go to the home and work directly with the parents of this same child. Until we are willing to finance this type of program, we will continue to perpetuate a system in this country in which failure is guaranteed at an early age and the dropout is an inevitable result.

Not only must we enroll the minority child in schools early, but these schools must be integrated. The dilapidated, rat-infested schools in the ghetto must be torn down and large campus type schools must be built to replace them. We must stop procrastinating on this subject and act. We must integrate our schools during the early years of a child's life. Integration at the secondary level, while useful, is locking the door after the horse has been stolen. Effective integration occurs best when the child is young, before he is brain-washed with the phobias and myths perpetuated ignorantly by much of our adult society. States refusing to move on integration should be denied all federal help, and national boycotts of their manufactured products should be instituted.

The most logical way to integrate our schools would be through fair housing policies. The onus cannot be thrown on boards of education by telling them "to mix all the schools up." It frequently is impossible for boards to do this. We know what happened in Berkeley, where the board had to fight for its very life after taking the first step. So let us not put the responsibility completely on the board of education. Let us really think about fair housing. This is the best way to integrate our schools.

Let us also look at the world of work. You cannot move a poor Negro or Oriental or Caucasian from the slum. He has to find a job, and he has to have the economic and vocational skills that we are talking about in order to do this. So let us look at labor and industry. If they will employ these minority groups, we will integrate neighborhoods, and when we integrate neighborhoods, we will integrate schools. I suggest that we are not going to solve our problems if all of the initiative must come from boards of education.

There are ways, however, in which we as school people can act to prevent dropouts from occurring. First, we must start by humanizing instruction in every classroom. It is altogether too easy for a child to get lost and lonely. We must root out these conditions.

Second, we must organize our schools so that students will

be challenged and not threatened. Whatever cuts down a person's self-image, cuts down the effectiveness of his intelligence. This is one of the basic reasons why homogeneous groups, keeping one group of children together in a tight band, must be discouraged. Children should be grouped in compatible groups in each of the disciplines, regrouped in the fine and practical arts, in the home room, and again in physical education.

Third, we must teach the truth to our children. We can do this by including material on the contributions of all minority races in our textbooks. Stories in reading books should cover every racial group and avoid exclusive emphasis on the middle-class Caucasian child in his own nice private environment. The dilemma associated with civil rights and the myriad of complex problems surrounding this subject should be fully aired in texts dealing with American history.

Fourth, in areas where children are taken by bus out of ghetto areas, we should face up to the rest of the problem by building libraries, playgrounds, and swimming pools in the ghettos. Let us give them something to come home to.

Fifth, we must pass strong legislation requiring all students to attend school until they reach a minimum age of eighteen. Schools should be given the freedom of permitting individual students to accept proper employment during part of the school day, if these students agree to attend school on a flexible basis until completing requirements for a high school diploma.

Sixth, in cases where the parent does not have the money to finance a college education, students with academic ability and college potential must know that full college scholarships are available to them on completion of high school. Every college and university must have a plan for accepting hundreds of minority children under special conditions each year. I grow tired of the university that tells me there is a plan—if the youngster has that college board score. There is a better way of evaluating the child. If we continue to use the college board test results exclusively, we are never going to see Negroes on our fine school campuses. These tests are not adequate measures of the children about whom we are speaking.

Seventh, schools should carefully review vocational offerings.

The trend is to focus attention on auto mechanics and machine shops for men, with heavy emphasis on office skills for women. These courses, while extremely important, require fine skills not possessed by many men and women. As a result, students either fail or avoid the course offerings. We must offer a diversity of courses, many of them requiring only simple abilities. These courses should include teaching of skills that will make the student eligible for immediate employment. They should be developed with the full cooperation of committees composed of local businessmen, educators, and labor leaders.

Eighth, we must give attention to our extracurricular programs. One characteristic of the dropout we are discussing is his failure to engage in these activities. The number of activities engaged in is not important, but what is important is the mere fact of being associated with extracurricular programs. Potential dropouts should be encouraged to participate. If the available activities are not of interest to them, the program is inadequate and should be redesigned.

The schools, the police, the courts, our government agencies at every level, our churches, business, and industry must join together to develop and implement procedures that will reduce the dropout incidence in our schools. The issue is too fraught with moral implications to be capable of solution by legal or educational means exclusively.

Not too many years ago I served as high school principal in a New England community where the dropout rate was sixty per cent. The reason was simple; the industries were employing youngsters at the age of fifteen. I developed a plan working with the industries and local leaders whereby no child would be employed until he had a high school diploma. We overcame almost the entire dropout problem in that community.

A full mobilization of America's moral and economic resources is required now. Any delay could be calamitous. If we are to refute the communistic belief that man is merely material and temporal, devoid of inalienable rights, to be used or abused for political or economic reasons, then we must demonstrate that we not only know why children drop out of school, but that we are willing to take the necessary steps to overcome the peril. We must prove to ourselves and to our neighbors everywhere that we can develop plans that are workable and better for all people generally.

We have made the studies. We have developed the research. We have identified the problem. We have the wealth in this country. We know what should be done and how we should do it. The time to start is now.

PART FIVE

FULL EMPLOYMENT AND LABOR MARKET POLICIES

13. The Role of Employment Policy

HYMAN P. MINSKY

INTRODUCTION

The war against poverty is a conservative rebuttal to an ancient challenge of the radicals, that capitalism necessarily generates "poverty in the midst of plenty." This war intends to eliminate poverty by changing people, rather than the economy. Thus the emphasis, even in the Job Corps, is upon training or indoctrination to work rather than on the job and the task to be performed. However, this approach, standing by itself, cannot end poverty. All it can do is give the present poor a better chance at the jobs that exist: it can spread poverty more fairly. A necessary ingredient of any war against poverty is a program of job creation; and it has never been shown that a thorough program of job creation, taking people as they are, will not, by itself, eliminate a large part of the poverty that exists.

The war against poverty cannot be taken seriously as long as the Administration and the Congress tolerate a five per cent unemployment rate and frame monetary and fiscal policy with a target of eventually achieving a four per cent unemployment rate. Only if there are more jobs than available workers over a broad spectrum of occupations and locations can we hope to make a dent on poverty by way of income from employment. To achieve and sustain tight labor markets in the United States requires bolder, more imaginative, and more consistent use of expansionary monetary and fiscal policy to create jobs than we have witnessed to date.

Incidentally, tight labor markets, by making all labor something of value will go far to building morale among our urban and rural poor. The community facilities program may be a poor substitute for tight labor markets, even for the social objectives it is trying to achieve.

The war against poverty must not depend solely, or even primarily, upon changing people, but it must be directed toward changing the system. However, the changes required are not those that the traditional radicals envisage. Rather they involve a commitment to the maintenance of tight full employment and the adjustment of institutions, so that the gains from full employment are not offset by undue inflation and the perpetuation of obsolete practices.

To anyone who has a deep commitment to a liberal pluralistic democracy, a policy of changing the system rather than changing people is most attractive.

Job creation in the context of the American economy means the sophisticated use of expansionary monetary and fiscal policies. Irrational prejudices, to which even the recent highly professional Councils of Economic Advisers have catered, exist against spending, deficits, and easy money. Ignoring these prejudices, are there any serious barriers against using expansionary aggregate-demand-generating policies to achieve tight full employment? In addition, if barriers do exist, can expansionary policies be designed which get around or over them? These are the problems upon which this paper will focus.

Other papers at this conference have considered the various definitions as well as the characteristics of poverty in America. We will just note that the Council of Economic Advisers estimated that in 1963 the heads of 30 per cent of the families living in poverty were employed all year and another 30 per cent were employed part of the year.[1] A program of ending poverty by generating tight full employment will mainly affect these families, as well as those which will have members drawn into the labor force as a result of jobs being available.

It is also estimated that the heads of some 40 per cent of the families living in poverty were not in the labor force during 1963. Obviously, expanded, improved, and modernized programs of transfer payments and income in kind for the aged,

[1] Council of Economic Advisers, *Economic Report of the President,* 1965, p. 166, Table 21.

the infirm, the disabled, and needy children are necessary. As I see it, this has little to do with the war on poverty; it has mainly to do with our national conscience and affection for man. Simple decency calls for a system of transfer payments and income in kind for the case book citizens that lifts their lives well above any "poverty line."

This paper is almost exclusively concerned with the problem of generating enough job opportunities of the right kind, at the right place, and with sufficiently high incomes so that all who are willing and able to work can earn enough from jobs to maintain themselves and those for whom they are responsible at a level above some poverty line. Some adjustments and additions to our system of transfer payments may be required; in particular, family allowances may be in order. However, from the perspective of this paper, such changes are peripheral elements; the fundamental element in any war against poverty is jobs.

Of course, sane adults should be free to choose poverty, but no one should have poverty thrust upon him.

TIGHT FULL EMPLOYMENT

The single most important step toward ending poverty in America would be the achieving and sustaining of tight full employment. Tight full employment exists when over a broad cross section of occupations, industries, and locations, employers, at going wages and salaries, would prefer to employ more workers than they in fact do. Tight full employment is vital for an anti-poverty campaign. It not only will eliminate that poverty which is solely due to unemployment, but, by setting off market processes which tend to raise low wages faster than high wages, it will in time greatly diminish the poverty due to low incomes from jobs. In addition, by drawing additional workers into the labor force, tight full employment will increase the number of families with more than one worker. As a result, families now in or close to poverty will move well away from it. There may be a "critical minimum effort" that is needed to move families to a self-maintaining income growth situation, this effort bringing about a sharp move to a position well above poverty. Having multiple earners in a family is one way of achieving this.

That is, there is no better cure for poverty than family income, especially family income earned on a job.

There is a need for us to envisage what a tight full employment economy in the United States would look like. Many adjustments might be needed. For example, if we know that we can generate as many jobs as there are workers seeking work, then those programs, many of which are legacies of the Great Depression, designed to control the size of the labor force can be eliminated. In fact, the combination of a commitment to tight full employment and the view that income earned on a job is best indicates that programs to expand the labor force are in order.

Serious research on the attributes of tight full employment should be undertaken, not only because it is a weapon in the war on poverty, but also because it certainly is one of the attributes of any Great Society. In this section only three attributes of tight full employment will be taken up:

1. The size of tight full employment GNP in 1965
2. The effect of tight full employment on relative wages
3. The effect of the transition to tight full employment on the price level.

The "interim" employment goal set four long years ago by the Heller Council of Economic Advisers and reaffirmed by the Ackley Council this year is a four per cent unemployment rate. On the basis of Swedish and other European experience, this is a very slack employment goal. Even if we allow for considerably greater voluntary mobility and random industrial changes in the United States than prevail in Europe, the Swedish equivalent unemployment rate in the United States might be a measured 2.5 per cent unemployment rate (Table 1). As an interim definition of tight full employment, I shall use a 2.5 per cent unemployment rate. This is lower than the measured annual rate for any year since World War II.

The Council of Economic Advisers, which has been congratulating itself for the performance of the economy in 1964, admits that even with its slack four per cent definition of full

Table 1. UNEMPLOYMENT RATES, BY MONTHS, FOR SWEDEN, 1956–1963 (IN PER CENT)

Year	*Jan.*	*Feb.*	*Mar.*	*Apr.*	*May*	*June*	*July*	*Aug.*	*Sept.*	*Oct.*	*Nov.*	*Dec.*
1956	2.4	3.6	2.4	2.1	1.3	.7	.5	.7	.7	.9	1.3	1.9
1957	2.9	2.6	2.6	2.7	1.9	1.2	.8	.9	.9	1.2	1.7	2.7
1958	3.8	3.6	3.6	3.8	2.6	1.3	1.0	1.3	1.3	1.7	2.4	3.3
1959	4.3	3.4	2.6	2.7	1.9	1.2	1.0	1.2	1.2	1.3	1.6	1.8
1960	2.8	2.5	2.0	1.9	1.2	.8	.6	.8	.8	.8	1.1	1.4
1961	2.1	2.0	1.5	1.6	1.1	.7	.5	.7	.7	.9	1.2	1.4
1962	2.1	2.2	2.0	1.9	1.3	.8	.6	.8	.8	1.0	1.2	1.3
1963	3.6	2.5	1.9	1.8	1.1	.7	.6	.8	.9	—	—	—

Source: Sammanställning Arbetsmarknadstabeller, Kungl. Arbetsmarknadsstyrelsen, Stockholm, October, 1963.

The percentage unemployed is based on the number of registered unemployed within the unemployment insurance system. This number is considerably less than the total number of unemployed. Sample surveys of the labor force are also taken to gain more complete information about the number of the unemployed. The estimate of the total percentage of all unemployed as opposed to the actual percentage of insured registrants who are unemployed indicates a minor upward revision is necessary in the percentages in the table. For example, the estimated unemployment rate for all workers in November 1961 was 1.7 per cent compared to 1.2 per cent for workers covered by unemployment insurance. To adjust Swedish unemployment rates to American definitions, an upward adjustment of about 0.3 to 0.5 per cent is necessary.

Source: Joint Economic Committee, *Economic Policies and Practices, Paper No. 5, Unemployment Programs in Sweden*, Joint Economic Committee, 88th Congress, 2d Session, 1964, p. 16.

employment, the gap between the potential and actual gross national product was $27 billion in 1964.

What would GNP be in a tight full-employment United States in 1965? The forecast GNP is $660 billion, but the Council does not expect any reduction in the unemployment rate. Okun's rule of thumb is that for every one percentage point decline in the measured unemployment rate there is roughly a three per cent increase in measured GNP.[2] If we apply his rule to the difference between 5.2 per cent and 2.5 per cent unemployment rates, we get a gap of $53 billion. If we modify Okun's rule so that it holds only for unemployment rates down to four per cent, after which there is a one-one relation between percentage point declines in the unemployment rate and the percentage increase in GNP, we get a gap of $34 billion. No matter how it is estimated, the gap is much larger than the $11 to $12 billion which has been used as the amount it would take to raise the incomes of all those now living in poverty above the poverty line.

The pattern of relative wages in the United States reflects the past of the economy and present institutions as well as present labor market conditions. It is important to recall that relative wages are related to relative value productivities, and there is an interrelation between relative wages and relative prices.

The general rule seems to be that during periods of extreme labor market tightness wage differentials narrow, and that during periods of slack they increase.[3] The widening of the differential during a period of increasing slack in the labor market is illustrated by the relative gross average hourly earnings in the primary metal industry and in retail trade.

Since World War II, the ratio of primary metal to retail

---

[2] Arthur Okun, "Potential G.N.P.: Its Measurement and Significance," *1962 Proceedings of the Business and Economic Statistics Section,* American Statistical Association, pp. 98–104.

[3] A study which summarizes the evidence with regard to the effect of slack and tightness is Lloyd Ulman, "Labor Mobility and the Industrial Wage Structure in the Postwar United States," *Quarterly Journal of Economics,* LXXIX (February, 1965), pp. 73–97. The illustrative example used here is consistent with the results of Ulman's thorough analysis.

trade hourly earnings has risen from 1.54 to 1.70. In 1962, average hourly earnings in retail trade were $1.75, which is close to the $1.50 per hour that marks the poverty line. In 1947, wages in retail trade were two-thirds of those in the primary metal trade. If the same ratio ruled in 1962, given primary metal industry wages of almost $3.00 per hour, wages in retail trade would have been about $2.00 per hour. This is substantially farther above the poverty line than the $1.75 per hour that in fact prevailed. That is, if the 1947 wage ratio had been maintained, the contribution of retail trade employment to poverty would have been much smaller.

The cohesiveness of relative wages and the importance of key trade union contracts in setting a pattern for wage increases depend upon the over-all tightness in the labor market. In particular, wage gains in industries with weak trade unions—such as textiles—or with essentially no trade unions—such as retail trade—will keep up with or even improve on the bargains struck in highly organized industries such as steel and automobiles only if the labor market is tight.[4]

Between 1947 and 1962, employment in the primary metal industry fell by some 180 thousand, while employment in retail trade rose by more than 1,300 thousand. Over this period, as we have seen, the ratio of primary metal wages to retail trade wages rose from 1.54 to 1.70; that is, wages in primary metals rose relative to wages in retail trade, even though employment in primary metals was decreasing while employment in retail trade was increasing. This indicates that it was supply conditions rather than demand conditions that affected relative wages; for if it were demand conditions, the rising "demand" for labor in retail trade as compared with the primary metal industry would have led to retail wages increasing relative to primary metal industry.

Conceptually, we can think of two sets of industries—high and low wage industries. High wage industries exist because the

[4] Harold M. Levinson, "Postwar Inflation," *Study Paper No. 21, January 1960, of "Study of Employment, Growth and Price Levels,"* Joint Economic Committee, U. S. Congress, 86th Congress, supported this view.

employers want to be able to "select" their workers. Perhaps they invest so much in training or are so vulnerable to worker dissatisfaction that they are willing to pay premium wages in order to be able to select their workers and keep them happy. Since they award a prize whenever they hire, these high wage industries have an infinitely elastic labor supply at their going wage (L_s in the diagram below).

A simple model which generates the observed type of relative wage behavior follows (Fig. 1):

FIGURE 1

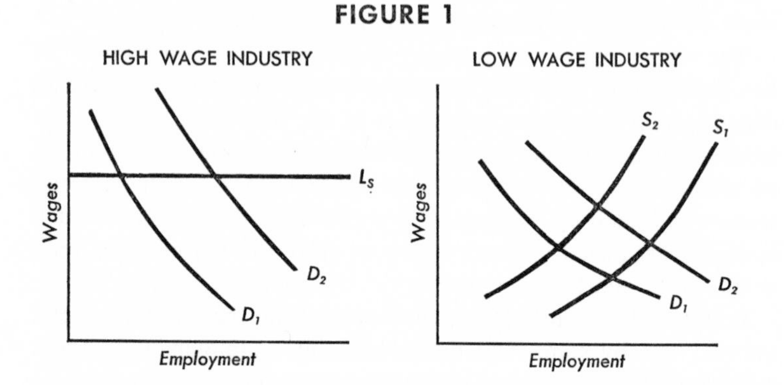

The supply curve of labor to the low wage industries is upward sloping—but its position depends upon the number of workers employed by the high wage industries. Thus, if employment by the high wage industries increases, the supply curve of workers to the low wage industries shifts to the left; and if the high wage employment decreases, the low wage industry's labor supply curve shifts to the right. If the demand curve for high wage industry shifts to D_1 from D_2, the supply curve of labor to the low wage industry shifts from S_2 to S_1. As a result, wages fall and employment increases in the low wage industry.

If, on the other hand, aggregate demand is increased, so that the demand for labor in both the high and low wage industries rises from D_1 to D_2, then the supply curve in the low wage industry also shifts, this time to the left of S_2. Total employment in the low wage industry may rise or fall, depending upon the reaction of labor force participation rates to higher wages and improved job availability, but its wages will rise while wages in the high wage industry would remain constant.

This "model" of the labor market is static. It ignores the fact that in general real wages will rise over time. We can, as a first approximation, assume that in the high wage industry money wages will rise at the same rate as labor productivity. Thus, in a dynamic context, the fall in low wages, associated with labor market slack, and the rise in low wages, associated with labor market tightness, must be interpreted as a rise or fall relative to wages in the high wage industry.

One of the intermediate policy objectives of the anti-poverty campaign should be to facilitate the rise of wages in low wage industries while constraining the rise of wages in high wage industries. A problem that arises in implementing such an incomes policy is that it is also necessary to constrain the rate of increase of nonwage incomes. The proud boast of Gardner Ackley, Chairman of the Council of Economic Advisers, that corporate profits after taxes rose by 18 per cent in 1964 shows either that some policymakers are not serious about eliminating poverty, or a strange belief on their part that poverty has nothing to do with income distribution.

The anti-poverty campaign carries an implicit commitment to a rapid increase of those wages that are close to or below the poverty line. A more rapid increase in these wages than in the physical productivity of the workers implies a rise in the prices of the products or services that use these workers. For the measured price level to remain constant, offsetting decreases in some other prices—the prices for the products of high wage industries—would have to take place. That is, for price level stability, wages in high wage industries would have to rise by less than the increases in the productivity of their workers, and management in these often oligopolistic industries would have to pass this decline in unit costs on to their customers.

The existence of nonlabor costs and incomes makes the programming of declining prices when wages rise less than labor productivity difficult. Assume that the productivity of labor increases in our high wage industries, but wages are kept constant. Let us also assume that this is a truly disembodied increase in productivity: no increase in the capital stock or visible change in technique occurred. If prices per unit fell by the same percentage as did wages per unit, then gross profits per unit of output would also fall by the same ratio. However, the capital value of the firm and its ability to meet contractual financial commitments depends not upon the mark-up on wages, but rather on the flow of gross profits after taxes. Only if the elasticity of demand for the product is equal to or greater than one will such a fall in relative prices lead to a gross profit flow that is large enough to maintain capital values and meet financial commitments.

As firms tend to be risk averters, the usual assumption they will make is that the demand for their output is inelastic. They will attempt to cut price by a smaller percentage than the fall in their labor costs, thereby raising profit margins. Given the deviations from competitive conditions that exist in much of our economy, they will succeed in this effort. Thus, the distribution of income between profits and wages will shift to profits. This is not desirable both on policy and aggregate demand grounds, and given the generally strong position of trade unions in high wage industries, it is also not stable.

The outcome we can hope for with tight full employment and a commitment for low wages to rise more rapidly than high wages, is for high wages to follow some productivity guideline. As a result, prices of the products of the high wage industries will not fall, and prices of the products of the low wage industries will rise. The transfer of a larger proportion of the over-all productivity gains to the workers in the low wage industries will take place by way of rising relative prices for the output of the low wage industries.

We can look at the effect of relative wage changes in another way. The high wage workers, and other affluent citizens, have been subsidized, by way of low product prices, by the poor. If the poverty campaign results in tight full employment, it will lead to a cost push inflation; for the removal of the subsidy will lead to a rise in the measured price level.

This inflation is a phenomenon of the transition from a slack to a tight full employment economy. Once a tight full employment economy is generated and sustained, this source of inflationary pressure will cease. (Whether or not there is inflationary pressure in a sustained tight labor market will be discussed in the next section.) Given the highly emotional and thus irrational opposition to inflation that exists, those committed to the elimination of poverty in America will have to prepare to hold to their objectives while this transitional inflation occurs.

Incidentally, the position that the Administration (as well as many economists) has been taking—that the likelihood that inflation will occur increases as the unemployment rate gets to or below four per cent[5]—is in the nature of a self-fulfilling prophesy. By repeatedly stating this view, they are "brain washing" business and labor into believing that inflation is unavoidable at low unemployment rates. If business and labor begin to act as if inflation will take place once unemployment rates are down, then inflation will take place.

Part of the task of those committed to the success of the war on poverty is to enlighten all concerned that the rectification of relative wages—which is necessary for the success of the war—will be accompanied by a rise in the measured price level. This inflation is quite a different kettle of fish from an inflation which either maintains or perversely changes relative wages. Our slogan must be: not all inflations are bad!

BARRIERS TO USING AGGREGATE DEMAND AS AN ANTI-POVERTY MEASURE

There is no doubt that the expected aggregate demand for 1965 is insufficient to generate tight full employment. A tight full employment GNP would be in the neighborhood of $700 billion. The Council of Economic Advisers forecast a GNP and thus an aggregate demand of $660 billion for 1965. They also predicted that no appreciable reduction in unemployment rates would be achieved. The estimated $660 billion GNP is below the slack employment definition of capacity the Council uses.

---

[5] Kermit Gordon, Director of the Bureau of the Budget, was cited by the *Wall Street Journal* of February 24, 1965, as holding this view.

A minimal aggregate demand policy for 1965 consistent with the objectives of the war against poverty is to use monetary and fiscal policy to raise demand to at least the four per cent unemployment capacity level, if not the tight full employment capacity level.

Three purported barriers to the effectiveness of measures to increase aggregate demand in the war on poverty will be discussed. One is that labor and product markets will operate so that an increase in aggregate demand will be dissipated in price increases. The second barrier is that urban white non-aged poor families are in the "tail" of the income distribution, so that an upward shift of median income will not appreciably reduce the proportion living in poverty. The third is that a rise in income, with or without an accompanying rise in prices, will quickly bring on a balance of payments crisis.

These three barriers are quite different. The first two are based upon technical characteristics of the economy; the third, the balance of payments barrier, is based upon legislated institutions and a policy objective. The dissipation via inflation argument depends upon assumptions as to the nature of labor demand and labor supply. The income distribution argument follows from an assumption that a move to tight full employment is equivalent to growth at full employment insofar as the distribution of income is concerned. These two arguments lead to the propositions that further increases in demand will merely result in inflation and in improving the lot of the already well-to-do.

As will be indicated below, it is not certain that these two barriers exist. Thus, they do not constitute a good reason for failing to take additional measures to increase aggregate demand, such as measures to ease the money market or an additional tax cut. Such programs should be adopted even though it can be shown that they would not be as effective in eliminating poverty as a correctly distributed increase in spending. However, they can be put into operation more quickly and thus should be used. If these technical barriers do exist, then the only cost of the experiment would be a once-and-for-all increase in the price level.

However, there is a real barrier to such an experiment with aggregate demand. It is the impact not only on our balance of payments, but also on our position as an international banker. Monetary ease as a means of expanding our economy is ruled out by the need to keep foreign (and domestic) short-term deposits in the United States. Since convertibility of European currencies has been achieved, the location of certain deposits is sensitive to covered interest rate differentials. Thus, the active use of monetary policy to expand demand is constrained by the banking aspect of our balance of payments problem. Under present arrangements, the monetary authorities must see to it that United States short-term interest rates are high enough to keep short-term balances—foreign as well as domestic—in the United States.

Thus the only really available devices for expanding aggregate demand are fiscal.

Underlying the Council of Economic Advisers' commitment to a four per cent "interim" unemployment goal is a belief that the "Phillips curve" for the United States is such that rapidly rising wages and prices occur whenever United States measured unemployment is below four per cent.[6] That demand increases are dissipated by price increases when unemployment is below four per cent is not a well substantiated argument. In the first place, the only type of tight labor market that has ever been observed in the United States is the transitional type. We move to tightness and back away. We have never observed the results of moving to a tight labor market and staying there. The evidence from World War II is not relevant; for unconstrained

[6] The "Phillips curve" is a relation between unemployment and wage or price increases. See A. W. Phillips, "The Relation Between Unemployment and the Rate of Change of Money Wage Rates in the United Kingdom, 1861–1957," *Economica,* XXV (November, 1958), pp. 283–299. See also, R. G. Lipsey, "The Relation Between Unemployment and the Rate of Change of Money Wage Rates in the United Kingdom, 1862–1957: A Further Analysis," *Economica,* XXVII (February, 1960), pp. 1–31; R. G. Lipsey, "Structural and Deficient-Demand Unemployment Reconsidered," in A. M. Ross (ed.), *Employment Policy and the Labor Market* (Berkeley and Los Angeles: U. C. Press, 1965), pp. 210–255; Paul Samuelson and Robert Solow, "Analytical Aspects of Anti-Inflation Policy," *American Economic Review,* L (May, 1960), pp. 177–194.

demand was far greater than potential supply, and of course great premiums were being paid to achieve desired labor mobility.

The evidence from Europe should be examined from the point of view of what labor market institutions would be needed in order to constrain inflationary pressures under conditions of tight full employment where the condition is expected to persist. It seems as if even in Sweden there still is a wage rate-unemployment relation similar to the Phillips curve, although, of course, the Swedish government does not use this type of inflation as an excuse for not maintaining tight labor markets.

The argument that tight full employment cannot be achieved by measures to increase demand is a structuralist argument. For the standard income determination models, it is assumed that labor is homogeneous and fluid. In such models, as long as there is any unemployment, the labor supply to any and all occupations is infinitely elastic at the same going wage rate. It does not matter how demand is increased: no matter where or what kind of initial impact occurs and no matter what the pattern of final output may be, the employment and wage effects are the same.

Obviously, labor is not homogeneous and fluid. The gestation period of a worker with particular skills in a particular place may be quite time consuming and the gestation process quite costly. At every date there is a need not only to generate the right kinds of labor, but also to make do with the available labor force. In theory, slight changes in relative supply prices of the various kinds, or qualities, of labor could lead to a considerable amount of substitution in production, that is, in making do. Such substitution in production would tend to narrow wage differentials. However, for many outputs the technical possibilities of substitution are limited.

Since labor is actually heterogeneous and viscous, the efficacy of different demand-generating instruments in raising employment depends upon where the initial change in final demand takes place, what the immediate derived demands are, and what is the ultimate change in final demand. In addition, it does not pay to train workers unless it is felt that the demand for a particular type of trained labor will be sustained. Thus, the expected length of time for which labor markets will be tight is a determinant of the extent to which labor will be trained to conform to the pattern of demand.

The standard theory of aggregate demand generation glosses over the differences in effect of the various demand-generating policy actions. Monetary ease, increased spending, and decreased taxes are perfect substitutes insofar as their effects upon GNP, employment, and prices are concerned. A conventional argument is that fiscal ease can be used to offset the effects of tight money; and seemingly, tax reductions are perfect substitutes for spending programs. But this, in fact, is not so.

All of the policy instruments have "what kind" as well as "how much" dimensions. Proper attention to the "what kind" is necessary in using monetary-fiscal measures, and the "what kind" should be determined in the light of the contribution it makes to the war against poverty.

As was mentioned earlier, the use of expansionary monetary policy is constrained by the international position of the dollar. Thus, we need not discuss it, except to note that the path from monetary ease to aggregate demand is not particularly favorable for the war on poverty.

The Administration emphasized tax reductions in its expansionary fiscal policy of 1964 and again in 1965. From the perspective of the war against poverty, this is a poor choice. The initial impact of tax reductions is through the increased spending power of those with incomes. The present poor are not direct beneficiaries; they benefit only to the extent that jobs are created, by way of the spending of the affluent, that they can get. Given the regional and ethnic concentration of poverty and income, the immediate demand for labor resulting from the spending by the beneficiaries of the tax cut will have only a small component of demand for the services of the present poor. From the point of view of the poverty campaign, it matters where the initial spending takes place. The "trickle down upon them" approach of tax cuts is not efficient; Harlem is not Scarsdale.

In order to use expansionary monetary and fiscal policy in

an efficient program against poverty, it is necessary to recognize the heterogeneity and the viscosity of the labor force. This means that the emphasis should be upon the spending side of fiscal policy, and an object of the spending should be to have the largest primary and secondary impact upon the present poor. Thus, spending should be directed at the communities with low incomes, and the spending programs should directly employ the low-income worker.

If we look at the pattern of increases in government spending in the postwar period, it has been biased against the poor. The most rapidly growing sector of federal government spending has been upon research and development, which has been growing at the rate of 20 per cent per year. This has biased labor demand toward the highly educated and well trained. Another rapidly growing sector of final demand has been in education. The number of teachers increased by 48 per cent in the decade of the 1950's, while the labor force grew by 14 per cent. These policy-determined changes in the composition of final demand help to explain why the belief has grown that from now on job markets necessarily will be biased to the highly trained. A different emphasis in final government demand would have changed the trends in employment. After all, during the Great Depression the lament was, "I used to be on the daisy chain, but now I am a chain store daisy."

That is, there is nothing sacred about the pattern of demand for labor.

As a result of economic growth, the median family income of nonfarm white families whose head was aged less than 65 years had increased to $6,582 by 1960, and less than 10 per cent of this group had incomes in the poverty range. Even though the incidence of poverty in this class is small, it is a large group and contains some 30 per cent of all the poor. Locke Anderson advances the argument that for this large group of the poor, further increases in over-all income, resulting

[7] Locke Anderson, "Trickling Down: The Relationship between Economic Growth and the Extent of Poverty Among American Families," *Quarterly Journal of Economics,* LXXVIII (November, 1964), pp. 511–524.

from economic growth, will not appreciably decrease the incidence of poverty.[7] He based his argument on the fact that, in terms of the distribution of income, these present poor are in the long attenuated tail of the income distribution. An upward shift of the entire distribution will not draw a large number of these poor across the poverty line.

However, there is a difference between the growth of income that occurs in a persistently slack labor market, such as we have had in the recent past, and the shift from a slack to a tight full employment economy. There is no necessity for a tight full employment economy to grow any faster than a slack economy. The emphasis upon growth of the Heller era (which is persisting now that Gardner Ackley is Chairman of the Council of Economic Advisers) was a mistake. What needs to be emphasized is that the shift from a slack to a tight full employment economy would be accompanied by a once-and-for-all jump in GNP and a change in relative wages favoring the low wage industries. That is, the increase in average income which would occur during this period would be of such a nature as to reduce substantially the lower tail of the income distribution. Thus, the shift to tight full employment would lead to a marked reduction in poverty. This would be followed by a further slow decrease in poverty under conditions of continued growth with the new income distribution.

This can be illustrated by referring again to the argument about the relative wages of primary metal workers and retail trade workers. In 1962 the average hourly wage of primary metal workers was approximately $3.00, and retail trade workers averaged $1.75 per hour; that is, the median annual income was roughly $6,000 in primary metals, and approximately $3,500 in retail trade. Given this median income, a very small percentage of the primary metal industry workers would be likely to earn less than $3,000 per year, whereas a substantially greater percentage of the workers in retail trade would fall below the same poverty line. The change in relative wages which would occur in a tight labor market would increase the average annual income of retail trade workers relative to that of primary metal workers and markedly reduce the percentage of retail trade workers with incomes below the poverty line. On the other hand, an increase of, let us say, $500 in annual incomes of primary metal workers would not markedly change the number lying below the poverty line.

In addition, if the high aggregate demand resulted in shifting workers from low to high wage industries, then the incidence of poverty would be markedly reduced; i.e., the relative weights of the different occupations and industries in the determination of the over-all income distribution would change as tight full employment became the way of life.

Thus there is no real conflict between the proposition that tight full employment will lower poverty markedly and the proposition that further growth of capacity GNP will not quickly reduce poverty.

Fundamentally, tight full employment is inconsistent with the Administration's balance of payments objectives. An international monetary system with fixed exchange rates based upon the dollar is incompatible with tight full employment and the rapid elimination of poverty in the United States. If, for example, the marginal propensity to import equals the average propensity when imports are four per cent of GNP, then a GNP $50 billion larger than that achieved in 1964 would have resulted in additional imports of about $2 billion. Moreover, the move to tight labor markets would entail a rise in prices, which would further affect the balance of payments. A balance of payments deficit of $5 billion in any one year tends to generate a flight from the dollar; and a tight full employment economy would tend to create such a deficit.

To a considerable extent, ever since 1958 the needs of the dollar standard have acted as a constraint upon domestic income. We have not had tight labor markets because of the peculiar bind that the dollar is in internationally. It is apparently appropriate to allude to William Jennings Bryan by saying that, in part, the cross that the American poor bear is made of gold.

A Program Against Poverty

The reason we need to understand the barriers to pursuing a tight full employment policy is to enable us to design efficient policy strategies to overcome these barriers—not to enable us to shrug our shoulders and prepare excuses for failure. In this section some suggestions will be made as to how the federal government's tax, spending, and monetary controls can be used to generate tight full employment, although, obviously, it will not be possible to include a complete catalogue of what should be considered.

The solution to the gold standard barrier is simple: get rid of the gold standard. If, for some subtle reasons understood only by bankers, the Department of State, and the Treasury, we cannot do this, then we can buy economic breathing room by raising the price of gold. An even better move would be to announce once-and-for-all that a "dollar is a dollar," that the U. S. Treasury will sell gold as long as it has any, but it will no longer buy gold. Within a very short time an international monetary system rooted firmly in the dollar's ability to command goods and services in the U. S. would arise—and we would be able to proceed to build the great society at home.

To the extent that we continue to try to live with the gold standard, expansionary monetary policy is not available as a weapon to achieve tight full employment. In fact, monetary constraint might have to be increased as income increases to compensate, as far as the balance of payments is concerned, for the greater volume of imports which accompanies the higher GNP.[8]

On the other hand, the argument that more rapid expansion will not improve the relative position of the poor is *not* a real barrier to more vigorous monetary and fiscal measures; it just asserts that it will not be effective. The answer to this objection is "let us try tight full employment and see what happens."

The function of intervention in a free enterprise economy is to make the economy behave so as to achieve the best of at-

---

[8] Obviously, all of the complexities of the international monetary problem cannot be considered in this paper, where it is but one of many issues. Many suggestions for modifying the present monetary system are being discussed, most of which are designed to bring greater flexibility into the world's monetary arrangements. It is important to note that we have brought "flexibility" into our international monetary arrangements by devices such as the interest rate equalization tax. The question is not one of fixity versus flexibility, rather it is "what type of flexibility."

tainable situations. "Best" often implies a choice, or at least a tradeoff, among objectives. The war against poverty as a "new" policy objective implies that the relative weights given to other policy objectives need to be reconsidered. In particular, the war against poverty requires both a definition of full employment as tight full employment and the inclusion of a relative wage or relative income policy objective in the set of policy goals.

Economic theory asserts that no appreciable inflation will occur until aggregate labor demand exceeds aggregate labor supply—the homogeneity and fluidity of labor will guarantee this result. However, labor is not homogeneous and fluid, and, in addition, effective production functions seem to be such that marked substitution among types of labor does not take place in response to small wage differentials. Thus, economic policy should devise interventions that make labor more homogeneous and that generate demand for the unemployed, relatively low wage workers.

The emphasis upon job training, labor relocation, and other similar programs is intended to make labor more homogeneous. However, there are limits to the capacity of such programs to transform particular types of labor which are in excess supply into the types that are in excess demand. Thus, as excess demand appears for particular classes of labor, further expansion of demand for labor should be concentrated on other types of labor. Once generalized excess supply of labor disappears, the choice between tax cuts and government spending as alternative fiscal stimuli becomes important. Whereas the ability to stimulate the demand for particular types of labor by way of generalized tax cuts is limited, the ability to tailor-make government spending to conform to the particular excess supplies is not limited. In other words, although tax cuts and spending are largely equivalent in stimulating recovery from a depression, they are not fully equivalent in generating full employment during a period when a substantial amount of unemployment is the result of structural changes.

Along with job training and labor relocation policies, programs to encourage the substitution of labor that is now in excess supply for labor now in excess demand should also be undertaken. Aside from industry relocation, such programs might very well take the form of breaking complex jobs down into simpler jobs—for example, using park patrolmen as supplements to completely trained police. If we ever do get an urban extension service (comparable to the agricultural extension service) one of its tasks might be to look at an area's demand and supply of labor to determine how complex jobs might be divided into jobs within the grasp of the existing unemployed.

Dynamic economics is primarily concerned with differential reaction and gestation periods. We are learning that what happens to a child between the ages of three to five is of vital importance in determining the capabilities of the adult. Thus, preschool training is necessary to break the vicious circle of poverty. But if this view is true, then it takes 18 to 20 years to realize the benefits from such programs. Similarly, we cannot stimulate the demand for labor of a 20-year-old high school dropout by increasing appropriations for the National Institutes of Health, the Atomic Energy Commission, space programs, and the like. Programs must be designed which hold out a promise of a useful and productive life for our high school dropouts.

Spending programs aimed at directly employing those in the labor market who are poor, and opening up job opportunities for second earners in the families of the present poor, would have a strong impact upon poverty. Only in the second and subsequent rounds of spending following the original round will there be a demand for other kinds of labor, and, as indicated earlier, primary jobs for residents of Harlem will generate retail and service jobs in Harlem. The present poor are more likely to get such jobs than they are to get similar jobs in the suburbs.

The New Deal, with its WPA, NYA, and CCC, took workers as they were, and generated jobs for them. Sweden today generates public works jobs for the seasonally unemployed in its north country. We could easily do the same in areas such as Northern Wisconsin and Michigan, and for poor farm families throughout the country. The resurrection of WPA and allied projects should be a major weapon of the war on poverty.

Note that WPA was a labor intensive approach to unemployment, and it did tailor-make its projects to the capabilities of the available labor. There was another expansionary spending approach during the depression—PWA were its "initials" during at least part of its life—which went in for massive public works. Public works are favored by the trade union movement and by contractors as a solution to unemployment programs. In the context of the war against poverty, programs of expanding standard public works are inefficient; for they mean providing jobs for already affluent workers. "Public works" is not much better than a tax cut as an anti-poverty measure.

Work should be made available to all who want work at the national minimum wage. This would be a wage support law, analogous to the price supports for agricultural products. It would replace the minimum wage law; for, if work is available to all at the minimum wage, no labor will be available to private employers at a wage lower than this minimum. That is, the problem of coverage of occupations would disappear. To qualify for employment at these terms, all that would be necessary would be to register at the local public employment office.

Various national government agencies, as well as local and state government agencies, would be eligible to obtain this labor. They would bid for labor by submitting their projects, and a local "evaluation" board would determine priorities among projects. Because skilled, technical, and supervisory personnel are needed, the projects should be allowed to average something like $4,000 per worker. The federal government should put in some funds for materials, but the allocation for materials should be a fraction of the labor costs—let us say, 25 per cent.

Not so long ago, economists and other social scientists thought disarmament was a possibility. Daniel B. Suits used the Michigan model of the United States economy to estimate employment effects of various alternative programs. He found that if the government used $1 billion to employ some 260 thousand workers—i.e., a spending program concentrating on low income jobs—the result would be a rise of 322 thousand in employment (Table 2).

Let us assume that there are some two million more unemployed than there would be if we enjoyed tight full employment. As-

TABLE 2. MULTIPLIERS FOR SELECTED ACTIVITIES (BILLIONS OF DOLLARS)

	Government purchases	Government employment[a]	Federal income tax		Social security transactions	Private investment in plant and equipment
			level	yield		
	+$1.0	+$1.0	+$1.0	+$1.0	+$1.0	+$1.0
Gross national product	1.304	1.903	−1.119	−1.798	0.825	1.690
Consumption expenditure	0.295	0.738	−0.915	−1.470	0.674	0.382
Unemployment insurance benefits	−0.160	−0.390	0.091	0.146	−0.069	−0.137
Tax recipts						
Federal	0.458	0.220	0.622	1.000	0.274	0.586
State and Local	0.030	0.034	−0.045	−0.072	0.033	0.058
Social Insurance	0.030	0.051	−0.024	−0.039	0.018	0.038
Employment (millions of persons)	0.089	0.322	−0.076	−0.122	0.056	0.115

[a] Additional government wage expenditure of $1.0 billion to hire 260,000 employees.

Source: Daniel B. Suits, "Econometric Analysis of Disarmament Impacts," in E. Benoit and K. Boulding (eds.), *Disarmament and the American Economy* (New York: Harper and Row, 1963), p. 104.

sume that the remaining "2.5 per cent" unemployed are short-term transitional unemployed who would not take advantage of such a program; standard unemployment insurance is sufficient protection for these unemployed. An expenditure of $7 billion per year, resulting in direct employment of 1,820,000, on the basis of Suits' estimates, would eliminate the excess unemployment. However, with a wage support law, workers making below the minimum wage—including many low-income farmers and people not now in the labor force—would join the program. Perhaps a $10 billion gross expenditure employing some 2,600,000 workers would be a more appropriate initial amount for the program.

Given that some 25 per cent of the labor cost would be available for material spending, the gross cost would be $12.5 billion per year. This would lead to a rise of $22.3 billion in GNP. Although it is a relatively unimportant consideration, federal tax receipts would rise by $3.3 billion; thus, the net cost of such a program would be some $9.2 billion per year.

This path to tight full employment generates a GNP that is smaller than the estimated tight full employment GNP used earlier. This is so because these workers are fed into the value of output at less than the median labor income.

Needed improvements of transfer and income in kind programs might cost an additional $5 billion per year. Thus, the total cost of a meaningful war against poverty might be $17.5 billion per year.

Incidentally, many of the proposed community development type projects might fit into the set of approved WPA type projects. Certainly a directive to the local evaluation body to weight such programs highly would be in order.

Once such an artifically created tight labor market existed, the pattern of excess demands for labor resulting from generalized measures to expand aggregate demand would indicate the job training and work relocations that should be undertaken. These training and relocation programs are really valuable within a context of tight labor markets. Lifelong learning for all is a necessary policy objective in our complex and ever-changing economy and society. Programs making this possible and appealing to all should be instituted. But this is not solely or even primarily a concern of the war against poverty.

In the process of achieving tight full employment, low wages in the private sector would be pushed up, hopefully, more quickly than high wages. (If this did not take place, tight full employment would have to be supplemented by an incomes policy.) Under these conditions, the national minimum wage could be raised. If, for example, $3.00 per hour is the median gross wage, the wage support level could be raised over time from its present level of 40 per cent of the median wage to 60 per cent. However, raising the minimum wage now is not particularly desirable; it is more important, first, to make the present minimum wage effective for all.

Many workers in both private and public employment are paid at or below the poverty line. Since an effective anti-poverty war would raise low wages relative to high wages, a question as to whether the rise in wages should be passed on to prices is in order.

For example, such workers as hospital attendants and orderlies require relatively little skill and can be trained easily. They also tend to receive incomes close to the poverty line. To raise their incomes and *not* raise the price of hospital care, the "public" nature of such employment should be recognized. It would strike a visitor from Mars as odd that in the United States the federal government can support the building and equipping of hospitals, but it cannot support the pay of the operating personnel. A scheme under which the federal government paid a percentage of the wages of workers in industries such as hospitals should be part of our permanent package of price- and income-determining measures.

Another aspect of the problem which I will just mention is that people can become impoverished, even though they are not poor. A skilled worker or an engineer, for example, may lose a job because of technical or program changes. If no fully equivalent job is available, this worker will suffer a capital loss—equivalent to the loss by fire of an uninsured house. Some integration of programs to cope with this dynamic and high level impoverishment into our unemployment compensation system seems to be in order. Perhaps the capital value of such contract revisions should be available as compensation to victims of technical change.

The line between what is private and what is public is narrow and arbitrary. Subsidized employment opportunities for the present poor and ill-trained are just as useful as subsidized employment opportunities for the people like us in conferences such as this, or in government supported research institutes. We are rich enough to afford boondoggles for the poor as well as the affluent, and I would expect the gains in welfare to be at least as great, per dollar of expenditure.

To conclude, the way to end the biggest chunk of poverty is to generate jobs at adequate incomes for the people in poverty. Some improvements in transfer payments, such as children's allowances and medical care for all without means tests, would help; but the basic approach must be to provide jobs for all who are willing and able to work—taking their abilities as they are.

Once tight full employment is achieved, the second step is to generate programs to upgrade workers. I am afraid that in the poverty campaign we have taken the second step without the first; and perhaps this is analogous to the great error-producing sin of infielders—throwing the ball before you have it.

14. Labor Market Strategies in the War on Poverty

FREDERICK HARBISON

There is today an explosion of concern over poverty in the United States. As stated in the declaration of purpose of the Economic Opportunity Act of 1964, the nation's policy is to eliminate the "paradox of poverty in the midst of plenty . . . by opening to everyone the opportunity for education and training, the opportunity to work, and the opportunity to live in decency and dignity." This concern is in part the result of upheavals generated by the civil rights issue which has brought in its wake a "job movement" for underprivileged minority groups. It also stems from a new awareness by the American people that, even with unprecedented business prosperity, poverty and unemployment seem to be permanent ulcers in a prosperous economy and that measures must be taken to cure them. As a consequence, there has been a burst of new legislation which affords a wide range of programs to attack unemployment and poverty. The compelling need now is to build appropriate strategies for the integrated use of the various means now available for the so-called War on Poverty.[1]

The prevailing policy of the exponents of The Great Society is to act first and think later. In implementing the anti-poverty legislation, action has the highest priority; there is a premium on getting programs initiated and moving; there is reluctance to wait for carefully documented findings of research. On balance, this approach is good. There are lessons to be learned by ac-

[1] In addition to the Economic Opportunity Act of 1964, which is directed squarely at poverty, various provisions of other legislation have a bearing on the poverty program, i.e., MDTA, ARA, the Vocational Training Act of 1963, and the Civil Rights Act of 1964.

quiring experience as rapidly as possible. Some programs will be successful; others may fail completely. Some investments will win high returns, and others may end in complete loss. Even though there may be chaos in the war on poverty, this chaos can be productive if there is systematic evaluation of on-going action programs. Fortunately, in the new legislation sizable funds have been set aside for research, and, if these are used with discretion and vigor, wisdom will prevail in the long run.

Poverty can be alleviated only in part by labor market policies. The heads of many poor families are not members of the labor force. The aged, the indigent, and the mentally incapacitated are beyond the reach of the labor market. Poverty among these groups must be attacked by public assistance, medical care, social security programs, and other measures for income maintenance. Labor market policies can affect only those who are actually or potentially members of the labor force. And, the availability of jobs for the poor depends significantly upon the maintenance of high aggregate demand which must be a primary concern of general economic policy.

Let us then examine some of the areas where labor market policies may have a significant role to play. Some families are poor because the breadwinners are unemployed. More are poor because the breadwinners, though employed, are not earning enough to provide adequate support for the family. Poverty is also in part attributable to unemployment of youth. Many youngsters are unsuccessful in finding employment, and some of the others who are neither in school nor seeking work, may be motivated to get and hold jobs.[2]

In the aggregate, perhaps, teenage unemployment may not be a major cause of poverty, since most teenagers live at home and have few family responsibilities. Yet, according to the 1965 Manpower Report, almost half a million teenagers were the primary wage earners of families and about 200,000 were teenage family

---

[2] According to a recent study by Bowen and Finegan, about 27 per cent of teenage males (5 per cent of all teenage males) not in school were not in the labor force, i.e., not working or actively seeking work. See William G. Bowen and T. A. Finegan, "Labor Force Participation and Unemployment," in A. M. Ross, editor, *Employment Policy and the Labor Market* (Berkeley: University of California Press, 1965), p. 140.

heads. The family incomes of these two groups were very low, averaging less than $2,200. Unemployment of teenagers in this category, therefore, is a major cause of poverty, and this is particularly true in the case of the nonwhite teenagers. For example, whereas about 12 per cent of white teenagers are from poor families (with incomes of less than $3,000 per year), 43 per cent of all nonwhite teenagers are members of poor families. Thus, the nonwhite youth who is either unemployed or out of school and not in the labor force is very likely to be from a poor family.[3] Obviously then, poverty can be attacked by concentrating on the improvement of employment opportunities for nonwhite teenagers.

I think that in an anti-poverty program quite different strategies may be necessary to attack the problem of unemployed youth on the one hand and the problem of unemployed adults on the other. My argument would be as follows:

A *long-range strategy* is necessary to deal with the problem of unemployed youth. Its top priority objective should be to prepare underprivileged, undereducated, and undertrained youth for *self-sustaining employment* in reasonably well-paying occupations with a future. The placement of young people in low-paying, unskilled jobs, though perhaps important as a temporary expedient, should *not* be the long-range goal. The central objective should be to enable young people to rise permanently from the ranks of unskilled employment into occupations where the pay is sufficient to support a family in decency and dignity. This means that somehow or other these young people must be induced to make "a critical minimum effort" to acquire the education and training necessary to get good jobs in areas of expanding opportunity. Here, the *development of capacities* should take precedence over the mere finding of work, although the latter may be one means of achieving the former. Thus for the teenagers, employment as service station attendants or orderlies in hospitals should be thought of only as a means of motivating these young people to prepare for higher-level occupations such

[3] See U. S. Department of Labor, *Manpower Report of the President and a Report on Manpower Requirements, Resources, Utilization and Training,* 1965, p. 28.

as master mechanics, foremen, or medical technicians. Young persons should not prepare for permanent employment in occupations which pay only a minimum wage.

In pursuing this strategy, it must be recognized that some teenagers may not have the capacity nor even the will to make the necessary "critical minimum effort." Some hard-core unemployment among youth will remain even if the war on poverty is generally successful. The best results will be achieved by concentrating on those disadvantaged young people who have the intelligence, the capacity and the will to upgrade themselves. And a major function of anti-poverty programs should be to identify these individuals and to give them intensive assistance in their efforts at self-development. Also, because of the high incidence of poverty and unemployment among nonwhites, it would be appropriate to give priority to increasing the employment capacities of Negro youth.

The machinery is now being created to implement a strategy of this kind. Under the Economic Opportunity Act, work-training programs are provided by Neighborhood Youth Corps. In these programs, young people live at home and work on jobs created by nonprofit organizations or state and local governments. Some of the participants are in school part time, and others receive special training as part of the program. The Job Corps offers more intensive education and training for a smaller number of persons in camps or other residential training centers. And there is the Work-Study program which provides part-time employment for students in colleges and universities. According to the 1965 Manpower Report, during the fiscal year 1966 over 430,000 youths will be participating in these three programs.[4] In addition, the U. S. Employment Service is establishing a network of Youth Opportunity Centers to provide special testing, counselling, and job placement services for young people. Opportunities for both general and vocational training are being expanded. Finally, a number of private employers are setting up programs for the employment and on-the-job development of high school dropouts and others with inadequate education and training.

---

[4] *Ibid.*, p. 37.

Thus, success in preparing disadvantaged youth for self-sustaining employment is likely to come from the building of appropriate strategies for activation and integration of programs already available rather than from creation of new machinery. Most of the youth programs provide for "outreach techniques" to find, recruit, and motivate youths who would not otherwise seek assistance through regular channels. They provide for heavy emphasis on training, and for opportunities to pursue both formal and informal education. At present, possibly more money is available than can be spent productively, and additional resources would probably be forthcoming for clearly demonstrated needs. But, the more pressing problem today is the need for a clearer sense of direction, a consensus on long-range objectives, and above all the development of qualified personnel to implement the vast array of new centers and programs which are being established at a breath-taking pace.

The elimination of poverty which stems from the inability of adult breadwinners to earn enough to properly support their families calls for a somewhat different and perhaps more short-run strategy. In this case, greater emphasis should be placed upon providing jobs for the unskilled than upon education and training for higher-level occupations. Particularly in the case of older workers, unskilled employment even at low pay may be a legitimate end in itself. The capacity of older workers for upgrading is not as great, and the social need for developing their skills is not as pressing as in the case of young people who must prepare to participate in the labor force for a lifetime.

The creation of unskilled jobs for adults is likely to be retarded by existing and perhaps rising minimum wage standards. For this reason, it might be appropriate to consider the possibility of paying a wage subsidy to employers who agree to employ at the minimum wage the breadwinners of poor families for work which otherwise would not be performed. Under the Economic Opportunity Act, provision is made for wage subsidies of this kind in some nonprofit and government organizations. Within limits, the idea might be extended to small private enterprises particularly in the services field. The savings resulting from taking otherwise unemployed persons off public assistance rolls would offset in part at least the subsidies to support employment at the minimum wage. In any case, the idea might be worth trying on an experimental basis.

There are now many programs designed to enable the adult poor to participate more effectively in the labor force. The Community Action Programs which are being set up in many rural and urban areas are beginning to offer specialized services in finding jobs, testing, counseling, and training. The Adult Literacy Program will assist adults whose inability to read and write is a real barrier to finding employment. Experiments are being made with relocation allowances to move workers and families to areas of expanding employment opportunity. And the Civil Rights Act of 1964 provides a measure of new protection from employment discrimination against nonwhite workers. Here again, much of the machinery for attacking the problem of the adult poor is available or is in the process of establishment. The critical need is for well-designed strategies to utilize it and competent people to operate it.

In conclusion, I would like to emphasize once again that one should not expect too much of labor market policies in alleviating poverty. Their role is limited to enabling the poor to find suitable employment. A certain amount of poverty will persist even under conditions approaching full employment. In essence the major function of labor market policy is to select from among the poor those persons who are capable of being productively employed and to render assistance to them in finding and holding jobs. Programs such as the Job Corps, neighborhood youth centers, adult literacy classes, vocational training, and rehabilitation projects are mainly selection devices. Persons who successfully complete such programs become more employable, not merely because of the training received, but more importantly because they have demonstrated a will and capacity for employment. The adult illiterate who makes the effort to learn to read and write in effect becomes a member of a select group. The teenage dropout who returns to school after work-training thereby increases his chances to be selected when applying for a good job. In the end, the crucial test of the various work and training projects connected with the anti-poverty program is their effectiveness in selecting the poor who are employable from those who are not. This means, of course, that these projects will help those who are best able to help themselves. They will concentrate on people who are the most intelligent and the easiest to motivate. And this is a proper strategy for freeing the largest possible number of persons from the chains of poverty by means of labor market policies. The hard-core of unemployables, of course, will remain unemployed. For these, other solutions will need to be found which probably lie beyond the scope of practical labor market policy.

The strategies suggested in this paper are certainly tentative, and in no sense are they comprehensive. In an action-first program, one must learn by accumulating experience. Intensive research is called for, and fortunately is provided for financially in the new legislation. Strategy building should be given high priority in forthcoming research efforts.

15. Trends and Perspectives in Manpower Policy

GÖSTA REHN

In Western Europe, most countries have long had manpower and labor market adjustment programs, including retraining, stimuli to geographic mobility, area redevelopment, and public works. At the same time, it must be recognized that these programs, in general, have been rather small. Even now, they cannot be regarded as an important contribution to the solution of the dilemma involved in reconciling full employment with price stability and equilibrium in the balance of payments. In some countries, however, the activities devoted to improving employment are more comprehensive, in the midst of full employment, than similar measures to *attain* full employment in America.

Moreover, in recent years there has been an expansion of measures to improve manpower adaptability in most European countries. In part the driving force has been the need for overcoming rigidities, as a means of neutralizing inflationary tendencies and balance-of-payments difficulties. In part it has been the realization of sustained structural problems—pockets of unemployment, underemployment, and low productivity, along with shortages of labor in rapidly expanding and highly productive sectors and areas.

The reduction of trade barriers has also given impetus to government action, and to approval of such action by groups which earlier would have resisted it, on both the management and labor sides. In addition, the creation of the European Social Fund within the Common Market has been a stimulating factor.

More fundamentally, however, the driving force seems to be the need for measures to offset the negative influence on economic growth of the anti-inflationary policies which countries have occasionally had to enforce. A few examples will illustrate some of the newer European developments which constitute a sort of break-through for the idea of an *active manpower policy.*

UNITED KINGDOM

In the last few years there has been a sharp change in attitude toward both the training of young people and the retraining of adults in the United Kingdom.

Under the provisions of the recently adopted Industrial Training Act, responsibility for vocational training is to be collectivized through industrial training boards, whose programs are financed by a levy on all firms in the industry covered by each board. To a certain degree, the legislation is modeled after a system which has long existed in France, where there is a general levy of 0.4 per cent of payroll on employers, to the extent that they cannot show that they spend at least that much for vocational training. However, the United Kingdom system will be more logical, differentiating by industry according to the costs of providing needed training in each industry.

The English reform was inaugurated under the previous Conservative government. The earlier attitude in government as well as in employer and union circles had strongly supported the notion that vocational training was to be an affair between an apprentice and his employer. Gradually, however, it came to be realized that the system yielded too limited a supply of skilled workers and practically no possibilities for upgrading or retraining of adults.

The new government has repeatedly declared that it wants to attack the fundamental difficulties of the British economy through measures aimed at reducing the rigidities of the country's social and industrial system. Steps have been taken in this direction in order to strengthen and enlarge support for both geographical and occupational mobility. Moreover, the famous "declaration of intent" by government, unions, and employers includes a statement recognizing the need to liberalize the longstanding restrictions which have been aimed at protecting jobs and which have hampered the expansion of training and retraining programs.[1] The loosening up of these restrictions would help to pave the way for occupational and other changes which are inherent in technical progress.

As part of this program of expanded manpower measures, the capacity of the government training centers has been substantially expanded in the last few years to permit an accelerated program of retraining adults. Furthermore, the system for redistribution of industries (aid to distressed areas) is becoming more and more oriented toward the idea of growth points, which also implies more labor mobility.

In the concerted action to create an atmosphere of *acceptance of change,* the introduction of an economy-wide redundancy compensation scheme (giving a half to a full week's severance pay per year worked with the employer) is regarded as particularly important. It is seen as a corollary to the present disinflationary policy with its presumed effect of reducing employment in some sectors. The efforts to encourage shifts to more desirable employment are at the same time indicated by an expansion and improvement of the public employment service, which has to administer many of the mobility-promoting measures mentioned above. It must be recognized, however, that a successful program of this sort requires constant pressure to upgrade the labor force through a combination of policies aimed at expanding total demand and increasing the possibilities for individuals to get generous help for adaptation when they need it.

France

The creation of the National Employment Fund implies a sharp expansion of existing aids for the retraining of displaced workers or for their relocation to other areas. Resettlement allowances, which formerly were very limited and not very much used, have been increased so that they may reach an amount exceeding two months' earnings. In addition, the scheme for accelerated

---

[1] For further discussion of some of these restrictions, see Margaret S. Gordon, *Retraining in Western Europe* (Washington, D. C.: U. S. Department of Labor, Office of Manpower, Automation, and Training, forthcoming).

training of adults, which used to provide training—in courses lasting up to six months—for about 25,000 persons annually (chiefly young men) is now in the process of being doubled in the course of a few years. Moreover, the existing government scheme for supporting intra-firm retraining in cases of reconversion was radically enlarged in 1964. The total number of adult trainees in government-sponsored schemes (with income maintenance at 75 to 90 per cent of former earnings) is expected to reach one half of one per cent of the labor force in 1966.

All these measures, as well as various improvements in the area redevelopment program, have been proclaimed by the French Government as expressions of a *politique dynamique* for the labor market, which is regarded as part of the anti-inflationary growth policy.

WEST GERMANY

A debate over the entire vocational training system, which is largely based on apprenticeship, appears likely to lead to a reform in the near future that would secure a better adjustment of output of skills to the economy's needs. A good deal of emphasis has been placed on specific efforts to provide housing for those who move to labor shortage areas, not least with respect to immigrants from abroad. In recent years, also, seasonal unemployment has been rather spectacularly reduced through a specific system of allowances, paid by the unemployment insurance fund, to stimulate winter work in the building industry.

BELGIUM

A whole set of new provisions relating to employment policy was adopted in 1961–63 and is gaining increasing quantitative importance. The programs include, among other things, government participation in the costs of retraining workers in cases of redundancy. The subsidies are particularly generous, amounting to 35 to 60 per cent of the costs, in those situations in which older workers are hired and trained or when expansion of firms takes place in development areas. Moreover, the utilization of existing private facilities for industrial training is being stimulated by government grants.

SWEDEN

The Labor Market Board has proclaimed as its next target the doubling of the system of retraining for unemployed adults, which already includes about one per cent of the working population every year, in courses averaging six months in length. A government commission recently recommended the extension of government retraining grants to employed persons, particularly when there is a need for overcoming labor shortages in highly productive industries. Interestingly, this recommendation was adopted with unanimous support from labor, management, and most political parties. The commission also recommended a substantial increase in subsidies for intra-firm training, which have previously been of importance mainly as a stimulus to industries moving into depressed areas.

A new law contemplates considerable government financial support for an area development program which will concentrate on localities with particularly "bright prospects" within a vast area characterized by difficult employment problems. As in the British case, the Swedish policies will involve a combination of "workers-to-jobs" and "jobs-to-workers" policies.

In order to promote geographic mobility in those cases in which a worker is tied to an area with poor employment prospects because of ownership of a house that is difficult to sell without a loss, the government can come in and buy the home. Frequently this is cheaper than keeping the jobless worker on unemployment insurance or relief work. Furthermore, the allowances given to stimulate geographical mobility have been sharply increased and are utilized more and more to draw people away from labor surplus areas to areas where, e.g., construction workers are needed to overcome the mobility-hampering shortage of housing.

NORWAY

Previously, Norwegian policy has emphasized regional development of a relatively undifferentiated type, directed toward the North. More recently, however, the emphasis has shifted to policies which would provide a stimulus to the development of growth centers. The Norwegians have also begun to expand and strengthen measures to promote labor adaptability, e.g., retraining and resettlement allowances of the Swedish type. In addition, their old system of municipal employment services is being taken over by the state and thoroughly reformed.

DENMARK

Although an effort to revamp the present craft-oriented system of placement offices into a more modern employment service is continuing to meet strong resistance from vested interests, the Danes are developing an interesting program of training for the upgrading of laborers, i.e., those who did not have any apprenticeship training in their youth. The long-run objective of this program is similar to the attempt in the United Kingdom to get rid of "jurisdictional" craft rigidities, a problem which is particularly difficult in Denmark, because there are about 50 craft unions and one big union for laborers.

AUSTRIA

Austrian policy has been characterized by a rather strong tendency toward protection of existing jobs, irrespective of costs. Recently, however, the labor and management organizations have collaborated with the Ministry of Social Affairs and the Austrian counterpart to Britain's National Economic Development Council to propose the adoption of a series of labor market measures modeled after those that have become prevalent in other industrial countries. A driving force in this direction seems to have been the prospect of an increasing need to restructure the economy under the influence of the Common Market.

PRINCIPLES OF AN ACTIVE MANPOWER POLICY

In the OECD Manpower and Social Affairs Committee, we have launched the slogan "Active Manpower Policy," and we are naturally pleased to see that the President of the United States has explicitly adopted it in his recent Economic Report.

What do we mean by this expression? With regard to *goals,* we mean giving high priority to matching the ever-changing supply and demand for labor in such a way that a country achieves and maintains "full, productive, and freely chosen employment." [2] With regard to *means,* we recommend (1) forceful utilization of measures to improve the adaptability of labor geographically, occupationally, and socially, by making available the necessary facilities and stimuli to training and retraining, resettlement, and social adjustment; (2) selective action or employment creation in local areas when the "jobs-to-workers" approach appears more suitable; and (3) forecasting, planning, and administrative efforts to keep a high level of preparedness to meet all employment disturbances.

The following quotation from the OECD Recommendation on Active Manpower Policy (1964) may be appropriate:

1. Manpower policy should be given an important role in the pursuance of economic growth by contributing both to the increase of the productive capacity of the economy and to its utilization. Along with the basic program for education and training of youth there is need for training programs for persons of all working ages to help meet demands for new skills and adaptation to changes in the industrial structure. Along with scientific and technical progress there is need for measures to promote acceptance of new techniques by all concerned. Along with fiscal and monetary policies designed to maintain high levels of employment and business activity in general terms, there is need for more specialized and selective measures, creating jobs in labor surplus areas and encouraging the flow of manpower from such areas to expanding and productive industries.

2. By promoting the mutual adjustment of manpower needs and resources, an active manpower policy has the special advantage of being expansionist with regard to employment and production but anti-inflationary with regard to costs and prices.

3. The diversification of production, the increasing volume of technical research and innovations, the efforts to liberalize and expand international trade, and the appearance of a number of new countries as producers in the world market for industrial products tend to increase the multiplicity of economic changes, perhaps also their severity. If the necessary adjustments do not take place rapidly there

[2] The quoted phrase is from *Employment Policy, with Particular Reference to the Employment Problems of Developing Countries,* International Labor Conference, 48th Session, Report VIII (2), International Labor Office (Geneva: 1964), p. 70.

is a risk that they will give rise to economic contractions and unemployment. If the adjustments are not carried out in forms acceptable to those who are most immediately affected, protective and restrictive reactions can be expected. Since the benefits of such change accrue to the community as a whole, the community should bear a significant part of the costs of adjustment to economic and technical change and should also act to reduce the burden of such adjustment.

4. Countries sometimes accept the burden of large direct, or indirect, subsidies or measures of protection to maintain employment in declining and less productive sectors. Public money could often be better used to facilitate and stimulate workers' moving and retraining for better jobs or the establishment of industries with positive prospects in areas facing employment difficulties. Expenditures of the types envisaged here for the improvement of human resources and their readjustment should not be regarded as a cost to society, but rather as a sound "investment in adaptation." At the same time they promote important social values by increasing the individual's freedom in the choice of an occupation or workplace and his security against loss of income.

On this basis the OECD Council underlined the mutual interest of all countries in an effort on the part of each nation to increase its capacity to solve its employment problems through processes of internal adjustment rather than by a "beggar-your-neighbor" policy. All member countries, therefore, were urged to reappraise and re-examine their present manpower policies. Then, more specifically, the recommendations went on to advise the following types of action:

a) A more comprehensive employment service, which can be utilized by employees and employers of all categories.

b) An increased degree of preparedness for preventive or remedial action against employment disturbances.

c) Substantial enlargement of adult training facilities and reforms in the general education and training system to meet the rapidly changing needs of modern technology.

d) Forecasting of future occupational requirements to act as a guide for developing education and training programs.

e) The introduction or reinforcement of specific means for encouraging desirable geographical mobility.

f) More systematic support of industrial expansion in backward or depressed areas with development possibilities.

g) The intensification of measures to make it easier for marginal groups to take up and keep gainful occupation.

h) The development of income security programs, such as unemployment and redundancy compensation and special adjustment allowances.

CONCLUSIONS

The tasks of an active manpower policy are apparently formidable. In the American context, one may perhaps reformulate them to mean that the unemployment rate should be brought down to something like two per cent by measures which would not aggravate inflationary tendencies or the balance of payments problem.

We must recognize, of course, that even those European countries which have gone the farthest with their manpower policies have not created and kept full employment with sufficiently anti-inflationary methods. In the first heydays of full employment, European countries showed a tendency to reduce their manpower policy apparatus. If I dare to comment in America on this problem, I hope that this country will let its currently expanding manpower programs continue uninterrupted from the stage of attempting to achieve full employment on into the stage when its aim is to combine full employment with maximum growth and monetary stability.

On the other hand, it should be recognized that the economic benefits to society which can be gained through more vigorous manpower policies are very large. The differences in productivity, persisting over decades, among various geographical areas and sectors of the economy are often very wide. Efforts to speed up the shift from subsidized occupations in poverty-stricken areas to more efficient sectors of the economy would pay off very handsomely if governments were less inhibited about helping the labor market to function as it should. Here is a field for cost-benefit analysis which would be a challenge to any economist.

Nevertheless, we must realize that there will always remain

unemployment problems which it would not be rational to solve through measures of the type that I have been discussing. For this reason, and because I am also interested in promotion of personal liberty, I should like to close with a few comments on a rather different theme.

The fact that variations in the demand for labor result in awkward income variations for individuals often creates pressure for protective or remedial measures which do not actually provide substantial real benefits. To meet such situations, we should develop income maintenance programs which would give the individual income security over time but which would not require him to submit to those continuous controls which make unemployment periods, even if covered with very good insurance benefits, a rather awkward and destructive experience. We may presume that—with increasing wealth—the right to old-age pensions, to vacations with pay (including sabbatical periods of the type introduced by the American steelworkers), and to more or less subsidized education and training are being more and more developed. One way of obtaining an improvement in the mutual adjustment of supply and demand for labor (and at the same time increasing the scope for the individual's free choice) would be to permit the utilization of these rights to be optional to a certain extent and, through appropriate incentives, to stimulate people to utilize their rights in periods when this would be desirable in relation to variations in the economy's need for manpower. Such a buffer—absorbing the first impact of some of the variations in the demand for labor—would reduce the need for hasty, costly, and sometimes inflationary measures to stimulate local creation of employment and manpower relocation. In other words, it would reduce some of the difficulties which now stand in the way of stabilizing full employment, and thereby of abolishing poverty—in America as in Europe.

Discussion

WILLIAM HABER

Let me begin my remarks by expressing some thoughts that were stimulated by the three illuminating papers we heard this morning—those by Gordon, Glazer, and Harrington. The object of the anti-poverty program must be, at least in part, to deal with poor people now, as they exist today, using existing programs. I would certainly like to see over time a development of an attitude toward work, such as that advocated by Harrington this morning, in which we consider a graduate student as having an occupation. But, although that is an idea, it is a little hard to deal with this year, or the next year, or the year after, when we are talking about 30 to 35 million people—men, women, and children—of whom 60 per cent are in the labor market.

Let me go on to make a few observations that cut across this morning's discussion. Clearly, poverty is not primarily a labor market problem. Consequently, labor market adjustment policies are not necessarily applicable unless we define labor market and labor market adjustment policies very broadly—in such a frame of reference as to include basic education, secondary education, technical education, university education, minimum wage laws, shorter hour laws, family allowances, and social security benefits as well as the more obvious programs of training, retraining, mobility, placement, counselling, and testing. In general, we have not conceived of the labor market as encompassing all aspects of an individual's development. We have conceived of it as a rather narrow aspect of man's relation to work.

Now perhaps one of the first things the anti-poverty program suggests to us is that we ought to revise and enlarge our idea of what we mean by labor market adjustment policies. We mean the totality of those situations—education, work, and job—that create the marriage between the job-seeker and the job-giver.

The second idea that comes to me after this morning's discussions is that labor market adjustment policies are not the solution to the poverty problem. If I had to choose between the structural problem, to which Professor Gordon referred, and the aggregate demand problem, to which the Council of Economic Advisers has been referring—if I had to make that kind of choice by public or secret ballot—I would choose the aggregate demand approach, on the theory that the prospects of serious maladjustment problems, of serious dislocation problems, of serious unemployment are far greater under conditions of weak demand, with a semi-active rather than a vigorously active labor market, than with an active labor market. Given time, even marginal workers will find a job. But, in my own reflections on this matter, I try to avoid an either / or choice. I say that they are both problems, and I certainly completely associate myself with the view that one recession could wipe out all the gain that this program could achieve in five years. As this year's excellent report of the Council of Economic Advisers indicates, one recession adds 400,000 family units to the poverty category, i.e., pushes them down below the $3,000 family income level.

My third point is that some things are taking place in the labor market which will put to a severe test—perhaps the most severe test they have yet had—all of the programs and institutions of labor market adjustment which have been developed in the United States. Consider the fact that between 1965 and 1970 about a million and a half persons will enter the labor force a year, as against a million in the preceding five years. Consider, also, that there are 500,000 new young people, teenagers, entering the labor force each year. Many of them are high school dropouts, and most of them do not have specialized skills. Meanwhile, there is a tremendous shift in demand to occupations requiring much more education, much more training, much more skill. All this will mean a far more serious problem in the labor market barring a real boom. We also need to take into account the problem of color and the rapid growth in the number of female workers. If we consider all these trends, I think we must admit that automation has probably had a more serious effect than the statistics presently show.

There is no question, of course, that, over the last three decades, we have slowly been developing a labor market policy. Beginning in 1933, there was the Wagner-Peyser Act that established the United States Employment Service. Then, in 1935, the Social Security Act established old-age and unemployment insurance, as well as the public assistance program, which has a very important relationship to the poverty issue. A third measure, the Fair Labor Standards Act of 1938, adopted the minimum wage law, and it is rather interesting to observe that the first minimum wage was 25 cents an hour, while today we are debating whether the present $1.25 should be raised to $2.00. A fourth important measure was the Servicemen's Readjustment Act of 1944, which, as Harrington said this morning, pays students for going to school and learning.

In the more recent past, a fifth piece of legislation was the Area Redevelopment Act of 1961, which in a sense embodied a novel approach to the problem of structural unemployment. Under this measure, some progress has been made in bringing loans, grants, and technical aid to hundreds of communities classified as depressed. The number of such communities has declined, and the rate of unemployment in many of these communities has fallen. Whether this has been because of the general economic situation, or because of the unique features of ARA, it is a bit hard to tell, and I do not believe we should argue too much over which should get the credit. Certain it is, that, if the economy had not moved ahead as it has, these measures would not have been as successful.

My sixth measure was the Manpower Development and Training Act of 1962, which adopted a whole new program of retraining, aimed directly at the problems of structural imbalance, of automation, of young people, and of displaced older workers.

Another exceedingly important step was the passage of the Vocational Education Act of 1963, under which for the first time Congress began to take the whole idea of vocational education seriously and to pump a good deal of money into it—to be sure, not as much of a change in this type of program as I should like to see. Why we should still train literally hundreds of thousands of young people in agricultural occupations when every estimate for every single year from now until 1975 shows a decline in numbers employed in agriculture, I do not know.

Finally, there are three other measures: federal aid to education, the Economic Opportunity Act, which underlies the discussion at this conference, and Appalachia.

All in all, I have mentioned 11 items. If we reflect on this, we recognize that slowly, perhaps without plan, perhaps without any schedule, we have been developing a national manpower policy. Much of this legislation is the result of persistent unemployment, and of a growing realization that we have a continuing problem of poverty in the midst of affluence.

Now, most specifically, and this is the final point I want to make, about three-fourths of all the people who make job contacts do not need labor market adjustment policies. They do it themselves. They do not go through public employment offices or even to a private employment office. They have their own contacts. And that, incidentally, is not uniquely American, as I think our guests from overseas would agree. The British public employment service has existed much longer than ours, dating from 1910. Yet they have no more of an impact upon placement than we do, with a penetration rate in placement about equal to ours. The rates in Norway and Sweden are perhaps somewhat better, but not by a wide margin. It seems to me what we have to recognize here is that the overwhelming majority of Americans resolve their job-seeking and job-transfer problems without an appeal to public authority, or even to private agencies.

In my judgment, it is a great mistake to judge the success of the public employment service solely on the basis of the placement rate it achieves, as we have done historically. Because appropriations have been based too much on this one criterion of success, the agencies have been stimulated to make any kind of placement—short-term, long-term, or temporary, because the budget was related. This is a serious weakness in relation to the anti-poverty program, because the people in the poverty category often need counselling, testing, and guidance much more than they need immediate placement. In the long run, this type of help will result in much more satisfactory placements. It requires individual work with people in trouble—young or old, black or white, displaced by technological change or by some other kind of industrial dislocation.

This is the newest part of the employment service operation, and it is the part that is least understood by legislative appropriation committees. In 1963, for example, the employment service tested 500,000 seniors in high school. That is a healthy development. But when these tests are made in the employment office with dropouts who may not have finished grade school or two years of high school—and particularly if they are verbal tests—it is not an adequate measure of capacity. There are newer tests which may be more appropriate for impoverished, marginal, less educated, and disadvantaged people. The employment office needs adequate funds and competent staff resources for counselling, testing, guidance, and placement to a degree that it has never had. This is the problem that concerns me, and it is not, of course, novel, because a good deal has been done in this direction.

I am impressed, also, with the fact that some experimentation with mobility allowances has been started on a rather informal basis. I would like to see a much larger program. In fact, I would like to see, frankly, some money wasted. We have always shied away from it, pointing out that this is not Holland or Sweden or Norway but a huge country in which paying people to move from one area to another might be very wasteful. I would also like to see our retraining program converted from a temporary program to deal with persistent unemployment to a much more permanent training program for the kind of labor market we are likely to have in the next 10 or 15 years—namely a labor market characterized by a tremendous amount of technological change and by the entry into the labor force each year of half a million teenagers who have no work experience whatsoever. We must accept the fact that these problems cannot be solved overnight and somehow get public acceptance of the idea that labor market programs are one facet of a national manpower policy that encompasses all of the measures I have mentioned, which have developed over a period of 30 years.

As a final note, I was impressed by Nathan Glazer's observation this morning that the poverty problem of the United States differs from the British. It differs in this country largely because of the Negro problem and the civil rights revolution. I have often thought of the civil rights movement, really, as a job movement, and it is interesting to recall the experience of the March on Washington, with Martin Luther King's dramatic speech. The signs were about jobs and about discrimination in jobs, and I think this is a challenge for which we are ill-prepared. It requires a kind of intensive seminar exploration on the part of all of the experts involved in the Negro community, the employer community, and, also, I will say with great emphasis, the labor union community. If job opportunities are to exist for those who are least prepared for them, all of the groups are going to have to be prepared to adjust their attitudes and their practices.

PART SIX

INCOME MAINTENANCE POLICIES

16. Poverty and Income Maintenance for the Aged

CHARLES I. SCHOTTLAND

Poverty is today's current hit theme in the political, economic, and social arenas, and the elimination of poverty is now an accepted national goal of public social policy. We still have much to do if we are to eliminate poverty; but we are making progress.

In the past, poverty meant the simple scarcity of essential food, clothing, shelter, and services. Today, in the less-developed countries, it is still related to the hard economic reality of insufficient goods and services. But in the United States, the abolition of poverty is no longer a problem of economic capacity. Our economy is expanding (whether too slow, too fast, or at just the right tempo depends on one's economic philosophy); the percentage of our population in poverty is decreasing; productivity per worker continues to rise rapidly; the income of most Americans is on the increase; and evidences of our general economic well-being can be seen in the continued growth of home ownership, in the production of automobiles, in savings and other indices of general prosperity.

However, we have learned that neither increasing our gross national product, nor raising average personal income, nor increasing individual assets, will eliminate poverty unless specific measures are taken to raise the level of income of groups which do not participate fully in the general rise in the standard of living.

One of these groups is the 18 million aged in the United States today. Our aged will not automatically share in the general upward thrust of our economy. Unless we take specific action to provide for them an equitable share of our expanding economy and to replace the lost income of those unable to work, their economic condition can be expected to decline in the years ahead. For these 18 million, the problems of poverty, unemployment, and low income are persistent, not temporary.[1]

The reasons for widespread poverty among the aged are well known. They are related to our modern industrial society. The change from an agricultural, barter economy to an industrial, money-wage economy, means simply that money income, more than anything else, determines whether an individual shall be among the poverty-stricken. Since money income is related to employment, the aged are particularly vulnerable, for the relative number of aged in the labor market continues to decrease.

Prior to the turn of the century, two-thirds of the men over 65 in the United States were gainfully employed; today the corresponding proportion is less than one-third, and the relative number of employed men over 65 continues to decrease. Add to this the increase in the number of the aged, the growing number who are really "old," i.e., in their late seventies and eighties, the excess of women over men in the older population, the constant lowering of the age of retirement, and other circumstances such as the emergence of the nuclear family which has no place for the elderly as a member of the household, and we have the basis for the poverty of the aged. In a work-oriented society, the lack of income arises primarily from stoppage of income from work—and retirement in old age, whether voluntary or involuntary, is a major cause of poverty among the aged.

To alleviate this condition and to insure against the risks of stoppage of income in old age, almost every modern industrial state has established some kind of program for maintaining income, usually a form of social insurance whose characteristics are derived from the original German model of social in-

---

[1] Dorothy McCamman, "The Economics of Aging," *Lutheran Social Welfare Quarterly,* IV (September, 1964), p. 10.

surance of Chancellor Bismarck. Such programs are contributory, with employers and employees sharing in the costs; wage-related, with both taxes and benefits bearing some relation to earnings; compulsory, covering a large segment of the gainfully employed (and in the United States almost all); and they seek to replace the income lost by reason of retirement in old age. Some nations have emphasized "social assistance" measures rather than social insurance, and have based old-age benefits on need or age without the contributory or wage-related features.

The United States has adopted both systems. Its Old-Age, Survivors, and Disability Insurance program partially protects nine out of ten of the aged against stoppage of income. This is supplemented by other public programs, such as railroad retirement and the retirement programs of government employees. In addition, a public assistance program, similar in some respects to the social assistance schemes of other countries, provides income for the needy aged.

But in addition to these public programs, the maintenance of income in old age has taken a decidedly new turn in the United States in the past 15 years as a consequence of the rapid development and growth of private pension systems on a previously unprecedented scale.[2]

Thus we have established in the United States a variety of complex, complicated, public and private programs to maintain income in old age and to prevent the aged from living in poverty. But that we have not succeeded in preventing poverty among millions of them is attested by numerous studies, reports, and analyses of the past five years.[3]

While a few of those over 65 years of age in the United States are among the wealthiest people in the world, families

---

[2] Harold L. Orbach and Clark Tibbitts, *Aging and the Economy* (Ann Arbor: University of Michigan Press, 1963), p. 8.

[3] For example, see *1964 Annual Report of the Council of Economic Advisers; 1963 Survey of the Aged,* Social Security Administration; *A Staff Report to the Special Committee on Aging,* U. S. Senate, 1961; "Poverty in the United States," *Indicators,* U. S. Department of Health, Education, and Welfare, February, 1964, etc.

headed by a person aged 65 or over make up one-third of all families in the poverty class, although they constitute only one-seventh of the population.[4]

If the present war on poverty is to make the progress for which we hope, then more attention must be given to the aged, and measures must be devised to improve their lot. Let us proceed to consider the income status of the aged, the adequacy of present programs for maintaining it, and the next steps which need to be taken to rescue the aged *from* poverty instead of merely assisting them at a level which results in their remaining *in* it.

THE INCOME OF THE AGED [5]

The aged constitute a major group of low-income families in our increasingly high-wage economy: for most, Social Security benefits are now the major source of income.

About 13.5 million people over 65 years of age are now drawing Social Security benefits under the OASDI program. Another 1¼ to 1½ million aged are eligible for benefits, except that they—or their husbands—have not yet retired. Persons currently receiving benefits, or eligible to do so on retirement, make up about four-fifths of the total population over 65 and as much as 95 per cent of the population now reaching 65.

In addition, about 1¾ million persons between the ages of 62 and 64 are drawing Social Security benefits which, except in the case of widows and disabled workers, are reduced because of payment before the age of 65.

Social Security benefits payable in mid-1964 averaged about $77.00 a month to the retired aged worker, $40.00 to the spouse, and $67.00 to the aged widow.

Among most beneficiaries, the Social Security benefit is a

---

[4] Lenore A. Epstein, "Income of the Aged in 1962: First Findings of the 1963 Survey of the Aged," *Social Security Bulletin,* XXVII (March, 1964), p. 3. See also *1964 Annual Report of the Council of Economic Advisers.*

[5] The material in this section is quoted or obtained from *Background Facts on the Income Position of Older Persons,* The National Council on Aging, October 5, 1964; Epstein, *op. cit.; 1964 Annual Report of the Council of Economic Advisers.*

major part of retirement income; for many, it is the only source. According to a 1963 survey of the Social Security Administration, the benefit was practically the sole source of cash income for nearly one-fifth of the beneficiary couples and for more than one-third of the unmarried beneficiaries who had been entitled to benefits for a year or more. There has been little improvement in this respect since 1957 when the income of beneficiaries was last studied.

Employment was the largest single source of income for the aged population in 1962, despite the fact that 3 out of every 4 persons 65 or over did not work during the year. Half of all aged couples, including couples in which one member is under 65, and one-fourth of the unmarried had some earnings in 1962. For many of them, employment is part time and earnings are primarily a supplement to retirement benefits. But of the 2.3 million persons aged 65 or over who worked during 1962 at jobs that were usually full time, earnings made up about two-thirds of total income.

As we have seen, the labor force participation of men 65 years of age or over has decreased substantially since the turn of the century. The rate of labor force participation of men 65 or over was dropping before the enactment of Social Security; the rate of decline accelerated when retirement benefits became effective; rates of participation rose in the war years when job opportunities increased and competition from younger workers decreased, and resumed their decline thereafter. However, the proportion of aged women who work has been increasing slightly.

And, most significantly, there has been a decided increase in part-time employment. In October 1963, nearly two-fifths of the men aged 65 or over and half of the aged women employed in nonagricultural occupations were working part time (less than 35 hours in the survey week).

Private group pensions provided some income for 16 per cent of the married couples and 5 per cent of the unmarried. Persons with private pensions are the economic elite among the retired: their median total income of $3,400 was only one-sixth less than that of beneficiary couples with at least one member working at a full-time job. And for unmarried beneficiaries, a private pension did as much as full-time employment to raise the average level of money income.

Old-Age Assistance—which until early in 1951 was the major provider of income for the aged population—has increasingly taken on a supplementary role. Of the 2.2 million persons now receiving Old-Age Assistance, nearly two-fifths are the beneficiaries of Old-Age, Survivors, and Disability Insurance. Of all *new* applicants for assistance, about three-fifths are Old-Age, Survivors, and Disability Insurance beneficiaries.

The total income of the aged population is probably now between $38 and $40 billion. During the single decade of the 1950's, the income of the population over 65 more than doubled, rising from about $15 billion in 1950 to over $30 billion in 1959. This was a substantially faster rate of increase than was experienced by the younger population, and it was achieved despite the decreasing importance of earnings. Most of the increase came from Social Security benefits.

The share of the nation's aggregate income that is received by those aged 65 or over is only slightly less than their proportion in the total population. Nearly one-third of this aggregate, however, is in the form of earnings; most people of these ages do not share at all in this source and others have only small earnings to supplement retirement benefits. The retired aged—excluding the relatively few still working at full-time jobs—clearly receive a much smaller share of the nation's income than is justified by their number in the population. Earnings account for 32 per cent of the aggregate money income of all persons aged 65 or over and their spouses. Old-Age, Survivors, and Disability Insurance benefits run a close second: 30 per cent. Other public retirement benefits add 6 per cent and private pensions another 3 per cent. Thus, two-fifths of the aggregate comes from public and private retirement programs, combined. The aged receive 15 per cent of their income from interest, dividends, and rents. Public assistance and veterans' compensation account for 5 per cent and 4 per cent, respectively.

In spite of all of these sources of income—employment, Social Security, public assistance, private pensions, investments, and so on, the incomes of aged persons remain too low. The unmarried aged, who constitute about half of the population over 65, had a median income of $1,130 in 1962; for the married aged, who tend to be younger than the single aged, the median income was $2,875. However, about three in every ten couples had incomes of under $2,000, while incomes of one-third of the unmarried men and of half of the unmarried women were below $1,000.

PRESENT PROGRAMS OF INCOME MAINTENANCE

This recital of the plight of the aged makes it clear that our programs to maintain their income call for improvement. Increasingly, the income of the aged from employment will decline as the age of retirement falls lower—a trend which most authorities agree is inevitable. Therefore, if we are to maintain the aged on the "modest but adequate" level established by the United States Bureau of Labor Statistics at $2,500, our efforts must be concentrated on income maintenance programs, both public and private. In spite of the growth of these programs, in 1962 more than one in every three couples in which both members were over 65 had a cash income of less than $2,500.

Personally, I feel that even the figure of $2,500 is too low for a "modest but adequate" budget. My experience with these budget standards for the aged during the past thirty years convinces me that almost always they are not only too low but also fail to catch up with the rapid changes in the needs of the aged as a consequence of a changing society. What is an adequate budget is always a relative matter, and little profit will ensue from a lengthy discussion of the subject. But too little attention has been given to the trauma and dislocation taking place in our society when the aged family faces existing on only about half the income of younger families of the same size.[6] The oft-heard comment that the needs of the aged are

[6] In 1960, the median income of 2-person families was $2,530 where the head was 65 or over and $5,135 when the head was under 65. The difference was even greater among persons living alone: $1,055 in comparison to $2,570.

different is not borne out by studies of patterns of consumption. Available data indicate that the aged with substantial incomes continue to follow their earlier habits as consumers. However, when their income is sharply reduced, they are forced to spend relatively more for essential goods and services and must make sharp changes in the patterns of expenditures to which they are accustomed.[7]

Let us now examine the largest of the income maintenance programs: Old-Age, Survivors, and Disability Insurance. Its growth has indeed been phenomenal. Of the total public payments to maintain income of almost three billion dollars monthly, Old-Age, Survivors, and Disability Insurance accounts for more than 45 per cent, making monthly payments to almost 20 million persons, of whom 13.5 million are over 65 and an additional million are among the retired aged between 62 and 64. This relative position is indicated in the following table of expenditures for September 1964: [8]

Total Public Income-Maintenance Payments	$2,923
Old-Age, Survivors, and Disability Insurance	1,365
Railroad and public employee retirement	444
Unemployment insurance, temporary disability insurance, workmen's compensation, training benefits (ARA and MDTA)	357
Veterans' compensation and pension programs	333
Public assistance	424

The average monthly benefit paid to retired workers by Old-Age, Survivors, and Disability Insurance is $77.00. As previously stated, for almost a fifth of the beneficiary couples and more than a third of the unmarried beneficiaries, the Old-Age, Survivors, and Disability Insurance benefit was practically the sole source of income. Nor is this situation relieved to any great extent by the possession of assets among the aged. Interest, dividends, and rents made up more than 15 per cent of the total money income in 1962 of persons over 65, with three-fifths of the couples and almost half of the unmarried

[7] Sidney Goldstein, "Consumer Patterns of Older Spending Units," *Journal of Gerontology* (July, 1959), p. 332.

[8] *Social Security Bulletin.*

reporting some income of this type. About half of them had less than $150 per year from such sources.

One result of the low total income of Old-Age, Survivors, and Disability Insurance beneficiaries is that, as I noted earlier, nearly two-fifths of the persons now receiving Old-Age Assistance and about three-fifths of all new applicants for Old-Age Assistance are receiving Old-Age, Survivors, and Disability Insurance.[9] The early supporters of Social Security hoped that its growth would decrease Old-Age Assistance or relief programs—and it has done so to a significant degree—but it is disturbing to see that a majority of all new applicants for Old-Age Assistance actually are in receipt of Old-Age, Survivors, and Disability Insurance and destitute even by the strict definitions of need imposed by the majority of states in their Old-Age Assistance programs. Obviously, Old-Age, Survivors, and Disability Insurance benefits are insufficient, even when added to other programs, to keep many off the relief rolls. About two-thirds of the OASDI beneficiary couples have less than $2,500 in total retirement income. As a result of the small benefits, we are making OASDI payments to millions of aged at a level which maintains them in poverty and perpetuates the poor as a class.

Among the poor also are the more than 2,150,000 recipients of Old-Age Assistance. They are on the average 77 years of age, almost two-thirds are women, and their assets are negligible, apart from owning their homes. The average monthly payment is $79 but since this is a state-operated program, the monthly payments vary from $39.38 in Mississippi to $108.61 in California.[10] Seventeen states have average payments of less than $70 and only eleven states average more than $90. Many states have a maximum payment set by law at far below any standard of health and decency. Because of our insistence on "states' rights" and as much state autonomy as possible, we have permitted most of our states to support their needy aged

[9] Bureau of Family Services, *Reasons for Opening and Closing Public Assistance Cases, July to December 1962,* U. S. Department of Health, Education, and Welfare (Washington, D. C.: 1963).

[10] For September, 1964. See *Social Security Bulletin.*

on a standard which can find little justification in so rich and expanding an economy as ours.

Although the level of Social Security benefits and Old-Age Assistance payments has increased over the years, their failure to provide even a minimum level of reasonable subsistence has stimulated the growth of the private pension movement.

Many theories have been advanced to justify the expenditures for private pension programs in industry. Among other arguments, the concept of "human depreciation," the theory of deferred wages, and the belief that it will increase the worker's productivity have been advanced as the rationale for this expanding program. But these reasons come after the fact. The drive toward economic security and the small benefits for the retired aged in OASDI have been major influences in the growth of private pensions. It was easier for the labor unions to demand private pensions than to wait for more adequate benefits under OASDI.[11] Likewise, employers found that pension programs would stimulate the retiring of older and less productive workers and were increasingly necessary in the competition for workers.

Whatever weight is given to individual factors, the net result has been a phenomenal growth of private pensions.[12] In a sense, these private pensions represent an alternative to the expansion of Social Security and represent a philosophy of sharing the costs of retirement between public and private means.[13]

Approximately 23 million wage and salary workers are covered by private pensions. For this group, the prospects of economic security are far brighter than most persons would have ever dreamed a generation ago,[14] and among the retired OASDI beneficiaries, those with private pensions constitute, as

---

[11] Margaret S. Gordon, *The Economics of Welfare Policies* (New York: Columbia University Press, 1963), p. 61.

[12] For a comprehensive discussion of private pensions see Paul P. Harbrecht, S. J., *Pension Funds and Economic Power* (New York: Twentieth Century Fund, Inc., 1960). A critical review is to be found in Merton C. Bernstein, *The Future of Private Pensions* (New York: The Free Press, 1964).

[13] Orbach and Tibbitts, *op. cit.*, p. 8.

[14] *Ibid.*, p. 9.

remarked earlier, the economic elite.[15] To repeat: their median total income of $3,400 from OASDI benefits and private pensions was almost as much as that of OASDI beneficiaries with at least one member working at a full-time job. It is important to note that those benefiting most from private pensions are almost all receiving OASDI also. In other words: "To him that hath shall be given!"

Although private pensions still do not cover a majority of the gainfully employed and there are many problems and deficiencies yet to be tackled—including the lack of insurance for most plans, making them subject to the fortunes of the particular company, the lack of vesting, and the long service required for eligibility—they will certainly continue to grow and be increasingly significant in the economic security of the aged.

To summarize: the aged constitute a large part of the poverty class in the United States; their largest income is from employment, although this is likely to decrease in the future; the largest and most significant of the income maintenance programs is OASDI which, despite its growth and its assurance to America's aged of a minimum floor of protection, is in many cases still paying benefits too small to lift them out of poverty; over two million aged are on public assistance, many of whom are in receipt of benefits so small that they are definitely poverty-stricken; private pensions assist in supplementing these public programs.

In a sense, our retirement programs are a hodge-podge of public and voluntary efforts. Some workers reach old age with little protection at all; others may receive benefits from several programs, such as an individual who receives OASDI, a disability military pension, a pension from private industry, and a pension from a state employees' civil service retirement system. The development of such disparate and uncoordinated retirement plans could well result in disparities in retirement income far wider than differences in income among workers during their active lives.[16]

---

[15] Epstein, *op. cit.*, p. 12.
[16] Gordon, *op. cit.*, p. 62.

Action Needed

If we are to lift aged Americans out of poverty and insure a decent level of retirement income to those who have contributed to our society throughout their working lives, a number of things need to be done:

1. In the first place, we need to change the value system which equates work with well-being and come to grips honestly with the fact that the aged will constitute, increasingly, a non-working population whose income will not be derived from current employment.
2. Social insurance, which emphasizes the fact that the benefits are work-related and grow out of work and contributions from earnings, should be the main path through which the aged are prevented from sinking into poverty in their retirement. This is already our accepted public social policy, clearly enunciated in the past by government officials and Congress.
3. Social Security benefits must be increased substantially. The present proposals for a 7 per cent increase will not rescue several million aged from poverty. Minimum benefits should be doubled from the present $40 to $80. The present taxable wage base of $4,800 should be doubled, likewise, to $9,600, thus maintaining the wage-related nature of the American system. Until the higher wage-base has been in operation for some time so that higher benefits flow therefrom, general revenues should be used to make immediate substantial increases in benefits. These proposals are neither radical nor economically unsound. Approximately 3 per cent of our national income goes for Social Security benefits for the aged. But it is 5.3 per cent in Denmark, 5.1 per cent in Italy, 4.4 per cent in New Zealand, 4.6 per cent in Sweden, 4.7 per cent in Switzerland and over 8 per cent in Germany (or almost three times the expenditure in the United States). This one move will take several million aged out of poverty and reduce drastically the vast sums spent on Old-Age Assistance.
4. The level of payments in Old-Age Assistance must be raised substantially. In our affluent society it is difficult to jus-

tify some of the low standards of our state public welfare programs. So long as the federal government provides most of the funds, it should set minimum monetary standards sufficiently high to maintain the needy aged in health and decency.

5. Steps must be taken to insure the payment of benefits from private pensions. This involves a number of changes, including stricter regulation of pension funds and some form of vesting.

6. An adequate program of medical care for the aged is essential to keep them from poverty. Today, many persons apply for Old-Age Assistance only because of medical expenses. The imperative need of an adequate medical care program for the aged is so clear that even the American Medical Association now acknowledges the need for some new program or an expansion of existing programs. What has happened in this area is that some needy aged receive medical care through the Old-Age Assistance program, some through the Kerr-Mills program, others through local public or voluntary programs, and many fall in between available services and for a variety of reasons receive little or limited care.

Some rational approach to this potpourri of programs is essential. The most logical, in my opinion, is the use of the Social Security mechanism. In a work-oriented society such as the United States, the Social Security mechanism ties medical care for the aged to the individual's work and provides a means of paying for the care out of the earnings of the work. Elaboration of this thesis is unnecessary here because of widespread public discussion of this matter. It is to be hoped that Congress will pass the program of the Administration as a start in the right direction.

These six steps I have enumerated may not lift all of the aged out of poverty. If adopted, however, they would go far in this direction. It is a goal upon which we should look with favor, and toward which we should direct our best endeavors.

17. Poverty and Income Maintenance for the Disabled

HERMAN M. SOMERS

A recent survey by the Social Security Administration states that "the disabled are among the most economically disadvantaged members of the population." Their disadvantages are augmented by the relatively inferior treatment accorded them by existing public and private income maintenance programs. The situation varies with the time of life at which the disability occurs—the fate of the youthfully disabled being far worse than for those affected later in life—with degree of family responsibility, the character of the disability, and the degree of medical attention required. But, on the average, the fate of the disabled is among the worst even in the disadvantaged classes. And, generally speaking, we do least for those whose need is greatest. We also know less than we should about the disabled. They appear to have aroused less public and scholarly interest than other disadvantaged groups.

On an average day in 1963, more than five million persons, aged 14 to 64, were disabled—unable to work, attend school, keep house, or follow other normal activities. About two-thirds had been limited for more than six months in their ability to carry on their major activity because of a chronic impairment—the so-called "long-term disabled." We do not count the millions of others with chronic conditions who were partially limited in the amount of activity they could pursue.

Short-term Nonoccupational Disability

The customary programmatic classifications of disability distinguish between work-connected and nonoccupational, and between "temporary" and "permanent." Four states and the federal government, for the railroad industry, have programs to pay cash benefits for a limited period of time—usually 26 weeks—in the case of nonoccupational disability for normally employed persons. The first of these was adopted in Rhode Island in 1942 and the last in New York in 1949. There has been a complete cessation in the spread of such programs for 16 years. There has also been very little expansion of private programs during the past decade. The usual designation of these programs as "temporary disability insurance" is misleading since it is the period of payment (six months) that is temporary; the disability may or may not be, and the programs do not attempt to distinguish. The customary line between "temporary" and "permanent" is arbitrary, with no relationship to diagnosis or probability of cure, and leaves large gaps, as disabilities may last a year or two or longer but still not be permanent.

An estimated 1¾ to 2 million persons are prevented from working as a result of so-called short-term nonwork-connected disability in an average day. The count includes the first six months of what turns out to be long-term disability, as well as disability lasting a shorter time. The total income loss in 1962 due to such illness has been estimated at $9.6 billion.

If every form of individual or group accident and sickness insurance, as well as paid sick-leave provisions and government-operated plans, are included, almost 70 per cent of the civilian labor force have some protection against temporary nonoccupational disability. It is, however, more meaningful to consider group protection for wage and salary workers. Private group protection covered some 27 million persons at the end of 1962 and government-operated funds another 4.5 million. This total comes to about two-thirds of employees in private employment. In the states without laws, 53 per cent of the private wage and salary workers have protection. By contrast, in jurisdictions with temporary disability insurance laws, 95 per cent are covered. The situation in states without compulsory laws has not shown much improvement during the past decade; the proportion covered was just under 50 per cent in 1955.

The extent of protection varies widely, but the Social Security Administration estimates that, in 1962, benefits paid under private and public cash sickness plans (including sick leave) replaced about 19 per cent of income loss. This ratio showed very little change over the previous five years. In the states without temporary disability insurance laws, workers in the aggregate were compensated for an estimated 17 per cent of their wage loss through voluntary group provisions. This represented no change from the 1957 ratio. For workers covered by the five public laws, benefits replaced 25 per cent of wage loss.

Voluntary methods of providing sickness protection made their greatest stride in the decade following World War II, when the number of employees covered by group accident and sickness policies tripled. Collective bargaining pressures were the major factor. Since the mid-1950's, however, the growth of disability insurance protection has little more than kept pace with the growth of the labor force. All the signs indicate that it is highly unlikely, if not impossible, that we can achieve broad national coverage in the absence of compulsory legislation. But, as we have indicated, the states have resisted inauguration of programs since 1949, presumably because of fear that local employers would be put at a competitive disadvantage. There is no sign of change in that situation. It seems apparent that some kind of federal action is required if broad coverage is to be attained in the foreseeable future. There are many possible forms of such action, but it would be best to view them in connection with the interrelated problem of long-term disability.

Long-term Nonoccupational Disability

More than half—about 1.8 million—of the 3.3 million persons with long-term disabilities were receiving cash disability payments from public income-maintenance programs at the end of 1963. This is a considerable advance over the one-third which received such support ten years earlier. The major factor in the increase has been the inclusion of disability provisions in the federal OASDI programs since 1957. By the end of 1963, about a million persons were receiving disability benefits under this program, representing about three-tenths of all long-term disabled, aged 14 to 64, and 55 per cent of those receiving benefits from any public program. Very few additional persons received benefits from private programs.

Of the 2.3 million disabled persons who were receiving no disability benefits, an estimated 950,000 had worked in employment covered by the program, but failed to meet the insured status requirement of 20 quarters of coverage out of the 40 immediately preceding the onset of disability. Another 250,000 had work experience that had been confined to employment not covered by OASDI. About a third of all these ineligible workers were receiving benefits from another public program, most frequently veterans' benefits.

Another 400,000 who met the OASDI insured status requirements were not receiving benefits mainly because of failure to meet the rigorous definition of disability which requires that the impairment be total and expected to be of permanent or indefinite duration, or to result in death. Workers with disabilities that have lasted more than six months, but whose prognosis is favorable for some time in the future fall between the stools of eligibility. The remaining 700,000 had no gainful work history; for example, persons with childhood impairments that never permitted them to work regularly.

The inadequacies of the OASDI disability insurance system, which we must remember is a relatively new program, are readily apparent from these data and many of them could be corrected without great difficulty or excessive cost. If the requirement were removed that the disability be of long-continued and indefinite duration, a matter which usually cannot be foretold with any degree of precision in any case, some 50,000 disabled workers would benefit. Such a change would be similar to the provision in many private insurance contracts which provides that, if a total disability has lasted more than six months, it is presumed to be permanent. As a matter of statistical fact, most workers totally disabled more than six months are likely to be disabled indefinitely. The majority of those disabled for such a period and denied benefits because they can be expected to recover are younger workers likely to have dependent families.

The requirement that workers must have 20 quarters of coverage out of the 40 immediately preceding makes it difficult, and frequently impossible, for a worker disabled while still young, and whose need is likely to be greatest, to qualify for benefits. The recent Advisory Council on Social Security, whose Report I commend to your attention, recommended to Congress that the law be changed so that a worker disabled before age 31 would be eligible if he had worked half the time between age 21 and the onset of his disability, with a minimum of six quarters of coverage. This would be consistent with the principle that insurance protection be confined to workers who have had substantial and recent employment and with the present provisions under which the survivors of a worker, who died while young, can qualify for benefits even though he had only a short period of covered work. Such a change would immediately benefit some 15,000 workers and add only .02 per cent on a level premium basis to OASDI taxes; the increase would be less on the higher taxable wage base expected to be in effect next year.

The Council also recommended that the disabled widow of an insured worker, who became disabled before her husband's death or before her youngest child became 18, or within a limited period after either of these events, should be entitled to widow's benefits regardless of age. This would help some 40,000 disabled widows.

The present stern requirement that a worker be unable to do any type of substantial gainful work might be reconsidered for the disabled 55 years of age or over, to permit benefits if they are unable to do work similar to that performed during their lifetime. The severely disabled older worker generally finds that he cannot obtain work that is reasonably related to his skills or for which he might be trained. Such a provision would probably affect a majority of the 400,000 who have insured status under OASDI but are currently denied benefits.

The grim severity of the present definition of disability to qualify for benefits may be gathered from some comparative mortality rates. Death rates for disabled workers under age 50 in the OASDI program approximate those of the U. S. population 70 to 74 years of age. The difference in death rates relative to that of the population in the same age group is more than ten to one. Disabled beneficiaries 50 to 64 years of age had death rates higher than all persons 75 to 84 years of age. The OASDI definition is far more restrictive than that used in industrial disability pension plans and by most insurance companies.

The Advisory Council recommended that beneficiaries be covered by the same hospitalization insurance program proposed for the aged, which we hope will go into effect next year. The disabled, like the aged, are a low-income, high-health-cost group who rarely can obtain adequate private health insurance. Their health costs are at least as high as those of the aged and they have even less prospect of current outside income. The case for hospital insurance for these social security recipients is as persuasive as that for the aged. The Council's actuarial studies found that a satisfactory program covering both the aged and the disabled under Social Security could be financed at quite reasonable cost. Yet, this is one of the few Council recommendations which the Congress is unlikely to adopt—at least this year.

PUBLIC ASSISTANCE PROGRAMS

As no social insurance program can be designed which will meet all the needs of all the disabled, we will continue to require also the "last resort" federal-state public assistance programs. Aid to the Blind now furnishes assistance to about 97,000 persons a month and Aid to the Permanently and Totally Disabled to some 520,000. Liberalization of the basic social insurance program would, of course, diminish the need for public assistance. But these programs also require liberalization. For example, confinement of the APTD program to the permanently and totally disabled is not justified. Many other individuals are in need because of disabilities which constitute a serious handicap to their prospects of employment or to satisfactory functioning. The program could be expanded to include persons with significant and serious disabilities. A work incentive feature could also be introduced to give partial exemption on earnings as is now successfully done in the Aid to the Blind program which exempts the first $85 a month of earned income and one-half of the remainder up to a maximum.

The level of payments in the assistance programs is something of a scandal. Each state determines the minimum amount disabled and blind people need to live in health and decency, but very few make payments high enough to support that minimum. Federal reimbursements could be made contingent upon each state paying the needy disabled the full amount necessary to maintain the minimum living standard the state itself has set. This would raise benefits significantly.

Rehabilitation

It is only in recent years that we reached a delayed turning point in our conception of income maintenance programs, recognizing that they must go beyond cash and medical benefits to be effective. It is now accepted that, wherever possible, one of their major functions should be maximum restoration of work and normal living abilities. Technological advances of recent years have created previously undreamed of capabilities for restoration of the disabled which turn out to be not only humane and constructive, but economical as well. Such procedures can and often are operated at a net financial saving to the public programs.

Despite unqualified and universal lip service to the principle of rehabilitation and some modest progress, we have hardly begun to exploit its possibilities, to our great loss as a society. This is due to some lack of faith, lack of personnel and facilities, reluctance to make the initial capital investment, and to growing indifference as we become accustomed to living in a labor surplus economy. The disabled capture our concern primarily during labor shortage periods.

Even in the OASDI program, whose strict definition of disability means that there is less potential for rehabilitation than among other disabled groups, the Advisory Council recommended that money be made available from the Social Security trust funds to finance the rehabilitation of selected beneficiaries. Its studies showed that this could be done at no net cost because, it reported, "the savings from the amount of benefits that would otherwise have to be paid exceed, or at least equal, the money paid from the trust funds for rehabilitation. It is wasteful and shortsighted for the Social Security system to be paying benefits to disabled persons if a lesser expenditure of funds would assure their return to work."

Some OASDI beneficiaries do receive rehabilitation, but in the main the group receives a very low priority from state vocational rehabilitation agencies, and the Social Security Administration believes that only a small proportion of its beneficiaries, who could substantially profit from such services, receive them. The proportion in the public assistance programs is probably even lower. (Incidentally, most states do not pick up all the federal funds available to them for rehabilitation purposes, for failure to provide sufficient matching funds. In fiscal 1964, the states matched only 61 per cent of the federal allotment base, and only five states picked up all their federal allocations.)

The prospects for successful rehabilitation are generally directly related to early appropriate medical care and to early referral to rehabilitation authorities. This thought brings us back to the category of the temporary disabled. We have seen that organized temporary disability insurance programs are not available to most workers. The five public programs are oriented entirely towards the idea of short-term, nonenduring, incapacity. Yet, as I have indicated, many of these workers may have long-term or chronic malfunction. Among those who manage to qualify later for OASDI disability benefits, it will be a minimum of seven months before they will be eligible and usually a longer time before they are actual recipients of benefits and will face an agency that is oriented towards long-term care and the possibilities of rehabilitation. (Hopefully, the prospective hospital insurance program will also heighten the Social Security Administration's sensitivity to rehabilitation.) The delay could be costly and damaging.

One important reform of the OASDI system could go far towards correcting this deficiency while also helping to meet the problem of inadequate coverage of the first six months of disablement. At present a minimum waiting period of six months is required between the onset of total disability and eligibility for OASDI benefits. The intent is apparently to exclude from consideration temporary conditions that terminate within six months. Such a long waiting period, however, is not necessary to identify the character of disability. A three-month waiting period is long enough to keep the worker without income as well as to make reasonable determination of the extent of the disability. (After all, the decision will not be irrevocable; people can be cut from the rolls if unexpected recovery should occur.) This change alone would increase the number of disabled workers immediately eligible for benefits by about 250,000.

If this change were combined with the previous suggestion for removal of the requirement that the disability be appraised as of indefinite or permanent duration, we would bridge the present gap in protection for those disabled for six months or more but expected to recover some time in the future. We would also provide for the more serious of the "temporary disability" cases who now have no coverage, and it would be a significant boon to the restorative prospects of the seriously but not irreparably disabled.[1]

Disablement itself seems likely to increase in the years ahead, but we can reduce its personal griefs and we can, if we will, significantly diminish the extent to which it results in unnecessary removals from the labor force and destruction of productivity.

Occupational Disability

A paper on disability cannot omit occupational disability and workmen's compensation, the oldest of our social insurance

---

[1] Since the presentation of this paper, the House of Representatives passed H.R. 6675, for which Senate concurrence is expected, which would eliminate the requirement that a worker's disability must be expected to result in death or to be of long-continued and indefinite duration, and instead would provide that an insured worker would be eligible for disability benefits if he has been totally disabled throughout a continuous period of at least six calendar months. Also, the benefits would be payable beginning with the last month of the six-month waiting period rather than beginning with the next month.

programs, even though work-connected disability is a small proportion of the total, about five per cent. My comments on this topic will be reluctant and brief.

Some excellent studies of workmen's compensation have been made in recent years, some of the best at this University under the leadership of Mrs. Gordon and our chairman, Professor Cheit.[2] Such studies confirm that little progress and little change has taken place in the program in recent years. About a fifth of wage and salary workers are still not covered, a proportion that has remained stable over the past decade. In 13 states the ratio of actual to potential coverage is less than 65 per cent. In addition, many injuries are still excluded in many states. For example, 2 states fail to cover any occupational diseases (as distinguished from "accidents") and another 20 do not cover all.

Recent estimates indicate that, on the average, cash benefits do not replace as much as one-third of wage loss. The proportion is highest for temporary disability, averaging around 40 per cent, but for permanent and total disability it is probably less than 25 per cent. Despite the apparent intent of the laws to replace about two-thirds of wage loss, much the largest share of industrial injury still falls on the worker and his family, or on public assistance or private charity.

Medical benefits have been increasing in availability but their quality has long been under severe doubt and attack. In this program too, despite the almost universal verbal dedication of experts and administrators to the principle that rehabilitation should now be the primary goal of the compensation process, the programs have not proved adaptive to the new needs. Many of the program procedures or requirements are in apparent conflict with the rehabilitation process. Only half the workmen's compensation jurisdictions have any special provisions in their acts to encourage rehabilitation, and these vary widely in their adequacy. In practice, most workmen's compen-

[2] See Earl F. Cheit, *Injury and Recovery in the Course of Employment* (New York: Wiley, 1961); and Earl F. Cheit and Margaret S. Gordon, editors, *Occupational Disability and Public Policy* (New York: Wiley, 1963).

sation recipients who need such services do not receive them.

Internal decay often fosters fears and suspicions which not only paralyze capacity for self-reform but find comfort in conjuring up an imagined external culprit. The only excitement generated by workmen's compensation in recent years has been a massive propaganda attack on the federal disability insurance system as an alleged threat to survival of workmen's compensation, led by employer organizations and private insurance carriers, a campaign to which state administrators have been recruited. They allege that overlapping benefits from disability insurance and workmen's compensation result in "excessive" benefits, more than the full wages of the worker on his last job, and that the federal government is engaged in a deliberate scheme to replace workmen's compensation as the primary source of protection against occupational injury.

You will recall that when disability insurance was inaugurated in 1957 it carried a provision that the federal benefit would be reduced by the amount a beneficiary might be receiving at the same time from any other public disability benefit program. Congress, after finding that the requirement created severe inequities, that it was administratively very costly and cumbersome, and that the extent of overlap was trivial, repealed it two years later. Now great pressure is being directed at Congress to re-enact the offset. Several state legislatures have memorialized Congress for such action.

The alleged issue is, however, false and, significantly, is being pressed most vigorously by those who opposed the passage of any disability insurance program in the first instance. The documentation in the spate of literature being disseminated is made up of extreme hypothetical examples of what could possibly occur, and not real cases. The two programs, which cover different populations for different contingencies, for different purposes, overlap in only minuscule degree. A tiny fraction of compensation awards—probably considerably less than one-half of one per cent—involved the permanently and totally disabled and many of these cannot qualify for OASDI benefits. Of the OASDI beneficiaries less than two per cent also receive workmen's compensation.

Even among this small group, it is relatively infrequent that the sum of both benefits will exceed the 66 per cent of wages which workmen's compensation itself originally promised. The two benefits can in some cases exceed 100 per cent of previous wages, but this is almost always in the case of very low paid workers or workers permanently disabled while very young and with a dependent family, where the need is greatest. And it should be recalled (1) that the destroyed future earning potential of the young is not taken into account in these figures, (2) that about half the states pay workmen's compensation benefits to the permanently injured only for a limited period of time, and (3) that workmen's compensation is intended to compensate the worker for the injury itself as well as for lost wages.

Many other factors could be recited to illustrate the absurdity of the allegation that the survival of workmen's compensation is threatened by the federal program, but it is unnecessary here. The Advisory Council on Social Security studied the question with care and concluded that no real problem justifying federal action exists at present. This member's judgment is that the only major threat to workmen's compensation is its own neglected dry rot.

This episode illustrates that there are influential forces that not only oppose improvements in provision for the disabled but would turn the clock back. The leading advocates for deliberalizing the federal program do not, I should add, favor strengthening workmen's compensation. On the contrary, the same literature which attacks the federal system often alleges that compensation is just dandy as it is.

CONCLUSION

In conclusion, there is not much cause for optimism in regard to the plight of the seriously disabled. A look at the present poverty program as well as our established public programs indicates that they have a relatively low priority. They do not excite the imagination of most reformers or have high public appeal. This is understandable in an economy with so many able-bodied and youthful unemployed, with a lifetime ahead, who seem to deserve prior attention. It is not widely understood that many of the disabled workers have established work habits and often have skills that are translatable into new work patterns, and thus with relatively small investment they can often be made self-supporting. Many are relatively young. Also there is less appeal to the self-interest of the general population than in other programs. For example, everybody expects to become old and a potential beneficiary of enlightened programs for the aged; very few people expect to become permanently and totally disabled. There are other reasons as well.

I thus must end on the pessimistic note that the disabled are likely to remain among the most unfortunate disadvantaged in our population for the foreseeable future. Hopefully, an enlarged and comprehensive poverty program could invalidate that forecast.

18. Poverty and Income Maintenance for the Unemployed

MARGARET S. GORDON

INTRODUCTION

It is now more than seven years since the annual average unemployment rate in the United States has been below five per cent. During those seven years we have moved slowly and haltingly toward a national policy of combatting unemployment through a combination of measures aimed at stimulating aggregate demand and promoting labor market adjustment. But we have done very little to overcome the glaring inadequacies in our system of income maintenance for the unemployed, and, in neglecting this policy area, we have failed to take advantage of an approach which could easily have prevented millions of families and individuals from falling below the poverty line at one time or another since 1957.

To what extent is poverty in the United States attributable to unemployment experienced by the family breadwinner in the course of a year? It is not easy to arrive at a reliable answer to this question on the basis of existing data, and, in any case, the answer would vary from year to year with changes in the amount of unemployment. A report recently published by the Social Security Administration suggests that nearly a fifth of the families and about a tenth of the individuals with incomes too low for a bare subsistence level of living in 1963 owed their poverty at least in part to involuntary unemployment experienced by the family head or the individual at some time during the year.[1] Leon Keyserling has estimated that 20

[1] These estimates have been developed from data included in Mollie Orshansky, "Counting the Poor: Another Look at the Poverty Profile," *Social Security Bulletin,* XXVIII (January, 1965), pp. 3–29.

per cent of all families and 40 per cent of all persons living in poverty in the United States are in consumer units whose heads suffer substantial unemployment during the course of the year or who are not in the civilian labor force because of scant job opportunities.[2]

In 1961, the average income of all persons who had some work experience during the year was $3,700, but among the 9.6 million workers who experienced five or more weeks of unemployment during the year, average income *from all sources* was only $2,300, while, for those with 27 or more weeks of unemployment, income averaged only $1,443.[3] The loss of income associated with unemployment in 1961 would undoubtedly have been greater were it not for the fact that early in that year Congress authorized a temporary system of federally financed extended benefits for unemployment insurance recipients who exhausted their rights to benefits during the 1960–1961 recession.

The low incomes of the unemployed are attributable in part to low unemployment insurance benefits and limited duration of benefits. But what many Americans, I suspect, do not realize is that large numbers of unemployed persons cannot qualify for any type of public income maintenance payment at all under existing legislation. Only about three-fifths of all workers are covered by the federal-state unemployment insurance system, and in 1961 barely more than half of those who experienced five or more weeks of unemployment received unemployment insurance benefits. For those who exhaust their rights to benefits, or are not eligible in the first place, our public assistance system provides inadequate protection. This is a subject to which I shall return at a later point.

Retraining and Unemployment Compensation

The failure to take decisive action to improve our income maintenance system for the unemployed is not hard to explain.

---

[2] Leon H. Keyserling, *Progress or Poverty* (Washington, D. C.: Conference on Economic Progress, 1964), p. 52.

[3] Robert L. Stein, "Work History, Attitudes, and Income of the Unemployed," *Monthly Labor Review,* LXXXVI (December, 1963), pp. 1405–1413.

There are a number of factors involved. However, I believe that part of the explanation is confusion on the part of many well meaning people about the relationship between retraining and unemployment compensation.

Retraining, these people will argue, is far superior to "relief." The important thing is to equip people to get back to work rather than to encourage them to exist in idleness for months on a public "hand-out."

Although I am a strong advocate of retraining, and am on record in favor of a permanent and expanded retraining program,[4] I would urge that a large-scale retraining program is no substitute for an adequate system of income maintenance for the unemployed.

In the first place, by no means every unemployed worker should be retrained. Much unemployment is of a short-term nature, attributable to frictional or seasonal factors, and entailing no need for a change in occupation. Cyclical unemployment is likely to last somewhat longer than the frictional or seasonal variety, but, again, does not invariably call for retraining. It is primarily those workers whose skills are obsolescent, or who lack any skill at all, who should be referred to retraining. In 1963, despite continuing and quite justified concern about the problem of long-term unemployment, 44 per cent of the unemployed were out of work less than five weeks.[5]

Secondly, a large-scale retraining program cannot be developed overnight. The number of vocational training instructors must be greatly expanded, and, particularly in the case of special remedial programs for disadvantaged groups, counsellors and other types of personnel must be recruited and given specialized training. In many situations, training equipment must be acquired, and buildings to house training classes must be rented, purchased, or constructed. In the light of these considerations, it is scarcely surprising that our MDTA program was

---

[4] See my report on *Retraining and Labor Market Adjustment in Western Europe,* (Washington, D. C.: U. S. Government Printing Office, 1965).

[5] Susan S. Holland, *Labor Force and Employment in 1963,* Special Labor Force Report No. 43 (Washington, D. C.: U. S. Bureau of Labor Statistics, 1964), p. A–39.

slow to get under way in the first year or two. One of the conclusions I drew from my recent study of the postwar development of retraining programs in Western Europe was that we would have been far better off if we had developed a retraining program some years ago, before we were confronted with the persistent unemployment problem that has prevailed in the last seven years. We have tended to look upon our retraining program as an emergency, crash effort to deal with an unemployment problem, whereas it is really more appropriate to view retraining as a means of encouraging adaptation to structural changes in employment, which are a continuous phenomenon.

The MDTA program, as authorized by Congress, contemplates the training or retraining of about 700,000 workers and total expenditures of nearly a billion dollars over the four-year period, 1962–1966. Put in these terms, the program seems large, but when one considers that this implies retraining 175,000 workers annually, on the average, and that 175,000 workers represent only about five per cent of the unemployed and about two-tenths of one per cent of the labor force, one gains better perspective on its dimensions. Actually, during the first 11 months of the program, through the end of June 1963, only 59,000 trainees were approved for training, and during the following fiscal year, 128,000 were approved. Since there is often a delay between approval of a training project and the beginning of a course, the number who had actually enrolled in courses was considerably smaller, and the total number who had successfully *completed* training under the program by the end of May 1964 was only about 44,000.[6] The training program conducted under the Area Redevelopment Act has been considerably more limited, involving a total enrollment of about 27,000 during the period from November, 1961, through June, 1964.[7] The Economic Opportunity Act of 1964 also provides for training and retraining activities, but chiefly for young people.

---

[6] *Training Facts,* Report No. 14, Office of Manpower, Automation, and Training, U. S. Department of Labor, October, 1964, pp. 3 and 21.
[7] *Ibid.,* p. 21.

We could, of course, develop a considerably larger retraining program on the basis of expanded appropriations, but it would take time. Moreover, the more rapidly we attempted to expand the program, the greater would be the risk that no jobs would be available for those completing training. If there is a need for both expansionary fiscal and monetary policies and labor market adjustment policies to combat unemployment, there is also a need to maintain an appropriate relationship between the two approaches.

Finally, it is important to recognize that the training allowances paid to workers undergoing MDTA or ARA training do provide income maintenance for the relatively small number of unemployed persons in training programs at any one time. But the training allowances under ARA are equal only to average unemployment benefits in each state and those provided under MDTA cannot exceed $10 more than the average benefit in each state or the individual's own benefit, whichever is higher. We shall see just how adequate such compensation is under existing state laws.

THE FEDERAL-STATE UNEMPLOYMENT INSURANCE SYSTEM

Gaps in coverage

Although the situation varies somewhat from state to state, approximately two-fifths of the labor force and more than a fifth of all wage and salary workers are excluded from the federal-state unemployment insurance system. Moreover, many of those who need protection the most are among the uncovered. The exclusions apply to nearly all farm and domestic workers, many workers in small firms, a substantial proportion of state and local government employees, and employees of nonprofit institutions.[8]

Inadequate benefits

Although most state laws aim at providing benefits equal to 50 per cent of a worker's previous earnings, the actual benefit

[8] *Comparison of State Unemployment Insurance Laws as of January 1, 1964,* U. S. Bureau of Employment Security, BES No. U–141 (Washington, D. C.: 1964), pp. 1–15.

received is well below 50 per cent in a large proportion of cases as a result of the restrictive effect of the ceiling on benefits. These ceilings, or maxima, have become *more* rather than *less* restrictive over the years, despite legislative action to increase them from time to time, because the increases have failed to keep pace with the rise in wage levels. Largely as a result, average weekly benefits have declined from 42 per cent of average weekly earnings in 1938 to about 35 per cent in recent years.

An unfortunate aspect of the erosion of benefit ceilings has been its relatively severe impact on heads of families, whose earnings are likely to be higher than those of single beneficiaries and secondary wage earners. Beneficiary surveys conducted in five labor market areas in various parts of the country in the middle and late fifties indicated that benefits received by heads of four-person households averaged a third or less of lost earnings in all five areas.[9] If federal provisions were to require states to raise their maxima gradually to two-thirds of *average* weekly earnings (while retaining a benefit standard of 50 per cent of the *individual's* weekly earnings), it would be chiefly male family heads who would tend to benefit. Such a provision was embodied in legislation submitted to Congress by the Kennedy Administration[10] and is likely to be included in anticipated Johnson Administration proposals.

The fact that male family heads would derive the greatest benefit from an increase in unemployment compensation standards is an important consideration in the light of recent evidence that children—and, among them, the children of the unemployed—constitute a larger proportion of impoverished persons than had previously been thought.[11] This new evidence has tended to lend support to proposals for a modified negative income tax, which would restore perhaps 14 per cent of

[9] See *Unemployment Insurance and the Family Finances of the Unemployed,* U. S. Bureau of Employment Security, BES U–203 (Washington, D. C.: 1961).

[10] Since this was written, the Johnson Administration proposals, similar in most respects to the 1963 proposals of the Kennedy Administration, have been sent to Congress.

[11] See Orshansky, *op. cit.*

the gap between a substandard income and a national minimum standard which would vary by the number of dependents in a family. Such a program would make a modest contribution to the level of income of impoverished families and would benefit particularly the families with large numbers of children.

Although there are arguments in favor of such a scheme, it would, in my opinion, be no substitute for a more adequate system of income maintenance for the unemployed or for major improvements in other aspects of our existing Social Security system. It would be most unfortunate, indeed, if the effect of a negative income tax were to hold back needed improvements in existing programs—a result which would be highly likely in view of the heavy costs involved.

Let us consider, for example, the case of Bill Crawford, who has been earning $5,200 a year, has a wife and three children, and is out of work 15 weeks in 1965. Typically, at present, he might receive unemployment benefits of some $35 to $40 a week after a week's waiting period, and his total income for the year would be cut to approximately $4,200. The negative income tax would not assist him at all, since it is most unlikely under current proposals that the minimum standard would be as high as $4,200 for a husband-wife family with three children. On the other hand, an increase in his weekly benefit to $50, or 50 per cent of his earnings, would raise his total income for the year to $4,400, thereby reducing the severity of the necessary cut in the family's level of expenditures. A higher benefit standard and/or the provision of dependents' allowances—now paid in only a small minority of states—would improve his position a good deal more.

In this connection, it is important to keep in mind the fact that unemployment insurance benefits, inadequate as they are, have been a highly significant and quick-acting means of maintaining purchasing power in recessions. The negative income tax would be far less effective in this respect.

Duration of benefits

One of the disturbing aspects of our unemployment problem in the last seven years has been the extent of long-term unemployment. Although those with 15 weeks or more of unemployment constituted less than a seventh of the unemployed on an annual average basis in the early 1950's, they have accounted for more than a fourth of the unemployed in the years since 1957. In the last few years, moreover, about a half of these long-term unemployed persons have been out of work 27 weeks or more.

It is this latter group, in particular, which suffers from the fact that the maximum duration of benefits under most state unemployment insurance laws is 26 weeks. In both the 1957–1958 and 1960–1961 recessions, Congress enacted legislation to extend the duration of unemployment insurance benefits on a temporary basis. These measures were designed to meet an emergency situation, but there has been increasing recognition of the need for a permanent federally-financed system of extended benefits, along the lines of the provisions included in the 1963 Kennedy Administration proposals. Under this type of provision, a worker who had been unemployed more than 26 weeks and had exhausted his state unemployment benefits would be eligible for up to 26 additional weeks of benefits, but only if his employment record showed substantial attachment to the labor force in the last three years as well as at least 26 weeks of employment in the state base period.

There has been much criticism of the unemployment insurance system on the ground that married women who move into and out of the labor force, as well as other workers with loose labor force attachments, have been able to qualify for unemployment benefits. It is extremely important to emphasize the point that such individuals would typically *not* be able to qualify for extended benefits under the 1963 proposals. Moreover, although the added protection for the long-term unemployed with strong labor force attachments would be available both in prosperity and in recessions, the impact on the purchasing power of the unemployed would be particularly pronounced in recessions, when the number of persons exhausting their regular state benefits tends to rise sharply.

Financing

One of the obstacles to achievement of these needed improvements in unemployment insurance has been our virtually exclusive reliance on an employer payroll tax as the means of financing the scheme. In this respect, our American system is unique. In almost all other countries with an unemployment insurance system, the program is financed either by a tripartite combination of employer, employee, and government contributions or by some combination of two of these three sources of funds. With employer payroll taxes set chiefly at the state level and unemployment insurance costs varying widely from state to state, largely as a result of wide variations in unemployment rates, strong employer resistance to increased state payroll taxes which would raise their labor costs in relation to those of competitors in other states is altogether to be expected. This problem would exist with or without the added complication of experience rating, which is deeply imbedded in our financing system and I suspect is here to stay. Although I think that substantial changes in our system of financing unemployment insurance are highly unlikely, I can see no good reason why at least the federal portion of the existing payroll tax, which would increase from 0.4 to about 0.7 per cent if a system of federal extended benefits and other improvements were adopted, should not be shared among employers, employees, and general government revenues.

PUBLIC ASSISTANCE FOR THE UNEMPLOYED

What protection do we provide through our public assistance system for an unemployed worker who has exhausted his insurance benefits or was not eligible for insurance benefits in the first place? There is probably more confusion and misinformation on this point than on almost any issue of public policy in the United States. I am convinced that the average man on the street thinks that most unemployed workers who cannot get unemployment compensation promptly go to the county welfare office and start collecting relief checks.

The fact is that until recently our public assistance provisions were such that in many parts of the country relief was either unavailable to the unemployed worker or was available only on the most meager, restrictive, and humiliating terms. Partly for this reason, and partly because the typical American worker has a deepseated aversion to "going on welfare," the proportion of the unemployed receiving relief payments has tended to be very small. A nationwide survey of the unemployed in the 1957–1958 recession showed that the proportion who went on relief rose gradually from *none* of the families whose heads were unemployed one to four weeks to eight per cent of the families whose heads experienced 27 or more weeks of unemployment.[12]

Our policies toward relief for the unemployed show many vestiges of the Elizabethan notion that it is dangerous to provide "outdoor relief" to able-bodied persons lest they remain content to live slothfully on these "handouts" and refrain from seeking work. By contrast, many other advanced industrial countries have unemployment assistance or some other type of public assistance that is quite generally available to unemployed workers who have exhausted their insurance benefits or were ineligible for them in the first place. And the extremely low unemployment rates prevailing in many of these countries, such as West Germany and Sweden, bear eloquent testimony to the fact that in modern industrial societies most workers have a strong preference for the increasingly satisfying level of living that is available to those who *work* as compared to the meager level of consumption that is available to those who are subsisting on relief.

Under the public assistance provisions of our Social Security Act, federal grants-in-aid to the states are available only for certain categories of needy persons, and until 1961 those categories did not include the unemployed, who had to fall back on general assistance, which was financed either by the states or by the counties or some combination of the two, and was generally considerably more meager than the federally aided categories of assistance. A 1959 study showed that 23 states had no general assistance available to the unemployed and their families, while elsewhere the means test was typically so severe that a person had to be practically destitute to get

[12] W. J. Cohen, William Haber, and Eva Mueller, *The Impact of Unemployment in the 1958 Recession* (Ann Arbor: Institute of Labor and Industrial Relations, University of Michigan and Wayne State University, 1960), p. 40.

relief.[13] Even in the relatively enlightened and progressive state of California, I have been informed, there was at that time not a single county in which an individual could qualify for relief if his only reason for being in need was unemployment.

In 1961, Congress extended federal grants for the Aid to Dependent Children program to the families of unemployed parents on a temporary basis, and in the Public Welfare Amendments of 1962 these provisions were extended for another five years, or until 1967. However, only 18 states have taken advantage of these provisions. At the end of 1964, only about 67,000 families in the entire country were receiving such aid, at a time when total unemployment amounted to nearly four million.[14]

Moreover, these provisions do not meet the problem of the unemployed worker without minor children. Thus, they do little to help older unemployed workers, who are unlikely to have minor children but are particularly susceptible to long-term unemployment.

If time permitted, I could go on to enumerate other antediluvian features of our relief policies as they relate to the unemployed, particularly the curiously short-sighted practice found in many parts of this country—so unlike policies of Western Europe—of offering the relief recipient *no* incentive in the form of higher weekly compensation if he enters a training program in order to increase his employability.

CONCLUSIONS

There are a number of other aspects of income maintenance for the unemployed that could be mentioned if more time were available, including a variety of proposals that have been made in recent years relating to special allowances for unemployed youth and older workers.

I should like, however, to close on a broader note. If we are really serious about our intention of moving forward with

[13] *Public Assistance: Report of the Advisory Council on Public Assistance Containing Findings and Recommendations,* p. 10; and *Daily Labor Report,* No. 199, November 12, 1959, pp. A-5 to A-7.

[14] *Welfare in Review,* III (March, 1965), p. 29.

a vigorous anti-poverty program in the United States, we shall need to emphasize, at one and the same time, national policies which stimulate the growth of the economy and affect the distribution of income and more locally oriented training and job corps programs, such as those authorized by the existing Economic Opportunity Act. We must also recognize that certain approaches, e.g., liberalization of income maintenance policies, will achieve immediate results in terms of improving the lot of the poor, whereas others, such as certain types of reforms in our educational system, may yield results only in the long run. In my opinion, we need an appropriate blend of all these approaches. Clearly, however, the main theme of this paper has been that we could substantially and quickly improve the level of living of a significant segment of the poor by moving toward a system of income maintenance for the unemployed more in keeping with the needs of the latter half of the twentieth century.

PART SEVEN

WELFARE SERVICES AND REHABILITATION

19. New Techniques in the Rehabilitation of Welfare Dependents

RAYMOND M. HILLIARD

Within the last six or seven years a new concept of poverty has made its impress upon American society. This concept of the "new poor"—those made dependent directly or indirectly by the vast and immutable changes taking place in America's economy—was, it seems to me, long overdue.

During the previous decade, emphasis was centered on the increasing productivity and growth of the economy, and upon the consequent affluence of the majority of our population. Little noticed was the development of an increasing army of people at the bottom end of the economic scale, who found themselves either phased out of the work force directly by technological innovation, or "bumped" from their menial occupations by those who had descended from higher, but now obsolete jobs.

We have now begun to see that poverty as we had defined it in previous years and decades was not a realistic concept to use in trying to deal with the situation at hand. The older concept, at least in the public mind, centered on the individual's immediate lack of income, with no particular penetration into the long-term causes and effects of his dependency on the public treasury. We have begun to understand that modern-day poverty is a complex interlocking set of circumstances, which cause and in turn reinforce each other, combining to throw the unlucky individual into idleness, dependency, and eventually into apathy and social deterioration. We have begun, too, to realize that this new kind of poverty was going to demand a new set of approaches to the business of public welfare; a set of approaches that would do more than merely hand out checks in the hope that if dependent people could be kept from suffering physical deprivation they would somehow find their way back into—or simply into—the mainstream of American economic life.

An indication of the changing nature of poverty was seen in 1959 when the economy was recovering from a recession. Normally the number receiving general assistance quickly declines during such recoveries; yet in 1959 the number continued to rise. This fact led to a series of intensive studies in Cook County into the nature of the local unemployment problem and the educational qualifications of those receiving public assistance.

The first of these studies showed us that nearly 71 per cent of the applications for general assistance could be attributed, either directly or indirectly, to unemployment and not to social, psychological, or physical factors. The study also revealed that the main characteristic these persons had in common was a low level of education and training. The second study—and this one analyzed the reasons for the loss of last job held and of job held for the longest time—showed that directly and indirectly unemployment due to automation accounted for a significant 59 per cent of the total reasons reported for loss of the last job held. The third study, carried out early in 1961, revealed the continued and growing impact of these economic changes. As I said, this idea of a new configuration of poverty is now fairly well accepted by economists, government officials, and progressive public welfare administrators. Having accepted the premise that a new poverty exists, we had to turn our attention next to the means of dealing with it. This is the subject I want to talk to you about today.

The Problem of Illiteracy

Obviously, in trying to develop techniques to rehabilitate welfare dependents, we are confronted with the whole range of economic and social factors affecting individual performance. The more apparent areas for treatment, such as lack of job skills, degenerative physical surroundings, and emotional abnormality, naturally suggested avenues of treatment. Not quite as evident to my agency in particular, until a study of welfare recipients was carried out in the Woodlawn area of Chicago in the spring of 1962, was the educational factor. The Woodlawn study revealed that, although only 6.6 per cent of a group of recipients in the area had less than five years of education, almost 51 per cent were functioning at reading levels below the fifth grade, which is considered to be the minimum literacy level necessary to function in modern society.

So it became apparent that a broad attack on illiteracy was necessary to raise these people to a point where they had even a chance of attaining self-support. In fact, any meaningful assault upon poverty must have education as its basis. Lack of literacy skills means not only a poor chance to be economically productive, it means being out of touch with society at large, not sharing in the cultural, social, or intellectual life of the nation or the community. In a very real sense, the poor illiterates are living in another world; a world of bleak ideas and deadening apathy. I believe there are few communities in this nation that would not benefit from an intensive campaign against illiteracy. I also think that the total costs of educational programs are easily offset by the long-term profits in the form of economic productivity as well as social and cultural uplift.

To move from the abstract to the concrete, let me discuss briefly some of the methods we in Cook County are using to give many of the thousands who are receiving public assistance the wherewithal to become productive. I shall confine myself to a brief mention of our work training programs, because I want to devote more emphasis to the educational aspects of rehabilitation.

TRAINING PROGRAMS

As far as vocational counseling, placement, and training are concerned, we have for many years maintained a facility—known as our Welfare Rehabilitation Service—as a center for these activities. Created shortly before World War II, this service is organized to train the marginal worker in a variety of tasks, to help unemployed persons with work skills find jobs, and to counsel potential workers who have particular emotional or psychological problems. The program has had what we consider a fine record of accomplishment over the years in helping thousands of dependent persons to self-support. Included as part of this service is an extensive work relief program, in which unemployed men work on public projects for pay up to the amount of their assistance grants.

Welfare Rehabilitation Service carries out its functions primarily through a counseling and placement program and the Industrial Training Center, where recipients learn a wide variety of industrial skills by actually working at jobs which have been subcontracted by a number of firms. Other programs run by the Welfare Rehabilitation Service are licensed practical nurse training, nurse's aide training, and clerical, maid service, and porter training. I should add at this point that these and all the other special work-oriented training programs I am going to mention are services provided entirely by our Cook County Department; in this respect I believe we have pioneered among public welfare departments across the country.

Increasingly complex occupational patterns and economic relationships of contemporary society have made us aware that the services I have just mentioned are not enough to make up an effective rehabilitative program. It has become obvious to us that this greater complexity requires more sophisticated training programs. In answer to this need, we have started a series of specialized training programs over the past few years. We have tried to tailor these programs to train men and women in work for which there is a demand. In this way the training not only fills a need in the economy, but the trainees have the added incentive of knowing there is a job "at the end of the line," so to speak. Let me mention a few of these programs to you.

First, there is the Yellow Cab Driver Training Program. This is an ongoing voluntary program of training and rehabilitation in cooperation with the Yellow Cab Company of Chicago, which operates 3,000 cabs on a double-shift basis. Our general purpose is to rehabilitate unemployed men by training them to become independent wage earners who at the same time fill a need in the industry. The two-and-a-half week training includes instruction in traffic safety, place locations, accident prevention, cab operation, practice driving, working with the public, and basic arithmetic, as well as special talks on budget planning and credit buying by department specialists. When they have finished their training, and have passed a routine police and FBI records check, these men are helped to obtain state and city chauffeur's licenses, and are then hired as drivers by the company. Supportive casework service is provided during the training period and we supplement earnings made until the man becomes fully self-supporting. Since the start of this program in November 1962, more than 1,300 men have been graduated from the course, most of whom are now self-supporting members of the community.

Next, we have a food preparation training program, geared to furnish trainees with the skills needed to qualify as salad and pantry assistants, sandwich and grillman assistants, breakfast cooks, and chef's helpers. This program, which has turned out some 150 graduates in less than a year, features lectures, demonstrations, trainee participation, and work-training experience. In the course of a year, this program can train 175 people at an estimated cost of $45,000 resulting in an estimated saving of $438,000 in assistance grants—an almost ten-to-one return on the investment.

Third on the list of programs is service station attendant training, which is being administered in two separate efforts, one sponsored jointly with the Shell Oil Company and one with the Sun Oil Company. Fundamentally these programs are the same, with training including instruction in the gasoline and oil products of the companies, station operation procedures, mechanical repairs, salesmanship techniques, safety, bookkeeping, and so on. One of these companies even gives a trainee the opportunity to become an independent station owner if his performance is good enough. Fourth, there is a custodial training program, developed in cooperation with the Chicago Urban League to offer training for maintenance and janitorial jobs. Last, there is an eight-week program which is designed to prepare men for a career as wood finishers.

Another technique in rehabilitating men for productive performance in the economy is screening and referral to other agencies and programs. For example, we have been referring many people through the State Employment Service for training under the Manpower Training and Development Act of 1962. Job skills are taught in the clerical and sales, metal trade, general and industrial, hotel and restaurant, service office, and professional and managerial categories. To give you some idea of the scope of this program, in our department alone, as of December, 1964, 1,941 persons had entered 26 different Manpower Development programs; by the middle of January, 791 had been graduated, and no fewer than 640 of these had been placed in jobs.

Still another phase of our rehabilitation efforts involves a broad home economics service, which attempts to raise the level of housekeeping and homemaking skill of the mothers receiving assistance. Our purpose here is not so much aimed at self-support through earning as it is at the social and cultural uplift to be gained from greater know-how in the everyday tasks of living, from household sanitation to credit buying. The whole gamut of home skills is taught to women on our rolls to help them become better housekeepers, better mothers, and inevitably, better citizens. This service incidentally trains women as domestic workers, homemaking aides, and housekeeping teachers.

Attacking Illiteracy

However, job training and placement mean nothing if the people you're working with lack the fundamental tools of learning. A person who cannot read or write cannot very well be expected to profit from vocational training. Here I am reminded of a friend of mine who owns a good restaurant in my neighborhood. I had been speaking of the growing need for higher levels of education when he said to me:

> I know just what you're talking about. Almost a year ago, I hired a Negro kitchen man and he turned out to be about the best employee I ever had—industrious, dependable, and cheerful; willing to tackle anything. He showed a definite flair for cooking and I began to urge him to get into the cooking end of the business.

He kept backing away from it and finally I sat him down and said, "Look, I can make you my head chef—you can make twice your present salary. I know you can cook; now, what do you say?" The man gulped for a moment, and then in obvious embarrassment, looked up and said, "Mr. Fulton, I'd love to be a head chef and I know I can do it, but you see, I just can't read those orders." He couldn't read recipes either.

I am firmly convinced that this kitchen man, even while he holds his present job, can be taught enough reading in an accelerated course to enable him to read orders and recipes and then move into the job of chef and vacate a job for a kitchen man that can be filled from the present relief rolls.

I have already mentioned our growing realization of the dimensions of the problem of illiteracy in our community. The fruit of this realization was the creation of a vast program, in March of 1962, to train people on relief to read and write. Adult recipients, who are referred to the program by special education workers in our 19 district offices and suboffices, attend classes in nine Chicago public schools and four suburban Cook County schools. This effort, conceived in conjunction with the Chicago Board of Education, proposed to help the great number of functionally illiterate recipients obtain the necessary reading and arithmetic skills that would enable them to compete in today's expanding economy.

To give you some idea of the dimensions of the program, as of the end of last year there were 8,121 persons enrolled—5,308 in the basic literacy classes, and 2,813 in high school classes. Elementary classes are held for two hours an evening, two evenings a week; high school classes take place four evenings a week for two hours. Those placed in the elementary school advance from grade to grade at their own pace; those in high school proceed on a semester basis. So convinced are we of the value of this program that we're making plans to expand to full-time day classes. These classes, which will have a vocational orientation, are geared to provide accelerated learning for the adults in them. Feeling that a certain degree of social discipline was necessary for the program to stay alive, we decided that every person receiving assistance whose basic literacy level was found inadequate would be required to participate as a condition of receiving aid.

In our experience with this program so far, several facts have emerged. We have found that we have very seldom had to use compulsion; attendance has been excellent. Also, the general level of interest and eagerness to learn of these people has been encouraging. I think there is a real zeal on the part of many of the untrained to "make up for lost time," so to speak, and gain the skills to make themselves economically independent. We have learned not to try to fit our recipients into regular school classes. Differences in age, social and economic status, and so on make these people shy and hesitant to participate in the learning process; we have much greater success when we assign our people in groups where they are among themselves. The need for education is underlined by the fact that we can no longer afford to train people narrowly; the man trained to do one job and one job only may very well find himself out of work altogether. An individual today needs a broader background in terms of which he can adjust to new fields in general and new occupations in particular.

A recent survey showed that nearly 90 per cent of all employable adult males who are on the country relief rolls are school dropouts of yesterday. The school dropout has become one of the nation's most pressing social as well as economic problems. As we know, the school dropout is headed not only for chronic unemployment, but for the greater evils of street gang association, delinquency, and eventual contact with the courts, and in many cases, the prisons. The vast majority of these persons, young and old, do not have enough education to qualify for the upgraded jobs that are available in today's labor market, and it's certain that they will be unable to keep pace with constant job upgrading if they themselves remain static in educational skills. In other words, these people do not have reading ability to understand the instructions to operate the machines which may replace them, or to get a job vacated by somebody who has moved up the line of occupations.

We have had a program we call "Target . . . Dropout" in

effect for some time. This program is aimed at keeping young people of high school age in school by providing them with part-time job opportunities or work-study programs. Specifically, employers agree to hire young people if they will agree to stay in school.

The Problem of Prevention

However, adult literacy training and dropout placement services fall in the category of *cure*. What we are most interested in at this point is *prevention*.

This leads me into still another facet of the long-term rehabilitative effort—the effort, you might say, to rehabilitate society itself, not just the individual. Adult functional illiteracy is the product of cultural deprivation in the formative years—or simply the lack of adequate education. In the case of a great number of our recipients, the basic educational opportunity simply was not there. On this premise, we have been directing our attention to the children of people receiving assistance. Children of illiterate parents begin school at a distinctly lower level of preparation, and they face a tremendous uphill fight if they are ever to reach the same level as their classmates. In order to break the natural cycle of culturally inherited illiteracy, we are exploring the possibility of using an automated educational technique for youngsters in these families. We are presently planning a demonstration training study of preschoolers with this system, known as a responsive environment device. I have great hopes for this technique as a means to give these children an equal chance for competing successfully in school, and in life.

For a long time I have advocated the creation of a youth corps similar to the depression-era Civilian Conservation Corps. You will recall that this organization achieved truly marvelous results in making many public improvements as well as giving thousands of young men an invaluable sense of usefulness and common effort. Sociologists, welfare workers, and experts from many other fields will testify that this kind of organization is the single most effective measure that could be taken to check the rising tide of juvenile delinquency. Preference should be given to young men and women from broken or unfit homes or from a bad community situation. A high priority, I think, also should be given to youths rejected for military service.

The provision for a Job Corps in the Economic Opportunity Act of 1964, while it doesn't duplicate the proposal I have just mentioned, in the main hits at the heart of the problem and to that extent it is valuable.

I think it is vital at this point to mention some of the federal government's current proposals for aiding education in this country. To summarize very briefly, the administration's new bill calls first for $1 billion for the first year of a three-year program to help public school systems where three per cent or more of the pupils are from families earning less than $2,000 per year; secondly, for $100 million for the first year of a five-year program to provide books and other teaching materials for public and private nonprofit schools; and similar proposals to create supplementary educational centers, to establish educational research laboratories, and for strengthening state departments of education.

This program, in the words of Health, Education, and Welfare Secretary Celebrezze,

> directs special and notable attention to the education of the children of the poor and, at the same time, enhances the quality of the whole of education. It is unprecedented in size and in scope. It is imaginative and eminently practical, seeing first things first, and focusing funds where the needs are greatest.

It appears to me that the increasing commitment of the federal government in this area is perhaps the only way in which we can raise the general level of social, cultural, and economic life in our country.

However, I want most emphatically to insert a word of caution here. Federal participation in a war on poverty is certainly welcome, but not at the expense of efficient, intelligent administration. If we are going to be bogged down in a morass of red tape the program becomes self-defeating. I am very much afraid it looks this way already. The Department of Health, Education, and Welfare, as a condition of authorizing projects under the new legislation, has sent us an eleven-page form, entitled, mind you, as follows: "Appendix H.T. No. 38 (12-7-64) Page E-1 of 11 pages, BFS-WA-D/HEW FS 181, Form Approved Budget Bureau No. 122-R-092, Title V of the Economic Opportunity Act of 1964; Work Experience Program, Project Proposal." There follows a painstakingly minute breakdown of administrative service costs, occupational classifications of persons needed to participate, and characteristics of the people to be served by the program. As if this were not enough, there is also a four-page form to be filled out on every single prospective trainee. If we took the time to gather and enter all this data, we'd hardly have time to render any service!

To use other words, what I am saying is that some way has got to be found to reduce the amount of paperwork, particularly at the federal level, or all our programs will one day be nothing more than elaborate formal exercises in futility. I hope my words are not taken as a symptom of negativity; it is precisely out of a desire to be positive, to achieve positive results, that I am making this statement.

CONCLUSION

The techniques I have mentioned today by no means exhaust the list of possible approaches to disintegrate the somber shadow of poverty, ignorance and dependency which has hovered over this country too long. In a day when we can call on the resources of all the social and physical sciences to provide us with ideas for penetrating the stubborn enclaves of social decay, there is no reason not to experiment boldly. Government and private organizations alike have command of a broad range of techniques which can be applied to make the free enterprise system a truly democratic institution.

Naturally, we are dealing not only with what is theoretically possible but also with what is politically feasible. Nevertheless, I see the day when growing public understanding of this problem, together with the marshalled resources won by academic discovery, will give us the strength to reduce the proportions of poverty to an insignificant dot on the landscape.

20. A National Program for the Improvement of Welfare Services and the Reduction of Welfare Dependency

NATHAN E. COHEN

The "War on Poverty" is essentially a phase in the American historical process of attempting to correct a growing imbalance of power which is creating a sense of powerlessness in an ever-increasing "underclass." The solution to the problem, therefore, goes beyond the question of individual inadequacy and involves change in our social institutions. As in previous generations such as the Jeffersonian Revolution in 1800; the Jacksonian in 1828; the Lincolnian in 1860; the Rooseveltian in 1932, we are entering a period when a fight is being made to give the common man his "share of the good life, of opportunity, of the American dream." [1]

The war, therefore, is not a new one, but rather a stepped up campaign in the nation's effort to combat and reduce dependency. It has been waged over the years in the name of charity, social reform, the purchasing power necessary to keep the economy going, the waste of human resources, and more recently, social justice. It has gained momentum from the Negro revolt and the intimate relation of the solution of the racial and poverty problems. It is also being fed by the changing nature of our society and the fears emerging from the growing impact of automation on work and jobs.

It is a complicated war in that both the purpose and method lack common agreement. There is no agreement on the defi-

[1] J. T. Adams, *Frontiers of American Culture* (New York: Scribners, 1944), pp. 113–114.

nition of poverty even among those who have joined the battalions prepared to do battle. Because it is not a problem which lends itself to a simple cause and effect analysis which would permit priority decisions along biological, psychological, economic, social, or environmental lines, the solutions being projected vary greatly. Some are satisfied in taking arms against symptoms whereas others view the problem within the larger context of the scientific and technological revolution which is engulfing us.

Viewed within the most measurable yardstick, the economic, one arrives at a figure of "more than 30 million Americans, almost a fifth of the Nation, living in poverty." [2] A further breakdown reveals that one-third of the poverty group is made up of aging and their families; another third includes widows, divorced women, and unmarried mothers with their children; other groupings are the sick and the disabled, the underemployed and the casually employed, the small farm owner, the tenant farmer, the farm worker, and the small shop owner. In brief, a sizable segment are not able to hold a regular job and the solution to their problem would rest with changes in the social insurance system and a more successful effort in the implementation of the 1962 welfare amendments. Another sizable group would include the millions of men and women now employed but earning less than $3,000 a year. For this group the solution is related to upgrading their skills and changing the wage structure.

A major effort to help a large segment of the present poverty group, therefore, would involve higher payments in the old-age insurance system and the aid to dependent children program; a comprehensive system of pensions for invalids; a comprehensive system of health insurance; a national program of unemployment benefits; minimum wage legislation for the 16,000,000 workers without coverage; low-cost housing programs for the disadvantaged living in 11.3 million houses and

---

[2] "Converging Social Trends," *Emerging Social Problems,* U. S. Department of Health, Education, and Welfare Administration, Division of Research, Washington, D. C., p. 18.

apartments classified as slum dwellings; and expanded health and social services.[3]

Employment has been the major channel for overcoming poverty. As noted above however, there are millions now employed within a wage structure which is below the poverty line. Race and sex weigh heavily as discriminating factors in the competitive job situation and as handicaps to earning power. The most crucial factor which is emerging is education. The growing number of high school dropouts is automatically disadvantaged in an economy where expansion of job opportunities is coming in fields which require as a bare minimum a high school education.

Many of the programs to combat poverty are predicated on an identified poverty group and do not take into account the growing impact of scientific and technological revolution. Unemployment through increased automation can result in adding substantially to the one-fifth of the nation living in poverty and to the additional one-fifth living close to the poverty line. The problem viewed within this context demands a more fundamental look at some of our basic societal concepts. For example, we are in the interesting situation in which we may be able to eliminate poverty and yet not solve the problem of unemployment, for within our present conception of work there is no assurance of jobs for everyone. This problem strikes at a deeply rooted value in American life, namely, that we must work competitively to live. There may be forms of work and service which do not fall within the context of our usual concept of work and its role in our society. We are so geared, however, to a theory of motivation related to survival and meeting basic needs that it is difficult for us to envision other patterns.

The present War on Poverty as evidenced by government programs to date, therefore, would have to be considered as an important launching of a series of battles, but not as a full-scale attack. One of the strengths of the Economic Opportunity Act is its emphasis on young people and its stimulation

[3] Gunnar Myrdal, *Challenge to Affluence* (New York: Random House, 1963), p. 59.

of community action programs. Through such efforts may come greater clarity as to the nature of the problem, the level of commitment of the American Public, and the true targets of action. Perhaps the soundest view of the present War on Poverty is as a strategy for obtaining support for a number of existing important health, education, economic and welfare programs whose full implementation, expansion and reorganization have been resisted in recent years.

The way in which the war is waged may have a profound effect on future developments and directions. If the approach is primarily task-oriented without relation to basic institutional rearrangements essential to dealing with the long-range implications of the problem, we may win a few battles but lose the war. It is important, therefore, to define the parameters within which the war should be waged.

What are the essential premises on which we might proceed? They might include the following:

1. Poverty, like other social problems, does not lend itself to a single cause and effect etiology. It is a problem of multiple causation and its solution demands a multiple approach.
2. Poverty cannot be dealt with adequately unless a community thinks and acts as a total community rather than as sharply divided public and voluntary sectors.
3. Since the causes and solutions of poverty are no longer just local in nature, there is need for new local, state, and national patterns of organization.
4. In the mounting of any comprehensive efforts to deal with the problems of poverty the functional relationship between organizations and services is crucial.
5. The problems of poverty demand not only institutional rearrangements, but also a new look at our methodology in dealing with people.

An analysis of a social problem like poverty reveals that we are dealing with a profile of factors running the entire gamut of the economic, social and psychological. Policies and programs which seek a one-dimensional approach are bound to fail. Job training without the availability of jobs can lead to further frustration; creation of opportunities for job training will not automatically guarantee the use of these resources; expanded social services are not a substitute for adequate budgets to meet the basic needs of food, clothing and shelter; adequate budgets, on the other hand, are no automatic guarantee of reducing the sense of dependency. What is needed is a comprehensive approach which takes into account the importance of all of these factors.

The Responsibility of Public Agencies

One of the most difficult phenomena to face, and yet one of the most important, is the growing "sense of powerlessness" found in the poverty group. As pointed out by Myrdal, we are developing an "underclass that is no longer an integrated part of the democratic structure but a useless and miserable substratum." This group does not have the mobility or strength to move through our social institutions essential for preparation for our type of society. Myrdal states that this development is "not only demoralizing for the individual members of this underclass," but that "it is fatal for democracy." The danger to democracy is that they have become "so mute without initiative that they are not becoming organized to fight for their interests." His crucial point is that "for its own health and even preservation an effective, full-fledged democracy needs movements of protest on the part of the underprivileged." [4]

In brief, our policies and programs should reflect approaches that involve doing with others rather than for others. A society by the affluent for the poor is not the democratic pattern, but rather one which places the concept of charity ahead of social justice. Lincoln's point that a democratic society cannot live half slave and half free applies to our present predicament—a democratic society cannot live half affluent and half poor, half powerful and half powerless.

Public agencies will be carrying the major responsibility for the poverty program. The attitude of the public toward these agencies has not been a positive one. As they attempt to help the poor overcome their apathy and help preserve their hu-

[4] *Ibid.*, p. 10.

man values they will be faced with public criticism and protest. Marvin Larson, Director of the Kansas State Department of Social Welfare, pointed up the issue clearly in a recent speech at the 1963 biennial conference of the American Public Welfare Association. He stated that:

> You and I have a very real responsibility to our nation. Our responsibility is to defend the poor, and to do it with courage and conviction. The extreme rightists, the ignorant and those who are thoughtlessly selfish cannot be appeased. I am sorry to say that public welfare administration has too frequently and too long been a matter of mealy-mouthed appeasement and of apology. I am very sure everyone who administers public welfare, those in the federal agency, those in the state agency and those in the county agency, stand on an important outpost for the preservation of democracy and for the preservation of our nation as we know it. I hope all of us develop a little more knowledge—above all I hope we all develop a little more guts and courage.[5]

The public agencies will need the support of the vast network of voluntary agencies, including the welfare councils, if they are to succeed in their efforts. The professionals in the nonpublic sector can make a vital contribution by constantly educating their lay leadership about the nature of the problem and what its solution entails. They can also help recruit a cadre of volunteers both to assist the public agencies and to become better informed about the poor through direct experience. Without this type of backing the public agencies can easily slip into a task-oriented program and fail in the efforts to help the poor help themselves.

COOPERATION BETWEEN PUBLIC AND VOLUNTARY AGENCIES

This brings me to my second major concern, namely the need for a community to think and act as a total community rather than as public and nonpublic sectors. The dichotomy between the public and the voluntary has haunted the American scene for generations. The ideological revolution of the thirties drove home the realization that one could no longer

---

[5] Marvin E. Larson, "Public Welfare and Public Policy," *Biennial Conference Papers,* American Public Welfare Association (1963), pp. 5–6.

think of these two sectors on an either / or basis, but rather as both / and. As pointed out by Eric Goldman, this concern to bring about security through legislation, this conception of a "protective state" was indeed a break with reforms of the past.[6] Although progress has been made there is still a strong tendency in the voluntary welfare field to refer to the public sector as "they" and to their own sector as "we."

One reason for the continuation of the dichotomy was the artificial division of function which emerged in the thirties. With the expanding role of government in social welfare, the voluntary agencies were forced to review their functions. In some circles the view remained that we were dealing with a piece of pie which could be cut into *x* number of slices, and that as the public sector increased its slices, there would be that much less for the voluntary sector. This represented a static concept of society and its changing pattern of needs, rights, and responsibilities.

The division of function which took place was unreal, and in some respects contributed to the problems we face today. The public sector was given the responsibility for dealing with the physiological needs of food, clothing, and shelter, and the safety needs of protection against danger, threat, and deprivation. Their clientele was to be the poor. The voluntary agencies took unto themselves responsibility for dealing with social, ego, and self-fulfillment needs. Their clientele was to be the middle-class. It represented a dualism between catering to the body and catering to the soul.

Although the voluntary agencies, as they drifted away from the poor and became more engaged with the middle-class, gave lip-service to the entire continuum of needs, they shifted their emphasis more and more toward "treatment" and away from concrete services. The public agencies, because of inadequate budgets, lack of trained personnel, and the negative attitude of the public toward economic dependents, worked with enormous caseloads which permitted only infrequent contact with clients. They were able to give only lip-service to social, ego,

---

[6] Eric Goldman, *Rendevouz with Destiny* (New York: Knopf, 1952), p. 287.

and self-fulfillment needs. The voluntary agencies, proud of the truism that "man does not live by bread alone" lost sight of the important fact that "man lives by bread alone only when there is no bread." [7] Immersed with ministering to the middle-class where the problem of bread was secondary, it was easy to state and restate the truism.

The impact of the expanding role of government in social welfare also forced the voluntary planning organizations such as the welfare councils to review their function. There was a growing realization that the public sector had to be included in local community planning. The first efforts were to accommodate the expanding public agencies within the existing co-ordinating machinery by broadening the base of membership beyond agencies receiving support from the Community Chest. In many respects the public programs were regarded as auxiliary to those of the voluntary agencies, and the role of the public agencies in the councils as one of accepting the leadership of the voluntary groups. Not enough effort was made to create a structure which would break down the dichotomy, a structure which would reflect a total community outlook and approach.

Until recent years this pattern of community planning dominated by the voluntary agencies was possible since, as stated above, the public programs dealt with economic dependency, leaving to the voluntary agencies the area of social, ego, and self-fulfillment needs. The increased social problems, emerging out of a rapidly changing society in the throes of a scientific and technological revolution, have militated against the continuation of this artificial separation. Furthermore, with the advent of an increased concern and role by the federal government with problems like poverty and mental health, the inadequacy of local planning machinery has become evident.

A pervasive barrier to no longer viewing a community as part public and part voluntary, but as total community, is the fear of government. An expanding role for the federal govern-

---

[7] Douglas M. McGregor, "The Human Side of Enterprise," in Warren G. Bennis, Kenneth D. Benne, and Robert Chin (editors), *The Planning of Change* (New York: Holt, Rinehart and Winston, 1961), p. 425.

ment is becoming a new value. The basic question to be answered is, are there other ways of solving the growing social problems, or is the choice that of less centralization and less solution? The phenomenon of increased bigness is not a diabolical plot conceived by a group from another planet, in fact, not even from a particular political party. The principle of solving problems by beginning first at the local level, then moving to a state level, and finally to a national level is deeply imbedded in our American heritage. With the growing impact of the scientific and technological revolution have come myriad social problems which are national in scope, and in solution. Our challenge is not to deny the reality of change but to help find creative ways for the flow of authority to move in both directions.

New Patterns of Organization

This brings us to our third concern, namely, the need for new local, state, and national patterns of organization. As local communities have attempted to accommodate their structure to the large governmental programs the approach has been more that of emergency than seeking structures which would have long-range meaning and usefulness. The voluntary planning bodies possess some of the know-how but are hampered by their inability to overcome their concerns about expanding role of government and for the survival and maintenance of their system. The public groups, on the other hand, with new access to resources and power and lacking in experience in coordination and planning tend to follow the primitive pattern that given three agencies you can always get two to agree on what the third one should give up. It also becomes clear that the sources of policy- and decision-making vary greatly in the public arena from that in the voluntary field. In public efforts involving the city, the county, and the state, and special bodies within these structures such as education, health, welfare, and economic development, it is difficult to determine the sources for different levels of policy. Is it the paid staff, is it the elected officials, or is it the political party itself? The entire effort is frequently handicapped by an atmosphere of distrust and a lack of understanding of an essential ingredient in the solution of major social problems which face us, namely, basic institutional rearrangements.

Like the voluntary system, the public arena is still suffering from an attempt to protect the old rather than seek new organizational patterns more related to present-day problems. Furthermore, public agencies have lived under a fragmented task-oriented approach for so long that it is not easy for them to move toward comprehensive efforts. Arlin Adams, from his perception on the state level as Secretary of Public Welfare of Pennsylvania, describes the condition as follows:

> First, there is the organization of programs along categorical service lines rather than in ways which facilitate the solution of multifaceted human problems. For example, we organize to give money. We have a separate organization for health services, another for housing, another for social service. Each is its own little empire.
>
> Secondly, there is the unrealistic allocation of funds. Money flows through highly restricted channels. Funds coming through a public assistance channel or a health channel or a mental health channel or a housing channel must be expended in terms of the limited service for which the agency receiving the funds was established.

This leads to highly restricted programs at times, like the organized home medical care programs limited to patients suffering from one particular disease.

> Third, there seems to be lack of communication. We need devices for making communications more effective. There has been less than full acceptance of the notion that interdepartmental or interagency action is part of the normal business of program administration. Too often interagency action is looked upon as something abnormal and a device which only leads to the loss of agency sovereignty. Therefore, we fail to provide easy channels for it.
>
> Fourth, there is lack of knowledge of the values of other disciplines, and lack of administrative courage. Coordination does not occur spontaneously or without delineation of issues. Where there is honest disagreement over principle, arbitration by some coordinating authority may be necessary.
>
> Good coordination of programs flows from sound staff work. Too

frequently this is not available. Agencies tend to respond competitively instead of coordinately.[8]

On the federal level, coordination and planning in the area of social problems is also a new venture. Only in recent years has there been an effort to coordinate services within a structure like Health, Education, and Welfare. And only very recently has there been evidence of an interest in focusing on social problems which cross the lines of several departments. There has not been much energy devoted to long-range planning. As pointed out by Myrdal what we have is "a widely dispersed system of economic planning of a pragmatic and, as yet largely uncoordinated type."[9] He states that "what is now becoming an urgent necessity in America is in the first place a much better coordination of already existing government policies, that is, their integration into a more perfect, deliberate and rational long-range planning."

It is no longer possible to develop a planning system on the local level without a more adequate system of long-range planning on the state and federal levels. This is becoming more crucial with the growing ties between the local and federal efforts to deal with social problems which are national in scope. The nature of our social problems, the sources of funding, and the need to develop manpower to deal with them have overflowed local boundaries and can no longer be dealt with on an isolated local level. A system of planning, therefore, which is purely local in character represents a fragmentation and is meaningless in relation to a comprehensive effort. At best it can represent a mechanism for better management of inadequate resources and meet the conscience of the policy-makers more adequately than the needs of the consumer of the problems.

Because of the interrelationship of local, state, and federal planning, and because of the power of the federal effort, the federal government has great responsibilities in the way it develops a comprehensive program such as the war on poverty.

---

[8] Arlin M. Adams, "Public Welfare Can Move Ahead," *Public Welfare* (October, 1963), pp. 177–178.

[9] Myrdal, *op. cit.*, p. 23.

The program has given new strength and power to the public sector and, at the same time, has sharpened the conflict of goals in the voluntary sector. The method being utilized to challenge and change old patterns is often that of compliance. The leverage of federal funds becomes the power for forcing a new arrangement within the public sector and between the public and voluntary sectors. Frequently, there is insufficient time devoted to study and analysis of the problem through a process which might provide a rational base for new policies, programs, and structures. Machinery is at times created for the purpose of becoming eligible for the funds, but not always with assurance that there is a full understanding of the problems and acceptance of the new patterns necessary to deal with them. Thus, new organizational patterns may be emerging not out of a rational plan, but rather as a ticket of admission to obtain funds, with a hidden agenda to utilize these funds so that the equilibrium of the old systems can be maintained. There are very few examples where local communities have seized the opportunity of the availability of new resources to search for new patterns around common goals and values. Such an approach demands a new stance in planning and is predicated on a resolution of the fears of an expanding role of government on the part of the voluntary sector, and an understanding of the importance of citizen participation on the part of the public sector.

Unless the local machinery established for the war on poverty is more clearly defined in long-range as well as immediate terms, it can become a holding company for the distribution of federal funds without making any impact on essential institutional rearrangements. Furthermore, if the goals and functions are not clearly defined, the staff will find itself caught in the morass of trying to be a funding, coordinating, and operating body at one and the same time. In fact, it will find it impossible to establish meaningful criteria for the selection of projects and for evaluating the success or failure of these major efforts.

Lack of clarity of structure in relation to need and function can also cloud the cooperative roles of the public and voluntary sectors. In some communities the pattern is for the public agencies to contract for special services with the voluntary agencies. This is utilized as a way of bringing trained personnel into the program especially in the area of treatment. There are several difficulties with this type of plan. First, it is used as a substitute for the expansion of trained personnel in the public setting. Secondly, it is dealt with by the voluntary agency as a special project, often without clearly defined lines of administrative authority and without the sustained commitment necessary to provide ongoing services in the community. The reverse pattern is also found in the poverty program, namely, Settlement Houses which have contracted with various governmental agencies for special service units to operate as part of their program. Here again the question of administrative responsibility becomes complicated and what seems like an integrated program may be nothing more than common housing.

The war on poverty has, as a positive influence, its pervasiveness as a problem and its inherent demand for better planning if a solution is to be found. It could well become the vehicle for a fresh look at planning on the local, state, and federal levels, and at the structures necessary to relate these levels in a way which would encourage full participation in the process of decision making, in the flow of authority, and in the flow of resources. It could help create the structure necessary to meet myriad social problems emerging out of this period of rapid change.

A Comprehensive Effort

My fourth concern is that there be sufficient recognition that a comprehensive effort is more than the sum total of a number of services, and that the functional relationship between these services is crucial. Much of our depth of knowledge has come from an era of great specialization. We know a great deal about particular problems and have organized our agencies and services along these fragmented lines. Families living in poverty over a period of time, however, are like the chronically ill who need a continuity of care involving many types of services. It is too much to ask of anyone to be able to find their way through the maze of specialized services, let alone the poverty group. In a sense we are asking the client to be a good diagnostician so that he can locate the service essential to his problem.

The war on poverty demands that agencies change to meet the needs of families fighting economic dependency and all its attendant social problems, rather than ask the families to fit the needs of the agencies. It will also require that sizable numbers of professional people expand their traditional roles and spend their time in unfamiliar ways.

One of the major criteria for determining how much of the program can be carried out through existing agencies is the flexibility of the agency and its willingness to face change. If the agency begins with its existing structure as an end in itself and seeks merely to find some aspect of the poverty program which will fit into its present arrangements the program will serve the needs of the agency more than the needs of the poverty group. Furthermore, unless some machinery is established for a generalist approach with continuity of plan and service for the family the program will not be successful. Specialized services can enrich a program but are not a substitute for the family-oriented workers who view the problem as a whole and who are concerned with continuity and coordination of services.

The establishment of multiproblem centers with board and committee structure from the poverty area may well be the hub. These centers would be related to specific poverty projects and to programs in existing agencies through a council structure. Total planning for the area would be through the council. Linkage could be assured by having the core staff of the multiproblem center augmented by staff on loan a day or two a week from the various special poverty projects and existing social agencies. This would provide the necessary structural underpinning for insuring a proper flow of programs and services between the multiproblem center and other agencies. Such a structure would also provide a plan for funding projects in the areas and avoid viewing them as separate entities competing for new resources.

Key to the establishment of these new patterns and emphases will be the various professions. If they too become ritualistic about traditional roles they can become a barrier. The programs will demand the use of lesser trained people including indigenous aids and auxiliary help. It will also necessitate an interdisciplinary concern that focuses on the problem and the ways of tackling it, more than on professional boundaries.

SOCIAL WORK THEORY AND METHODOLOGY

This brings me to my final concern, namely, our theory and methodology for working with people in trouble. Private social work, like other helping professions, has tended to disengage itself from the poor.[10] Theoretically, social work began with a sociological period and then, with the impact of the psychoanalytic, shifted to a heavy emphasis on individual treatment. In its sociological period, there was a strong current of social reform reflecting the influence of pragmatism with its view that man was master of his own fate, and collectively could build a brave new world. The Freudian emphasis shifted the focus toward a Hobbesian view of man, but tended to abstract the individual from the power struggle of the various social institutions of which he was a part. This created a dualism in social work thinking.

Freud, from whom social work borrowed much, was pessimistic about the value of applying the therapeutic approach to the poor. As stated by Friedenberg,

> His tangibly compassionate reservation about using psychoanalysis to treat working class patients suggests that he felt that, for most individuals, the candle really did cost more than the game would be worth; and that people who in reality had very little opportunity to lead richer lives might better be left with their defenses and illusions.[11]

---

[10] Richard Cloward and Irwin Epstein, "Private Social Welfare's Disengagement from the Poor," for publication in Pearl and Riessman (editors) *Poverty and Low Income Culture.*

[11] Edgar Z. Friedenberg, "Neo-Freudianism and Erich Fromm," *Commentary,* XXXIV (October, 1962), p. 309.

For Freud, the emphasis was on the individual and his adjustment to society. Not enough consideration was given to a changing society as well as a changing individual, and to the importance of the socioeconomic structure and its impact on the character development of the individual. Fromm has pointed this up sharply. For Fromm a pervasive socioeconomic structure which runs counter to the basic nature of man, with "its inherent need for love, human solidarity and the development of reason" can result in a "socially patterned defect" in the total society. Such a condition, states Fromm, "inhibits his faculty for critical thought, and tends to transform him into an automaton, into a marketing personality who loses the capacity for genuine and profound feeling and thought, and whose sense of identity depends on conformity." [12]

The need to break out of the narrow treatment context has become evident even in the work with middle-class. It has been made most visible, however, in dealing with the problems of poverty. There is growing recognition that poverty cannot be viewed only in psychological terms, that it also has its roots in "structural" problems in our society. Furthermore, it is not just a problem for the individual poor, it has become a challenge to the survival of our democratic society as an institution of the people, by the people, and for the people.

Not only has there been disengagement from the poor on the part of private social work, but this sector has absorbed the major part of the trained manpower, and has greatly influenced the direction of social work education. Thus, even in work with the poor there has been the tendency to regard them as enroute to middle-class and to deal with them more in relation to what they might become, than where they are at the present time. It is not uncommon, therefore, to find ourselves in the embarrassing situation best described by the story of the policeman who finds a dead horse on Kosciusko Street. He has a report to write, but can't spell Kosciusko. His solution is to drag the horse over to First Street so that he can write the

[12] Erich Fromm, "Psychoanalysis," in James R. Newman (editor), *What Is Science?* (New York: Simon and Schuster, 1955), p. 380.

report. We have been dragging the problems of the poor over to our middle-class methodology without adequate results. Often we find that when we move in with some of our services the people do not flock to them. There results a gap between the availability and the usability of resources.

There is need to understand this gap in terms other than resistance and lack of readiness to utilize the services. We must seek the reasons for the gap in social institutional terms as well as psychological. What may be needed is a community development model as well as the community organization model found in the general urban community.

The poor are concentrated in subcommunities which do not possess the resources necessary to meet the problems of education, health, welfare, jobs, and social control. These resources must come from the larger community including the state and federal levels. The availability of resources alone, however, will not insure usability. We are also dealing with a problem of motivation and the development of a greater desire to overcome the "sense of powerlessness" and work toward an interest in self-help. This demands a community development model.

There is need to integrate our sociological and psychological knowledge if our programs are to be effective. Programs dealing with poverty are veering away from the psychological and placing a heavier emphasis on the sociological. Opportunity theory, for example, has been given great prominence. Greater access to educational, job training, and employment opportunities is being stressed. This change in direction is important, but there is danger of throwing out the baby with the wash. As stated earlier, experience shows that there is often a gap between the availability of resources and usability. The original cause may have a strong sociological base, but once internalized the problem may be psychological in nature. There is need to take our total knowledge into account and utilize it within patterns of service which have meaning in poverty areas.

In brief the two approaches merge even in the area of services. We know, for example, that the traditional family casework agency will not be too effective in a poverty area. If we take a hypothetical ethnic subcommunity identified as a poverty area the plan might be as follows:

1. Begin with the premise—Community Development fashion—that every community has a system for dealing with human problems. The system may be informal and may not have the recognizable characteristics of our formal organization patterns. People helping each other is as old as civilization itself. The first step, therefore, is to study the community and identify possible channels of linkage in launching a program.
2. *Step two* would involve developing the basic projects agreed upon as essential for attacking the poverty problem, namely, education, job training, job finding, etc. In setting up these programs, however, knowledge of the community and its subsystems, and knowledge of the ethnic characteristics, would be taken into account in order to insure usability as well as availability of these services.
3. *Step three* would consist of providing support for those who begin to lose their motivation and become dropouts. They would be helped in direct relation to the goal of the project, the goal being to help them complete the objective of education, job training, job finding, etc.
4. *Step four* would be to provide a more intensive service for a smaller percentage who, even with supportive help, could not make it. This group would become the caseload for more intensive psychological help.

Provision of services and help with motivation around specific programs is not enough. To overcome the "sense of powerlessness" prevalent in the "poverty" community, the poor must be helped to understand their rights and responsibilities as well as their needs. Such efforts would involve social and political action in relation to problems which affect them directly. This would include problems such as housing violations, voting rights, and rights in relation to the various departments of government such as police, sanitation, health, welfare, and education. Such projects may bring them into direct conflict with the existing establishment. This in turn may strain relationships with those sponsoring or funding the program.

There is sufficient evidence that the moment one proceeds to help the poor become self-directing, including the challenging of existing institutions, resistance and hostility result.[13] But, do we have any alternative, if the problem of poverty is to be attacked not in remedial terms, but within the context of prevention? One of the key factors will be the role of local, state, and federal bodies who serve as sponsoring and funding groups. Unless these groups understand the dynamics of change and the importance of overcoming the apathy of the poor, the war may turn out to be one of containment rather than an all-out war on poverty. As stated earlier, the role of the lay leadership in the voluntary agencies will be crucial in providing the kind of backing that protects the freedom of the various demonstrations and programs, and avoids running for cover when conflict emerges. Conflict in the positive sense of the term is an integral dynamic of change. Funding from outside the community should provide a necessary leverage for bringing about institutional rearrangements which cannot be accomplished if the resources are totally from within the existing structure of the local community. This means that the role of the state and federal governments must go beyond that of dispensing funds.

The war on poverty has as its major targets the inducing of change, change not only in the lives of the poor, but also in the social institutions through which they function. We are at a beginning level, unfortunately, in our theory and methods for inducing change. A theory as dynamic as the psychoanalytic, for example, has until recently, dealt primarily with defense mechanisms. Sociology, until the growing interest in developing countries began to emerge, dealt more with how to describe and transmit a culture than how to change it. Theory and method, however, are beginning to evolve. I refer to the work of such people as Festinger[14] in the realm of the intrapsychic,

---

[13] The recent attack on the mobilization for youth project in New York is a key example.

[14] Leon A. Festinger, *Theory of Cognitive Dissonance* (New York: Row, Peterson and Company, 1957).

Kelman [15] in the area of the interpersonal, Merton's [16] work on modes of adaptive behavior, and Hall's [17] writings on culture as a system of communication. There are also several new volumes on planned social change.

Time does not permit an analysis of these developments. Running through these different approaches, however, is the thread that change at the level of internalization of new values and goals is slow. The fastest change comes through compliance, that is, where the individual or group expect to gain specific rewards or approval and avoid specific punishment or disapproval by conforming. This level of change, however, may be temporary and may fade when the pressure is removed. Much of the efforts at this point are at this level, and will have meaning only if they are related to long-range goals. If they become an end in themselves, a few skirmishes may be won, but the war on poverty may be lost.

As stated in the beginning of this paper, an essential core of the war on poverty is the recurrent business of liberalism, namely, how "to correct imbalances of power and to organize social institutions in such a way that no one has too much power." [18] The war on poverty is providing an opportunity for us to reach democratic maturity, that is, a greater fullness of economic and social as well as political democracy. To grasp the opportunity means giving up our *status quo* mentality and showing a willingness to approach the problem with a sense of innovation, creativity, and adventure. Our democracy, which was founded in freedom, can be destroyed by a state of mind which resists innovation and can be strangled by the closing of frontiers in the realm of ideas. *Status quo* was not the state of mind of our founding fathers. Theirs was a spirit of change

---

[15] Herbert C. Kelman, "Compliance, Identification and Internalization: Three Processes of Attitude Change," *Journal of Conflict Resolution,* II (March, 1958), pp. 51–60.

[16] Robert K. Merton, *Social Theory and Social Structure* (Glencoe, Illinois: The Free Press, 1957).

[17] Edward T. Hall, *The Silent Language* (New York: Doubleday and Company, 1959).

[18] Charles B. Frankel, *The Case for Modern Man* (New York: Harper, 1955), p. 30.

in the cause of a society which would provide an orderly way to meet man's continuing quest to overcome economic, political, and social poverty. The responsibility of meeting today's challenge does not belong exclusively to the public sector or to the voluntary sector, but to the total citizenry and the total community. There can be resistance to change or innovation in either sector, since neither is the province of a group from another planet. Both efforts are but different sides of the same coin, and have meaning only if backed by a common currency, namely, social justice.

21. Some Demographic Aspects of Poverty in the United States

KINGSLEY DAVIS

A crucial problem in dealing with impoverished people in the United States is how to help them without making them more dependent on help. From this standpoint, the most hopeful objects of welfare are the children and youth in poor families. A sizable portion of impoverished adults are either beyond self-help for one reason or another (e.g., old age, chronic illness, mental defect) or are capable of independence only after rehabilitative efforts that are long, costly, and problematic in relation to the years of useful life remaining. With most children, on the other hand, the potential gain from intelligently administered aid is very great.

Yet it must be admitted that, to deal with the children of the poor, one must also deal with adults—that is, with the *parents* of the children. Inevitably the limitations of outlook and circumstances on the part of the parents affect the children as well. To overcome the defects of the family milieu, to keep poverty from generating poverty, one must therefore arrange the welfare system so that parents are favorably influenced at the same time that children are so influenced.

These considerations certainly apply to the particular aspect of poverty being considered in this paper. In analyzing demographic behavior in relation to welfare needs, we must necessarily deal with the rate and circumstances of reproduction—that is, with the creation of children in the first place—in poor families. Briefly our thesis is that, on the whole, such families still have children more abundantly and under worse circumstances than is beneficial to either the parents or the offspring.

Too often, it seems, the question of children in poor families is posed simply as a problem of maintenance. The poor are said to "have more children than they can support," and the welfare task is seen as how to help them care for these children. That this view is oversimplified is suggested by two criticisms: first, it says nothing about prevention, thus running counter to the rising demand for more birth control among those who cannot care for children adequately; second, it views the problem of children in quantitative terms, as if it were a matter of a given family income divided by the number of members in the family. It seems quite possible that the demographic problem of the poor is not solely the number of children they have but also the circumstances under which they have them. Furthermore, it may be that both the volume and the conditions of reproduction do more than simply tax the ability of the poor family to support itself; rather, that they *erode* that ability, reducing the economic capacity and the opportunities of both parents and children below what they would otherwise be. The rest of the present paper presents evidence bearing on these possibilities, beginning first with the total rate of reproduction among disadvantaged families.

The Rate of Reproduction

Just how many children people in varying economic circumstances should have is of course a debatable question. Most people would doubtless maintain that couples in better circumstances should, other things equal, have the higher birth rate, because they can give more advantages to their children. Be this as it may, the fact appears to be that in the United States the more disadvantaged couples are still having more children than those who are not so poor. Although the difference is less than it was during the first part of this century and is probably diminishing further, it is still observable, and it still represents a deviation from the more common condition of mankind prior to the urban-industrial revolution. Before that time, the lower strata tended to have a lower birth rate and/or a higher death rate than the other strata, leaving them with fewer living children to contend with.[1] Today, evidence that the inverse correlation between family income and fertility of the wife still distinguishes our industrial society is found in the 1960 census results. For instance, in 1960 the average wife aged 35 to 39 had borne the following number of children according to the 1959 family income: [2]

Family income	*Children ever born*
Under $2,000	3.7
$2,000–7,000	2.9
$7,000+	2.5

There is a widespread impression that the inverse correlation between income and fertility has disappeared. The reasons for this impression are several: First, as noted, the differential has been decreasing and in two or three European countries has

[1] Generalizations concerning differentials in fertility and mortality are necessarily hazardous, especially for such a broad category as pre-industrial societies. Not only are there various ways in which people differ economically and socially (e.g., by rural-urban residence, nativity, income, occupation, education), but the indices of fertility and mortality are themselves varied. Nevertheless, it seems undeniable that mortality has been in the past, and still is, negatively correlated with socio-economic status except for special circumstances. The question of fertility is harder, but the rule that it was positively associated with socio-economic status in pre-industrial times receives some support from the following lines of evidence: first, data for the early periods of industrialization in the now-industrial countries show lesser differentials than those that prevailed at a more advanced stage of economic development. For the United States, see Wendell Bash, "Differential Fertility in Madison County, New York, 1865," *Milbank Memorial Fund Quarterly,* XXXIII (April, 1955), pp. 161–186; Yasukichi Yasuba, *Birth Rates of the White Population in the United States, 1800–1860* (Baltimore: Johns Hopkins Press, 1961), pp. 169–177. For France, see J. J. Spengler, *France Faces Depopulation* (Durham: Duke University Press, 1938), Chapter 4. For Europe in general, see Dennis H. Wrong, "Class Fertility Differentials Before 1850," *Social Research,* XXV (Spring, 1958), pp. 70–86; J. T. Krause, "Some Neglected Factors in the English Industrial Revolution," *Journal of Economic History,* XIX (December, 1959), pp. 531–534. Second, data for present or recent times in traditional peasant societies often show a positive rather than a negative relationship between fertility and socio-economic status. See United Nations, *Determinants and Consequences of Population Trends* (New York: United Nations, 1953), pp. 94–96.

[2] Computed from United States Census of Population, 1960, *Women by Number of Children Ever Born, Special Reports,* PC (2) 3A, Table 38.

virtually vanished. Second, on theoretical grounds it can be *expected* to disappear, because it presumably rests on less contraceptive knowledge and accessibility among the lower than among the upper strata, a condition that could be expected to subside gradually. Third, it does in fact tend to disappear, and even reverse itself, when only fecund couples who plan all their births are considered or when the degrees of success within a particular stratum (e.g., college graduating classes) are dealt with.[3] But for the nation as a whole at present the inverse pattern still holds through most of the income scale. Table 1, which covers the most significant ages, shows that for each age-group of wives the number of children ever born goes down with income except for the highest income class ($15,000 and over), which shows a slight increase over the next-lower income class. The $15,000-and-over class, however, embraces only a small percentage of the wives; it includes, for example, only 5.7 per cent of the wives aged 35–39, according to the 1960 data.

The generally inverse correlation between reproduction and income holds whether we take all wives or only those who have borne at least one child (mothers); in general the inverse relation is sharper for the latter, suggesting that childlessness (undoubtedly due mainly to involuntary causes) has more connection with fertility than it does with income. The inverse relation between reproduction and income also holds for both racial categories, and it holds particularly for families in which

[3] For evidence of these points, see the following references: Gwendolyn Z. Johnson, "Differential Fertility in European Countries," in National Bureau of Economic Research, *Demographic and Economic Change in Developed Countries* (Princeton: Princeton University Press, 1960), pp. 36–72; Clyde V. Kiser, "Differential Fertility in the United States," *ibid.*, pp. 77–113; Gary S. Becker, "An Economic Analysis of Fertility," *ibid.*, pp. 209–231; Ronald Freedman and Doris P. Slesinger, "Fertility Differentials for the Indigenous Non-farm Population of the United States," *Population Studies,* XV (November, 1961), pp. 161–173; Deborah S. Freedman, "The Relation of Economic Status to Fertility," *American Economic Review,* LIII (June, 1963), pp. 414–426; O. D. Duncan and R. W. Hodge, "Cohort Analysis of Differential Natality" in International Union for the Scientific Study of Population, *International Population Conference, New York, 1961* (London: 1963), Vol. 1, pp. 59–66.

the wife was in the labor force.[4] The women in Table 1 have had all or virtually all of their reproductive experience since 1940; the data therefore represent the post-depression and postwar baby boom. During this period differential fertility declined but clearly did not disappear.

The income class that includes a high proportion of impoverished persons is that with family income below $2,000 per year in 1959. Age for age, wives in this group have a much higher birth rate than other wives. The percentage by which their number of children born exceeds the average for wives in all income classes is as follows: [5]

Age	*Percentage excess above average* *Wives*	*Mothers*
20–24	13.3	7.4
25–29	21.0	17.5
30–34	23.2	23.1
35–39	24.1	25.0

The excess is greatest at the older ages, because the wives of the poor less consistently reduce their childbearing after some years of marriage, as more prosperous wives do. Although the excess reproduction of the poor is in general not so great at younger ages, it is noteworthy that, at these ages, there is a greater discrepancy than at later ages between wives in general and "mothers." The reason for this is probably twofold: the poor marry somewhat earlier and hence (in the youngest age span) the "wives" have had more time for children to be born, and more of the poor wives were already pregnant (hence on the way to being "mothers") when they married.

[4] The effect of labor-force participation by the wife is evidently to make the reproductive differentials by income sharper, because the wife's work tends both to raise the family income and to lower the reproductive performance. Many wives are doubtless in the labor force because their fertility is low, rather than vice versa. However, the labor-force data in this case relate only to the week preceding the census enumeration, whereas the fertility data pertain to the woman's lifetime. Data on past work experience show that wives who never worked after getting married tend to have higher birth rates than do those who have worked at some time or other after that event. See Table 30, p. 141, of United States Census of Population 1960, "Women by Number of Children Ever Born."

[5] Computed from Table 1.

TABLE 1. CHILDREN EVER BORN PER 1,000 WHITE WIVES OF FAMILY HEADS, BY AGE, RACE, FAMILY INCOME, AND LABOR-FORCE PARTICIPATION OF WIFE

Family income	*Age of women* 20–24 Per 1,000 wives	20–24 Per 1,000 mothers	25–29 Per 1,000 wives	25–29 Per 1,000 mothers	30–34 Per 1,000 wives	30–34 Per 1,000 mothers	35–39 Per 1,000 wives	35–39 Per 1,000 mothers
All wives								
White	1,394	1,844	2,204	2,497	2,606	2,861	2,672	2,953
Under $2,000	1,579	1,980	2,666	2,933	3,210	3,523	3,316	3,691
$2,000–3,999	1,533	1,890	2,492	2,702	2,954	3,180	3,053	3,365
$4,000–4,999	1,519	1,864	2,373	2,557	2,782	2,966	2,811	3,066
$5,000–5,999	1,494	1,856	2,315	2,500	2,699	2,876	2,747	2,969
$6,000–6,999	1,337	1,791	2,216	2,437	2,609	2,800	2,675	2,901
$7,000–9,999	1,044	1,713	1,937	2,335	2,412	2,696	2,515	2,793
$10,000–14,999	962	1,752	1,675	2,289	2,228	2,628	2,377	2,749
Over $15,000	1,201	1,828	1,977	2,393	2,501	2,833	2,603	2,889
Nonwhite	2,086	2,498	2,854	3,325	3,315	3,868	3,321	4,059
Under $2,000	2,373	2,772	3,559	3,988	4,404	4,974	4,432	5,273
$2,000–3,999	2,164	2,506	3,101	3,531	3,590	4,134	3,537	4,309
$4,000–4,999	2,020	2,393	2,865	3,262	3,192	3,720	3,214	3,967
$5,000–5,999	1,931	2,325	2,606	3,009	2,970	3,497	3,104	3,776
$6,000–6,999	1,665	2,214	2,259	2,750	2,701	3,238	2,813	3,489
$7,000–9,999	1,357	2,013	1,862	2,424	2,402	2,906	2,527	3,158
$10,000–14,999	1,385	2,059	1,742	2,410	2,106	2,628	2,328	2,884
Over $15,000	—	—	1,892	2,481	2,415	2,785	2,410	2,940

	Col 1	Col 2	Col 3	Col 4	Col 5	Col 6	Col 7	Col 8
Wives not in labor force								
White	1,668	1,896	2,435	2,575	2,819	2,972	2,901	3,104
Under $2,000	1,689	2,008	2,768	2,977	3,343	3,620	3,472	3,828
$2,000–3,999	1,695	1,923	2,609	2,757	3,083	3,261	3,215	3,487
$4,000–4,999	1,724	1,910	2,496	2,610	2,893	3,035	2,921	3,134
$5,000–5,999	1,731	1,903	2,451	2,551	2,809	2,936	2,864	3,048
$6,000–6,999	1,666	1,862	2,400	2,508	2,754	2,883	2,830	3,006
$7,000–9,999	1,495	1,791	2,287	2,444	2,688	2,833	2,789	2,968
$10,000–14,999	1,437	1,813	2,169	2,405	2,630	2,804	2,749	2,944
Over $15,000	1,428	1,832	2,226	2,451	2,724	2,913	2,812	3,000
Nonwhite								
Under $2,000	2,324	2,607	3,262	3,565	3,830	4,227	3,903	4,507
$2,000–3,999	2,489	2,825	3,776	4,106	4,729	5,163	4,846	5,555
$4,000–4,999	2,320	2,577	3,354	3,667	3,912	4,353	3,872	4,540
$5,000–5,999	2,247	2,494	3,128	3,402	3,551	3,936	3,607	4,257
$6,000–6,999	2,265	2,501	2,955	3,216	3,363	3,749	3,492	4,006
$7,000–9,999	2,042	2,361	2,777	3,031	3,307	3,618	3,426	3,871
$10,000–14,999	1,842	2,262	2,496	2,819	3,122	3,369	3,393	3,815
Over $15,000	1,983	2,281	2,572	2,826	2,723	3,030	3,232	3,552
	—	—	2,266	2,570	2,941	3,040	3,087	3,405

TABLE 1.—Continued

Family income	Age of women: 20–24 Per 1,000 wives	20–24 Per 1,000 mothers	25–29 Per 1,000 wives	25–29 Per 1,000 mothers	30–34 Per 1,000 wives	30–34 Per 1,000 mothers	35–39 Per 1,000 wives	35–39 Per 1,000 mothers
Wives in labor force								
White	775	1,625	1,530	2,188	2,044	2,519	2,203	2,609
Under $2,000	1,071	1,794	2,094	2,646	2,597	3,039	2,675	3,100
$2,000–3,999	964	1,712	1,978	2,421	2,476	2,853	2,554	2,968
$4,000–4,999	930	1,653	1,863	2,302	2,388	2,701	2,498	2,858
$5,000–5,999	888	1,651	1,796	2,263	2,315	2,648	2,419	2,733
$6,000–6,999	733	1,544	1,658	2,168	2,194	2,537	2,335	2,656
$7,000–9,999	522	1,516	1,282	2,032	1,901	2,384	2,111	2,506
$10,000–14,999	458	1,573	949	1,968	1,554	2,233	1,894	2,389
Over $15,000	625	1,810	1,146	2,074	1,653	2,417	1,943	2,469
Nonwhite	1,618	2,233	2,401	3,137	2,629	3,322	2,666	3,488
Under $2,000	1,990	2,588	2,938	3,611	3,677	4,501	3,586	4,624
$2,000–3,999	1,789	2,311	2,553	3,194	3,046	3,726	3,068	3,954
$4,000–4,999	1,605	2,168	2,359	2,952	2,601	3,312	2,665	3,514
$5,000–5,999	1,454	2,010	2,087	2,652	2,445	3,113	2,642	3,463
$6,000–6,999	1,309	2,028	1,773	2,420	2,181	2,850	2,330	3,130
$7,000–9,999	1,047	1,791	1,495	2,134	2,014	2,608	2,106	2,782
$10,000–14,999	949	1,793	1,313	2,098	1,808	2,396	1,974	2,574
Over $15,000	1,497	2,140	1,491	2,347	1,955	2,508	1,896	2,516

Source: Compiled and computed from U. S. Census of Population 1960, *Women by Number of Children Ever Born*, Final Report PC(2)3A, Table 38, pp. 187, 188.

The figures in Table 1 also show that the reproductive excess of the poor holds for wives *in* as well as *out* of the labor force. Labor-force participation is of course strongly associated with a lower rate of childbearing, both because sterile wives tend to work and because working wives tend to control conception. Statistically, the effect of sterility in the comparison can be partially overcome by considering only "mothers," but the fact that the wife's working contributes to the family income, and thus tends both to lift the family out of the "poverty" group and to lower the fertility, cannot be dealt with so easily. Yet it is significant that, for *mothers not in the labor force,* the poor still show an excess reproduction in just about as great a proportion as for mothers who *are* working:

Age group of "mothers"	*Percentage by which "under $2,000" group exceeds average of all income classes in children ever born*	
	White	*Nonwhite*
Not in labor force		
20–24	5.9	8.4
25–29	15.6	15.2
30–34	21.8	22.1
35–39	23.3	23.3
In labor force		
20–24	10.4	15.9
25–29	20.9	15.1
30–34	20.6	35.5
35–39	18.8	32.6

A substantial number of mothers, it seems, are working in the poorest class both because they have numerous children and because they are so desperately poor that, even with their earnings, the family income is slight. One effect of their above-average reproduction is doubtless to make the poor poorer. This is suggested by dividing the family income by the number of family members.[6]

[6] Computed from Bureau of the Census, *Trends in the Income of Families and Persons in the United States: 1947 to 1960,* Technical Paper No. 8 (Washington: Government Printing Office, 1963), p. 114. In computing the figure for the 6+ group, it was assumed that families with six or more children had, on the average, 7.6 children, since this was the figure found in *Women by Number of Children Ever Born,* p. 6.

Number of children	*Median income per member*
None	$2,536
1	1,897
2	1,497
3	1,206
4	935
5	702
6+	523

Unfortunately, these figures do not take account of age of parents. (If they did, they would show a sharper differential.) [7] This can be done in a rough way by assuming that the mid-point of the range for each income-class is the average for that class, and dividing it by the number of children ever born plus two (for the parents). When this is done for families in which the wife is aged 35 to 39, here are the results: [8]

Family-income class	*Income per person*
Under $2,000	282[a]
$2,000–3,999	594
$4,000–4,999	935
$5,000–5,999	1,159
$6,000–6,999	1,390
$7,000–9,999	1,883
$10,000–14,999	2,856
$15,000+	n.a.

[a] Average income taken as $1,500.

Between the "under $2,000" class and the $10,000–14,999 category, the spread in family income is 8.33 times as against a spread of 10.13 times in per-person income. If the family-size scale were reversed—that is, if the lowest income group had the small family-size of the top group and vice versa—the spread in per-person income would be 6.85 times instead of 10.13 times.

Excess reproduction in the poorest households tends to subject the next generation to poverty conditions in greater degree than is called for by the existing distribution of income. This fact can be seen more clearly if we take, not the income of

[7] The reason is that both income and number of children ever born tend to rise with age.

[8] *Women by Number of Children Ever Born,* Table 38, p. 188.

parents but their education. In 1960 the ever-married women aged 35 to 39, distributed according to their educational achievement, had borne the number of children shown in Table 2.

TABLE 2. EDUCATION OF WOMEN AGED 35 TO 39 EVER MARRIED COMPARED TO NUMBER OF CHILDREN EVER BORN, 1960

	Children born per	
Education of Women	*Woman*	*Mother*
None	2.9	4.7
Elementary		
1–4 Years	3.5	4.5
5–7 Years	3.2	3.9
8 Years	2.8	3.3
High School		
1–3 Years	2.6	3.1
4 Years	2.3	2.8
College		
1–3 Years	2.3	2.8
4 Years	2.2	2.7
5+ Years	1.5	2.5

Source: Computed from U. S. Census of Population, 1960, *Women by Number of Children Ever Born*, Final Report PC(2)3A, Table 25, p. 100.

With the exception of those ever-married women with no education at all (largely confined to the feebleminded in present-day society and tending not to stay married long) the average number of births declines steadily with education. This means that a disproportionate share of the next generation is being reared by the under-educated women of the present generation. Among the ever-married women aged 35 to 39 in 1960, 21.9 per cent had only an elementary education or less, but they had borne 26.4 per cent of the children reported for this cohort of women. On the other hand, the women with some college education comprised 16.4 per cent of the total in this age-group, but they had borne only 14.1 per cent of the children.

WHITE-NONWHITE COMPARISON

The connection of excess reproduction with poverty can be seen in another perspective by looking at disadvantaged groups.

For example, the Negro population in the United States has regularly had a higher birth rate than the white population and has shared in the general rise in the birth rate. In fact, in spite of improvement in relative education and relative income, the rise in its birth rate has been greater than that in the white population. This fact, together with greater gains in life-expectancy, has given the Negro population a rising superiority in replacement rate, as follows: [9]

	Net reproduction rate		*Nonwhite exceeds white*
	White	*Nonwhite*	*Per cent*
1935–39	.96	1.13	17.3
1940–44	1.12	1.29	15.3
1945–49	1.35	1.55	15.6
1950–54	1.50	1.91	27.1
1955–59	1.66	2.17	30.6
1960–62	1.63	2.07	27.2

During the last two and a half decades the nonwhite population has been bearing children at a rate which, if continued along with the existing mortality, would double its number each generation. If this group had a net reproduction rate 27 per cent *lower* than that of the white population, instead of 27 per cent *higher,* its average income per person would be raised by approximately one-third, other things being equal.

Of course, not all nonwhites in the United States are poor. In 1960 the proportion of nonwhite families receiving less than $2,000 per year was about 32 per cent.[10] This particular group, however, had an extremely high birth rate. In 1960 its wives aged 35 to 39 had borne an average of 4.4 children, as compared to 3.3 children for white wives in the same income class. (Since these are "wives" in the census, the data do not include illegitimate children; the latter, as we shall see

[9] For dates from 1935 to 1954, computed from Clyde V. Kiser, "Fertility Trends and Differentials among Nonwhites in the United States," *Milbank Memorial Fund Quarterly,* XXXIV (April, 1958), p. 154. For later dates, computed from *Population Index,* XXX (April, 1964), p. 273; and National Center for Health Statistics, "Natality Statistics Analysis, United States, 1962," Series 21, No. 1, p. 42.

[10] Census Bureau, "Income of Families and Persons in the United States: 1960," *Current Population Reports—Consumer Income,* Series P-60, No. 37 (July 17, 1962), p. 35. The figure for whites is 11 per cent.

in a moment, further burden the poorest section of the nonwhite population with children.) In fact, the differences in class fertility among nonwhites are greater than among whites. For wives aged 35 to 39 in 1960, for example, the differentials for the two groups were as follows: [11]

Income	*Children ever born*		*Index*	
	White	*Nonwhite*	*White*	*Nonwhite*
Under $2,000	3.32	4.43	100	100
$2,000–7,000	2.81	3.28	85	74
$7,000+	2.48	2.47	75	56

It is hard to avoid the conclusion that a factor in the poverty of low-income nonwhite families is their reproduction, and that one way in which upper-class nonwhite families achieve and maintain their status is by a low rate of reproduction.

A similar conclusion is reached by analysis of data on educational achievement. Below, for ever-married women aged 35 to 39, are the fertility comparisons from the 1960 census: [12]

Years of school completed	*Children ever born*		*Index*	
	White	*Nonwhite*	*White*	*Nonwhite*
None or 1–8 years elementary	3.13	3.71	100	100
1–4 years high school	2.53	2.82	81	76
1 or more years college	2.42	2.00	77	54

THE CIRCUMSTANCES OF REPRODUCTION: ILLEGITIMACY

The demographic disadvantage of the poor does not lie solely in the number of births but also in the circumstances surrounding reproduction. For instance, although we have talked so far about "wives" or "ever-married women" we know that illegitimate births are more numerous among the poor than among others. This is hard to document in a precise way, because there is little information on illegitimacy in the United States. Sixteen states—including some large ones like California and embracing more than 65 million, or a third of the nation's total population—gather no information on illegitimacy at all. Furthermore, a substantial but unknown portion of illegitimate

[11] *Women by Number of Children Ever Born,* Table 38, p. 188.
[12] *Ibid.,* Table 25, p. 100.

births are not recorded as such even in those states that do report.[13] Thus little can be said about the class incidence of illegitimacy.

Indicators, however, that illegitimacy occurs more frequently among the poor are as follows: (a) The percentage of babies weighing 2,500 grams or less is much higher for illegitimate than for legitimate births.[14] (b) An amazingly large number of illegitimate children are being cared for at public expense. Excluding those living with adopted parents, approximately 35 per cent of all illegitimate children in this country are recipients of public relief funds,[15] suggesting that the natural parents are poor, especially in view of the fact that only about three per cent of legitimate children are receiving public relief. An illegitimate child, if not adopted by other than his natural parents, is about ten times as likely as a legitimate child to be on relief. (c) The illegitimacy ratio is high for very young mothers. According to 1962 estimates, one out of every five illegitimate births occurs to a mother under 18, which means that for the most part conception took place prior to age 17, whereas only one out of 30 legitimate births occurs to a mother that young.[16]

---

[13] For instance, births to married women are often not reported as illegitimate even when the father is clearly not the woman's husband, much less when there is no external evidence that this is so. Some illegitimate births to unwed women are probably not recorded at all, and in others the fact of illegitimacy is concealed by one ruse or another. See National Office of Vital Statistics, "Illegitimate Births, 1938–1947," *Vital Statistics—Special Reports; Selected Studies,* Vol. 33, No. 5 (February 15, 1950), pp. 81–82; similar report for 1938–57, *ibid.,* Vol. 47, No. 8 (September 30, 1960), pp. 246–248.

[14] In 1955 the percentages were:

	Legitimate	*Illegitimate*
All births	7.2	13.0
White births	6.6	11.2
Nonwhite births	11.0	13.7

"Illegitimate Births: United States, 1938–57," *op. cit.,* p. 241.

[15] Derived from estimates by Helen E. Martz, "Illegitimacy and Dependency," Health, Education, and Welfare *Indicators* (September, 1963), p. xxiii.

[16] The percentage of legitimate births occurring to mothers under 18 is 3.3; illegitimate births, 20.9. Computed from National Vital Statistics Division, *Vital Statistics of the United States, 1962,* Vol. I—Natality, pp. 19, 79–81.

(d) An association of illegitimacy with poverty is further suggested by the fact that the nonwhite illegitimacy ratio is greater than the white. In 1962 nonwhites accounted for 11.6 per cent of the total U. S. population but for 61.2 per cent of the illegitimate births during that year.

If the indirect evidence is correct, it follows that illegitimacy is an aspect of reproduction which tends, in many cases at least, to complicate the lives of young people in poor families and to handicap them (as well as their parents in many cases) in their struggle to complete an education and get started economically. The illegitimate offspring in turn tend to receive deficient training and to perpetuate poverty.

A curious aspect of illegitimacy is that it is increasing. Thirty years ago one might have prophesied that illegitimacy would decline almost to the vanishing point in an advanced country such as the United States, where contraception is readily available, where marriage occurs early, and where there is considerable stigma attached to unwed motherhood. Yet the fact is that the estimated illegitimate births per 1,000 unmarried women aged 15 to 44 has tripled since 1940, rising from 7.1 in that year to 21.5 in 1962.[17] In the latter year the birth rate among unmarried women was more than one-seventh the rate (147.2) among married women. The ratio of illegitimate births to all births has also risen, though not so fast, since the proportion of the female population married has increased. The percentage of illegitimate births among all births rose from 3.8 in 1940 to 5.9 in 1962.

If one takes the women at younger ages, one finds that the

Age of mother	*Percentage of all live births illegitimate*
Under 15	74
15–19	16
20–29	4
30+	3

[17] National Center for Health Statistics, *Natality Statistics Analysis, United States, 1962,* Series 21, No. 1, p. 47.

ratio of illegitimate to legitimate births looms quite large. According to 1962 data, the ratios were shown on page 313.[18]

However, the fastest rise in the illegitimacy rate for unmarried women has not been at the younger ages but at ages 25–34. Comparing 1940 with 1962, we find the results shown in Table 3.

TABLE 3. ILLEGITIMATE BIRTHS PER 1,000 UNMARRIED WOMEN

Age	*1940*	*1962*	*1962 ÷ 1940*
15–19	7.4	14.9	2.0
20–24	9.5	41.8	4.4
25–29	7.2	46.4	6.4
30–34	5.1	27.0	5.3
35–39	3.4	13.5	4.0
40–44	1.2	3.4	2.8
Combined: 15–44	7.1	21.5	3.0

Source: National Center for Health Statistics, *Natality Statistics Analysis, U. S. 1962,* Series 21, No. 1, p. 47.

These figures imply that, although illegitimacy is a substantial problem among youth (as witness the fact alluded to above that 74 per cent of births to girls under 15, and 16 per cent to those aged 15 to 19, are illegitimate), it has been moving in a direction that suggests it is chronic in some strata. This is further shown by analysis of illegitimate births according to birth order. Between 1955 and 1962 the proportion of illegitimate births which were first births to the mother declined,

[18] The proportions are approximate. Illegitimate births by age of mother are available only for reporting areas. To get national estimates I assumed the same age distribution in the country as a whole as in reported figures. Computed from *Vital Statistics of the United States 1962,* Vol. I— Natality, pp. 1–45 and 1–120. Running the percentages the other way, we get the following:

Age	*Legitimate births*	*Illegitimate births*
Under 15	—[a]	2.2
15–19	12.9	39.2
20–29	60.7	44.7
30+	26.4	13.9
	100.0	100.0

[a] Less than one-half of one per cent.

while those which were of higher order, especially fifth or over, rose sharply: [19]

Births to mother	*Percentage of illegitimate births* 1947	1962
First		
White	73.7	62.6
Nonwhite	52.0	39.6
Second to fourth		
White	22.6	28.9
Nonwhite	37.8	39.0
Fifth and above		
White	3.6	8.2
Nonwhite	9.9	21.1

The rise in illegitimacy has been greater for nonwhites than for whites. For instance, the ratio and rate of illegitimacy changed by race as follows:

	Per 1,000 total births		*Per 1,000 unmarried women*	
	White	*Nonwhite*	*White*	*Nonwhite*
1940	19.5	168.3	3.6	35.6
1955	18.6	202.4	7.8	90.1
1962	27.5	229.9		

Neither the rise in illegitimacy nor the tendency for it to become chronic in some cases is helping the poor to cope with their circumstances. Since during this period the general level of living of all classes has been rising, there is little warrant for the claim advanced in a recent report by the U. S. Department of Health, Education, and Welfare that "evidence has mounted that economic improvement results in the adoption of new social patterns and standards of sexual behavior." [20]

EARLY MARRIAGE

Another complication of family formation more frequent among the poor is early marriage. This is more closely related to illegitimacy than one might think at first, because a good

[19] *Ibid.*, p. 51, and National Office of Vital Statistics, "Illegitimate Births: United States, 1938–56," *Vital Statistics—Special Reports, Selected Studies,* Vol. 47, No. 8 (September 30, 1960), p. 238.

[20] Marz, *op. cit.*, p. 28.

share of the early marriages are, like illegitimacy itself, a product of premarital conception. In other words, short of an abortion (spontaneous or induced), a pregnancy prior to wedlock can lead either to an illegitimate birth or to marriage. That marriages have been getting more youthful in the United States at the same time that the illegitimacy rate has been rising suggests either that premarital conception has been sizably on the increase or that abortion has been declining.

If children born prior to eight months after marriage are defined as conceived before wedlock, the rate of premarital conception has apparently been rising. Rele finds the following among white women: [21]

Period of first marriage	*First births within eight months or less per 1,000 ever-married women*
1900–09	74
1910–19	89
1920–24	83
1925–29	81
1930–34	90
1935–39	86
1940–44	80
1945–49	103
1950–54	119
1955–59	160

During this half century the age at marriage has generally tended to decline.[22]

The United States now has the lowest age at marriage of any industrially developed nation. That some of these marriages

	Median age, first marriage	
	Grooms	*Brides*
1920	24.6	21.2
1930	24.3	21.3
1940	24.3	21.5
1950	22.8	20.3
1960	22.8	20.3
1962	22.7	20.3

[21] J. R. Rele, "Some Correlates of the Age at Marriage," *Eugenics Quarterly,* XXXXIII (April, 1965.)

[22] Bureau of the Census, *Statistical Abstract of the United States,* 1963, p. 70.

are brought on prematurely by premarital pregnancy seems probable. The results given above are confirmed by additional studies done in recent years. Harold Christenson, for example, by linking marriage and birth registrations, finds that at least 12 per cent of the first births are premaritally conceived in Utah and 19.8 per cent in Ohio.[23] Monahan has found, for domestic court cases in Philadelphia in 1954, an average of 20.1 per cent of white couples pregnant before first marriage and 45.6 per cent of Negro couples.[24]

By taking all first births and assuming a fifth of these to be premaritally conceived, we can add these to the illegitimate births to get what may be called a "social tragedy conception rate"—that is, the rate of conceptions prior to marriage which lead either to an illegitimate birth or a forced marriage. This rate in 1962 was more than double the illegitimacy rate—being 47.5 per 1,000 unmarried women as against 21.5 for illegitimate births. The legitimate birth rate necessarily drops somewhat by this calculation, the ratio of legitimate to illegitimate births becoming more nearly equal. Of course, this rate does not measure premarital conceptions per se. Undoubtedly, a high proportion of such conceptions end in abortions, although nobody knows what the proportion actually is.

Monahan discovered that, among his cases, the rate of premarital pregnancy varied according to past mobility. For the white couples, the highest rate was for those born in Philadelphia but married elsewhere (presumably they left town to get married quickly—possibly in Maryland); for Negroes the highest rate was for those marriages in which both parties were born in Philadelphia itself, and the lowest was for both parties born in the South and married in the South. His figures are shown at the top of page 318.[25]

Monahan's data afford no confirmation of the theory that illegitimacy is a rural "culture pattern," or that it is inherited

[23] Harold Christenson, "Child Spanning Analysis Via Record Linkage: New Data Plus a Summing Up from Earlier Reports," *Marriage and Family Living,* XXV (August, 1963), pp. 273, 274.

[24] Thomas P. Monahan, "Premarital Pregnancy in the United States," *Eugenics Quarterly,* VII (September, 1960), pp. 133–147.

[25] *Ibid.,* p. 141.

	Percentage of couples with premarital pregnancy	
	White	*Nonwhite*
Both parties born in Philadelphia		61.0
Married in Philadelphia	19.5	
Married elsewhere	26.6	
One party born in Philadelphia	17.6	
Spouse not born in South		47.2
One party born in South, but spouse not born in South		49.0
Both parties born in the South		
Married in the South		33.6
Married elsewhere		44.9
Both born outside Philadelphia	17.9	

from the South "because of slavery" or is a hangover from a prior regime. It is an urban phenomenon flourishing in all sections and reflecting the social conditions of the nation with the world's highest standard of living.

Monahan also discovered that, among his domestic relations cases, premarital pregnancy was highest for those marriages in which the wife was very young (see Table 4). For Negroes the

TABLE 4. PREMARITAL PREGNANCY BY AGE AT MARRIAGE OF WIFE,[a] PHILADELPHIA, 1954

Age of wife at marriage	*Per cent pregnant before marriage*	
	Whites	*Negroes*
Total	20.1	45.6
Under 16	(29.5)	54.4
16	26.1	59.0
17	28.1	52.2
18	23.3	56.8
19	22.4	44.0
20	17.0	40.9
21	18.2	39.4
22	16.2	39.4
23	(14.4)	(25.0)
24	(15.6)	(26.5)
25–29	12.4	31.9
30+	(16.7)	(23.4)

[a] Primary marriages. Percentages based on fewer than 100 cases are shown in parentheses.

Source: Thomas P. Monahan, "Premarital Pregnancy in the United States," *Eugenics Quarterly*, VII (September, 1960), p. 140.

marriages in which the bride was under 19 years old were forced marriages in more than half the cases; for whites, those in which the bride was under 20 were forced in more than a fifth of the cases.

An early age at marriage is associated with a low educational level when, as has been done in our research office,[26] we correct for the trend in educational achievement of the population as a whole. Also, the earlier the marriage, the higher the fertility of that marriage tends to be for any given duration of marriage. Furthermore, early marriages tend to reduce the labor-force participation of women in two ways: first, single women have substantially higher participation rates compared to their married counterparts, age by age, except for those below 18. Second, those who marry earlier, especially before age 21, experience comparatively much lower participation in the labor force during their first five years of marriage than do those who marry later. This loss of the working power of the wife among poor families is a contribution to poverty, as well as the cost of the extra children. When we add that premature marriage is an important cause of school dropouts among high school and college students, especially among women, we can see a further disadvantage.

CONCLUSION

It still seems true in the United States that the poor are poor in part because they have too many children. In addition they have them under circumstances that further damage their own and their children's opportunities. This is seen particularly with reference to illegitimacy and early and forced marriage.

---

[26] Rele, *op. cit.*

PART EIGHT

URBAN RENEWAL POLICIES

22. Poverty in America--the Role of Urban Renewal

ROBERT C. WEAVER

"Poverty," said that Shavian humanitarian and munitions maker, Andrew Undershaft, "is the worst of crimes."

This being the case, we have some 9.3 million such so-called criminal families in the United States today, and over five million of these are living in cities. The impoverished have been historically the city's most enduring trademark. The poor have helped build cities, and they have despoiled them. Most important, though, the poor have been the main object of the democratic city's greatest purpose: to provide the fullest opportunities for the civilization of man.

The American city has, on the whole, performed this civilizing function rather well. It has escalated millions of immigrants to relative affluence, or at least to considerably better conditions of living than could have been hoped for in the "old country." But, in recent years, we have come to see that this historic role of the city has deteriorated badly. Its humanizing function seems to have broken down. In some cities neighborhood blight and poverty have existed, hand-in-hand, for three generations or more. And for the people involved, escape from the slum and the clutch of impoverishment no longer seems likely. The slums have become ingrown, their denizens increasingly isolated—through lack of education, skills, and opportunities—from the growing affluence of the larger society.

These conditions afflict particularly groups of the impoverished who labor under special difficulties—nonwhites, the elderly, and the handicapped. Since the end of World War II, with the acceleration of the suburban exodus and expanding affluence of most of society, the poor have increasingly become impacted into large central city areas. The reasons for this—available housing, mass transportation, and a broader range of job opportunities—are the same reasons which have traditionally kept the poor in the slums, but there were some significant differences. For one thing, the city slums began to collect an increasing number of nonwhites. The postwar immigration to central cities from small towns and rural areas clogged older central areas with millions of families and individuals in search of the same dream which had drawn earlier immigrants—opportunity for a better life.

The types of obstacles which the nonwhite immigrant encountered were more severe and enduring than those met—and often superseded—by his predecessors. The deadly barriers of prejudice and discrimination have trapped the nonwhite poor in ghettos just as surely as barbed wire.

During the postwar period, while most of America grew more prosperous, the cities continued to catch the residue of those at the tail end of the affluence parade, or out of it altogether: a large proportion of the Negroes and Puerto Ricans, the elderly, and the handicapped. The only group, for instance, which did not show a decline in impoverishment (as measured by income of $3,000 in constant dollars) during the postwar years were the elderly. And, while the number of poor white families declined by 27 per cent from 1947 to 1962, the number of poor nonwhite families declined a bare three per cent.

A particularly related statistic is that while the number of poor families with male heads of the household decreased by 30 per cent in the 15 years after 1947, those poor families with *female* heads of household actually increased by 19 per cent. Situations where mother is the only breadwinner—and these are much more common, relatively, among nonwhite than white families—or on relief, represent the fastest-growing sector of poverty in the nation. And this has been happening at a time when the total number of poor families has been declining from 32 per cent of all families to only 20 per cent.

Within a few short years after World War II, it was apparent that cities were in serious trouble. The path to affluence seemed to head right into suburbia, and millions of aspiring white families took it. The slums—which had never been an unbearable burden on the American conscience anyway—proliferated, and the city's physical condition decayed in consonance with its fiscal condition.

In fact, the city became caught in its own particular cycle of poverty. As the middle-income white families left and were replaced by lower-income families, real estate values—and the subsequent municipal tax take—dropped, and the city's capacity to meet its economic problems declined, too. As municipal services and particularly schools deteriorated, more middle-class families were motivated to leave. And so it went.

URBAN RENEWAL

In the midst of these massive geographic and economic shifts, the Federal Government proposed a new solution to the slum problem—urban renewal. Basically, the Housing Act of 1949 made funds available to cities for the acquisition and clearance of slum properties and the resale of the cleared land to private builders who would redevelop such land according to a publicly conceived and approved plan.

The slum clearance and rehousing approach had its roots in the public housing program enacted in 1937. With this program, the Federal Government proclaimed its intention to get rid of bad housing, and reconstruct new housing which low-income families could afford. Although the program was born in the midst of a period when the nation's social consciousness was particularly active, it was sold also as a public works endeavor. It seemed, even in the bloom of New Deal idealism, that the nation could not bring itself to embrace the notion that clearing slums and rehousing the poor was in and of itself reason enough for public housing.

Public housing was just gathering steam when World War II came, and our efforts were turned to defense living. After the war, public housing continued to be opposed by the private building industry. So, the thought naturally arose to harness private industry to the social objectives of clearing slums through urban renewal.

Within urban renewal's first five years, it was apparent that there was more to this than met the eye. Most of the early projects were started in or near the worst slums. Most of these slums were heavily Negro or, in the case of New York, also Puerto Rican. These areas were not only about the worst, but they were often easier to handle than other, more affluent neighborhoods. For the newer breed of urban poor had been remarkably quiet. They were not likely to fight city hall. And, for a while at least, they didn't.

At the same time, the desperate need for more city tax revenues pressed cities to strain for high-value land uses. This translated into high-priced housing, or at least housing priced well above the capacity of neighboring residents to pay. Even when, as in Chicago and Washington, the original redevelopment plans specified moderate-income housing, there were no effective financial tools to facilitate it. The anomalies inherent in this situation did not escape the urban poor. With public housing, at least there resulted, after slums were cleared, housing which was within the means of the poor. But this new business knocked down the slums and then rebuilt for the class which needed it least—the affluent.

This is, of course, an over-simplification. But it was nevertheless the urban renewal image. And it is this image which we must understand and deal with today, when our whole approach is so very different from what it was then. But before I get to that, we should consider for a moment the repercussions of those earliest renewal efforts upon the poor.

The most important effect renewal had upon the city's poor was to identify them. Not that people didn't know where the poor lived—slums *are* pretty visible even though commuters headed for the suburbs try to hide behind their newspapers. This country has generally not become preoccupied with the problems of the poor, although there have been occasions when a Jacob Riis or Jane Addams could stir strong reform sentiment. By and large, though, the nation's guilt about its poverty-stricken has been assuaged by simply sweeping them under the rug—into the slums.

But urban renewal lifted the edge of the rug; it helped identify the poor in several ways:

1. By delineating impoverished neighborhoods for municipal action.
2. By displacing impoverished families.
3. By attempting to relocate these families into decent housing.
4. By rebuilding renewal areas for families or individuals who are, by and large, not poor.

An under-appreciated facet of renewal's role in identifying the poor has been simply this: urban renewal was the first federal program which promised to find better homes for those families displaced by government action.

In our democratic tradition, governments are conscious of such public promises, and the people have a way of guaranteeing their enforcement. In fact, urban renewal's record in this regard is unique and outstanding. Reports from all cities with federally backed renewal programs have indicated that the great majority of families moved out of renewal areas were located into decent housing.

To check further the progress that is being made in this regard, the Housing and Home Finance Agency contracted with an outside agency for a new relocation survey, which is not completed. With the results of this study, we and the public have a sound basis upon which the current practices and consequences of relocation in urban renewal can be evaluated.

In the summer of 1964, the U. S. Bureau of the Census attempted to interview all families relocated by urban renewal in cities having such relocation as a consequence of projects going into execution in 1962 and 1963. Some 2,840 families were involved—about 60 per cent of all those relocated by urban renewal during the summer of 1964. Of the 2,840 families in the sample, 2,300 were interviewed by the Bureau of the Census —the remainder had moved from the city, could not be located, or refused to respond. Of those interviewed, 94 per cent had been relocated in standard housing. But the study also showed that relocatees often pay higher rents in their new quarters. This is precisely why President Johnson proposed, and the Congress enacted last year, relocation adjustment payments to displaced families of modest means.

Relocation, in identifying the problems of the urban poor, showed us that, unless renewal considered more than real property, it could never be wholly successful. It became obvious that unless the program could reclaim the human spirit, as well as the land, it could not play its proper role; it could never live up to that promise, enunciated so ringingly in 1949, of a "decent home and suitable living environment for every American family."

It obviously was not enough simply to raise the quality of a poor family's living accommodations. This is a must, but it is not the whole story. These suspicions have been verified by several studies, carried out with public housing residents. One such study, for instance, showed that whereas public housing residents often feel that their position in life is improved due to their better living quarters, their aspirations for their and their children's future are not necessarily raised.

If other conditions of life—low income, disorganized family situations, and problems of physical or mental handicap—continue to be the same, then better housing can only ameliorate these conditions, but hardly abolish them.

At the same time that these human considerations were increasingly impinging upon the urban renewal program, other things were happening which we realize today constituted a revolutionary reorganization of American society.

For one thing, the civil rights movement suddenly came alive. Its leadership impressed, with vivid strokes, the absolute necessity for equality upon the American consciousness. More important, that American consciousness reacted, through its legislators and civic leaders, and—catching the cry for equality—echoed it back in the form of landmark legislation. Tremendous legislative strides were taken in a few short years.

The verve and drama of the civil rights movement swept over some of our city slums last summer. We saw peaceful demonstrations as well as violence. We saw hoodlums, Negro and white, prey upon the situation with calculated ruthlessness. But through it all, I think most of us saw that progress was being made. Civil rights, equality before the law, are far from a full-fledged reality in every "Middlesex village and town," but the American people, Negro and white, know it is coming. You will get few arguments on that point. The arguments turn over whether or not the revolution is happening fast enough.

Just as better housing is not the whole answer to rooting out poverty, neither are civil rights. Freedom to stay poor is no freedom at all. Or, as a young Harlem man put it, "What does it mean to be integrated into poverty?"

And so we must have better housing, we must eliminate slum living. And we must have equality for all citizens before the law. But that is still not the whole story on poverty. The most critical need remains: the need to maximize human opportunities. Or, sticking to urban renewal terms, the need to restore fully the city's primary function: the fullest opportunities for the civilization of man.

THE GRAY AREAS PROGRAM

Just about the time that the federal urban renewal program was entering its second decade, several cities deeply involved in the program began to devise the means for expanding opportunities. In Oakland, California, New Haven, Connecticut, and a few other cities, perceptive men began to dig away at the root causes of poverty and slum living. These were men who had worked hard in urban renewal, and learned well its strengths and weaknesses. For financial aid, they turned to a great nonprofit institution, the Ford Foundation. Other benefits aside, this threw a powerful new force into the battle against slums and poverty.

The Gray Areas program of the Ford Foundation set the pattern for what is called today the war against poverty. It called for all the institutional forces of the city—private and public alike—to rally together in that conflict. The ultimate objective: to break the deadly poverty cycle.

Not surprisingly, the program gave priority to young people. Job clinics were established to find work for those under 25 or so, and to train them. In the case of many dropouts, they were encouraged to finish high school, while still holding jobs. The key to success was quickly found to rest with developing aspirations—give a young person a meaningful, realizable goal to shoot for, and watch him (or her) succeed. These young people were not trained in skills alone. They were made to realize their value to the larger community.

While programs of job opportunities, schooling, and training proceeded with young men and women, other programs were engineered for the very young. Educators had learned that many dropouts suffer primarily from a low learning capacity. By second or third grade, it was already obvious that some children simply were not going to learn very much. Most tragically, in the overcrowded classrooms characteristic of impoverished neighborhoods, many overworked teachers simply gave up on such children.

The new approach aimed to solve this problem by catching the child when he or she is very young, well before kindergarten age. Three- and four-year-olds were placed on an experimental basis, into "learning situations." Tots, not long out of crib and cradle, were read to and permitted a wide variety of self-expression in art, music, and speaking. Much of what happens in these sessions seems shockingly rudimentary. But for many of these children, the book in teacher's hands is the first one they have ever seen in use. Out of these classrooms, hundreds of small children are already taking the first uncertain steps away from the poverty cycle.

There is another aspect of the pre-kindergarten schooling I should mention. In New Haven, Boston, and other cities, the parents are very much a part of this approach. Teachers and parents meet weekly, discuss the children or just general problems. Many teachers serve coffee and cookies. The atmosphere is relaxed. The child sees its parent and its teacher talking together, enjoying the chance. It is the sort of thing, the psychologists tell us, that children long remember.

Moreover, the parents learn, too. For some of them, it is the first time in a school since *they* dropped out. The lesson of the role education plays in shaking off the chains of impoverishment is not usually lost on them.

There are many other aspects to the Gray Areas approach—special aids to fight juvenile delinquency, providing legal assistance to the poor, promoting special activities for the elderly and handicapped. These programs are, at the local level, usually engineered and operated by existing social service agencies. In some cases, new agencies have been established.

The Gray Areas approach pointed squarely at erasing the causes of poverty. It established the pattern for the federal program which followed. Last year, the Congress passed the Economic Opportunity Act, which threw the weight of the federal government into the war against poverty on a much broader scale than ever before. Not only were new programs enacted to attack the causes of poverty, but the new Office of Economic Opportunity became a rallying point around which many other programs—of several federal departments and agencies—could form up for a concerted assault.

With the establishment of OEO, the Federal Government announced its purpose to deal comprehensively with the total urban environment. The social as well as the physical fabric of cities would be repaired—and, indeed, must be repaired—if cities are to function at the highest level.

Last year, our housing programs reflected the impact of the anti-poverty approach. For one thing, relocation payments were increased and, perhaps even more important, a new element was introduced into the whole notion of relocation aids. For the first time, the federal government provided supplemental rent payments for up to one year for relocated families or individuals in need. Also, special urban renewal demonstration programs in Pittsburgh and New York are helping identify the problems and potential solutions for families to be relocated in large areas of those two cities.

URBAN REHABILITATION

Another important feature of the "new look" in renewal is the increased emphasis on rehabilitation, with a new program of special, low-interest loans for homeowners and renters alike. Although funds were not authorized for the administration of this program last year, President Johnson has requested that Congress provide appropriations for the rest of this year as well as 1966.

Rehabilitation in the most impoverished areas of large cities continues to be a major difficulty. Now, with community action programs being initiated in those areas, we shall have to bend our efforts—federal and local, public and private—to provide higher housing quality. The new programs will help. And some other approaches, which I shall mention in a moment, should also get us closer to our goal of providing decent housing to *every* American family and individual, regardless of income.

In this regard, I think a slight digression on the workings of the housing market is in order. Recently, we have been pressing for more low and moderate income housing on urban renewal sites. In this regard, the program of below-market interest rate loans, called Section 221(d)(3), has been markedly successful. At interest rates of 3⅞ per cent and 40-year mortgages, this housing is built to rent for $15 to $20 per month less than corresponding homes built with typical FHA financing.

This housing is obviously still above the economic reach of the very poor or the lower moderate-income sector of the market. But we have recently had some insights into the workings of the housing market which lead us to believe that such housing can be of decided help to poor families. This is not to say that the old filter-down theory, in its pure form, works. The unqualified premise that any new housing can, after sufficient depreciation, serve as decent housing for the poor has been discredited by experience. By the time this housing is "depreciated" enough to get its cost down to where the poor can afford it, it is pretty terrible housing.

But if new output is priced fairly close to what the poor are paying for their bad housing, then you are likely to get some families moving out to the newer supply and consequently loosening up the older supply. This process involves a relatively brief period of time and is quite different from the old-fashioned filter-down theory. It seems to be working.

New Directions

Today, urban renewal and other housing and community development programs are working with anti-poverty programs to provide a comprehensive approach to the problems of the poor. I think I can best illustrate the comprehensiveness of the approach by telling you something about the new directions we contemplate in federal programs for housing and urban development.

In the first place, we do not intend to stop repairing the city's physical condition just because we have learned that such action alone will not solve all our problems. The fact is that we must prosecute the physical rebuilding of our cities more vigorously than ever. But we must be more careful about what we build and where we build it. Obviously the market for high-priced apartments is not unlimited. And certainly such housing does not provide for the poor.

But there must be much more new housing production in our cities, and we shall propose programs to accomplish this. There must also be a higher order of rehabilitation—more production, as well as more realistic standards. We must make a more pronounced effort at code enforcement, as a means of upgrading the quality of the housing stock. Now, under urban renewal, cities can declare large areas to be code enforcement areas, and receive federal aid for their upgrading.

For new housing aimed at moderate- and low-income families, we shall develop a new program of rent supplements. We also propose to step up the public housing program and make much more use of existing units for low-income families. This will ameliorate the problems of finding large sites for new construction and also provide a more flexible supply of subsidized housing. It will also provide low-rent housing more quickly than can new construction.

Public housing can serve the poor in ways other than simply giving them a roof over their heads. We have initiated a program, on an experimental basis, of concerted social services in public housing projects. Through this program, we have brought badly needed social services to poor families, the elderly, and the handicapped. And we intend to expand these efforts.

Largely through our urban renewal experience, we have learned the vital role that sound neighborhood facilities can play in the redevelopment of old sections. One of the earliest such projects was in the Wooster Square of New Haven, where a community center was established in an urban renewal area stressing rehabilitation. I might remind you again that this pioneering project occurred in a city with a long renewal history—and the same city which was among the first to realize the need for a broad-gauge attack on social as well as physical problems.

So we shall propose direct capital grants for neighborhood facilities to serve the gray areas and districts where the anti-poverty programs are operating.

Other new programs will be recommended by President Johnson to improve the physical condition and enhance the beauty of neighborhoods in our cities. Obviously, such activities mean little without coincident attention to expanding job opportunities and educational training, but now we are proceeding on all these fronts.

Conclusion

There can be no Great Society if any significant portion of our population continues to suffer want and impoverishment. The expansion of opportunities which will lead us to the goal of a Great Society can only come through a concerted attack upon the social as well as the physical disorder which blight our cities. Such an attack is now being mounted, and the urban renewal program plays a key role.

I shall not, in closing, have the temerity to predict the utter abolition of poverty in this nation in the foreseeable future. Earlier seers are still choking on such high-flown predictions as "No slums in ten years."

These objectives which we have set for ourselves will take unremitting effort. They shall have to be prosecuted just as we prosecute war. The analogy is apt.

And Oliver Wendell Holmes has provided us with some guidelines for war, which are particularly appropriate:

> To fight out a war, you must believe something and want something with all your might. . . . More than that, you must be willing to commit yourself to a course, perhaps a long and hard one, without being able to foresee exactly where you will come out.

23. Social Action Programs in Urban Renewal

BERNARD E. LOSHBOUGH

In laying the groundwork for this discussion of "Social Action Programs in Urban Renewal," I will state immediately my conviction, based on ACTION-Housing's experience in Pittsburgh, that a social action program needs to engage both the resources of the city and the energetic participation of the neighborhood people. Without both elements, a social action program cannot be effective.

People need to understand and desire renewal and development of their neighborhood before the undertaking of large programs. This is a business-like approach to problems. The first step in engaging participation and developing understanding is the drawing up of a balance sheet of community assets and liabilities, a balance sheet to be made by the neighborhood people concerned, with professional guidance. Short-range goals must be established, as well as long-range goals reaching many years ahead.

Then comes the formulation of a detailed physical plan, hammered out building by building and area by area in partnership with the Urban Redevelopment Authority, City Planning Department, Board of Public Education, Public Health, local businessmen, and residents. It must fit into comprehensive planning for the over-all metropolis.

Concurrently, it is necessary to develop an over-all, workable social plan, taking into account the economic status and basic needs of the people, and placing particular emphasis upon education in the broadest sense, opening up and training for employment opportunities, and widening of cultural horizons.

Today, social action programs can be soundly and realistically based. Money and tools for detailed physical planning are available through governmental urban renewal. For the first time, money and tools for wide-scale social planning can be attained through the Economic Opportunity Act of 1964.

Today's citizens are faced with a host of confusing urban problems, with little faith in their ability as individuals to solve them. Through social action, urban renewal and war on poverty programs, the citizens, who are the consumers of public and private services, can find the allies and resources to meet the problems. In the process, they can be armed with the sophistication and the knowledge of the proper channels through which to utilize the public and private resources available. Their first need is for information and guidance, followed by joint action with their fellow citizens.

This intensive participation of all neighborhood people, including the poverty-stricken, is basic to the success of any social action program. People themselves must take part in planning, decision-making and implementation of programs for their own betterment, or we may end up with modern, antiseptic cities and alienated people.

This participation, with co-related aid from education, government, foundations, private enterprise, social agencies and other institutions, is what Pittsburgh's ACTION-Housing has been striving to bring about for the past six years through a community development process. This process is called Neighborhood Urban Extension.

It is one of a number of approaches to social action that have emerged in the United States and have been and are being tested under operating conditions.

THE GRAY AREAS PROGRAM

Through the "Gray Areas Program," the Ford Foundation has given financial assistance to experiments in a number of cities, including Boston, New Haven, Washington, D. C., Philadelphia, and Oakland, California; and also in one state, North Carolina, where the concern includes rural problems. Although it provides grant funds to these programs, the Ford Foundation does not enter into selection of staff, administration, or methodology. This autonomy gives operating responsibility to the grantee, where it should be, and allows for testing of various methods in various cities.

The approach is one of systems analysis and "social invention," in the words of the Foundation's Director of Public Affairs, Dr. Paul Ylvisaker. It places "the Foundation's first bet on the city's school system, and more on school outlook methods than on buildings; on employment systems; administration of justice; and a growing list of similarly critical production processes which are currently bottlenecks in the process of citizen building."

The courage and foresight of the Foundation in funneling $15 million into these projects over several years has been of great significance to urban development in the United States. It has jolted public indifference to urban problems, and, I would venture to speculate, greatly accelerated the formulation and passage of the Economic Opportunity Act of 1964.

These Gray Area projects are operated by a new kind of urban organization, a melding of the public and private sectors, called "half-way houses," on whose boards sit public officials, high-level representatives of commerce and industry, and other civic leaders. In these cities local philanthropy also has been active.

Careful research and professional planning are done by staff specialists, and imaginative efforts are undertaken to modernize school systems, streamline employment services, and rejuvenate other urban resources. In most project areas, particularly in Boston and New Haven, this social development program goes hand-in-hand with massive urban renewal, and in most of the communities there have been some impressive changes in urban institutions and creation of effective new services. However, the governing philosophy is usually to work with and strengthen existing agencies, rather than to replace them.

These Gray Area projects, which usually encourage the formation, cooperation and support of citizen groups, are making creative and substantive contributions to urban renewal and development. The projects have concentrated on changing and improving the concept and performance of executive agencies—public and private—which already had public mandates and acceptance; for example, mayors, governors, school boards, and the like.

Two Other Approaches

Another approach is New York City's neighborhood conservation program, which involves direct action by city government. Localized planning and expanded services are brought to the people out of "neighborhood city halls."[1]

In New York City, a settlement house, church, hospital, or university is asked to co-sponsor the program in each neighborhood—and even to take over the program after it is well under way. The intent is to provide large-scale housing, code enforcement, narcotics control, family welfare, recreation, and other services as needed. This approach has been particularly successful in improving the social and physical health of Chelsea, Bloomingdale, and Morningside.

Chicago has the Industrial Areas Foundation, which has organized thousands of citizens to do their own planning and to use their power to obtain the services they need. This approach uses protest methods to the point of conflict, such as marching, picketing, packing city council hearings, and the like. It, too, has produced some good results.

Neighborhood Urban Extension

Pittsburgh has ACTION-Housing's Neighborhood Urban Extension approach through which, I believe, we are finding a way to enlist both people and resources in effective programs of social action.

Neighborhood Urban Extension derives much of its philosophy and methodology from agricultural extension techniques developed more than 50 years ago in the United States under the direction of M. L. Wilson.[2]

ACTION-Housing defines this approach as follows:

> Neighborhood Urban Extension is a planning-education-action process for vitalizing and revitalizing urban areas through extension of

[1] An Interim Report on Neighborhood Conservation in New York City, The Housing and Redevelopment Board, City of New York, June, 1963.

[2] M. L. Wilson, Retired Administrator of Agricultural Extension and former Assistant Secretary, U. S. Department of Agriculture, Washington, D. C.

the resources of the metropolis to the people of neighborhoods who are alerted and assisted to utilize these resources in programs to help themselves achieve a better living environment.[3]

My own four years of work in the community development programs of rural India convinced me of the need for involvement of people in planning social action programs for urban America. Planning for neighborhood urban extension in Pittsburgh began back in 1959. It included short-term action-research projects and conferences, with citizens, as well as specialists and officials, many from the Ford Foundation, participating from the beginning.

Numerous conferences and meetings were held with local officials, national and international specialists in community development, members of citizens' councils, settlement house officials, officials of the Pennsylvania State Agricultural Extension Service, and other educators from major universities throughout the country.

Eleven action-research projects of six weeks' duration included home making, parent-school relations, neighborhood business, home modernization, church-community relations, and a neighborhood youth corps, and were carried out with citizens in a number of neighborhoods in 1962. Programs in both cities were studied. In one declining old neighborhood in Pittsburgh, where neighborhood leaders had been asking ACTION-Housing for assistance, a comprehensive pilot program was carried out for three years.

Based on this preparation, a full-scale, five-year demonstration was begun in 1963 in three large Pittsburgh neighborhoods. The Ford Foundation has granted a total of $475,000 for the five-year demonstration in the three neighborhoods, an amount more than matched by grants from Pittsburgh foundations and corporations and from the neighborhood people themselves, making a total of more than $1 million.

ACTION-Housing, as an across-the-board civic organization with representation of powerful interests and considerable city

---

[3] Plan of Operations, Neighborhood Urban Extension, Pittsburgh, March, 1963.

and county backing, regardless of political affiliation, mobilizes the resources of the city so that they become available to neighborhood people. Citizen groups in the neighborhood determine their own needs, do their own planning, establish relations with the resources that can meet their needs, and get them extended into the neighborhood, where they are coordinated and utilized. Citizens are assisted to organize, plan, and act by neighborhood extension workers supplied by ACTION-Housing and other public and private agencies' staffs, with subject-matter specialists.

The relationship between ACTION-Housing and the citizen group in each neighborhood is delineated by a signed agreement which specifies mutual goals, and the responsibilities and rights of each party. The written agreement provides for joint decisions on planning and programming, and for joint financing of the program. Both parties enter the relationship freely and voluntarily. The heart of the relationship is the written agreement.

Before any worker is hired and assigned to a neighborhood, he is interviewed by citizen leaders. If they have valid objections, he is not hired. The final decision, however, rests with the Executive Director of ACTION-Housing.

This demonstration is now in its third year in two of the three neighborhoods, and in its fifth in the other. Many hundreds of citizens participate diligently in planning, decision-making, and action in each of the three neighborhoods.

These citizen councils act with great independence, having regular and direct negotiations with department heads, the Mayor's Office, City Council, and other officials. Their method is one of harmonious cooperation when possible, but militant action when absolutely necessary. This was the case last summer when, after years of broken promises from Pennsylvania's Highways Department concerning the building of a new bridge, and many fruitless negotiations, housewives and men of one neighborhood blockaded the old bridge for weeks and forced the State to act. The bridge is now being built.

Similarly, following repeated charges of laxity in law enforcement made by a neighborhood urban extension council, the Mayor of our City has asked the International Association of

Chiefs of Police to undertake a "comprehensive study into all phases of Police Bureau administration" in Pittsburgh.

Militant action by these Pittsburgh citizens councils is a method to be used on occasion, rather than a permanent operating philosophy. The Neighborhood Urban Extension approach is one of "consensus" rather than one of pre-determined and inevitable conflict.

CONSENSUS—A SPRINGBOARD

As President Johnson observed, in a scantly publicized speech last month:

> A consensus can produce varied results. Consensus can become a comfortable cushion on which a nation simply goes to sleep. Consensus can also be an active, dynamic, rolling credo. It can be a springboard, providing a take-off for resolute action toward generally agreed upon goals.

In planning, decision-making and prompt implementation, Neighborhood Urban Extension works to create such a consensus of all the neighborhood people, including the hard-core poverty-stricken, government, universities and public and private school systems, commerce and industry, churches, social agencies, and the other major urban resources.

At a Ford Foundation conference I attended in December, Jack Conway, now the Deputy Director of the Office of Economic Opportunity, stated:

There are three basic strengths for a Community Action Program—

1) Strong public commitment,
2) Involvement of the private community, including business, labor and civil rights groups, and
3) Involvement of the poor themselves.

He predicted, "Without participation of the poor this Program will not be a success."

ACTION-Housing's experience bears out another contention that is coming to be widely recognized. This is that social and economic issues cannot be separated. The nurturing of social responsibilities goes hand-in-hand with the development of a sound economy.

In times past, slums in the United States, made up largely of successive waves of millions of immigrants, were not the nearly hopeless traps they have become in recent years. Poverty, hunger, discrimination, and intolerable conditions were prevalent, certainly. Although the aged, for the most part, accepted their lot, they worked and prayed for their children. For the ambitious, energetic youth, there usually was opportunity to set forth and find employment and decent housing elsewhere than in the slums—in a country that was building and expanding, with some pauses, in every direction. Many of these sons and daughters of immigrants have become the professional, political, and business leaders of modern times.

In recent years, racial discrimination and radical technological changes have fundamentally worsened the situation in the blighted, gray areas and slums of our inner cities. Today, the future of the untrained, deprived white dropout seems bleak enough, but if such a youth's skin also happens to be black, there may seem to be no way out.

As a large proportion of middle and moderate income families have rushed out to suburbia, large areas of our inner cities have become festering reservations of the unskilled and helpless. The functionally illiterate, the apathetic aged, the displaced victims of a rapidly industrializing society, racketeers, dope pushers, and delinquents, are crowded into an environment of inadequate, deteriorating housing in neighborhoods deficient in educational, social and recreational facilities.

This describes, in general, two of the three large Pittsburgh neighborhoods in which ACTION-Housing's Neighborhood Urban Extension process is being demonstrated. In one neighborhood, incidentally, the population is 70 per cent Negro, many of whom are citizens with highly developed educational and professional qualifications as well as adequate means. But others have all the problems that emerge from neglect, deprivation and poverty.

Pittsburgh is almost across the continent from California. Few persons here can be expected to know intimately the neighborhoods concerned and their special circumstances and problems. It, therefore, would be inappropriate and time-wasting for me to attempt to itemize in detail the activities of the neighborhood extension councils over the past years. Instead, I will summarize their major accomplishments, with reference to the difficulties faced, and then try to illustrate with a few brief examples what these social action programs have meant to all the participants, particularly to the neighborhood people themselves.

ACCOMPLISHMENTS

All three neighborhoods are well along in comprehensive physical and social planning. In one, the people themselves, with the support of local industry, hired their own professional planner, and after three years of seeking agreements and threshing out details in cooperation with the City Planning Department, the plan was approved by Pittsburgh's City Council and is now being implemented. It calls for the razing of some 2,000 houses, all this decided by the residents and owners and others concerned. It becomes a part of the over-all Pittsburgh Community Renewal Program being developed by the City. It includes a $3-million, 96-acre, 27-block conservation project being worked out by the Urban Redevelopment Authority, with the aid of federal and city financing—the first such urban renewal project in the city putting major emphasis upon modernization rather than clearance.

In the same neighborhood, to implement this over-all physical plan, the Citizens Renewal Council has worked for months, with the cooperation of the City Planning Department, to obtain badly needed zoning changes. Last month, Pittsburgh's City Council approved these drastic zoning changes, which had been the subject of long controversy and struggle. In certain key areas, where conflict might later have arisen, these changes, in effect, assure that the general physical plan for the neighborhood, developed by a consensus of the neighborhood and city planning, will be adhered to. In these areas any new building or rebuilding must conform to the plan.

Each neighborhood has had and is conducting massive housing code enforcement campaigns, obtaining cooperation from the County Health Department, and a high percentage of voluntary compliance. The citizens' councils have made appearances before City Council against slum landlord practices. Although much remains to be done, many abandoned and dilapidated houses have been razed, and there has been some alleviation of overcrowded tenement housing.

Committees of the councils have been instrumental, with substantial cooperation from local government, in obtaining improved and broadened public services, notably in the areas of police and fire protection, removal of abandoned automobiles, better lighting, repair and cleaning of streets, more attention to sewage problems. Contracts were signed recently by the University of Pittsburgh's Institute of Local Government, ACTION-Housing, and a neighborhood for a ten-month program which should produce an over-all plan for model public services for the community. This contract has the approval of the Mayor's Office.

Pittsburgh's major universities, the Board of Public Education and the parochial school system have been represented from the beginning by leading educators consulting on the over-all program, and have participated, usually under contract, in aiding in the carrying out of many of its important phases. There are such programs as the following:

1) Tutorial courses in remedial reading and motivation for elementary school children, staffed by hundreds of volunteer high school and college students, and now on a year-round basis in several public and parochial schools.
2) Courses in merchandising and marketing for neighborhood merchants.
3) In-the-home day-care for pre-school children of working mothers.
4) Home economics courses for housewives.
5) Research projects in evaluation and the role of the churches in urban renewal.
6) Extension courses leading to diplomas for high school drop-outs.
7) And a number of others.

The councils have worked with the Board of Public Education in determining sites for new school buildings, as well as obtaining temporary demountable school classrooms to meet emergency situations.

For the past several years, the councils and their employment committees have pioneered in retraining and placement of the unemployed. In two of the neighborhoods, employment centers, staffed by professionals and aided by the Federal Government and the State Bureau of Employment Security, have been established in convenient locations. Through volunteer counselors, neighborhood people who know the problems, more than 1,500 of the unemployed have registered and have received counseling. Some have found jobs on their own. Approximately 200 actually have been placed in jobs, and hundreds more are finishing or are entering upon retraining courses in such fields as hospital aides and dieticians, research technicians, and machine tool workers.

However, training for employment is often an uphill job. Among its other training programs, ACTION-Housing is now in its eighth month of carrying out a Special Group Manpower Demonstration Project under contract with the Office of Manpower, Automation and Training of the United States Department of Labor. This demonstration project proposes to test the practicality of training young men, grade school graduates between the ages of 17 and 22, for placement in jobs as research aides and service station mechanic-attendant-dealers. As a further purpose, it tests the effectiveness of the neighborhood-based employment centers and volunteer counselors.

These men are residents of two of the declining Pittsburgh neighborhoods, mostly hard-core unemployed, half of whom are married and half single, few with more than an eighth grade education, many with racial frustrations, heavy marital obligations, police records—though often for minor infractions—and little previous job experience.

In this special group, the preliminary findings have been that many of the young men are hostile to school authority, unpunctual, even afraid to work. Often they are unable to adjust to classroom teaching methods and drop out. Some just don't know what they want to do; some just become belligerent at being told what to do; some indicate a fear of going through the training, working hard to finish, then finding themselves still on the jobless rolls. Some dropped out, however, because they found other jobs, in a climate where unemployment has declined in Pittsburgh, though this may be a temporary situation.

There seems to be a need for intensive changing of attitudes, perhaps through pre-training work in the neighborhoods. The volunteer counselors are proving their worth, particularly in recruiting and in stimulating trainees to attend the courses. Some trainees have completed their courses and have been placed. One young man wrote to his neighborhood volunteer counselor:

> I would like to extend a sincere thanks for my training and employment. It's a rewarding thought to know such an organization as yours exists, that will turn despair into hope.

This summation, which recounts only the high spots of the Neighborhood Urban Extension demonstration, may afford some indication of its scope.

As Pittsburgh's Mayor Joseph M. Barr has said:

> I am not reluctant to acknowledge that Pittsburgh's Community Action Program, which was one of the first funded under the Anti-Poverty Program and which Federal officials have indicated is sound in concept, borrowed heavily from the Ford-sponsored urban extension program run by ACTION-Housing in this city.

INSIGHTS

However, for deeper insights into the meaning and value of this comprehensive social action program, it may serve well to cite a few examples of participation, such as:

> The experience of one man who had worked for 23 years to end an overflowing sewage problem which had damaged his house and those of his neighbors. When a block club was organized, one of hundreds which are active, the whole matter was satisfactorily resolved, and new sewer lines put in, in a matter of months. Since the offending sewer lines were on private property, individual families had to be persuaded to invest $600 each to repair the sewer and end the nuisance.
>
> The white realtor, head of the planning committee in a predominantly Negro neighborhood, who invested his own money to buy up two rows of dilapidated houses, landscaped and placed a

courtyard between them, rewired, installed new doors, windows, plumbing and kitchen facilities, repainted, and now rents these two-bedroom modernized houses at rentals between $65 and $75 per month. It is not unusual in Pittsburgh to pay $90 per month rent for slum dwellings of the same size.

The personnel director of a large steel company and the head of the local steelworkers union who worked together supplying space and training for the volunteer counselors who have been instrumental in placing of unemployed in retraining and jobs.

The neighborhood volunteer counselor who not only aided a number of people in the evenings on his own time, but who made it a point to call at the house of one notoriously absent trainee every morning to see that he got off to class.

The volunteer college student tutor who told of her three slow-learner elementary school pupils phoning her and coming to her house at odd hours for story reading, and her remark that, "these children don't need a teacher; they need a friend."

The neighborhood owner who was inspired to modernize his house and who told of how his nearby neighbors all followed suit.

The 15 young women, all without previous training or work skills, who braved Pittsburgh's worst snowstorm of last winter to attend the opening class in machine shop skills, held many miles from their homes. Incidentally, all but two of these girls finished the course. The two dropouts found jobs in the meantime. However, these girls, all Negro, have had difficulty in finding jobs in the field in which they were trained.

There is evidence that, with proper organization and guidance, social action programs in which the people themselves participate can do much to bring about the revitalizing of the declining neighborhoods of the inner city, if they utilize and coordinate all the resources of the community, particularly education. However, the key to effectiveness is the local leadership and active participation of the people themselves, and their desire for a better way of life.

In his Special Message to Congress of February 9, 1965, President Johnson said:

> I have recommended a community extension program which will bring the resources of the university to focus on problems of the community just as they have long been concerned with rural areas.

Among other things this program will help provide training and technical assistance to aid in making our communities more attractive and vital.

In the three Pittsburgh neighborhoods, ACTION-Housing has, in effect, been acting as the extension arm of our universities in some phases of urban renewal and development, notably in social action programs. With the support of private enterprise, public and private agencies, and a broad panel of civic leaders, it has been engaged in pioneering its own war on poverty since 1959. It has been most active more recently in setting up programs, under contract, with the Office of Manpower, Automation and Training, and last week signed contracts with the Mayor's Committee on Human Resources, Inc., which has received a major grant to carry out Pittsburgh's Community Action Program under the Economic Opportunity Action.

No city has exactly the same problem, but it is hoped that ACTION-Housing's experience in the evolving of the Neighborhood Urban Extension process will be useful to this Conference and to other cities throughout the nation in formulating and developing programs of social action in urban renewal and development. It is not only the poverty-stricken and the people of the gray areas, but all the citizens of our urban areas who will benefit from effective social action programs.

In conclusion, I am reminded of the remark made by the president of one of Pittsburgh's largest corporations, with plants all over the world, who inquired about the progress of Neighborhood Urban Extension. When told, he made this pronouncement: "If such programs as these can't succeed, our economy—indeed our entire society—is in deep trouble."

24. Relocation—Opportunity or Liability?

PHILIP M. HAUSER AND MARY B. WIRTH

The free enterprise system has provided the American people with the highest mass level of living in the history of man. This achievement, however, has not been without its problems and costs. Among these has been the propagation of the slum and the slum-dweller. Through the process of urban growth in the United States, inner and older zones of cities, housing lower-income families, have become progressively obsolescent and blighted.

The lower-income families have characteristically included newcomers to the urban community, as well as that part of the older resident population which, because of various types of handicaps or deficiencies, fared badly in the competitive American society. The newcomers were mainly foreign immigrants largely from Northern and Western Europe during the nineteenth century and, after the turn of the century, from Southern and Eastern Europe. In more recent decades, the newcomers to metropolitan areas have been primarily in-migrants from rural and nonmetropolitan areas—including the Negro, the Appalachian White and, most recently, the American Indian. They have, however, also included immigrants from Mexico and migrants from Puerto Rico.

Prior to the emergence of relocation services by government or private agencies, slum dwellers who were able to escape their poverty relocated themselves. Or, it may be said, relocation was effected through the process of competition, which among other things, involved competition for the more desirable residential locations and housing. As immigrants and in-migrants acquired literacy and education and obtained better jobs and renumeration, they were able, family by family, to improve their residential location and the quality of their housing. This process constitutes in fact, an important part of the history of this nation and represents a significant element in this country's contribution to the story of man. For the process of the "Americanization" of the immigrant and the acculturation of the in-migrant in our urban areas embodies what may well be the two major contributions of the United States to the history of man. These are the achievement of unity out of diversity and the demonstration of an open society—one in which successive newcomer groups have, from humble beginnings, been able to rise in the economic, social, and political orders, subject to limits set only by their own individual capabilities.

To be sure, the slum dwellers also included a "hard-core" precipitate of the handicapped or defective—a conspicuous example of whom were the residents of skid rows. But, until recently, this hard core seemed to constitute a relatively small proportion of the population. The chronically poor were regarded as virtually a part of the natural order and were ignored once their base subsistence needs were met through the resources of private or public agencies.

In the postwar world, a number of developments combined to break down the traditional competitive method of effecting the relocation of newcomers resident in our urban slums.

First must be mentioned the unprecedented magnitude of in-migration to urban areas during World War II and its aftermath. Second, the newcomers were disproportionately a different racial group—the Negro. He was not only highly visible upon his arrival but he also remained visible in subsequent generations. Third, the Negro in-migrant, by reason of his opportunity-deprived past in this nation, often lacked the incentives and motivation to get ahead found among the immigrants. For the latter came largely from culturally intact backgrounds embodying varying but, usually, well-defined goals.

In addition to these changes in magnitude and type of migration, there were also economic, social, and political developments which led to the abandonment of the traditional competitive system of relocating slum dwellers. These included: (1) accelerating technological advance which increasingly displaced human labor, especially unskilled labor; (2) increased urban demolition for highways, expressways, parking lots, and other requirements of the automobile, and for public works in general—schools, parks, playgrounds, etc.; (3) the emergence of public housing and urban renewal programs as slums became a matter of national and international disgrace and entered national politics. They included, also, (4) the impact of Franklin D. Roosevelt's "New Deal" which made the nation welfare and security conscious; (5) the increasing educational level of the American people; (6) the changing attitude of the American people toward the Negro—increasing recognition of his qualities as a human being and increasing guilt feelings about the injustices to which he had been subjected in his history in the United States. These types of developments, together with the increasing urbanization of the Negro (from 73 per cent rural in 1910 to 73 per cent urban in 1960), the emergence of a sizable Negro middle class, and the growing political consciousness of the Negro community culminating in "the Negro revolt," have drastically altered the process and problems of relocation.

Initially the postwar developments created the specter of a caste-society emergent in the United States, manifest in a new urban structure—an inner core of slum inhabited by the in-migrant Negro and an outer core of middle and upper income white population. With the passage of time, however, the developments outlined generated new forces to cope with the new and unprecedented problems. These included public housing and urban renewal and related programs on the physical side; and, also, many social and economic programs consolidated now in President Johnson's anti-poverty program—projects for education, rehabilitation, retraining, and the general civil rights program. The relocation function is to be understood as an element in the emergent new concept of "social renewal" to accompany physical urban renewal. Relocation as a public function is to be understood against these perspectives—and only in this light can relocation be considered as suggested in the title assigned to this paper—that is, as "opportunity" or "liability."

The Relocation Process

Relocation has emerged as a function of public agencies because government has undertaken to raze our inherited slums and to renew our cities. These objectives embodied in urban renewal and related programs required demolition of residential structures and, therefore, the clearing of sites of all human inhabitants. Site clearance dislocated families *en masse* and created problems of mass relocation.

The history of relocation began in the early 1930's with the clearances under the Public Works Administration. It continued through World War II when clearance was necessary for war workers and for public housing sites; and through the 1950's and 1960's for slum clearance and conservation projects. The Federal Housing Act of 1949 set the standard by making the approval of federal funds dependent upon the adequacy of the supply of housing for those displaced. They were to be placed into "decent, safe and sanitary housing in areas not generally less desirable in regard to public utilities and public facilities, within their financial means and reasonably accessible to their places of employment." The act of 1949 has been amended to meet many of the problems which were encountered—in 1950, 1954, 1962, and 1964. That is, as we gained experience and knowledge, the laws were changed to meet the new needs.

Although the principle of public responsibility for the relocation of families displaced by governmental activities emerged early, a full understanding of the extent and complexity of the relocation process was slow to develop. The goal as stated in the Housing Act of 1949 has been difficult to achieve. The reason for this may be perceived by first examining the relocation process.

In general, the process of relocating families and individuals by governmental action, as carried on by a special staff assigned for this specific purpose can be described as follows:

1. Surveys and home visits are made to answer questions about the reasons for the clearance, to give information about the time allowed for relocation, to indicate what the legal rights

of tenants are and what financial assistance they may have. In continuing visits and interviews it is ascertained what the housing needs and desires are—what the economic and the social status is, and eventually, with the assistance of specialists in various fields, an evaluation of the social situation is made.

2. Since the relocation assignment to move families into "decent, safe housing in good neighborhoods" is interpreted to mean "into standard housing" which is usually described by the housing and zoning codes, it is also necessary to convince the slum dweller of the desirability of living in standard housing. It is necessary to tell him what it is, help him look for it, and generally be available to him for a given period of time while his problems are complicated by the necessity of moving.

3. Records are kept and reports made on the details of inspection, supervision of moving, payment of cost of moving, and the results achieved.

PROBLEMS OF RELOCATION

It is not possible to separate the problems faced by relocation agencies from the whole renewal process. Failure in relocation may result from inadequate planning on the part of city officials many years earlier; or from lack of knowledge and training in a new field of endeavor.

The first obvious fact—sometimes arrived at too late—is that there must be adequate available standard housing—at the time the clearance begins. This means that the estimates made at the time of the conception of the program must be accurate. Federal and local renewal agencies are giving more attention to improving these estimates, planning new housing in advance of clearance, or in providing for the rehabilitation of areas without clearance. There are indications that the requirements of the "Workable Program" are being met more conscientiously each year. The technical difficulties of forecasting reliable displacement projections over uniform time intervals are great and complicated. Cities must assess the adequacy of the housing supply to meet the anticipated demand for housing resulting from governmental displacement in competition with the normal nondisplacement demand, plan new housing or improved housing if there is a shortage, and establish comprehensive relocation programs. Moreover, they must stimulate special programs for providing such social assistance as may be required well in advance of any clearance. In assessing the adequacy of housing, the cities must face the fact squarely that there are at least two housing markets, white and nonwhite, and often a third housing market—that in the suburbs.

In many cases, enthusiasm for launching new projects, whether expressway, public works, or urban renewal, has led to widespread demolition without adequate regard for the problem of relocation. Without question the most serious and numerous complaints about relocation have resulted from the deficiency in the supply of adequate standard housing into which to place dislocated families.

Under the requirements of the "Workable Program," however, this enthusiastic approach to improvement without adequate planning is less likely to occur. Moreover, aside from the federal requirements that have to do with the allotment of funds to the local communities, there are other safeguards. It is becoming increasingly difficult to secure official city approval for any project for the use of public funds for any kind of development such as highways, parks, schools or renewal, without community approval and active community participation. Neighborhood agencies and organizations are alert to their needs and more experienced in presenting their cases to the city fathers. The best sounding plans can fail to get off the ground, for example, if the local community refuses approval because there is "no place for people to move" or because their moving will be likely to have "an unfavorable impact on adjacent communities." Public protest undoubtedly slowed up the approval of many improvement schemes but has produced increased community participation in, and understanding of, the entire program, from the planning through the clearance process.

Experience shows that one of the most frequent sources of criticism is the impact of relocatees on the communities to which they move. Although very little information is available on the matter, it appears that in the past relocation agencies have not seriously attempted to avoid the overcrowding of the receiving communities. In Chicago, we can say that in the third large clearance on the south side of the city some families were relocated who had been previously relocated from both the first and second clearances. The problems which have been created and the studies that have been made are bringing about a more cautious and reasoned approach to this problem.

The fact that different levels of government are involved in clearance and relocation has also created difficulties. Not only do procedures vary from state to state and city to city, but within cities separate agencies relocate families for the various programs. In Chicago, a bureau under the City's Housing Coordinator was responsible for the first clearance for the highways. The Housing Authority had its own relocation unit for the clearance of its own sites. The Land Clearance Commission cleared sites for the first big renewal projects and, finally, the Conservation Board got into the act for its program.

There were demands in Chicago, and across the country in many other cities, for a centralized relocation service with uniform regulations and procedures. By 1959, a number of centralized relocation departments had been set up. There were usually a few hold-outs—agencies or authorities that would not amalgamate.

Even when there was a central or combined service established, however, uniform procedures did not necessarily follow. The problem that gave the most concern in poverty stricken areas or slums was the variation, depending upon the sponsorship, in the amount of money available to displaced persons and families for moving expenses, loss or damage of property, utility deposits, and other expenses connected with moving. There was no federal money for the payments to families displaced for highways. Moreover, since highways ran through the state, county, and city areas, each level of government had different arrangements on the same highway. Many large cities, to make the relocation process more successful, added financial aid to that provided by the federal government. The relocation personnel in Chicago, for example, looked with envy upon New York City's report on the relocation of the first 500 families for the clearance of the Lincoln Center of the Performing Arts. There have been instances of the payment of bonuses to families for moving quickly, payment of rent in new quarters, cleaning and decorating of the new location, money paid to real estate agents as "finding fees," as well as the regular moving costs. While it is true that money cannot buy happiness, it is generally conceded that it helps. This seemed to have been proven by the fact that, the more money spent in payments to relocatees, the fewer were the complaints about the forced moves.

Other problems have arisen from variations in record keeping and reports. The Urban Renewal Administration requires a continuing report on the moves into substandard or undesirable housing. In order to make such reports the local housing agencies must keep a close watch on the displaced families' moves; assist in finding suitable housing; inspect vacancies before making referrals; inspect housing units after, as well as before, move-ins; know the housing and zoning laws; and report on the results of the program. Hundreds of thousands of people, however, have been moved in this country to make way for the auto and the highway without any reporting on where or how they were relocated—since that program was not conducted under the Housing Acts of Congress. The laws have been changed recently to make money available to the local agencies clearing for highways, but it is necessary for the various states to pass enabling legislation. Thus far, this has not been done in many states.

These problems are among those which have generated criticisms of the relocation programs. But the laws have been amended as governmental agencies and legislators have been persuaded to deal with them. Furthermore, a wealth of objective studies, reports, and recommendations are appearing every year which give rise at least to the hope that these types of problems will be solved as they are better understood.

The major problem of relocation, however, transcending all other problems, derives from the fact that relocation involves more than physical moving from a substandard to, presumably, a standard housing unit. Relocation necessarily involves social, as well as physical, uprooting.

THE SOCIAL PROBLEM

From the beginning of the Urban Renewal Program, there were many who felt the need for trained social workers in the relocation process. Opinions on this, however, varied. Some administrators were interested only in site clearance. They believed that social workers would delay clearances by taking too much time on individual social problems. Other administrators, however, felt that the whole relocation process should be a social service task.

Certainly, it is clear that site clearance necessitated dislocation of families—families that were disproportionately in the lower-income brackets, including those in the poverty category. Hence, it was not surprising, as experience itself has indicated, that the dislocated population consisted often of "problem families." The experience of relocation agencies has indicated that the displaced families fall mainly into the following four categories:

1. Families with inadequate financial support.

This group includes most of the families living on relief budgets, the unemployed, unemployable, unskilled, and broken families without male breadwinners. These families range from those with little or no income to family groups on a full public assistance budget.

2. Families with health problems.

These families contain persons who are seriously ill, chronically ill, or physically handicapped, including those who are emotionally or mentally handicapped.

3. Families in need of protective services.

This group includes families with criminals, drug addicts, abandoned and neglected children, illegitimate children, and the like.

4. Families with problems of old age.

These families include persons who need nursing home care or companionship and friends; or persons who require special kinds of housing units, in special areas; or persons needing special medical care for diseases of old age.

Dislocation, added to the other problems of families in bulldozed areas, may sometimes tip the scale to the breaking point for many families in which relationships are already precarious. Every relocation office has records showing "breakup of the family group" as the end of the relocation process. Even for relatively well established families, relocation is a difficult experience. It is a traumatic experience for the elderly, destroys the roots of ethnic groups, requires new adjustments on the part of all family members, and exaggerates whatever problems may already exist.

As a result, the mistake has often been made of attributing the problems which exist among the slum families to the need for relocation. The relocation process does not create the problems that affect these families; it merely uncovers them. Their problems have been developing for many years. Often social service agencies have been working for 20 to 30 years with some of the families—sometimes with their parents and even their grandparents. Many of these problem situations have not only been known for many years, but, also, they represent the "consolidated failures" of the agencies and the community. Some of the problems of these families have been dormant, and erupt again in the period of stress occasioned by moving. Some problems are, of course, uncovered for the first time. There are relocation records showing that children have been mistreated or neglected for years, and only the forced move to other quarters brought the situation to the attention of the courts for placement of the children in foster homes or in institutions.

A problem deserving of special attention, and of growing concern is that relating to the relocation of elderly people. Ten years ago this concern was centered in the planning, architecture, construction, management, and maintenance of projects. Now the social and personal problems of the aged are in the limelight. Relocation experience has helped to point out not only the residential needs of the elderly but, also, their personal and social problems.

Similarly, relocation discloses the many problems of small businesses, the specific problems of ethnic and racial groups. In general relocation discloses almost always, for slum families, the need for social services and medical care.

In view of the above, the need for social workers in relocation is obvious. Even in the cities where it is difficult to secure trained social service staff, it is possible to follow social work advice and techniques. Among the many things that the social workers can ascertain are answers to such questions as: How deep are the people's roots in the area to be cleared? Is it a neighborhood of an ethnic group with attachments to certain schools and churches? Is it segregated racially? How long have they lived there? Do they appear to be eligible for public housing and what is their attitude toward public housing? Are they employed or are they receiving some form of aid? Do they need and want assistance in finding a place to move? Are they home owners or tenants?

Some relocatees have a life centered around the institutions of the neighborhood. But others have only been living in site areas because they could do no better for themselves. Some have the kind of social and health problems that make it difficult to relocate them into any good area. The problems proliferate, and trained personnel is required to find solutions—long-run solutions as well as immediate emergency solutions requiring the assistance of community welfare agencies and health and protective groups.

In the cities in which social problems of slum clearance were acute, services of social workers, either in supervisory or field work, have been incorporated into the relocation program. It is not surprising, however, that in many areas relocation workers turned out to be untrained, political appointees, sometimes uneducated and often underpaid. The acquisition and retention of personnel with knowledge and experience in housing and relocation has become a serious problem. Moreover, it is often impossible to control renewal projects so that there is no lag between developments. At one period a city may be in need of a large number of social workers and, in between projects, there may be little for them to do. As the work load decreases or the money runs out, the experienced staff moves on, and the process of recruitment and training must begin over again for a new program. Certain it is that the work of relocating families may often be among the most complex of the tasks that the trained social worker may be called upon to perform.

THE RACIAL PROBLEM

The problems of relocation are greatly exacerbated when compounded by the problem of race—as they are in most of metropolitan United States. As has been indicated above, among the newest newcomers to urban and metropolitan slum areas, and the most visible and numerous, are Negroes. Like other newcomer groups, the Negro has found the inner, older, blighted zones of the city his port of entry and area of first settlement. Because slum clearance, urban renewal, and other clearance projects have developed chiefly since large-scale Negro inmigration began, it is the Negro who is typically bearing the brunt of the displacement and who is disproportionately the relocatee. Thus, added to all the other problems of relocation, physical and social, are the problems generated by racial prejudice. This is why urban renewal has often been labeled "Negro removal."

That the Negro's burdens have been greatly increased by reason of urban renewal and other relocation programs cannot be denied. Moreover, it is also clear that the unsatisfactory relocation of Negroes who have been uprooted constitutes perhaps the most conspicuous failure of the entire program. That is, even though Negroes have admittedly achieved better housing by reason of the public housing and urban renewal programs, they have also paid a fearful price in being physically and socially uprooted and relocated, sometimes more than once; and in being concentrated, in many cities, in large and segregated public housing units, which, while they have solved some physical problems, have created monstrous social problems. Certainly the concentration of segregated high-rise public housing, such as that along State Street in Chicago, constitutes one of the most dramatic and conspicuous failures of the effort physically to renew the city. It represents a solid and lasting monument to the prejudices and shortsightedness of the American people and their political leaders.

Yet, to acknowledge this is not to hold that the entire effect of urban renewal and public housing was negative—even from the standpoint of the Negro. The alternative of no urban renewal, no public housing, and no dislocation would not have led to less segregation, and it most certainly would have doomed the poor Negro to perpetual residence in slums. Moreover, it would have doomed our cities to perpetually decayed inner cores. There can be no justification for condemning public housing, urban renewal, and other clearance programs by reason of the inept form that public housing took for the Negro; and by reason of our having failed, thus far, to utilize the urban renewal program to effect integration and to build better social communities. The alternative of stopping urban renewal and other clearance projects and cutting back public housing would be much worse than even the evils we have created for our cities and for the nation as a whole, as well as for the Negro.

The Challenge to Our Society

The need for the relocation of families has been a by-product of efforts to achieve other objectives—largely the physical planning objectives of urban renewal or expressway and public works construction. The relocation process, however, has itself posed major social problems by uncovering the sorry accumulation of personal, familial, and societal failures over the years. Moreover, the clumsy handling of relocation has opened up an urban Pandora's box of unprecedented proportions.

In uncovering the social problems glossed over and ignored over the years, relocation is presenting unprecedented opportunity for our society to deal with its accumulated failures. In part, the most difficult problems of relocation are the best indexes of the opportunity that is ours. Just as exploratory surgery points to incipient fatal disease, so the relocation process points to mortal threats to our society. It is ironic, indeed, that the physical planner, often oblivious of the social consequences of his planning, should have forced upon us the need for social planning through his efforts to rid the urban area of its physical blight.

The personal, family, and racial problems unveiled in the relocation process are almost always associated with poverty. For that reason the problems of relocation have a special significance at the present time. In the United States, for the first time in human history, we have conjured up an image of a "great society" in which poverty and its concomitants will be eliminated. It is generally agreed that the United States is the first major nation with the technological and economic ability to justify the fixing of such an objective.

Relocation must then be regarded as opportunity rather than liability in forcing us to face our accumulated social, as well as physical, problems. Far from interpreting the problems of relocation as evidence of failure of urban renewal, public housing, and related programs, we should be utilizing the experience we have gained to date to avoid repeating the mistakes we have already made and, in due course, to undo those mistakes. The vision of the great society, founded as it must be on the elimination of poverty, necessarily requires the linking of physical and social planning, to the end that social as well as physical slums are eliminated. It holds forth the vista of a society which continues to achieve unity despite diversity—a pluralistic social order in which integration is achieved across social, as well as religious and economic differences; and in which real equality of opportunity will enable us to demonstrate that our society can continue as an open society for all within its boundaries.

SELECTED BIBLIOGRAPHY

Abrahamson, Julia. *A Neighborhood Finds Itself.* New York: Harper and Brothers, 1959.

Abrams, Charles. *Forbidden Neighbors.* New York: Harper and Brothers, 1955.

American City, "Relocation is Not a Numbers Game" (October, 1956).

Anderson, Martin. *The Federal Bulldozer, A Critical Analysis of Urban Renewal, 1949–1962.* Cambridge: Massachusetts Institute of Technology Press, 1964.

Aronovici, Carol. *Housing the Masses.* New York: John Wiley & Sons, Inc., 1939.

Baker, Carolyn E., Marcella C. Blaetus, *et al. Relocation: People and Problems.* Howard University, M.S.W. dissertation, June, 1960.

Baltimore Urban Renewal and Housing Agency. *The New Locations and Housing Characteristics of Families Displaced from Area 3-C.* Baltimore, Maryland: March 1961.

Bauer, Catherine. *Social Question in Housing and Town Planning.* London: University of London Press, Ltd., 1952. Also appears in "Social Questions in Housing and Community Planning," *Journal of Social Issues,* VII (1951), pp. 1–34.

Buell, Bradley, and Associates. *Community Planning for Human Services.* New York: Columbia University Press, 1962.

Carpenter, William, The Pittsburgh Plate Glass Foundation. *What Our Cities Need Most: Brains.* New York: 1963. Available from Action, Inc., New York.

Chicago Urban League, "Urban Renewal," pp. 11–12 of the *Negro in Chicago.* (Chicago: Chicago Urban League, August 1961).

Colborn, Fern M. *The Neighborhood and Urban Renewal.* New York: National Federation of Settlements and Neighborhood Centers, 1963.

Community Service Society of New York, Committee on Housing. *Not Without Hope, A Report and Recommendations on Family Relocation.* New York: March 1958.

Community Surveys, Inc. *Redevelopment, Some Human Gains and Losses.* Indianapolis, Indiana: February 1956.

District of Columbia Redevelopment Land Agency. *Community Services and Family Relocation.* Washington, D. C.: 1964.

Drake, St. Clair, and Horace R. Cayton. *Black Metropolis.* New York: Harcourt, Brace & Company, 1945.

Dudley, Otis, and Beverly Duncan. *The Negro Population of Chicago.* Chicago: University of Chicago Press, 1957.

Duncan, Beverly, and Philip M. Hauser. *Housing a Metropolis—Chicago.* Glencoe, Ill.: The Free Press, 1960.

Federal Housing Administration. *An Evaluation of the Section 221 Relocation Housing Program.* Washington, D. C.: December 1959.

Fiser, Webb S. *Mastery of the Metropolis.* Englewood Cliffs, N. J.: Prentice-Hall, 1962.

Gans, Herbert J., "The Human Implications of Current Redevelopment and Relocation Planning," *Journal of the American Institute of Planners,* XXV (February, 1959), pp. 15–25.

Handlin, Oscar. *The Uprooted.* Boston: Little, Brown & Company, 1951.

———. *Race and Nationality in American Life.* New York: Doubleday & Company, 1957.

———. *The Newcomers.* Cambridge: Harvard University Press, 1959.

Hauser, Philip M. *Population Perspectives.* New Brunswick, N. J.: Rutgers University Press, 1960.

Hemdahl, Ruel. *Urban Renewal.* New York: The Scarecrow Press, 1959.

Housing and Home Finance Agency. *Federal Laws—Urban Renewal,* Excerpts from Housing Act of 1949 and Related Laws as Amended through June 30, 1961. Washington, D. C.: 1961.

Hudson Guild Neighborhood House and New York University Center for Human Relations and Community Studies. *Human Relations in Chelsea, 1960.* Report of the Chelsea Housing and Human Relations Cooperative Project.

Institute for Urban Studies, University of Pennsylvania, and National Association of Housing and Redevelopment Officials. *Essays on the Problems Faced in the Relocation of Elderly Persons.* National Association of Housing and Redevelopment Officials: June 1963.

Jacobs, Jane. *The Life and Death of Great American Cities.* New York: Random House, 1961.

Lanpher, Henry Coe. *Welfare Aspects of Housing.* Virginia: Alexandria Community Welfare Council, March 1962.

Lichfield, Nathaniel, "Relocation: The Impact on Housing Welfare," *Journal of the American Institute of Planners,* XXVII (August, 1961), pp. 119–203.

Lieberson, Stanley. *Ethnic Patterns in American Cities.* Glencoe, Ill.: The Free Press, 1963.

Mackelmann, D. C. *Recommendations on Relocation.* Chicago: City of Chicago, Office of the Housing and Redevelopment Coordinator, 1950.

McEntire, Davis. *Residence and Race,* Final and Comprehensive Report to the Commission on Race and Housing. Berkeley: University of California Press, 1960.

Meltzer, Jack, and Sheilah Orloff, "Relocation of Families Displaced in Urban Redevelopment: Experience in Chicago," pp. 407–459 of Coleman Woodbury, editor, *Urban Redevelopment: Problems and Practices.* Chicago: University of Chicago Press, 1955.

Metropolitan Housing and Planning Council. *Housing the Economically and Socially Disadvantaged Groups in the Population, Recommendations.* Chicago, Ill.: January 1961.

Meyerson, Martin. *Politics, Planning and Public Interest: The Case of Public Housing in Chicago.* Glencoe, Ill.: The Free Press, 1955.

Montgomery, Dorothy S., "Relocation and Its Impact on Families," *Social Casework* (October, 1960), pp. 402–407.

National Association of Housing and Redevelopment Officials, *Saving Cities Through Conservation and Rehabilitation.* NAHRO Publication N 391, August 1961.

National Association of Housing and Redevelopment Officials in Cooperation with the Urban Renewal Administration, Housing and Home Finance Agency. *Community Renewal Program Experience in Ten Cities.* NAHRO Publication N 480, August 1964.

Panuch, Anthony J. *Relocation in New York City: A Special Report to Mayor Wagner.* New York: City of New York, Office of the Mayor, December 1959.

Philadelphia Housing Association, "Relocation—The Human Side of Urban Renewal," *Issues* (November, 1958).

President's Advisory Committee on Government Housing Policies and Programs. *Recommendations on Government Housing Policies and Programs, A Report.* Washington, D. C.: U. S. Government Printing Office, December 1953.

President's Executive Order 11063. *Equal Opportunity in Housing.* Washington, D. C.: Housing and Home Finance Agency, November 20, 1962.

Rapkin, Chester, and William G. Grigsby. *Residential Renewal in the Urban Core.* Philadelphia: University of Pennsylvania Press, 1960.

Redevelopment Agency, City of Sacramento. *A Demonstration Project, Relocation Plan.* Sacramento, California.

Redevelopment Authority of the City of Philadelphia, The. *A Report Concerning Certain Aspects of Relocation.* Philadelphia, August 1961.

Reynolds, Harry W., Jr., "What Do We Know About Our Experiences with Relocation?" *Journal of Intergroup Relations,* II (Autumn, 1961), pp. 342–354.

———, "Human Element in Urban Renewal," *Public Welfare Journal* (April, 1961).

Rossi, Peter H., and Robert A. Dentler. *The Politics of Urban Renewal.* Glencoe, Ill.: The Free Press, 1961.

San Francisco Redevelopment Agency. *Preliminary Program for the Rehousing of Residents, Western Addition.* San Francisco, California: 1962.

Sarchet, Bettie. Cited in Millspaugh, Martin and Gurney Breckenfeld. *The Human Side of Urban Renewal.* Baltimore: Fight-Blight, Inc., 1958.

Schorr, Alvin L. *Slums and Social Insecurity.* Washington, D. C.: U. S. Government Printing Office, 1963.

Sears, Roebuck and Company, Urban Renewal Division. *ABC's of Urban Renewal.* Chicago: 1957.

Tenants Relocation Bureau, City of Chicago. *The Homeless Man on Skid Row.* Chicago: City of Chicago, September 1961.

Unwin, Sir Raymond. *Housing and Town Planning 1936-Lectures-1937.* New York: Columbia University School of Architecture, 1937.

Urban Renewal Administration, Urban Renewal Service. *Technical Guide No. 9.* "Determining Local Relocation Standards." 1961.

———. *Technical Guide No. 2.* "Questions and Answers on Relocation Payments." 1960.

Van Huyck, Alfred P., and Jack Horning. *The Citizens Guide to Urban Renewal.* West Trenton, N. J.: 1962.

Weaver, Robert C. *The Urban Complex.* New York: Doubleday & Company, 1964.

Whiting, Robert F., and Gerald S. Newman. *Rehousing Residents Displaced from Public Housing Clearance Sites in Chicago, 1957–58.* Chicago: City of Chicago, Chicago Housing Authority, November 1955.

Wirth, Louis. *Community Life and Social Policy.* Chicago: University of Chicago Press, 1956.

Wood, Elizabeth. *Housing Design; A Social Theory.* New York: Citizens' Housing and Planning Council of New York, 1961.

Woodbury, Coleman. Editor. *The Future of Cities and Urban Redevelopment.* Chicago: University of Chicago Press, 1953.

PART NINE

AREA REDEVELOPMENT AND RURAL POVERTY

25. The ARA Program

WILLIAM L. BATT, JR.

In May of 1961, culminating a six-year struggle, the Congress and the President created the Area Redevelopment Administration and gave it a specific purpose in life. The Congress declared that:

> . . . some of our communities are suffering substantial and persistent unemployment and underemployment; that such unemployment and underemployment cause hardship to many individuals and their families and detract from the national welfare by wasting vital human resources; that to overcome this problem the Federal Government, in cooperation with the States, should help areas of substantial and persistent unemployment and underemployment to take effective steps in planning and financing their economic redevelopment. . . .

In order that the new organization could make some headway on its mission, the Congress authorized, and later appropriated, about $300 million for loans to new or expanding factories and businesses, for building the access roads, water supplies, and other facilities needed for operating the new enterprises, for training and retraining workers in the areas, and for making technical studies of the resources and industrial development opportunities on which a new economic base for the areas could be founded. Finally, the Area Redevelopment Administration was told not to extend any financial assistance to the areas designated as requiring redevelopment of their economies until they had developed and submitted an acceptable economic program looking toward solution of their problems.

The Experience with ARA

Now that the ARA has had three to four years of actual experience with its program, what have we learned, what has been demonstrated? Let me first summarize some of the positive aspects of our experience, and then I shall discuss what we need in order to improve our performance in the future.

First of all, our experience indicates that a pattern of cooperation between private businessmen, state and local groups, and the federal government can function and can produce new jobs. In this pattern, the initiative and the responsibility for both program and action rest with the local community and private enterprise. The federal role is a supplementary one—a role of stimulation and of financial and technical assistance. The pattern functions like this. The communities are encouraged to organize for economic development, to analyze their opportunities for economic growth, and to develop a program of action. ARA will help them to make promising resource and industry feasibility studies. When a businessman indicates interest in a specific opportunity—he may want to expand an existing facility or build a new plant—he is extended a long maturity, low interest loan in which the community economic development organization also participates to the extent of at least a ten per cent equity. This loan is often coupled with financial help to the local government to provide the public facilities necessary to service the new enterprise. It may be that the enterprise requires workers specifically trained for its operation. ARA, through the Department of Labor, provides this training; and the cycle from community planning to actual jobs is complete.

This may sound like a complicated pattern of cooperation, and it is. Even so, I have not mentioned the other federal agencies which participate—the Department of Agriculture helps the rural communities in their organization and planning efforts, the Small Business Administration helps in making the loans, and the Community Facilities Administration of HHFA helps on the facility loans. In Indian areas, the Department of Interior cooperates, and the Health, Education, and Welfare Department participates with the Labor Department in the vocational training.

The pattern can be improved, but it does work. As of January 31, 1965, the Area Redevelopment Administration has approved 548 projects which, when fully operational, will assist in the creation of over 115,000 jobs. More than three out of every four persons now working on ARA-assisted projects were not working full time prior to their present jobs. All of these jobs are in new, expanded, or restored facilities; not one has been relocated from another area.

A second major conclusion that can be extracted from our experience of the last several years is that the cost to the federal government of creating these jobs has been far less than the cost of continuing to support these workers and their families through public programs. When all the nonreturnable outlays ARA makes are taken into account, including a contingency for bad loans, the average cost to the Federal Government for each job to be generated on an ARA project is about $800. This is only twice as much as the Federal Government collects each year in taxes from the average employed person and from the average business per employed person. Even if the ARA-assisted business and the ARA-project wage earner would pay substantially less taxes than their national average counterparts, it is still only a matter of a few years before the Federal Government fully recoups the job costs of $800. This does not take into account the savings represented by payments for unemployment compensation or for welfare benefits. Nor is there any account taken of the most important national benefit of all—the added output of real wealth that the formerly unemployed person is now producing each year. Or the immeasurable factor, the restored self-respect to a man and his family when father goes back to a steady job.

A third demonstration from our experience has been that communities can be encouraged to work together to produce sensible programs. Under the ARA program, more than 1,000 local committees have been formed to work on over-all economic development programs. We have been pleasantly surprised by the many instances in which the self-help momentum and pride generated by this effort have produced community dividends completely unrelated to federal aid—such as a new library, a nursing home, a local recreation park, or a facelifting of Main Street.

A fourth major finding growing out of the experience with the ARA program has been that many areas, some of them quite extensive—for example, substantial parts of Appalachia—are badly in need of basic improvements in their infrastructure. These needs must be supplied before the pattern of local planning, private investment, and government assistance can be expected to produce long-term jobs in any significant numbers. This need was vividly pointed up by the voracity with which the redevelopment areas absorbed the projects made available under the temporary Accelerated Public Works program which was administered by ARA. The universal need, within our affluent society, for such essential community facilities as waste treatment plants, water and sewer systems, and hospitals, was eye-opening. We learned that these facilities are essential if private investment is to be attracted, but we also learned that we can get the greatest value from them in terms of economic growth if they are concentrated regionally to provide the widest possible benefit.

ARA AND THE ANTI-POVERTY PROGRAM

So much for the general lessons from our experience. What has this to do with poverty, especially of a rural type? The elimination of poverty requires that people must be able to earn a living at jobs which pay living wages. Two basic requirements must be met. First, those who are unemployed or underemployed must be helped to improve their employability. And second, more jobs must be created.

The program of the Economic Opportunity Act is largely directed toward helping the unemployed and underemployed improve their employability. The Manpower Development and Training Act also is focused on the people side of the equation. The program of the Area Redevelopment Act is directed at creating more jobs in the areas and regions where jobs are most needed.

Let me be more specific about this relationship, and cite the example of the Sequoyah Carpet Mill in Anadarko, Oklahoma. This ARA-assisted enterprise started operations last fall. It was expected to hire around 50 persons by the end of the first year. But it is over the 100 job mark right now. This, in itself, is heartwarming, but the real point of the Sequoyah Mill story is this: 90 per cent of the first employees were people who never before had had a permanent job!

These new workers are mostly Indians from a nearby reservation. The chairman of the board of this firm is also an ordained Methodist minister. He told us that when they were getting under way he was advised against hiring these people. They were pictured as deadbeats and unemployables. But once they obtained regular jobs, these workers became steady and dependable. The management tells us absenteeism is virtually nonexistent at the plant. In the past, only 20 per cent of these people had taken advantage of their rights as citizens to vote in an election. Now 100 per cent are registered to vote. Steady workers become active citizens.

New enterprises like the Sequoyah Mills at Anadarko, Oklahoma, may well prove to be one salvation of rural America. As mechanization has hit agriculture and the economic size of farms has become larger, owners of uneconomically small acreages have had to supplement their farm income or leave for already overcrowded cities, where they are ill-equipped to compete for jobs.

In those sections of rural America where industry is locating or expanding, like Chesterfield County, South Carolina, or Aroostook County, Maine, or Marion County, Arkansas, farm people can combine a factory job from seven to three-thirty with maintaining a family farm in the remaining daylight hours. Having the factory job income permits them to keep the farm.

For many who will eventually give up farming, it provides a vestibule in which to gain experience and confidence in factory work and small urban living.

In the South Carolina county, for instance, ARA has helped make available some 1,000 jobs. One new metal-working plant resulted from an ARA-financed study. Four others resulted from an ARA-aided water supply system and sewage treatment facility. An ARA-financed water supply saved a bleachery in a third town, and an ARA loan made possible a peach packing plant in a fourth.

In Aroostook County, Maine, ARA has helped create over 1,700 new jobs. In the Ozark counties of Arkansas, 800 more. Most of the jobs are being filled by people who would otherwise find it difficult if not impossible to stay and raise their families the way they want to in rural America.

ARA's role in fighting poverty is the essential one of helping create jobs in the nation's hardest hit areas. Since the act expires on June 30, and the program has amply demonstrated its usefulness, President Johnson has stated in the Budget, Economic, and Farm Messages his intention to ask Congress that this program "be improved and made permanent."

The President's Budget Message points to the improvements being planned.

1. Federal resources and efforts would be concentrated more heavily in areas of greatest need.
2. Special incentives would be provided to multi-county development regions which include areas especially suited to serve as centers for broader economic development.
3. More liberal grants and substantial increases in funds would be made available for those public facilities most essential for economic development.
4. In addition, a special fund would help local communities meet part of their share of the cost of projects undertaken under other Federal grant-in-aid programs.
5. Federal guarantees of working capital loans would be authorized for eligible industrial projects.

The Administration, during the debate on the Appalachian bill in the Senate, committed itself also to encourage other multi-state regional groupings where sections of neighboring states share similar problems of economic rehabilitation, as do those in Appalachia.

The Congressional decision on the President's recommendations will be known within the next few months. Present indications are that its finding will be favorable and that this pioneer effort to help the hardest-hit areas and regions in the United States rejoin the productive mainstream of our society will continue to be an accepted responsibility of government.

26. Area Redevelopment: A Tool to Combat Poverty?

SAR A. LEVITAN

The major thrust of the current attack on poverty has been aimed at rehabilitating the deprived and destitute. The goal of obliterating or reducing poverty is to be achieved by making available to the poor better educational facilities, by special training which would equip the unemployed and underemployed with skills needed in the labor market, and by improving the services that society offers directly to the poor and which minister to their special needs. The assumption is that the aid offered will prepare and motivate the poor to enter the mainstream of American life and adopt the prevailing values of American society. The architects of the war on poverty—or shall we say generals—anticipate that the viable American society will be able to absorb the rehabilitated poor, as it has done for millions of immigrants throughout our history.

The Area Redevelopment Act is unique in the arsenal of weapons provided by Congress during the past four years to combat unemployment and poverty. It directs its aid to employers, and not to the unemployed. The program is based on the belief that in order to combat area unemployment, federal aid should concentrate on the business community which will generate needed jobs and thus help the unemployed.

Thus, the bulk of the resources allocated by the federal government for the depressed area program concentrates on providing incentives to businessmen to locate or expand established enterprises in depressed areas. The program authorizes a total of $200 million of subsidized long-term loans to businessmen at 4 per cent interest. It also provides for the expenditure of

$175 million in grants and loans for the construction of public facilities in depressed areas. The improvement of infrastructure in these areas is tied to the specific needs of entrepreneurs and must be directly connected with requirements of business establishments. Eligible public facilities include the development of industrial parks, the development of commercial recreation and tourism projects, and the construction of utilities, including sewerage systems, water mains, and access roads. Excluded are such facilities as schools and recreational centers, which merely make the areas "a better place to live in."

The depressed area program also places heavy emphasis upon community economic planning. Only a relatively modest program is provided for the retraining of unemployed workers in depressed areas. The program authorizes the total expenditure of $375 million over a four-year period for loans to businessmen and the construction of public facilities, but only a maximum of $14.5 million per year for the retraining of workers and the payment of allowances to the unemployed workers while they undergo training courses. In brief, ARA uses the "trickle-down" approach to combat unemployment.

It is therefore surprising that the major sponsors and backers of the federal depressed area program included outstanding liberals in Congress and labor union spokesmen, who would no more be caught among the advocates of a trickle-down approach than they would favor a balanced annual budget or selling TVA. But such are the powers of semantics; by placing emphasis on aid to depressed areas rather than on aid to businessmen, the program becomes not only palatable to liberals, but deserving of their wholehearted support.

The federal depressed area program also reflects changes in attitudes experienced during the past few years concerning the appropriate programs of aid for the unemployed and deprived. When Senator Paul H. Douglas originally proposed the program to aid depressed areas nearly ten years ago, he was convinced that this was the best program he could sell to Congress. It took six years of Congressional debate, including two presidential vetoes in 1958 and again in 1960, before the Area Redevelopment Act was finally approved by President

Kennedy in 1961. And the funds allocated for ARA are dwarfed by comparison with the alleviative and preventive programs enacted to aid the unemployed and poverty-stricken during the four years which have elapsed since the passage of ARA.

JUSTIFICATION AND RECORD OF ARA

There are ample data to justify the trickle-down approach to combat unemployment and human deprivation in depressed areas. The close relation between unemployment, low wages, and poverty is well documented. The Department of Labor has estimated that 60 per cent of all poor family heads were in the labor force during 1963 and half of them were employed full time. Unemployment and low wages are therefore major causes of poverty and deprivation in the United States. In depressed areas, where the incidence of unemployment is much more widespread than for the whole United States and spells of unemployment are of longer duration, the relationship between unemployment and poverty is even closer. A sample study of income levels in 30 depressed urban areas indicates that in 1959 the per cent of families in these areas with an annual income of less than $3,000 was 29 per cent, compared with 20 per cent in nondepressed areas. In rural depressed areas, more than a third of the families had an annual income of less than $2,000, nearly three times more than for the nation as a whole.

In the Employment Act of 1946, Congress recognized the responsibility of the federal government to create an economic climate that stimulates maximum employment and production. But the 1946 Act was largely exhortation. The ARA committed the federal government to provide funds for generating new economic activity and employment, and the sponsors of federal aid to depressed areas have apparently concluded, and rightly so, that private enterprise is the best means to achieve this goal. The depressed area legislation therefore represents acceptance of additional government responsibility to the unemployed beyond the original intent of the Employment Act.

Aside from purely humanitarian grounds and the usual economic rationale of aid to the unemployed, proponents of federal aid to depressed areas have advanced a persuasive justification for the program. Considerable social capital is invested in depressed communities and the deterioration of the economic base of a community involves abandonment or underutilization of available facilities, thus involving great economic waste. The study of 30 depressed urban areas, referred to earlier, with a total population in 1960 of 2.9 million, disclosed that these communities lost nearly one-sixth of their total population as a result of net civilian migration during the fifties. Despite an excess of births over deaths, the total population in these areas declined by more than a hundred thousand. Out-migration tends further to deteriorate the economic base of depressed areas since it is highly selective and heavily concentrated among males in the primary working ages and among those with the highest educational attainments. But out-migration, despite the fond hopes of some economists, is not a solution to the economic problems that beset most of the unemployed in depressed areas. To be sure, our population is highly mobile, but exclusive reliance upon out-migration as a solution to the problems of depressed areas is as realistic today as Marie Antoinette's "Let-them-eat-cake" counsel.

We have now had nearly four years of experience under the federal depressed area program. Since ARA has spread itself thinly and scattered its meager resources over hundreds of areas, it is difficult to measure the impact of the depressed area program. We are indebted to Professor William Miernyk for some insights about the impact of ARA-backed projects. Miernyk has studied the employment background of 1,262 employees in 33 ARA-backed plants. While the study has not yet been published, an ARA summary indicates that only one of every four employees in those plants was fully employed at the time he was hired on the ARA-backed project. Forty-three per cent were unemployed, 11 per cent were employed on a part-time basis, and 22 per cent were not in the labor force. The study also shows that nearly half of the employees reported higher hourly earnings on their ARA-supported projects than they received in their previous full-time job. On the other hand, only 16 per cent of the employees hired on ARA projects were 45 years of age or older. In all U. S. manufacturing, employees in this age bracket account for 39 per cent of the total. The available data are too inconclusive to permit any definite judgment about the characteristics of employees hired on ARA-backed projects and the wages they receive. When Miernyk's study is released, we should be able to glean more adequate insights about the background of these employees.

The ARA publishes statistics on the anticipated number of jobs which will be generated as a result of its activities. According to these data, the ARA has committed or actually expended by the end of 1964 a total of $296 million, including $171 million of loans to commercial and industrial projects, $89 million for public facilities, $14 million for technical assistance, and $22 million for retraining. Based on estimates prepared by ARA clients, the agency's officials anticipate that when all the approved projects are fully in operation, they will add directly some 69,000 jobs in depressed areas. While the addition of 69,000 direct jobs within a period of less than four years would suggest no mean accomplishment on the part of the federal depressed area program, a closer examination of the official data raises a number of serious doubts about their validity and meaning. Even assuming that the estimated job-generation on ARA projects proves to be correct (and this may be a most generous assumption since ARA has backed many marginal enterprises, and it is only to be expected that a considerable percentage of these enterprises will go sour before too long), it would still be hard to believe that all the ARA-backed projects would not have succeeded without ARA help. ARA claims "credit" for each job generated by the projects it supports, though it contributes about a third of the total investment in those enterprises. No doubt, a great many of the projects would not have started without ARA help. It's the old story—for want of a nail a kingdom was lost. But we must assume that the converse is also true—that many a nail may be lost without having the slightest impact upon the progress of an empire. It is therefore impossible to guess the extent to which ARA-backed projects constitute net additions to the economy.

It is reasonable to assume that some of these enterprises might have been generated by other sources.

A judgment about the impact of ARA is therefore a matter of faith. The believers take ARA estimates at face value, while skeptics scoff at the claims. Yearning to be among the former, I would like to say "amen" to the claims, but the doubts keep gnawing.

Program Revision

Since an attempt at objective analysis of ARA accomplishments to date appears to be an exercise in futility, the examination of ARA statistics might appear to be superfluous. But the Area Redevelopment Act is due to expire in July 1965. President Johnson was committed to the continuation of the program, but not without changes. On the contrary, in the 1965 Economic Report the President stated that "the direction of this program can benefit from the experience of the last four years." It would also be reasonable to assume that the present Congress would follow the President's recommendations to extend the life of ARA. Acceptance of ARA claims suggest the wisdom of continuing the present program. Why change a good thing?

Whatever the true accomplishments of ARA to date may be, a close examination of the program suggests some serious weaknesses in the legislation and the desirability of revising the package of tools enacted in 1961. While the liberal proponents of the program accepted a trickle-down approach, apparently they did have some reservations about the package of tools they had devised, and this is reflected in a number of provisions containing inherent built-in impediments to realizing the full potential of the program. A psychiatrist might suggest that the architects of the program had displayed a "will to fail," and even an economist can see serious flaws in the program.

Credit for Private Loans

The success of the depressed area program rests upon attaining an active partnership between government, at all levels, and the business community. This would suggest that securing the active cooperation of conventional lending institutions is a *sine qua non* for achieving smooth operations of the loan program. It would appear, however, that the current loan provisions are intended to ruffle the feelings and interests of traditional lenders. ARA provides only for direct government loans, though the entrepreneur may secure part of the needed capital from banks or other private lending institutions. But by providing 4 per cent long-term credit the program offers an incentive to entrepreneurs to shun conventional lenders and to turn to the government for the maximum share of credit permitted under the law. Understandably, the lending community has not taken kindly to the ARA loan program and has resented the government's intrusion. It is also not surprising that established businesses have viewed with misgivings and frequent outright opposition ARA's practice of financing potential competitors at subsidized interest rates. On the other hand, there is no evidence that subsidized long-term credit is essential to induce new economic activity in depressed areas.

It is, however, recognized that conventional lenders in depressed areas are not adequately venturesome and that long-term credit is frequently not available in adequate amounts to finance new and expanding businesses. It is not necessary to have a direct government loan in competition with private lenders to remedy this situation. Credit resources could be expanded by a government guarantee program which would assure the conventional lender the repayment of his loan. However, adoption of this policy and its successful implementation might overload banks in depressed areas with excessive portfolios of long-term industrial and commercial paper for which there might not be any readily available open market. This situation already exists in some depressed areas, particularly in Pennsylvania. Similar conditions apply to local economic development groups which have raised funds to finance new industrial development in their areas and now find that there is no market for the long-term investments. A remedy for this situation can be found in the establishment of a federally-backed industrial and commercial mortgage association which would provide a market for long-term paper. It will be readily recognized that the above proposal is not original. A similar plan is now in operation, apparently quite successfully, in the housing field which enjoys the blessing and cooperation of conventional lending institutions.

It might also be recalled that when the original depressed area bill was discussed in 1956, Senator Ralph Flanders of Vermont proposed a loan-guarantee approach similar to the one suggested here. But his proposal was rejected because it would presumably provide a bonanza to bankers. The establishment of a mortgage association to provide a market for long-term industrial and commercial paper was proposed several years ago by Senator Joseph S. Clark of Pennsylvania.

A loan-guarantee program, in addition to securing the acceptance of the lending and business communities, would also make federal appropriations go much farther than a direct government loan program. It is estimated that for every dollar appropriated under a guarantee program, the banks could extend between ten and fifteen dollars worth of loans. Thus, the present $200 million loan authorization under the ARA could be stretched to provide possibly as much as $2 billion worth of guaranteed loans and still leave enough funds to establish a mortgage association to provide a market for the long-term industrial and commercial paper.

However, it should be recognized that in some areas banks do not have the resources, or are not in the practice of advancing long-term venture capital, and it is doubtful whether their practices will change even under a federal loan-guarantee program. Provision should therefore be made to retain a limited direct government loan program. But such loans should be restricted only to cases where there is clear evidence that credit would not be available from other sources.

The present act also contains a provision requiring community or state participation in every ARA commercial and industrial loan. The underlying rationale for this provision is that the local people would be best able to appraise the soundness of a new venture and that they should also be willing to make some sacrifices to expand the economic base of their area. However, experience has shown that the provision is unworkable.

In addition to requiring a minimum of 10 per cent local or state contribution to the cost of a given project backed by ARA, the law also proscribes the repayment of the local or state contribution until the federal share of the loan is repaid. It would appear that reducing local participation to 5 per cent would be adequate to indicate effective local interest in any given project, and scarcity of local funds will prevent excessive reliance upon government guaranteed credit. For purposes of repayment, the local contribution should be placed on the same basis as the federal share of the loan and be repaid concurrently with the latter.

It hardly can be expected that expanded availability of long-term capital will provide a cure to the economic ills of depressed areas. Availability of credit will not by itself create effective entrepreneurs, a scarce commodity in most depressed areas. Moreover, an excessively easy credit policy is bound to result in undue business failures which would damage the program.

PUBLIC FACILITIES

The public facilities provision of the ARA also proved somewhat unrealistic. The act provides for two separate public facility funds: a $100 million loan program and a $75 million grant program. The apparent reason for separating the loans from the grants was to weaken the attacks of opponents who charged that the proponents of the legislation were sponsoring a giveaway program. To indicate "fiscal responsibility," Douglas provided that grants would be made only in "extreme cases of need." Communities found little attraction in the 4 per cent public facility loans in light of the tax-exempt status of interest on loans which they could obtain in the open market. In practice, it didn't require sophisticated calculations to recognize that the 4-to-3 ratio of loans to grants hardly justified the conclusion that grants were to be made only in "extreme" cases. And ARA normally "sweetened" public facility loans with a grant. By the end of fiscal 1963, ARA had exhausted its grant funds, though nearly half of the grant authorization was never expended, since ARA did not use most of the grant fund appropriated during its first year of operations, and Congress determined that the unused portion could not be reappropriated. Once ARA lost the authority to make grants, communities shunned public-facility loans, and the Public Works Acceleration Act, which quintupled the funds available for public facilities under a 50 per cent minimum grant provision, filled the needs of communities seeking aid for that purpose. But even after the PWAA expired, the ARA public facility loan fund remained unutilized and about $50 million is still available for which the agency cannot find any customers.

It would appear, therefore, that if a public facility program for depressed areas is to continue—and the evidence indicates a need for such a program—it ought to be fashioned after the PWAA and provide for grants, rather than loans.

Training

The limited training program provided under ARA makes little sense in light of the much broader training made available under the Manpower Development and Training Act. ARA training is restricted to 16 weeks, compared with a maximum of 72 weeks provided under MDTA, and allowances paid to trainees under ARA are also less generous than those under MDTA. However, under current provisions, beginning with the next fiscal year, states will have to share one-third of most MDTA training costs. It is doubtful whether many depressed areas will be able to contribute the required share in order to benefit from MDTA training, and it is equally uncertain whether the states with a concentration of depressed areas would be able to allocate adequate funds to participate in MDTA training to the maximum extent allowed under the law. This indicates the need of a 100 per cent federally-financed training program for depressed areas, and the application of the broader training provisions of MDTA with whatever amendments might be enacted during 1965 to the depressed area program. It might also be desirable to add a special proviso to the depressed area program authorizing the allocation of up to 10 per cent of the total fund to subsidize mobility of unemployed workers from depressed areas, along the lines provided in the 1963 amendments to the MDTA.

OTHER FEDERAL GRANTS

Depressed areas frequently have difficulty participating in existing federal grant programs because they lack funds to supply the required share. One section in the Area Redevelopment Act provides that, for purposes of urban planning in depressed urban areas, federal funds would cover 75 per cent of the total cost, as contrasted with two-thirds in other areas. This provision might be expanded and adopted for other federal grant programs, e.g., construction of airports, the Hill-Burton Act, and others. The bill should specify the programs for which designated areas would receive a higher proportion of federal grants than is now allowed in the appropriate pieces of legislation. A special supplementary fund will have to be provided for these expanded grants.

TAX INCENTIVES

Consideration might also be given to the extension of special tax incentives to firms locating or expanding in depressed areas. Current ARA legislation fails to offer any inducements to established corporations, the major source of economic expansion and growth, to open branch plans in depressed areas. Large corporations normally finance expansion from reserve funds and rarely experience any difficulty in obtaining credit from traditional lending institutions; consequently, they do not qualify for subsidized ARA loans.

Two forms of tax incentive have been suggested to induce established enterprises to expand in depressed areas: accelerated depreciation and increasing the investment tax credit. The case for increasing the tax credit on investment may be of doubtful merit as far as depressed areas are concerned. It would presumably accelerate technological change and thus accentuate the short-run problems of labor obsolescence in these areas. Accelerated depreciation may present an attractive inducement for growing corporations to expand in depressed areas. The legislation could follow the provisions of the Defense Production Act of 1950, though not limiting eligibility only to defense-oriented industries. Whether the government should offer incentive to further expand corporate concentration is beyond the scope of this paper. Here we are concerned only with measures that would aid the rehabilitation of depressed areas. In any case, anti-trusters should not be excessively disturbed by the tax incentive proposal. Of all the provisions discussed in this paper, it has the least likelihood of receiving Congressional consideration, let alone approval. Tax measures have to obtain the blessings of the House Ways and Means Committee and the Senate Finance Committee. This would admittedly be a formidable obstacle under the best of circumstances, and, during the balance of this fiscal year—the deadline for extending the depressed area legislation—the two committees will be fully employed with medicare and reduction of excise taxes, to mention but two major bills now pending before Congress.

AREA ELIGIBILITY

One of the major criticisms voiced against the federal depressed area program is its overextension. More than a third of the total counties in the United States, with a population of some 38 million, are now eligible to receive ARA assistance. The suggested revised program would hardly make any economic sense if this situation were to continue. For example, it could scarcely be expected that truly depressed areas would benefit from a tax incentive system if major industrial complexes, such as Detroit, Pittsburgh, Buffalo, and others, would also be eligible to benefit under the program.

On the other hand, it is not realistic to expect that Congress would vote for an expanded program and agree to deprive communities of existing "rights." A possible solution to this dilemma is to base the extent of federal assistance on the relative need of each area. That is to say, some areas would be made "more equal" than others. The Public Works Acceleration Act of 1962 could be used as a model. Under this legislation, federal grants ranged from 50 per cent to 75 per cent of the total cost of a project, depending upon the level of chronic unemployment and the extent of poverty prevailing in the area. Under this approach, all designated areas could share on an equal basis in obtaining government-guaranteed loans to finance the expansion of industry. The share of federal grants for public facilities would range between perhaps 25 and 75 per cent of total cost, and the benefits of tax incentives or special supplements for matching grants would be reserved only for the most depressed areas.

REGIONAL PROGRAMS

The imminent passage of the proposed Appalachia bill has created considerable Congressional interest in regional programs. The Appalachia bill focuses on the improvement of the region's infrastructure. The bill authorizes $1,092 million of federal expenditure. The bulk of these funds, $840 million, would be allocated to the construction of 2,350 miles of developmental highways and 1,000 miles of access roads. These funds are to be spent over a five-year period, with the federal government contributing 70 per cent of the total cost. The authorized balance, $252 million, would be spent over a period of two years and would be allocated mostly for the construction and maintenance of hospitals and the construction of sewerage-treatment plants. Included in this amount is $90 million specifically earmarked to help local communities meet requirements for matching funds of federal grant programs.

It is only natural that the billion-dollar Appalachia program would whet the appetities of solons and plain citizens from other regions who are easily persuaded that their own depressed areas deserve equal consideration. The regional approach to depressed areas is therefore rather popular now in Washington. Aside from the potential federal largesse, the popularity of regional programs also reflects dissatisfaction with the ARA approach, which is largely restricted to designation of individual counties. In many cases these small political units have little relation to economic entities and are not in a position to embark upon meaningful economic development. But the ARA requires each county to prepare its own economic development plan, and a county cannot qualify for assistance unless it has first submitted such a plan to ARA.

A major inescapable implication of the regional approach is that some areas do not have an adequate base for developing a viable economic program and that the residents of such areas must band with their neighbors in continguous and even remoter areas to plan their economic future. Moreover, in many cases the employment potential for the residents in a depressed area may depend upon the growth and development of a community outside a county which may not be eligible to receive ARA assistance. Sound economic planning would dictate that a growing area be included as part of a designated area.

Still, the present regional kick may be overdone. The designation of growing areas—"growth points," to use the prevailing nomenclature—may extend the boundaries of depressed areas even beyond the present already unmanageable proportions. It should also be realized that Appalachia is a special case on the American scene and that most regions have already an adequately developed infrastructure for the expansion of local economies. Without negating the potential of rational regional planning, preoccupation with grand designs for large regions may force into the background the urgent needs of "little" economies which may need immediate help.

FUNDING

There remains the most difficult task, a discussion of funding or financing the depressed area program. The resources to be allocated to any single measure cannot be properly considered in isolation. In the limited area of programs in aid of the unemployed, the costs that should be allocated to rehabilitate depressed areas must be weighed in the context of resources required to provide for unemployment insurance, education, retraining, public works, public employment services, welfare, and related anti-poverty measures. As long as economics remains an art of allocating scarce resources—and this still holds true in a $630 billion economy—priorities for competing needs and goals have to be determined before the resources to be allocated for any specific program can be decided.

Although this broad question is beyond the scope of this paper, I might comment briefly that my close observation of ARA experience does not persuade me that too many eggs should be put into the depressed area basket. The President's

Budget calls for a $400 million depressed area program during fiscal 1966, without specifying how this amount will be parceled out among the several parts of the program. Based on four years of experience, this amount should be more than adequate to carry on with the present program. An expanded public works program might justify the allocation of additional federal funds.

27. Rural Poverty and Rural Areas Development

VARDEN FULLER

Rural poverty is intensive, extensive, and intractable. As elsewhere, being poor in the country is correlated with well-known factors—youth, advanced age, color of skin, technological impacts, poor education. In rural areas, these attributes come together in a maximum likelihood combination. Whether portrayed in photography or in statistical magnitudes, percentages, and index numbers, rural poverty is shocking. Yet, it is remote and obscure. The rural population—widely dispersed, racially and culturally heterogeneous, socially and politically incohesive—does not compete well for attention. Unemployment is easier to observe than is underemployment, and it is the latter which dominates the rural scene. Moreover, there is the widespread and mistaken notion that billions of agricultural subsidy dollars alleviate rural poverty.

As my interest is mainly in matters of policy, program, and organization in relation to rural poverty, I shall not dwell on statistical details beyond the mention of a few important magnitudes. Of 9.7 million families with less than $3,000 net cash income in 1959, 4.4 million, or two-fifths, were rural; one-third of the poor rural families were on farms and two-thirds were nonfarm. Over half of all rural poor are in the South.[1]

This nation has long had an uneasiness about rural problems. Some were concerned for the welfare of farmers; others

[1] There is considerable literature on low-income farming and rural levels of living; much less is known about low-income nonfarm people. A recent and useful source covering both is *Poverty in Rural Areas of the United States,* Agricultural Economic Report No. 63, U. S. Department of Agriculture, November, 1964.

were apprehensive that farm depression might spread to the rest of the economy. All parties involved centered their views, arguments, or rationalizations upon a sort of homogeneous perception called "the farmer" whose situation could be found in simple averages. Thus perceived and measured, "the farmer" suffered from comparatively lower income. The sources of his adversity were believed to be environmental and attributable to inherent inequalities of economic power. Government response, particularly since 1933, has been sympathetic. Many governmental and quasi-governmental approaches toward a more favorable environment have been proposed and adopted—reclamation, soil conservation, cooperation, credit, research, and extension programs. These have made up a considerable constellation, of which price supports ultimately became the center.

For all of these programs, "the farmer" was an undifferentiated homogeneity. Not until the advent of the Farm Security Administration in 1937 did a policy emerge which acknowledged that some farmers were poorer than others, that the poorest produced so little they could not earn a satisfactory income at any conceivable price; and, moreover, that hired farm laborers were also trying to earn a living in agriculture. In its short-lived career, Farm Security undertook to improve the resource base and the equipment of poor farms through loans and grants, and to relieve some of the most urgent shelter and medical needs of migratory farm workers. The demise of Farm Security, upon which comment will be made later, was a result of political assault.

Another Department of Agriculture program, contemporary with Farm Security and also short-lived, was State and Local Land Use Planning. While not intended to distinguish among economic classes of farmers, it sought through a grass-roots democracy idea to involve all segments of agrarian society in a local planning process into which the services of the various agencies would be integrated. Its brief life and demise will also be the subject of a deferred comment.

The New Dealers did not again make any serious effort to distinguish levels of prosperity or need within agriculture. But the Eisenhower administration did. The President's message to the Congress in 1954 declared that "the chief beneficiaries of our price support policies have been the two million larger highly mechanized farming units which produce about 85 per cent of our agricultural output . . . Special attention should be given to the problems peculiar to small farmers."

Thereafter, in 1955, Secretary Benson initiated a Rural Development Program that had many of the features now found in the Area Redevelopment and Rural Areas Development programs. His program depended upon local initiative and upon interagency response; it had no formal eligibility criteria but the concept was centered on pilot counties. Mr. Benson's five annual reports concluded in 1960 with the claim that:

> This program is now widely accepted as a major *national* approach to helping rural people improve farming, obtain off-farm work, and build better, more prosperous communities.

By 1960, the number of participating counties had grown to 210. There were reported to be 2,000 projects under way

> to improve farms, build new industries and expand existing ones, help both youth and adults to obtain the training they need, improve health, and accomplish other aims. . . . New businesses and service activities have added nearly 18,000 full- or part-time jobs. These include a whole range of enterprises, wood products manufacture, clothing, metal working, paper, chemicals, food processing, and many others.[2]

Nevertheless, the staff supplement to Mr. Benson's 1960 report leaves one to speculate whether many of the activities claimed as Rural Development achievements were not actually the result of trends in the economy.

Mr. Freeman built upon the rural development foundations laid by Mr. Benson. But not in candor or modesty, for the Freeman chronology of rural areas development has no entries prior to March, 1961.[3] Yet, the most readily observable differences between Freeman's RAD and Benson's RD are accel-

---

[2] *Rural Development Program,* 5th Annual Report of the Secretary of Agriculture, September, 1960, pp. 5, 7.

[3] *Report of the Secretary of Agriculture,* 1962, p. 40.

erated committee proliferation and increased flamboyance of political rhetoric.

The current RAD program,[4] now regarded as one of the major instrumentalities of the "Rural Renaissance" of the Great Society, does have some additional authority and resources. Part of these are derived from ARA, through specified eligibility of rural counties and through agency delegation of responsibility.[5] The other augmentation to RAD came in the Food and Agriculture Act of 1962, which, although mainly concerned with price supports, production controls, and surplus disposal, did provide small increments of authority for rural renewal, diversion of cropland into recreation facilities, and related activities. Other preexisting and general authorities are marshalled under the flag of RAD.

Within the Department of Agriculture, rural development is administered on a delegate-agency basis. General clientele, functional agencies only are involved—Farmers Home Administration, Rural Electrification Administration, Federal Extension Service, Farmer Cooperative Service, Soil Conservation Service, Forest Service, etc. The only identity within Agriculture that is directly and exclusively concerned with rural development is the Office of Rural Areas Development. In 1964, it had an eight-man staff, whose duties were to provide leadership, initiative, coordination, expedition, and liaison. This took $120,000 of the Department's 1964 budget of $5.7 billion. Additionally, under delegate agency agreement, Agriculture had $1.5 million of ARA's $145 million in 1964, of which approximately one-fourth also went into coordination-expedition-liaison-etc., while the remainder was sliced thinly among several of the regular agricultural research and program agencies. Including their own

---

[4] As this was being written, the President's farm message to the Congress (February 4, 1964) stated that: "The Secretary is creating within the Department of Agriculture a Rural Community Development Service, which will have no operating programs of its own but will devote its energies to assisting other agencies in extending their services." Since this "creation" was accomplished by renaming the Office of Rural Areas Development, there appears to be no real need to adjust names or tenses in the following text.

[5] Sar A. Levitan, *Federal Aid to Depressed Areas,* pp. 42–43, 61–64.

appropriations and transfers from ARA, the agricultural agencies in 1964 apparently spent some $40 million and lent $18 million for purposes generally directed toward (or expected to trickle down to) the rural needy.[6] These fragmental activities are the realized magnitudes and proportions of a program that in 1962 had been promisingly announced as follows:

The United States Department of Agriculture has directed that the combined resources of all its agencies be made available on a priority basis and in one concerted effort to assist the people in rural areas and towns to analyze their problems and make plans to improve their economic and social conditions. The first step is to help local leaders from all segments of economic and social life in the respective economic development areas to formulate over-all economic development programs for the use of available resources. This process of organizing, motivating, and servicing widely representative local committees in formulating and implementing overall economic development programs (OEDP's) is generally known as Rural Areas Development (RAD).[7]

As a concept of public administration, this suggests the endless tossing of a ball between bureaucrats and grassrooters, and, moreover, that it may be a ball of loose string which is vulnerable to unravelling. Subsequent explanations of RAD give no assurance to the contrary. Last November, Assistant Secretary John Baker told the Grange that:

The rural renaissance is a local cooperative endeavor, or it is doomed to be nothing. How much progress is made depends upon the drive and determination of people at the grassroots level. The challenge indeed is yours. Our role in government is to help you make your contribution as effective as possible. We accept fully our responsibility to encourage local leadership and initiative as we do through the Office of Rural Areas Development and Extension Service, and through the farmer committee system and soil and water conservation districts, and to provide through the several agencies of the Department the research, educational, advisory, and

---

[6] U. S. Congress, House Subcommittee of the Committee on Appropriations, 88th Congress, 2d Sess., Department of Agriculture Appropriations for 1965, Part 4, pp. 343–356.

[7] U. S. Department of Agriculture, *Helping People to Help Themselves in Country and in Towns,* September, 1962, p. 1.

financial assistance that will aid in the rural renaissance. . . . We can achieve a rural renaissance of creative living that will be one of the vibrant, dynamic forces of the Great Society. In the bountiful resources of rural America we have the economic potential. In the people, we have the necessary leadership and initiative.[8]

When the objective shifts from exhortation on possibilities to reporting accomplishments, official phraseology is less fervent. One of the regularly utilized measures of achievement is the number of local development committees that have been organized. According to the 1963 Report of the Secretary, more than 2,000 counties had such committees wherein "leading citizens—representing agriculture, business, finance, labor, schools, churches, local government, and other interested groups—are serving their area's assets and problems and organizing 'boot strap' operations to make the best use of their resources."[9] The statistics of committee organization are supplemented by details of conferences and of program actions by federal agencies, particularly those of the USDA.

Both the hortatory language of promise and the prosaic language of accomplishment imply that the problems of individual poverty are being met concomitantly with area (or community) development—all through the processes of grass roots democracy and local self-determination. Regretfully, it was left to the Commission on Civil Rights to inform the nation that in one major respect this was a delusion.[10] Neither as citizens nor as agency staff personnel are Negroes admitted into the local decision-making process. Carrying discrimination still further, program services and benefits to individuals have been unequal and inversely related to need. Beyond its findings of fact, the Commission reported that:

Underlying much of the failure to provide equal service to Negro farmers in the South has been the preconception, found in the

---

[8] Address by John A. Baker, Assistant Secretary, U. S. Department of Agriculture, before annual convention of National Grange, Atlantic City, New Jersey, November 11, 1964.

[9] *Report of the Secretary of Agriculture,* 1963, p. 17.

[10] *Equal Opportunity in Farm Programs,* A Report of the United States Commission on Civil Rights, 1965.

agricultural agencies, that Negro farmers have limited needs, capabilities, and aspirations. Starting with a view that Negroes cannot improve as farmers, many programs have not trained Negroes in the new technology nor encouraged them to diversify, to acquire larger acreage, or to make their small acreage more productive.[11]

Discrimination based upon race is not the only point of vulnerability to be encountered in relying upon local self-determination to overcome individual poverty and disadvantage. As Vidich and Bensman found in their study of class, power, and religion in a rural community,[12] the instinctive political reflex of local leadership is to insulate from change rather than encourage it, especially if it portends alteration in the structure of privilege and power. Trying to avoid this by sponsoring a community initiative outside of the established power structure or one that attenuates the positions of established leaders, as was done in Farm Security and Land Use Planning, offers no realistic prospect of success. Program approaches made through and with the power structure offer more hope for acceptance but also impose the obligation that benefit distribution must be in disproportion to need, i.e., of the trickle-down variety.

The inherent difficulty underlying government help to self-help in overcoming rural poverty is the lack of a cohesive, articulate clientele. As elsewhere, rural interest group organization and effectiveness are correlates of affluence. New Dealers in 1937 tried to serve the rural needy by creating an agency for a clientele having neither affluence nor influence. It did not survive.[13] Land Use Planning in 1938 was initially directed to program coordination, but it also had implications for allocation and priority. Milton Eisenhower was among the prominent individuals who in 1940 hailed local planning as "one of the momentous events in the history of agriculture in the United

---

[11] *Ibid.*, p. 101.

[12] Arthur J. Vidich and Joseph Bensman, *Small Town in Mass Society* (New York: Doubleday Anchor, 1958), originally published by Princeton University Press.

[13] The rise and fall of Farm Security Administration is well analyzed by Grant McConnel in *The Decline of Agrarian Democracy* (Berkeley: University of California Press, 1953).

States—probably far more important than any single agricultural program." [14] Two years later it was dead—from political assault.

The episode of Farm Security suggests the political impracticality of a clientele agency for the needy. Land-use planning initially was not so vulnerable. But when it began to appear that indigenous planning might go beyond coloring maps and preparing reports, the centers of power began to get nervous. Washington administrators and local well-established power groups reacted. Their collusion, though not flamboyant, was sufficient.[15]

I have other misgivings about local initiative as a satisfactory approach to poverty. Local initiative is supposed to start with the preparation of an Overall Economic Development Program (OEDP). Levitan's examination of a sample of them indicated a substantial proportion to be only pro forma submissions and quite useless.[16] What else could be expected? Even formally organized and regularly constituted groups notoriously find great difficulty in making comprehensive, all-embracing plans. Needs of information and of conflict reconciliation are too great.[17] The over-all development concept is another romantic, and impractical, idea. Is a disjointed, incrementalist decision for a road or a sewer worse than a synoptically made one if in fact the latter has to be compounded out of guesswork, supposition, and hypothecation? The OEDP idea rests upon three indefensible concepts: (1) suppositions of knowledge and community of interest beyond human capacities; (2) a philosophy of social and economic community microecology that ignores the realities of complex interarea and intergroup relationships; (3) the assumption that community needs and individual needs are one and the same.

---

[14] *Yearbook of Agriculture,* 1940, p. 1135.

[15] A detailed and penetrating analysis of land use planning and its termination is given by Charles M. Hardin, "The Bureau of Agricultural Economics Under Fire: A Study of Valuation Conflicts," *Journal of Farm Economics* (August, 1946), pp. 635–668.

[16] Sar A. Levitan, op. cit., pp. 195–200.

[17] David Braybrooke and Charles E. Lindblom, *A Strategy of Decision* (Glencoe: The Free Press of Glencoe, 1963), pp. 61–143.

Communities undeniably have needs—including the need to be pleasant and rewarding places in which to live, as well as the need to be prosperous. However, in an attack on poverty, as perhaps in most other contexts, community and individual needs are not wholly the same. There can be no guarantee that individual need will be met well or promptly if meeting it must depend upon achieving community concert and the filing of an OEDP.

I do not argue against community planning—it has its own merits. But if the war on poverty is to be more than a skirmish, opportunity must be available to the individual, regardless of what the community may or may not agree upon.

This argument implies direct access of individuals to program, which admittedly raises problems of public administration. Direct individual access need not require new agencies or programs wholly specialized to a needy clientele. Agencies and programs are probably best when specialized along functional lines. Since needs are multiple, it follows that agencies will be multiple. Overlapping, duplication, and interagency conflicts follow; coordination is called for. While coordination has its merits, it also has its price—and I believe the price can be too high. Isn't some degree of incoordination one of the luxuries an affluent society can afford?

Obviously, public administration founded on a federal-state-local participatory system cannot be completely vertical. Nevertheless, there is latitude of choice as to whether responsibilities will be direct or delegated, and whether selectivity will maximize individual or community option. And wherever the choice can be made, direct responsibility is to be preferred over delegated; in selectivity the individual is to be preferred over the area. Bachmura has been thinking along these lines and has suggested the G. I. Bill as a model,[18] which I believe is a fertile idea.

I would like to close by turning back to the rural community—as a community and not alone for the sake of its pros-

---

[18] Frank T. Bachmura, "Area Development: General and Selective Approaches," *Proceedings,* Association of Southern Agricultural Workers, Inc., February 3–5, 1964, p. 18.

perity. Depopulation of the countryside raises problems that are the reciprocal of congestion in the cities. Yet the rural area as a place to live and to be provided with social services seems to lag sadly in getting attention. Perhaps this is attributable to the lack of any widely shared concept of direction and purpose. We have had a serviceable national philosophy about farmers and farming. In the past, when farming dominated the countryside, this served also as a rural philosophy. But as farming becomes evermore a minor proportion of rural life, agrarian philosophy no longer services. National authorities are beginning to recognize this but the shadows of agrarian fundamentalism lie heavily upon their perceptions.

The President's farm message of February 4 incorporates the nuances of this ambivalence:

> I am determined that the farmers who have been efficient and successful in agriculture shall be fairly rewarded for their success. And I am equally determined that the rural community which has sustained the growth of agriculture shall have the chance to broaden its economic base and the range of opportunity which it can offer the children of its families.

As for rewarding the successful, the President's message is fulsome and fairly specific. For the more numerous others, including the agricultural poor and the three-fourths of rural Americans who are not farmers, the message is cryptic and sparse. The intent "to bring additional views to bear on the place of rural America" is mentioned. Incredibly, the President expects this to be done by his proposed new commission on food and fiber.

Food, fiber, and successful farming are doubtless an appropriate set of trifocals for viewing the national interest in commercial agriculture. But lenses of that prescription do not focus effectively upon the less privileged, in and out of agriculture. Consequently, if their use is continued, the causes and remedies of rural poverty will remain blurred. It will take an entirely different set of lenses to see clearly the individual prospects and needs of the rural poor. And it will take still another set to see the future of the rural community in an age when farming has become an integral part of the industrial system and is no longer *the* rural way of life.

PART TEN

THE ROLE OF THE POOR

28. Anti-Poverty Programs and the Role of the Poor[1]

FRANK RIESSMAN

The term "Community Action Program" means a program—which is developed, conducted, and administered with the maximum feasible participation of residents of the areas and members of the (low income) groups.

The Economic Opportunity Act of 1964, Title II Section A

NEW CAREERS FOR THE POOR

The Economic Opportunity Act of 1964 calls for the development of community action programs for the poor, with the poor, and by the poor. If appropriately implemented, this call for involvement and self determination by the poor can provide the basis for the development of millions of nonprofessional and subprofessional jobs and new careers.

The poor can participate in anti-poverty programs in a variety of ways:

1. The poor can be employed as nonprofessionals, particularly in the human services (health, education, welfare, recreation, etc.);
2. The poor can be employed to study themselves;
3. The poor can be involved in stimulating community and social action of various kinds; [2]

---

[1] A number of the ideas in this article are further developed in Arthur Pearl and Frank Riessman, *New Careers for the Poor* (Glencoe: The Free Press, 1965) (in press).

[2] The Alinsky model currently being applied in Syracuse and supported by a grant from the Office of Economic Opportunity is illustrative here as is the Mobilization For Youth Project. For a further discussion of the Alinsky Model, see Frank Riessman, "The New Social Action Trend and the Alinsky Model," *Trans-Action,* 1965 (in press). Later in the present article, I present an alternative to the Alinsky conflict model.

4. The poor can participate on local community action boards concerned with developing and implementing anti-poverty policy.

Hiring the poor to serve the poor is a fundamental approach to poverty in an automated age. Besides reducing the manpower shortage in the health, education and welfare fields, the employment of indigenous nonprofessionals can serve at least four other important functions.[3]

1. It can potentially provide millions of new jobs and careers for the unemployed in social service positions which are not likely to be automated out of existence. The major job types include: expediters whose function is to link services and people more efficiently—to mediate between the client and public and private agencies; direct service agents such as homemakers, teacher aides, mental health aides; community organizers or neighborhood workers whose function is to involve the residents of the area in community planning and community action.

2. It can provide more, better and "closer" service for the poor; it can reach the unreached, serve as a two-way communication bridge between professionals and the poor. Nonprofessionals can do things professionals cannot as easily do: they can be more "subjective," involved; provide more direct intervention, advice, companionship—they can be models for the poor. The nonprofessional has a number of unique characteristics that contribute to his potential effectiveness: local "know how," style of life, and peership.

3. It can rehabilitate many of the poor themselves through meaningful employment. This is based on the "helper therapy" principle.[4] People with a problem helping others with the same problem is an approach well known to group therapists. In fact, some people who do not seem to benefit from *receiving* help often profit indirectly when they are *giving* help. This may

---

[3] The discussion which follows is developed at greater length in Robert Reiff and Frank Riessman, *The Indigenous Nonprofessional*, National Institute of Labor Education Mental Health Program, 250 W. 57th Street, New York, Report #3, November, 1964.

[4] Frank Riessman, "The Helper Therapy Principle," *Social Work*, Vol. 10 (April, 1965).

be the case in a wide variety of group "therapies," including Synanon (for drug addicts), Recovery, Incorporated (for psychologically disturbed people), SCORE (Charles Slack's program for delinquents), and Alcoholics Anonymous. The "helper therapy" principle has at least two important implications for the indigenous nonprofessional of lower socio-economic background: since many of the nonprofessionals recruited for anti-poverty programs will be school dropouts, former delinquents, long-term ADC mothers and the like, it seems quite probable that placing them in a helping role will be highly therapeutic for them; as the nonprofessionals benefit personally from their helping roles they should become more effective as workers and thus provide better help. Such a cycle could be an important positive force in a depressed community.

4. It can help make the professionals' role definitions more flexible, creating an alliance and unity between professionals and nonprofessionals which will allow the professionals more fully to play their technical roles. In addition, it can stimulate the development of new creative professional roles as trainers, teachers, and program planners. The "objectivity" of the professional combined with the "subjectivity" of the nonprofessional can provide a new complementary unity of service.

In essence, then, the employment of indigenous nonprofessionals helps the poor as servers and served, as helpers and helpees.

SELF SURVEYS

Another way of involving the poor is by having them "surveyed" with regard to their reactions to public housing, welfare, education, etc. and by using their responses as guidelines for policy changes in these areas. For example, it is possible to have residents in low-income housing projects anonymously rate the housing manager and to have this information available to the housing manager and his administrative superiors. This could be done in many systems where the poor are served (welfare, for example) and could function to provide the poor with citizen or constituent power in systems in which they are typically powerless. Moreover, these surveys could be conducted by the poor themselves, functioning as nonprofessional research aides.[5]

Robert Reiff has proposed that various segments of the poor, including the most apathetic, be *employed to engage in social action and to study themselves in the process.*[6]

New Forms of Social Action—Inside the System

Before considering how publicly supported anti-poverty programs can play a role in the development of social action by the poor, it may be useful to consider the fact that there has been quite an upsurge of social action independent of government sponsorship in the last few years. One need only note the civil rights revolt, the rent strike movement (which spread to 25 cities in the United States), the renewed interest in Saul Alinsky's conflict model of community organization and the striking illustration of it in a Chicago-based community of the poor —The Woodlawn Organization (TWO)—and finally the recent emergence of a welfare rights group in California.[7] In this last illustration, people on public assistance have organized to demand their rights and to demand changes in the operation of the welfare system. Thus, social action appears to be on the move in America (outside of the system), and the poor have been increasingly involved in it.

It is in this context that government sponsored anti-poverty programs have arisen. I am not suggesting that the poor demanded these programs—that the poor demanded the Economic Opportunity Act. But it would seem that parts of this Act, particularly the community action section, reflect in some indirect fashion at least, the rising participation of the poor. In an article entitled, "The New Social Action Trend and the Alinsky Model," I have discussed some of these issues in more detail. Here I simply want to suggest that the poor are beginning to be or-

[5] Arthur Pearl has pioneered the use of indigenous nonprofessionals as research aides at Howard University's Center for the Study of Youth and Community and at the New York State Division for Youth.

[6] See Robert Reiff proposal for *Social Psychological Action Research for Change* (SPARC), 1964, Low Income Center, Albert Einstein College of Medicine, Bronx, New York.

[7] We would predict that before long "Councils of Unemployed" similar to those of the 1930's will appear again.

ganized by various citizen groups, who have an independence of action that cannot be emulated by publicly sponsored agencies. The independent political groups can more easily appeal to the potentially militant indigenous leaders in the community and can call for social protest action (including illegal boycotts of schools) with considerable freedom and certainly with no threat of withdrawal of public funds.

One of the great errors of Mobilization For Youth consisted in overlooking the fact that MFY could not long imitate the rent strike movement and the civil rights movement without "biting the hand that fed it." [8] MFY failed to recognize its potential "third force" role and instead attempted to "buy in" on the "second force," namely the civil rights and rent strike actions. It seems to me that government sponsored community action programs oriented toward the poor would do better to adopt a "third force" stance; that is to organize those sections of the poor who have not been appealed to by the protest models of Alinsky, the civil rights groups, and other independent political action groups. They can develop indigenous leaders who would not be developed via the protest route, and they can attempt to function as advocates of the poor, negotiating with the institutional structure, e.g., welfare department, housing department, etc.

But of course the relationship between "third force" and the "second force" is not a static one. Representatives of the "second force," civil rights leaders for example, will be invited to participate on local community action boards. Residents of the community being organized by the community action programs may in some cases move toward direct participation in the "second force," the civil rights movement, the welfare organizations, the housing movement, etc. Thus, it is clear that the two forces will articulate with each other, but it seems important to maintain a separation of function and goals.

Community action programs can play an important role in reaching segments of the poor who are unreached by the Alinskys, the Galamisons, the Jesse Grays, etc. This should be their

---

[8] See Frank Riessman, "Mobilization for Youth: What Went Wrong," *Commonweal* (May, 1965).

primary objective, rather than to incorporate the technology and focus of protest social action into government sponsored community action programs. Community action programs will have enough trouble becoming a "third force" without attempting to become a "second force." Moreover, these programs can emphasize two aspects which are less stressed by the independent militant groups: community action programs can stress the development of more effective service for the poor, including the expediting of this service, and they can also intervene more directly in the formal agency structure to produce institutional change. They have much more access to service technology, including the use of nonprofessionals as servers, and they have more access to the formal institutions through their negotiation role and through their public sponsorship and its associated sources of power, which are different than those of the protest groups.

They can use their service function as an instrument for the development of local community action. Thus, for example, in providing service via the rapidly developing neighborhood service centers (which are becoming a major structure for the use of nonprofessionals) community action programs can bring together in small groups those people who have common service needs, whether with regard to welfare, housing, schools, or whatever. These small groups can slowly emerge in the direction of broader community action.

It is interesting to observe that Mobilization For Youth bifurcated its service function and its community organization function so that service was provided through the neighborhood service centers, and the community section organized totally different people for social action. It is my contention that many of the people desiring service could be brought into milder forms of social action and that this is precisely the role that the community action program can meaningfully play. In developing this kind of service-based social action the role of the community action programs can be decisive. Indigenous nonprofessionals can be employed as community aides, in coordinating service-giving, small group development and larger community action. The Crusade for Opportunity (the non-Alinsky program) in Syracuse is developing neighborhood workers in this image. It would seem that indigenous nonprofessionals drawn from the community itself would be most sensitive to finding and involving members of the poor who are less responsible to protest forms of social action and have not been drawn toward the proliferating activist groups.

These indigenous nonprofessionals, however, will be faced by a unique problem in the training of these workers. They are being asked in a sense, to play a "third force" role and this is not their accustomed role in the community. Their style has in all likelihood been to talk to groups of people in the community, to help them express their anger, to mobilize them and perhaps in some cases to bring them toward "second force" groups—tenants' councils, civil rights groups, and the like. But now they are to be employed "inside" the system by a government-supported "third force" operation, and they have to develop a different posture in relation to the community and the agencies with which they will be working. These new nonprofessionals are being asked to play a two-way communication, bridge role. They are not being asked to organize the poor in order to smash the institutional structure, and they have to understand this thoroughly or else they will get into a great deal of trouble in their relationship with professionals and agencies as well as the people of the community. They may be rejected by the community as "finks," as has occurred in some cases in the Syracuse Crusade for Opportunity Project. Or they may be rejected by the agency structure as misinformed hotheads, as was the case in some instances with Mobilization For Youth nonprofessional workers. They must learn to walk a narrow line. This must be a crucial feature in their training, and training is essential for the development of the nonprofessional movement in America.

PARTICIPATION ON LOCAL COMMUNITY ACTION BOARDS

Another way in which the poor can have a voice in the anti-poverty programs is through participation on local community action boards. The tendency in selecting people from the neighborhood to participate on these boards will probably be to choose those residents who have already demonstrated leadership ability and interest. Thus, it was reported that in Syracuse the indigenous leaders who have been selected for various local boards have been well known for some time for their active participation in the communities of the poor. A small number of these leaders has already been chosen to be on many different local boards. This, of course, is a positive step in that it does involve indigenous leadership in programs related to the poor. Similarly, the involvement of minority group leadership will undoubtedly add an important voice to these community action programs. But here again, the leadership that is likely to be selected is the articulate, already developed leadership that exists in the communities. These are the leaders who are known to the professionals setting up the community action programs.

A much more important step, however, lies ahead. It should be possible to discover new potential leadership as the community action programs begin to function. If these programs are staffed in the main by nonprofessionals, indigenous to the area, there would seem to be a strong likelihood that new neighborhood leaders might be found and developed. After working with the potential leaders in various groups and capacities, it should then be possible to select people for the local community action boards who have had no previous experience at this "higher" level of participation. Board membership is an excellent method of developing various types of leadership skill, and thus participation on the board can be a technique for the development of new leadership.[9] This approach is entirely consistent with my philosophy throughout; that is, a concern for finding and developing people in the community who have not been sought out by previous social action and civil rights endeavors.

The new anti-poverty war should be able to enlist types of residents hitherto unreached by the growing social action movement in the United States. The new community action programs are not needed in order to reach the indigenous leaders who have been involved in the other more militant social action programs. These programs, whether developed by Alinsky or the civil rights movement, are quite capable of discovering and de-

---

[9] I am indebted to Rachel Robinson and Emanuel Hallowitz for the ideas expressed in the last paragraph.

veloping activist protest leaders. The community action programs supported by federal funds might do better to focus on the involvement of new untapped leadership. This is not to say that the new leaders developed through the community action programs will not to some extent become engaged in other types of social action taking place in the community—social action which is not led by government sponsored agencies. Some of the newly involved poor will move toward these groups and some will not. This need not, however, be the concern of the community action programs.

Thus, while I support the involvement of existing neighborhood leaders on local boards and in other forms of activity stimulated by the community action program, I think it is even more important that the community action programs search out and enlist less involved members of the poor and potential leaders who have not exerted this leadership. In this respect, I believe that Mobilization For Youth, for example, stressed far too much the involvement of known militant leaders in the community and did little through its service program in finding and developing new kinds of leaders.

It should be clear that the type of nonprofessional engaged in developing this local leadership and involvement of the community in planning and participation is a different type of nonprofessional, trained differently from the more service-oriented nonprofessional, such as the education aide or recreation aide. The type I am discussing here can be termed the community aide or neighborhood worker, as he is called in the Syracuse project.

Involvement of the poor on local boards assists the poor in two ways: it develops those who are selected as leaders and presumably indirectly aids the community by making the local boards more responsive to community needs as these boards become more truly representative of the area.

CONCLUSION

Four types of involvement of the poor in anti-poverty programs have been suggested, together with some of the potential benefits expected from this involvement. An alliance of professionals and nonprofessional representatives of the poor is urged as a "third force" mediating between the more militantly organized poor and the institutionalized agency structure. This "third force" alliance would begin to assist the unorganized, less militant, more apathetic poor in having their voices heard—through surveys, employment, group action, and participation on local community action boards.

The strong emphasis on employment of indigenous nonprofessionals as expediters, service aides, research assistants, and community aides, naturally leads to a great concern for appropriate training. It is hoped that many of the nonprofessionals themselves will rapidly move into positions as training assistants and trainers. Training is the key if the nonprofessional movement is to have a truly meaningful impact.[10]

---

[10] For a discussion of some of the training issues see Frank Riessman, "The Revolution in Social Work: The New Nonprofessional," *Trans-action,* Vol. I (November-December, 1964).

Discussion

PAUL JACOBS

Frank Riessman's paper reminds us of something that we often find convenient to forget: the war on poverty was conceived not merely to minister to the poor but to involve them in dynamic programs of self-help. Riessman offers us an analysis of the many ways in which the poor might participate in the anti-poverty program. Unfortunately, built into the very fabric of the poverty program itself are obstacles thrown up against just such full participation of the poor. This is true even when one takes into account the useful distinction Riessman makes between "second force" and "third force" community action programs.

The role of the poor in the anti-poverty program as it is now constituted ranges from a limited one to none at all. These limitations on the role of the poor are reflections of a whole set of circumstances and attitudes that have characterized the program from its administration in Washington to its implementation at the community level.

First, I think that the anti-poverty program as it is designed today is basically paternalistic in its view of the poor and of the role that they are to play in society. All too often the anti-poverty programs with which we are familiar tend to view the poor as clients, much in the way that traditional social service agencies do. Along with this goes a view of the poor, built into the program, which sees them as subjects rather than individuals.

Perhaps I can illustrate these points in a concrete way by an experience I had recently while working on an Indian reservation in the Southwest. I was on the roof of a building in this reservation, doing some rough carpenter work long with a group of Indians, mostly prisoners from the tribal prison, when a car drove up bearing an official from the Office of Economic

Opportunity. He had come to the reservation in connection with a decision that had to be made about an anti-poverty project on the reservation. He got out of the car with the governor of the tribe and looked up at us on the roof. So far as the Indians on the roof were concerned, there was no relationship between the man on the ground and anything that had any importance for the quality of their lives. They were totally indifferent to him, for on the basis of their experience, he was just another of the federal bureaucrats who was looking them over as objects of a program that had to be administered. Their response is one that will be characteristic of the poor in any situation in which they recognize that they are being treated as clients or objects in a program.

A second grave weakness of the poverty program vis-a-vis the role of the poor is that there is some unwillingness at the national level to run what are known as public relations risks. There is great concern in the OEO with the over-all public relations image of the program. The general principle that seems to operate is not to "get caught out" by some aspect of the project that might boomerang on the whole program. In the Job Corps, for example, the decision was made to exclude from the program young people with certain kinds of arrest records, based on this principle. The justification offered for the exclusion was that if such young people were brought into the Job Corps and then got into difficulties, the image of the Job Corps and the anti-poverty program would be damaged. In the MDTA program the same cautious spirit can be found to be operating as well.

However, it is clear that, if poor people are to be actively involved in the poverty program, many risks will have to be taken. Involving the poor in a program is inherently a bad risk to the public-relations-conscious administrator. The poor are, after all, generally inarticulate and uneducated. They will not always be as adept as administrators and social workers in smoothing over conflicts between various officials and agencies. Indeed, the participation of the poor may create all sorts of frictions and conflicts that will disrupt the public relations image created for the program in Washington.

At the local level, also, the desire to avoid risks leads to a retreat from the full involvement of the poor in the program. In the city of San Francisco a whole set of complicated political problems operate to interfere with the proper development of the poverty program. The Mayor, the Board of Supervisors, the Congressmen from the area, and the city welfare agencies all have something of an interest in the way in which the poverty program develops. Their interests are complicated by the extent to which active involvement by the poor begins to threaten these groups.

I can illustrate this best by describing an incident that occurred at a recent meeting of the anti-poverty council in San Francisco. In the course of the meeting, discussion was centered on neighborhood action centers. The director of the council was explaining that the purpose of such centers was to help stimulate the people in the neighborhoods to take their fate into their own hands. In connection with this purpose, he said, there would be a lawyer attached to the centers to help the people become aware of what their legal rights are. In the course of the discussion, someone raised the question of what would happen if the people in a neighborhood center voted, democratically, to resist the Redevelopment Agency of San Francisco, in its plans to redevelop the area in which the center was located. The director of the Redevelopment Agency happened to be present at this meeting, and his reaction to this hypothetical question was quite blunt and decidedly negative. It was his view that the use of government funds by one agency, the Office of Economic Opportunity, to disrupt the activities of another agency, the Redevelopment Agency, could not be handled inside the context of the poverty program.

Now this is a very serious question. It is a question that took a very sharp form in New York City with the efforts of Mobilization for Youth, and it will continue to be with us for the duration of the poverty program. The manner in which it is resolved will obviously have enormous implications for the possibilities of carrying out the goal of actively involving the poor in the various anti-poverty projects.

There is also the problem raised when the poverty program

involves the poor in conflict with private business interests. For example, what happens when Vista youth go into an agricultural community and help organize farm workers to get better wages, or into the Mission district of San Francisco to organize the laundry workers there in an effort to get better wages? These again are serious questions which affect the role of the poor in any anti-poverty program.

There are also problems within each of the particular communities in which the poverty program will operate. The Mexican-American community in San Francisco or Los Angeles, like the Puerto Rican community in New York or the Negro community in Chicago, has its own internal stresses and strains. Inside these communities, too, there are conflicts and group interests which may be affected by the manner in which the community is mobilized by the anti-poverty program. Again, because of these conflicts, there is a tendency for the professionals and the administrators to veer away from running the risk of upsetting the community too much, or antagonizing existing agencies.

This unwillingness to run risks at the national level as well as at the local level has, in my view, already truncated the poverty program. The only way in which the anti-poverty program will succeed in fundamentally coming to grips with the problem is to let the poor, the people with whom we are concerned, run risks and decide for themselves. They must be allowed to make their own errors and develop their own strengths. The importance of having the poor develop their own strengths is illustrated by a story that was told to me by Henry Miller.

The story concerns a guru, an Indian wiseman, who sat with a cocoon in his hand. He was watching the cocoon when a little boy came to him and asked him, "What is that?" And the guru said to the little boy, "It is a cocoon and inside is a butterfly. When the time comes for the butterfly to come out, he will break open the cocoon and come out to fly by himself." The little boy then asked the guru if he could have the cocoon. The guru said, "Yes, you can have the cocoon, but you must promise me, little boy, that when the cocoon splits and the butterfly starts to come out, no matter how much you want to help the butterfly you mustn't do it." The little boy agreed to this promise. He took the cocoon home and he sat and watched and finally in a little while the cocoon cracked open. Inside was a wet, moist butterfly beating against the shell of the cocoon and trying to get out. The little boy forgot his promise, and with all kindness opened the cocoon. The butterfly flew out, soared up in the air, and then suddenly fell down to the ground, dead. The little boy went crying to the guru with the dead butterfly. The guru said to the little boy, "You see, you must have opened the cocoon and helped the butterfly out because you felt sorry for it, but what you didn't realize is that the way the butterfly gets strong is by beating his wings against the side of the cocoon. And when you don't let him beat his wings that way, his wings will be weak and he must die."

What we have to remember about the poor in America, the people with whom we are so concerned, is that our society is the cocoon against which the poor must beat to gain their strength. And the only way in which the poor will get strong is if society is willing to take the risk of being beaten against.

Discussion

JEAN CAMPER CAHN

I want to start by talking to Paul Jacob's point about the risk involvement in helping the poor. Helping the poor is just about the riskiest thing that we, the American nation, could be doing. If we really mean to help the poor, if we really mean that we want people to get out of poverty, out of the cocoon, the ghetto, the caste of untouchables, then we are talking about something fairly dangerous because we are talking about social change.

We are talking about social change which is meaningful and which is within the best traditions of America. But we are also talking about social change which will disrupt and dislodge many vested interests. These interests will be disrupted and destroyed because poverty isn't something impersonal. Poverty is a very personal matter, and it concerns the poor and those who are not poor.

If the poor are ever given the power to hit back, they won't be hitting back at something impersonal called disease or lack of work or whatever the going name is for some symptom of poverty. The poor will be hitting back at the man who gives the credit down the street, or the welfare agency that withholds their checks, or the social board that fails to provide adequate education for their children, or the redevelopment agency, or all of the other vested interests in the American community. That means trouble. And if something is really going to be done about the 35 million people whom we say are below the poverty line, then we must realize that there are going to be millions of people who are disturbed in the particular worlds in which they live. And it is not going to be just the isolated case of the redevelopment official in San Francisco or of a welfare official in Louisiana who objects because he can't stand the sudden amplification of the voices of silence.

The impact of the confrontation will be valuable across this country. I wonder if we here at this conference, or anyone, has actually considered whether we are ready to take the risk—a very important risk and one which I think really tests whether or not we believe in democracy and what we say this country is all about. We like to talk about helping the poor. I prefer, for the sake of putting our problem squarely on the table, to discard the rhetoric and discuss particulars.

At one time I was a neighborhood lawyer. I sat in an office and things happened—for example, at six o'clock one evening a guy ran in, dropped a gun on my desk, and said, "I think I just shot my brother, help me." Or, another time, a woman whose child had just died in a fire said, "I think the hospital has been charging me five times for the same bill, help me." Or, several times, women said, "I just don't know what to do; I think I need a divorce." But what they were really talking about was that the bills had come to be too much to bear. I could recite other instances from personal experience, such as the case of the man who went out and stole a TV set because he wanted to go to jail. Why did he want to go to jail? If he went to jail, then there wouldn't be a man in the house and his wife could get welfare help under the rules of the Aid to Dependent Children program. In that way, she would be better supported than he could support her as a tree clipper for the city.

Nowadays, at the Office of Economic Opportunity, I have a different kind of experience. I don't meet people. I get letters instead. And the letters say to me, what can we, the OEO do? We have been getting a lot of letters from people involved in workmen's compensation cases. One of them states:

> For five years I have been trying to get this money. I am disabled, 40 doctors say I am disabled, but the one doctor on the workmen's compensation committee says I am not disabled. I can't get any money.

Or a daughter writes in for her father, who is confused about the fact that they paid for some sidings on the house and the contract which her father signed was, they thought, for $2,500. Instead, it is for $3,500, and they can't pay it. She writes:

We don't know anything about how we can get help, but we read an article in the paper that said that this war on poverty is to help us. Is there something you can do about it?

These are just examples. The stream of letters continues indefinitely. Some of them are very heartbreaking, because you know that you can search all the resources in this country, but you are not going to find anybody to help that person. I can sit at that desk in Washington, and make as many phone calls as I need to make, and I am still not going to find anybody to help in a little town out in Iowa, because I don't know what's going on out in Iowa. There is nobody there who is going to do the job, or to whom I can send this person and feel that I won't simply have sent him to one more rebuff.

These are the kinds of problems that have made me particularly sensitive to the role which the lawyer has to play in this society, and in the war on poverty. The lawyer is very important, because whether we are ready to admit it or not, we have become a very complex society, and in the urban areas—the areas that I know best—how a citizen ever gets what he wants without knowledge is beyond me. In fact, he doesn't. He just sits, and the forces of government, and of business, and of the community work on him. He doesn't know what to do about them. The people who really know what to do about them are the lawyers, or at least this ought to be the job of the lawyers. Right now, the lawyers really don't know what to do about many of the problems these 35 million people face. There haven't been enough lawyers interested in this kind of problem to stimulate the law schools to offer the kinds of courses that are needed or to help other lawyers feel that this type of work is not beneath them and will not damage their reputations.

In addition, there has been a question as to who would pay for such services? But, despite these problems, we do have enough technical knowhow at this point to go about developing ways of helping these people. Elizabeth Wickenden, one of the foremost social workers in this country, expressed the same point of view recently. She said:

I tell you this to underscore the fact that even though everyone sees the war on poverty in the light of his immediate task, in my own view the very heart of the problem for us in the United States is one of entitlement under the law: hence the primary challenge both to practicing lawyers and to all those who concern themselves with the frame work of the law within which we live.[1]

This general conclusion is the basic thesis of my presentation. I come to it from my particular point of view, for I am a lawyer. She, of course, came to it from the point of view of her long experience in social work. We are no longer voices crying in the wilderness. Others recognize the problem. Recently the American Bar Association passed what I think is an historic resolution. It decided that it was time for lawyers to do something about these problems, with the full recognition that this was going to hurt the pocketbooks of a lot of people and that it might be very unpleasant. The resolution, which passed unanimously, was very courageous, stating, in part:

> . . . whereas freedom and justice have flourished only where the practice of law is a profession and where legal services are performed by trained and independent lawyers, now therefore be it resolved that the American Bar Association reaffirms its deep concern with the problem of providing legal services to all who need them and particularly to indigents and to persons of low income who without guidance or assistance have difficulty in obtaining access to competent legal services at reasonable costs and authorizes the officers in appropriate sections, etc., to improve existing methods and to develop more effective methods for meeting the public need for adequate legal services.

Within a week after that time, ABA officials, together with other outstanding members of the legal profession, came to Washington to meet with representatives of OEO, and to offer their cooperation. Elizabeth Wickenden, Judge Pollier, and representatives of the Ford Foundation and other foundations were present. I have never participated in a meeting more action-oriented than this particular meeting.

---

[1] Proceedings of a conference on *The Extension of Legal Services to the Poor* (Washington, D. C.: U. S. Department of Health, Education, and Welfare, Office of Juvenile Delinquency and Youth Development, November, 1964), p. 41.

Now what does it all mean? Does the ABA actually realize what it means? Does the OEO realize? Do the participants in this session realize that what we are talking about is a basic social change? It is because people don't articulate these kinds of feelings that there exists this problem of risk avoidance which Paul Jacobs talked about, and which my husband and I analyzed in a recent article. Both locally and nationally it's being said, "Let's not take any chances, you know we've got to be successful in this first year. Let's look for success in modest ways, in little things, so that we can say to Congress or to the city council that we are producing something. Let's not train the people who are the worst hit by poverty. Let's first train the high school graduate who probably could get a job anywhere. And, of course, he must not have a record even though juvenile records theoretically are not criminal. Let's upgrade the 'good' guy, the one who has upward mobility."

But this really doesn't do anything for the problem of poverty. If we are not willing to engage in some experimentation and creativity, and in some programs that will cause a lot of problems and headaches, then we are not really serious about poverty. At this point, I find myself asking the same question of the OEO. Just how serious are you about this problem, and about the law program in particular? At this point, Mr. Shriver stands on the threshold of a great experiment. He has behind him the forces of the organized bar—not just the ABA, but the National Legal Aid and Defender Association and the National Bar Association, which includes Negro lawyers below the Mason-Dixon Line who are excluded from other associations. Will he go forward? The absence of any progress since the meeting of ABA officials and others in Washington to which I referred—which took place about two weeks ago—is not encouraging.

Let me repose my main question. Do we really want to take these people out of poverty or is our aim to make poverty more palatable to the people who are already poor? For if we want to take them out of poverty, then we have to be ready to do some pretty daring things and to put up with real unpleasantness. We shall have to listen to some boring speeches, perhaps, from poor people who can be very inarticulate and paradoxically quite vocal, and we must be prepared to see picketing and other troublesome developments. But we must make up our minds. And I think that America really hasn't made up its mind yet.

Discussion

EDGAR S. CAHN

As Frank Riessman spoke, I found myself looking at two sentences from my wife's and my article, "The War on Poverty: A Civilian Perspective":

—local leaders who feel that the program is doing too little too slowly can be silenced, undermined, discredited or hired.

I would venture to say that such a danger exists not just at the level of the poor—but in an even more dangerous sense at the professional level. It exists particularly because the temptations of government are great—and the most seductive of those temptations is the temptation to think that one can do good on such a grand scale that one forgets the individual. That is a danger not unique to the federal government. It exists at the local government level and the social agency level, where the resources available to help people always appear to have such mammoth potential for good that any distraction from operating on a grand scale appears insignificant and trivial.

One walks a tight rope—trying somehow to cope both with those individual demands for attention that flock to any official and, on the other hand, with those demands to utilize one's position in order to do good on a grand scale. And we forget—I think, often, that tomorrow is never promised—that the only good we can be sure we ever do is that which is done for particular individuals—no matter how insignificant, how annoying, or how demanding and ungrateful they may seem to be. And the larger question—the question of conscience for all officials, for those who are called members of the *establishment*—is how can one import the perspective of the individual, the citizen and maintain any fidelity to it given the seductive temptation of trying to do good and save the world—today, tomorrow, or the next day.

One thing we have not yet heard in this session is a satisfactory statement of why, speaking for the anti-poverty program, we want the involvement of the poor. I have heard somebody suggest that it would be nice to get them on the payroll, since this would, in effect, involve transfer payments to the poor, but transfer payments of three-quarters of a billion dollars one year, and a billion and a half the next, would scarcely make a significant dent on the problem of poverty.

Riessman has referred to a "bridging" function—that is, that we need the poor to translate our professional jargon or to perform a kind of sales job. This may work well if we are "selling" a product or service such as a vaccination, polio vaccines, or something about which we feel fairly confident. But I think that most of the time we don't have the right to feel very confident about the ideas or suggestions that we want to sell to the poor.

Actually, I believe, we want to involve the poor for two very different reasons. The first, and one of the most basic, is because we need to learn from them. We need to find out why it is that our system has failed so significantly for so many on so many dimensions, why our schools are not reaching many of the people whom they are supposed to help, why urban renewal is not really eliminating slums, and why welfare programs are not breaking the cycle of dependency. And I think we had better listen to the people who have knowledge of this first-hand.

Moreover, if we are talking about a rationale for involvement of the poor, we ought to start with a basic notion of democracy—that the people in their wisdom and in their folly know what is best for them, and that we had better listen to them, enfranchise them, and make sure that they have forums from which they can speak and compel response to their points of view. I was at a conference at which some poor people did get up and speak, and it seemed to me that the most significant achievement of that particular gathering was in providing a forum for these poor persons. And, in response to those who charge that the poor are inarticulate and apathetic, I would like to quote to you a statement which I took down as Mrs. Janice Bradshow from Pueblo, Colorado, spoke at a conference in Tucson:

> Poverty is a personal thing. Poverty is taking your children to the hospital and spending the whole day waiting there with no one even taking your name, and then coming back the next day and the next day until they finally get around to you. Poverty is having a landlady who is a public health nurse, who turns off the heat when she leaves for work in the morning and turns it back on at six when she returns. It is being helpless to do anything about that, because, by the time the officials get around to looking into it, she has turned the heat back on for that day, and then it will be off the next. Poverty is having welfare investigators break in at four in the morning and cut off your welfare payments without an explanation, and, when you go down and ask, they tell you it is because of a pair of men's slippers, house slippers, that they found in the attic when your brother visited you last Christmas.
>
> Poverty is having a child with glaucoma and watching that eye condition grow worse every day, while the welfare officials send you to the private agencies, and the private agencies send you back to the welfare officials. And, when you ask the welfare officials to refer you to the specialized division of the hospital, and they refuse, and you say it is because of prejudice since you are a Negro, they deny it flatly and shout at you to name one white child that we have referred there. And, when you name 25, they sit down and shut up, and they finally refer you, but it is too late then, because your child has permanently lost 80 per cent of his vision, and you are told that if only they had caught it a month earlier, when you first made inquiry, they could have preserved his vision.

Having heard her and others like her, I can't help but feel that the poor have a great deal to tell us about what is wrong with our society and about why poverty continues to persist.

The second reason why we want to involve the poor is because, in the most basic sense, we want to eliminate the phenomenon of the poor as a class apart—to eliminate the sharp dichotomy between "we, the fortunate" and "they, the poor," which divides America far more pervasively than we think.

Now I should like to shift to the question of the willingness of OEO to run risks—what we are prepared to do. I suppose nobody knows until the chips are down just what OEO will ultimately do. I do think it is a commentary on our nation at this time that so often radicalism takes the form of asking the government to subsidize radicalism. Moreover, we tend to overemphasize the responsibility of each of us as citizens and of the private sector of the economy to take the initiative and not to wait on the lead of government. I don't understand why it was the government that had to pinpoint or, in some sense, make sensational the problem of poverty to make it fashionable. The Government does have a responsibility. On the other hand, the entire responsibility for taking risks does not end with government, nor does it begin with government. And while we are busy asking government whether it is prepared to take the risks, I think we ought to turn around and ask ourselves the same question in our capacities as private citizens.

In a sense, the government has done one significant thing, much as it did in the civil rights movement, i.e., it has legitimated a grievance. It has legitimated the concerns and grievances and needs of a group of people whose concerns were never considered to be worthwhile or legitimate before. What has happened, then, is that a process has been unleashed—a process over which government cannot and should not have control or be permitted to maintain a kind of monopoly grip by virtue of its power or money.

If the Negro had left to the Justice Department the question of whether it should subsidize civil right demonstrations, the answer would have been clear. On the other hand, when one legitimates a grievance, one sets a force in motion. That has now been done, and we ought to have faith in our democracy and in the capacity of government to respond. The question now is what is OEO's role in that process.

I must say that I can't really agree with Riessman that our role is purely to mediate. I think there will always be an adequate supply of persons who will take a salary to be brokers between demand and supply. If we confined our role to mediating, to striking balances and compromises, I don't think it would be very meaningful. Let me put it this way. One of

OEO's chief functions is to coordinate all poverty-related programs on the federal level. On the local level, local community action programs are supposed to do the same thing. They are supposed to coordinate many different activities, many different agencies, many different jurisdictions in an attempt to deal with the multifaceted dimensions of poverty.

I suggest that that is one view of coordination, but it is an inadequate view. It supposes that there is a certain supply of services, or on the federal level a supply of federal programs and resources, that, if put together in a more sensible fashion, could deal adequately with a fixed amount of concern, of need, and of demand on the local level. This view implies if we could somehow rationalize that response, if we could get decisions made more intelligibly and more efficiently, existing resources at the local level and existing programs at the federal level, expanded a bit under new legislation, would be enough to do the job.

I believe that we should take a very different look at coordination. We might conceive of the role of coordination at both the local and federal levels as *increasing* demand, as stimulating pressures on local agencies and in turn on the federal government, and through OEO in turn on each of the departments within the federal government. In other words, rather than trying to keep the lid on demand or on concern, we ought to be interested in stimulating and in amplifying the voices of grievance and of protest in such a way that "heat" is put on local agencies, so that they would turn to their local sources of support and say that in a democracy it is your job to respond. And I think that ultimately OEO's role is to go to bat for the poor and for community agencies representing the poor, and to put pressure on the federal establishment to make it more accessible and more responsive to the needs of local government and of the poor themselves.

PART ELEVEN

A PROGRAM TO COMBAT POVERTY IN AMERICA

29. A Summing Up

GUNNAR MYRDAL[1]

This important conference on poverty, that has brought together such an impressive assembly of experts in many fields, is drawing to a close. And it has been left to two economists, my colleague Professor Fritz Machlup and myself, to make the concluding remarks. As a matter of fact, the first paper, as you will recall, was also given by an economist, Professor Gordon. I think Professor Machlup will agree with me that this honor given to our profession is hardly well earned. It is indeed remarkable how economists, as a profession, have succeeded in keeping themselves rather unaware of, and in many cases unconcerned about, the poverty problem in America. When the issue was raised to its present national importance, it was largely done by students in other social sciences, by practical people working in the wide field of social welfare, by the social reformers, and, ultimately, by the politicians. We cannot be particularly proud of our record in this field of study. It rather testifies to how economists have succeeded in keeping aloof from the worries of the nation.

I see in the choice of two economists to wind up the discussions of these two days rather a challenge to us. Undoubtedly, economic policies must take a prominent role in solving the intractable problem which is aptly described as poverty amidst plenty. Professor Gordon made the important point, which I would like to underline, that without rapid and steady economic growth, practically all other policies discussed here would be frustrated. If I should make any criticism of this beautifully organized conference, it would be that you have not

[1] Editor's note: The verbatim transcript of Professor Myrdal's statement at the final session of the conference has been only slightly edited.

devoted a session to putting the economists on the spot. What are the specific economic policies we have to suggest that would give reasonable effectiveness to the war against poverty?

I would first like to state my view of the place of this conference in the history of the nation. I believe that for about two years there has been in America a mighty change taking place in attitudes to social problems and that this change is going to result in a very different country. One good thing about America, which to me makes it particularly glorious, is that now and then it has a conversion. It is changing its mind, and is doing it rather whole-heartedly and radically. In this movement, new statistical investigations, conferences, books, articles, and speeches are like drops making up together a rapidly flowing flood. This conference is a particularly big drop, I might say—big enough to swell the stream through its effects and after effects in many localities, centers of learning, and government agencies to which the participants will now return.

This rapidly proceeding change in attitudes to social problems in America implies also an intellectual catharsis. It is not only that we are brought to see clearly what most of us have been able to conceal from ourselves: the relative prevalence and depth of poverty and its debilitating effects on those who are poverty-stricken—not least the children and the youth—and upon society as a whole. But it is also clear that the mythical and irrational conceptions we have built up over generations and preserved in order to defend laissez-faire, the do-nothing policy, are crumbling before our eyes.

Let me illustrate this point by reminding you that at the time the late President Kennedy first proposed the tax cut, a nationwide Gallup Poll showed a remarkable masochism on the part of the American people—the majority did not want to have lower taxes if it meant that the federal budget would go into the red. A year or so later, Congress decided on the tax cut. There are, as we know, many built-in mechanisms of reactionary inertia in Congress—incidentally, much more in practice than in the Constitution, which is not bad. Nevertheless, the American Congress, in my opinion, is more sensitive to public opinion than any parliament I know in the world. When it decided on the tax cut, therefore, this action testified to the fact that an astonishingly rapid change of public opinion in America had taken place—a change for which politicians and businessmen can take the credit more than the many thousand professors of economics in colleges and universities who should have had a special responsibility to educate the people.

And to take another example, when Congress is now on the verge of decreasing the requirement of gold cover for bank deposits, it is happening quietly, without creating the anxiety it would have caused a few years ago. The President is not gainsaid when he characterizes this requirement as arbitrary, unnecessary, and indeed harmful if it restricts the volume of credit needed to maintain economic progress in the United States. I foresee further relaxations in rigid, irrational concepts attached to gold, that dangerous metal which has always been the catalyst of superstitious beliefs and fears. Certainly, America is rapidly changing not only emotionally in attitudes but intellectually in its thinking.

In listening to the discussions during this conference, I have been struck by certain characteristics of the meeting, which, as I see it, provide further testimony of the maturing of American thinking. For one thing, I have heard little about two things which in recent popular discussion have been blamed as the major causes of the underutilization of labor, which, of course, is at the basis of the poverty problem in America. I refer to automation and the rapid population increase. As these two problems should not be left entirely aside in our deliberations, I should like to comment briefly on both.

AUTOMATION

Automation has, in my opinion, been given altogether too important a role in explaining the high unemployment rate and, consequently, poverty in America. To begin with, there are large sectors of the American economy which are not yet automated to any appreciable degree. We may just think through our daily routine of living and consider how many processes of producing goods and, particularly, services there are in which great savings of labor could easily be made. Capital investment, moreover, has not been high in relation to national income, which again does not indicate a particularly high rate of automation. The increase in productivity of labor, which should reflect automation most directly, has not been extraordinarily high in America, and, more specifically, has not been much greater in recent years than we should expect from all the research that is going on in industry and from the improved utilization of plants and machines.

Certainly, automation is occurring, particularly in manufacturing, in heavy transport, in banking and insurance, and even in retail trade, etc., but the same process is underway in all the rich countries. If the *level* of automation is considerably higher in America, which may be true, I would suggest that the *pace* of automation, which from an employment point of view is the important thing, is probably not faster here than, say, in France, Germany, or Sweden. In the full employment economies of Western Europe, automation is welcomed by employers as the only means of increasing production when labor is scarce. And it is welcomed by the employees as a basis for higher wages. It is the high unemployment rate in the United States which creates the danger that automation will leave workers unemployed.

Behind the popular idea that automation creates unemployment is chiefly the further thought that technological development is leading us to a situation in which very much less labor will be needed. This is, in my opinion, a mistake, or in any case a gross exaggeration. As we become richer, we will be in need of greatly expanded services of all sorts. Think of the improved education that we want to have. Think of the care we want to give to old people. We will soon be able to cure cancer, and we will live still longer. We are leaving the time behind us when old people could be taken care of by their daughters or younger sisters.

To illustrate what I mean, let me just refer to the fact that the number of hospital beds per 1,000 of population is higher in Sweden than in the United States and, in particular, that the rate of increase in that important index is higher. Nevertheless, we have in Sweden tremendous waiting lists to get into our hospitals, even of people who are seriously ill and for whom it is almost a catastrophe that they will have to wait. When it becomes possible for people to meet their needs, then the needs will emerge as very much greater demands that cannot be met. This means that when we make our manpower forecasts in Sweden and take into account all the teachers we need, as well as teachers of teachers and nurses and doctors, the conclusion is not that we will have too many workers, but just the opposite, that we have to speed up automation and rationalization even in hospitals and schools in order to be able to create the society we hope for.

Rapid Population Growth

I look upon the effect of the rapid rise of population and the labor force in America in very much the same way as the effects of automation. Whatever, in the long run, the effects are of having a rate of population increase of 1.7 per cent per annum in America, in the short run a rapid population increase should, in a country with plenty of capital, rather spur economic growth by raising the demand for more homes and related needs, as well as for production facilities for the increasing labor force. This was pointed out 30 years ago by the grand old man of American economics, Professor Alvin Hansen, and by many others, and I believe it is equally true today. If the rapid growth of the labor force in America is causing unemployment, it is because economic growth is not fast enough. In both regards—automation and rapid population increase—the situation can be described in the only superficially paradoxical terms that they render workers unemployed because the economy is not a full employment economy. Unemployment breeds unemployment in a vicious cycle. But it remains true that the rapid population increase in America necessitates a more rapid economic growth, if unemployment is not to be the result. That is a point to which I will return.

Deficient Demand or Structural Change?

Another intellectual advance in our thinking about unemployment which I believe is demonstrated at this conference is that we seem to have passed the stage when there was a conflict between two schools of thought about unemployment: the one school holding the view that unemployment was only a matter of lack of demand for labor, which could be cured simply by speeding up economic growth; and another school holding that unemployment had now become structural, so that there was a quality difference between the supply of labor and the labor demanded. The former school had its inspiration from a simplified Keynesian theory with its roots far back in neoclassical and classical, and incidentally also Marxian, economics, which regarded labor as a homogeneous entity. Until fairly recently, I am afraid, we must count the great majority of noninstitutional economists as part of that simplistic school of economics.

In America that school showed, however, a rather flagrant inconsistency in its thinking when it tended to consider very high unemployment rates, usually four per cent, as a level under which unemployment would not, or should not, fall. They never explained to themselves or to us in a satisfactory manner why such an extraordinarily high rate of unemployment should be normal in America, while in European full employment economies this rate was sometimes pressed down to one per cent, or occasionally even lower. Neither did they take adequate account of what I call "underemployment"—employees and self-employed workers with very low productivity and correspondingly low incomes—which in America probably accounts for at least as many as the unemployed. The underemployed are also in an abnormal situation as breadwinners.

The behavioral social scientists—incidentally one psychologist told me the other day that we economists were not empirical scholars, since we never came nearer to reality than when working with some figures, for example, which customs officials had collected—and the social workers and welfare administrators also are concerned about the underemployed and about those outside the active labor force, in addition to the large numbers whom economists normally consider to be unemployed. They, as well as many among the unemployed or the casually unemployed, often lack education and training. Many indeed are functionally illiterate, their physical and mental health is often deficient, their ambition and motivation is damaged, they are frequently discriminated against in the labor market on racial grounds, they live in slum surroundings, they constitute the hard core of the poor in America. To those among the poor in the age groups in which they could be an effective supply in the labor market in the absence of these handicaps, we must add the aged and the invalids and the many children in poor families.

So the approach characterized by the term structural unemployment opened a vista to that much larger problem of poverty which we have been discussing at this conference. It is a many-faceted problem, as has been stressed in many of the papers. And there is no simple cure, no panacea. Many things have to be done simultaneously, in a coordinated way, in the fields of education and the training of the children and the young, and in a vigorous program of slum clearance and low cost housing.

The social security system, including the provision of health facilities for all who need it, has to be reformed in a radical fashion. Incidentally, I believe somebody should look into the history of social security in America and how it is continually imprisoned in out-dated conceptions. I think it is too closely related to that old man Bismarck and our old friend Lloyd George, who were pioneers in this field, but who characterized the social problem as "eine Arbeiterfrage." I am proud that in my own country, Sweden, when we inaugurated an old-age pension reform in 1911, the labor party was eager to stress that we did not want to have the benefits subject to any condition except residence in the country. We wanted to give security to all as a right of citizenship. On that road we have continued. As a matter of fact, the richest banker receives pension checks; he will have to pay for them and more than that in his taxes. This, of course, also simplifies the whole administration.

Even after such a fundamental reform, the situation in America will remain one of serious social sickness. There will long be scope in the slums for what you in America call social work, and which, in the greater society of our dreams, will largely be unnecessary, as it already is in some countries. Social work tries to lift and remotivate individuals who are damaged by their experiences and their milieu. This raises problems that have been discussed in some detail during the several sessions of this conference. But that type of remedial action, directed to the individual, will be rather inconsequential if the basis of security of income is not created.

What the reformer is up to is to redirect policies in many fields in a rather radical fashion. Almost all social and economic policies in America—agricultural policies, taxation policies, housing policies, social security, minimum wage legislation, etc.—have in a queer way, as we now have begun to see, been following the perverse line of helping those who are not-so-poor while leaving the really poor in their poverty, and to state, local, and private charity, under one label or another. Insofar as we achieve success—and I am very optimistic about America in its present phase of rapid change of attitudes and thinking—we will increase the effective labor force, by which I mean those that have the capacity to meet the rising quality demands in the labor market.

In the present transitional situation with an oversupply of less skilled labor, I consider it almost fortunate that there is so much construction work which is needed in America: for slum clearance, low cost housing, transportation, and indeed reconstructing our cities. Even if for these needs, also, labor needs to be trained, this is easier than to train doctors or teachers or all the others in the service fields of which we need so very many more. The need for construction work gives us a possibility not only of changing the labor supply to meet the labor demand, but also of changing labor demand, at least for a time, to correspond more closely to the labor supply we actually have.

I regard it as an advance that we have left behind us the quarrel between the two schools—let me say, the conventional economist school and the new institutional school—about unemployment. What we need is to pool our insights, and then they will fit excellently together. On the one hand, it is clear that prolonged unemployment will result in less useful workers and sometimes in unemployables, partly because of the demoralization which follows unemployment. It creates a clientele for social work. On the other hand, it is equally clear that if we can create and preserve a brisk labor market, then young workers are given a chance not only to get a job, but to get training in the job. By far the greatest investment in training is normally carried out by private employers. They are, in America, providing most of what in a wider sense we could call vocational education. And a labor market in which labor is kept scarce provides a mighty inducement for employers to increase such investments in the nation's labor force. Thus, I have reason to underline again what Professor Gordon said in the first paper delivered at this conference—namely, that the most important thing is to maintain economic growth and the demand for labor. In the absence of that condition, almost every other effort to cure structural unemployment by education, by training, by retraining, etc., is foredoomed to be largely in vain.

ECONOMIC GROWTH

During the four years of the Kennedy-Johnson era, the GNP has, as we know, increased at an annual rate of five per cent, or about double the rate in the Eisenhower era. Even more remarkable than the duration of this period of more rapid economic growth is the fact that growth has been so balanced in all respects. Wholesale prices are at the same level as four years ago, wages have not risen faster on the whole than productivity, there has been no significant buildup of unfilled orders (and consequently no excessive pressure from the demand side), while inventory investments have followed a smooth growth curve and have constantly been falling short of final sales. In short, the picture of American business today shows remarkably few of the signs that, according to experience, forebode a recession. Even in the longer run, growth prospects look reassuring.

President Johnson ascribes, rightly in my opinion, this fortunate development to public policies. He said (I quote from his recent Economic Report to Congress): "Since 1960 a new factor has emerged to invigorate private effort. The vital margin of difference has come from government policies which have sustained a steady but noninflationary growth of markets." And the program of the government for the years to come is to continue courageously along this expansionist policy line.

The trend to rising unemployment has been stopped, but the unemployment rate has decreased only from a level above six per cent, to one around five per cent. I have, obviously, not the time now to discuss specific policies, though that should be done in a conference on the eradication of poverty in America. But concerning the growth rate of the GNP, I want to make two observations which I think are pertinent.

One is that, when we compare the economic growth rate in the United States with those in other rich countries, we have to subtract from the former a little more than one per cent. We all know that when we discuss underdeveloped countries, we regularly talk about income per head, while we prefer to speak in terms of total rates when we discuss conditions in the advanced countries. Now it so happens that the United States has, as I mentioned, a population increase of 1.7 per cent, while the rate is much lower in other rich countries. In Sweden it is only half a per cent. This implies that the growth rate in the United States is not very high, internationally speaking. It also implies that, in the Eisenhower era, the United States economy was in a virtual condition of stagnation, with only around one per cent annual growth of the national product per capita.

My second observation concerns more directly the problem discussed at this conference. We must aim at a speedier decrease of the unemployment rate in the years to come. We cannot stop at what the Council of Economic Advisers called the "temporary target" of four per cent, because this is an abnormally high figure. It is far above the level at which we can successfully pursue the war against poverty. The serious thing is, however, that the growth rate of the labor force will be increasing about 50 per cent faster from now on. During the four years when we only succeeded in reducing the unemployment rate by a little more than one per cent, the labor force was increasing on the average by one million a year. In the next five years, the labor force is expected to increase by over one and one-half million each year, instead of one million. Already, in order to prevent the unemployment rate from leveling off or even beginning to increase again, a higher growth rate of the GNP is needed. And in order to bring down the unemployment rate substantially, the United States will have to achieve a considerably higher rate of economic growth than just the five per cent of recent years.

As I said, this growth rate is not particularly high, internationally speaking, when we take into account the rapid rate of population increase. I cannot avoid the conclusion that what the United States now needs is to raise its sights. A gross economic growth rate, in the years to come, of seven, eight, or even ten per cent would not seem too ambitious. From the point of view of the problems discussed at this conference, this would almost seem to be a condition for any real success in eradicating poverty. Most efforts to lift the poor to participation in the nation's life and work, and, in particular, all efforts to raise the quality of labor by education, training, and retraining, will be largely in vain if the unemployment rate stays at its present level, and perhaps moves upwards again.

Some time ago, I would like to remind you, it was common among economists, when discussing planning for development in underdeveloped countries, to regard the huge reserves of unemployed and underemployed workers as an asset, and, indeed, as capital, which need not be wasted. By putting them to work, their economies could advance rapidly. Because of various defects in their political, institutional, and attitudinal structures, few of these underdeveloped countries, if any, have been able to accomplish much in this direction. But, for the United States, the abnormally high level of unemployment and underemployment undoubtedly presents an extraordinary chance to have durable, steady, and rapid economic growth without inflation, and consequently without the need for restrictionist policies. Whatever is done in the war against poverty to educate, train, and retrain workers and increase their mobility will increase that scope for expansion without inflation. I do believe that the United States now has the opportunity to speed up its economic growth and to keep this speedier growth balanced, without more planning and government control than the country is rapidly becoming prepared to accept under the Kennedy-Johnson regime.

When I say this, I would not be honest with you if I concealed the fact that I am now treading on controversial ground. Many of my colleagues, whose judgment I respect, would not follow me in this line. They agree, of course, that we now have the tools to give the economy the spurt to raise the rate of growth above five per cent a year, but they would not agree that it would be possible to achieve that speedier growth and still keep the economy balanced. Many would not even believe it possible to preserve the present low rate of five per cent a year without soon experiencing a recession. Their opinion implies, however—and I want to say this clearly—that we would then not see much further decrease in the unemployment rate, and that, instead, we would probably soon witness another upward trend in the rate, with the serious consequences that I have pointed out for all the efforts to eradicate poverty with which this conference has been concerned.

It is out of the question that, in these concluding remarks, I could specify in detail the considerations that give me a basis for my optimism and discuss the many problems related to what I have called the minimum requirements of planning and controls. I believe that the United States should now be in a position to speed up its economic growth so much that the unemployment rate could be brought down substantially, opening up opportunities for all the specific policies for eradicating poverty we have been discussing at this conference to be undertaken successfully and to have their maximum result.

The Role of Business Opinion

I cannot end without pointing to one more trend which I have discerned and which accounts to a considerable extent for my optimism. I am referring to the development of business opinion in this country. I feel that business, and in particular big business, is becoming progressive. Business has come a long way toward accepting and indeed actively promoting policies that would have seemed radical to most businessmen a few years or a decade ago. President Johnson is reaping, as I see it, what the late President Kennedy sowed. He can now safely come out against "conceptions of an earlier date that hamper rational action," while we all remember that the late President Kennedy's criticism of the "myths" was received coolly. The change is most noticeable in big business, but in a fairly disciplined way small business is coming along. This development can be authenticated from the opinion polls and from the systematic interviews carried out for business and other journals.

I leave it to my political science colleagues to study and explain this remarkable development, making only the single remark that an important factor has been the obvious effectiveness of policies pressed by the government during the last few years. The results of the present administration's unorthodox policies have turned out to be very beneficial for private business. Markets have been flourishing and profits have been growing. Business has, indeed, no reason to long for the previous era of relative economic stagnation.

Even the war against poverty is now seen as making sense to business. I would remind you that about a year ago, when President Johnson visited the National Manufacturers' Association, which we have not been accustomed to reckon among the more progressive organizations in America, he had the courage to speak about the war against poverty, and he was applauded. American businessmen, like government officials and some economists, are trained and accustomed to calculate in billions and to be prepared to wait for the returns on investments if they are high. They are beginning to see what a drag it has been on American prosperity and on their own profit rates that the United States, among the rich countries, has the highest unemployment rate, the biggest and most horrible slums, and the dirtiest subways, and that it is most niggardly with its old citizens, its sick, and especially its needy children, a very large part of the next generation's labor force.

To an extent this is, I would like to remind you, a return to tendencies in the twenties, when big business in the United

States was becoming more socially and economically progressive than its European peers. It was the Great Depression, with all its demoralizing effects, and then the conflict with President Roosevelt and the New Deal, which turned business opinion toward a reactionary mood. Since the war, there has been a steady trend in the other direction, and it is this trend that I now see speeding up.

It was big business that helped the politicians prepare public opinion for unbalancing the budget last year. It was big business that made it possible for the late President Kennedy to get Congress to pass the Trade Expansion Act, which nobody who knew America would have believed possible one year before. And I believe that we shall see big business take a leading part in the war against poverty. The change in business opinion is, in my opinion, one of the most significant trends in the United States, of particular consequence because of the extraordinary influence businessmen have in politics in this country. Potentially, it may be among the most important causes for allowing the rapid and steady economic growth in America that is the condition for success in the war against poverty.

30. Strategies in the War on Poverty

FRITZ MACHLUP

If I counted correctly, 33 speakers have preceded me on the platform at this conference. Some have spoken at the same time, in different rooms. Thus, if anybody in this audience has listened to as many as he could, he has heard what 15 experts had to say on the subject of poverty and poverty abolition in the United States. Coming at the tail end of this gabfest, I cannot reasonably be expected to say anything strikingly original. Indeed, the only way to be original at this conference would be to deny either the existence of poverty or the possibility of conquering it. Perhaps I was expected to do just that. When I received the invitation to make the concluding speech at this conference, I wondered why I was chosen for this spot. One of the hypotheses that occurred to me was that I was chosen because I have the reputation of being one of the few surviving individuals of an almost extinct species: an economist with value judgments firmly based on 19th century liberalism, or what most Americans now wrongly call "conservatism."

If this hunch is correct, and I *was* chosen as the anchor man because I might add a conservative counterpoint to a symphony of largely interventionist voices, I am afraid it will be only to a limited extent that I can satisfy the expectations behind that choice. For I do recognize that poverty exists in the United States. I do not believe that a policy of *laissez-faire* would eliminate it, and I favor certain government interventions to combat it. Perhaps, however, my old-fashioned liberalism will still show in some collateral judgments and proposals, and thus I will not let you down completely.

WHO IS POOR?

The question—"Who is Poor?"—calls for two different tasks: first, who is defined as poor, and second, who, on the basis of the chosen definition, are the types and kinds of people that compose the class regarded as the poor. The first question is one of convention or reasonable judgment; the second question calls for statistical fact-finding, for a descriptive inquiry, which may suggest some of the causes of poverty and perhaps also the directions of attacking it.

The definition of poverty is usually stated in terms of income and property available for meeting some "minimum" measure of consumption. An operational definition requires a numerical "poverty line" to be drawn, separating the poor from the non-poor. There are basically at least five ways of drawing such a line:

1. One might agree on a fixed consumption standard in terms of dollars of unchanged purchasing power; but if one had done this in a distant past, without later adjustments, poverty would have been eliminated several times over.
2. One might agree on a fixed place in the size distribution of income, for example, the lowest decile or quintile; but if this were done, poverty could never be eliminated or even reduced, for there will always be a lowest decile or quintile, no matter how well-off those in such positions may become.
3. One might agree on a standard, fixed as a percentage of the average or median income of the nation or community, for example, at one-third or one-half of the average or median; but in this case poverty could be reduced only if and as the earning power of the lowest-income recipients rose faster than that of the average or median earners—which we have no strong reason to expect. (Assume that the poor consist largely of aged or otherwise unemployable; why should their incomes increase at a faster rate than those of workers of average productivity?)
4. One might agree on a standard set at one time but rising annually at a rate fixed as a percentage of the rate of growth

of the average or median income of the nation or community; for example, the standard would be increased by one-half the rate at which national income per head had increased since the time of the original stipulation. (The relation of the relative uplift of the poverty standard to the relative growth of average income was called, by Theodore W. Schultz, the "society's income-elasticity of demand for services to the poor.")

5. One might agree periodically to adjust the standard of poor living to the standard of average living according to the social sentiment of the time, which could be more charitable or less charitable than it had been earlier but would most likely be increasingly generous; the upward adjustment of the poverty line would probably be between those indicated by methods 3 and 4.

Economic historians may find out what poverty lines were drawn or proposed at various times in various countries and compare them with estimates of average or median incomes (per family, household, or head) at these times and places. This might reveal some regularity in the relative differences between the poor and the average or median. (I understand that such a study has been made for New York City.) One should not expect, however, such regularity to be anything but rough, since the judgments about "subsistence levels" differ widely at any one time. For the United States today, some would reduce the poverty line to $2,000 per year for a family of four, others would raise it above the $3,000 proposed by the Council of Economic Advisers.

ONE-THIRD, ONE-EIGHTH, ONE-FIFTH

In the mid-1930's we used to speak of the ill-fed, ill-housed, and ill-clad, and we referred to them as the "underprivileged *third*." If the household budget that marked this poverty line had remained unchanged, merely being adjusted for the price changes of the last 30 years, we would be able to speak today only of the "underprivileged *eighth*." But we have adjusted the poverty line to a rising standard of living; as real national income per head increased, we have lifted the poverty line, if only by a smaller percentage. With the higher standard of poor living, we are invited—by the President's Council of Economic Advisers—to admit one-*fifth* of the household units to the class of the poor.

One may, of course, quarrel with the proposal of the $3,000 standard.[1] It fails to take account of the number of children in the family and, in concentrating on annual income, it disregards accumulated savings or property as well as the possibility of borrowing against future income. Of the $3,000 budget, regarded as the poverty line for a family, some $800 was taken to be the need for housing. Yet, 40 per cent of the poor households in 1962 had some equity in houses and therefore could meet part of their budget without drawing on current cash income. But I must stop haggling, lest you think I am a heartless reactionary.

War on Poverty

Only a relatively rich society can expect to wage a successful war against poverty. Where almost all the people are poor, the incomes of the few rich are not sufficient to alleviate poverty significantly by redistribution or to reduce poverty significantly through services raising the productivity of the poor.

In an affluent society, *redistributive, remedial,* and *preventive* measures are possible. Where as little as two or three per cent of the national income would suffice to supplement all low incomes and bring them up above the poverty line, poverty can undoubtedly be eliminated. This is especially easy to accomplish where society has been wasting financial and productive

---

[1] For a severe criticism of this standard, see Rose D. Friedman, *Poverty: Definition and Perspective* (Washington: American Enterprise Institute, 1965). Using the same general principles as were used in the studies on which the Council of Economic Advisers based the poverty line of $3,000, Mrs. Friedman computes a set of poverty lines, stating the "income levels at which households of different size achieve adequate nutrition" at 1962 prices. These are $1,295, $1,785, $2,195, $2,550, $2,855, and $3,155 for nonfarm households with 2, 3, 4, 5, 6, and 7 or more persons, respectively (p. 25). On this basis, only one-tenth of the households is poor. Yet, according to Mrs. Friedman, the difference "results neither from a different basic criterion of adequate nutrition nor from the use of different data. The high estimate by the Council results from the crudity of its analysis" (p. 46).

resources on useless programs and thus can achieve its purpose simply by putting good programs in the place of bad ones.

The United States is in this position and, hence, can win its war against poverty. We cannot, of course, do this in a *Blitzkrieg,* within a few weeks, but we can do it within a few years if we go about it in the right way.

Before one can reasonably examine the potential effectiveness of anti-poverty measures, one must examine the major characteristics of the poor. This has been done in several statistical studies, and we know now quite well that the chances of being poor are especially high for the aged, the disabled, the nonwhite, the uneducated, the families without male breadwinners, the Southern farmers. If a family suffers from several of these misfortunes at the same time—say, a family headed by an uneducated nonwhite farmer in the South—its chance of being poor becomes almost a certainty.

This does not mean that poverty can be eliminated in the shortest time if government tackles first the problem of those groups in which the incidence of poverty is highest. Assume, for example, a particular group in the country has an incidence of poverty of 75 per cent. To concentrate on this group may be called for on several grounds, but even the most effective measures can do little for the elimination of poverty in the nation if the particular group is very small. If this group represents, say, only 2 or 3 per cent of all the poor, complete elimination of poverty in that group would reduce poverty in the country by only 2 or 3 per cent. In the evaluation of a program to reduce poverty in the nation both criteria must therefore be observed: how high is the *incidence* of poverty in a group for which certain measures are designed, and how large is the *share* of that group in the entire population of the poor.

THREE MAIN PROBLEMS

If I may step back a little further from the statistical record presented by several investigators, I find it convenient to distinguish three main problems.

1. the problem of substandard earnings of employed persons;
2. the problem of unemployment of persons in the labor force; and
3. the problem of zero-earnings of persons not in the labor force.

This breakdown has the advantage of logical consistency: the member of the first group is in the labor force and has a job—but it pays too little; the member of the second group is in the labor force—but has no job; the member of the third group is not even in the labor force. This breakdown also helps us understand why some measures cannot solve all three problems. Higher unemployment benefits, for example, can help neither the first nor the third of these groups. Nor can full-employment policies help those who are permanently outside the labor force. (Let me mention that 39 per cent of all poor families in 1963 were headed by persons not in the labor force.) On the other hand, direct assistance to the poor, say, through cash payments, can help all three groups, although this may not be regarded as adequately remedial or preventive.

It may be useful to describe various types of measures that have been adopted or proposed to deal with poverty, that is, to relieve, to remedy, or to prevent poverty.

DISTINCTIONS

The usual distinction between *redistributive measures* and *measures increasing the earning power of the poor* misses some essential points. First of all, if the cost of measures to increase the earning power of the poor is paid by the rich, these measures are also redistributive; the difference singled out for attention is, evidently, whether the redistribution takes the form of transfer payments and / or relief in kind, supplementing the income earned by the poor, *or* of paying for actions that raise the market value produced, and hence the income earned, by the poor. Secondly, the usual distinction indiscriminately puts into the second category—raising the earning power—two economically different measures: those which really increase the *productive capacity* of the poor and those which merely raise, by subsidies or restrictions, the *market prices* of the products made with the labor of the poor. "Earning power" can be raised in both ways, but subsidies and other price supports must not be confused with increased efficiency.

To take account of these differences we should distinguish the following categories: (1) income supplements (relief, direct assistance), (2) income increases through indirect subsidies and restrictive and protective measures, (3) income increases through better use of the productive capacities of the people, (4) income increases through improvements of their productive capacities, and (5) income increases through measures to raise the aggregate demand for labor by means of general monetary expansion. Some of these categories should be further subdivided in order to bring out significant differences in approach. I believe that a catalogue of types of measures adopted or proposed in the war against poverty will help our discussion.

TYPES OF ADOPTED OR PROPOSED MEASURES AGAINST POVERTY

A. *Direct Assistance*

1. in kind—housing, food, clothing, medical care
2. in cash—
   - (a) for particular occupations
   - (b) for particular industries
   - (c) for particular age groups
   - (d) for disabled or handicapped persons
   - (e) for the "poor" regardless of group
   - (f) for low-income recipients without property (negative tax)

B. *Indirect Assistance through Subsidies or Protection to Particular Industries, Occupations, or Regions*

- (a) through price supports
- (b) through limitations of domestic competition (entry, minimum prices, etc.)
- (c) through limitations of foreign competition (tariffs, quotas, etc.)
- (d) through cash subsidies of various sorts

C. *Abolition of Discriminatory Exclusions from Jobs* (i.e., preventing discrimination on account of age, sex, race, color, nationality, ethnic origin, religion, and so forth)

D. *Abolition of Restrictive Laws and Practices Which Reduce Employment Opportunities* (especially for low-grade labor), including the abolition of
   1. (a) legal minimum wages
      (b) trade-union minimum wages
      (c) conventional minimum wages (employers' inhibitions)
   2. regressive employment taxes, pension contributions, and other deductions from wages
   3. restrictions of access to better jobs (direct barriers or wage contracts limiting the amount of labor demanded)

E. *Raising the Productivity of Low-Grade Labor* (both of poorly paid or of unemployed)
   1. Provision of complementary facilities (roads, factories in distress areas; loans to farmers and small business)
   2. Better job information, loans and assistance in moving
   3. Increasing skills (employability) through adult education, training, retraining

F. *Raising the Productivity of Future Recruits to the Labor Force*
   1. Family-planning assistance
   2. Prenatal and postnatal care
   3. Adding years of schooling (especially at ages 3 to 6)
   4. Preventing dropouts from school
   5. Accelerating and improving school programs
   6. Job corps for dropouts and high-school graduates
   7. Work experience for new entrants into the labor force
   8. Work-study programs in higher education
   9. Aid to education on all levels

G. *Increasing Aggregate Demand through Monetary Expansion*—especially
   1. Increased government spending
   2. Reduced taxes
   3. Increased credit availability to business and consumers

GENERAL APPRAISAL

Measures of types A and B in this catalogue are direct and indirect assistance; the measures of type B are likely to involve inefficiencies in the allocation of productive resources. Types C and D are measures which lead to a better use of available human resources, by making jobs available that do not exist at present (for example, jobs for unskilled, low-quality labor) and by making *better* jobs available to persons now forced to work below their productive capacity. Types E and F are measures designed to raise the productivity of our manpower—type E the productivity of persons now in the labor force, type F of persons joining the labor force in the future. Type G is not a specific measure against poverty, but rather a remedy in the nature of a cure-all. Let me note that many economists question its effectiveness in the long run, even if they recognize that it may work well for short periods. We shall have more to say about all seven strategies in the war on poverty.

There is only one way to appraise a program intelligently: to examine its benefits (to ask, especially, whether it is likely to achieve the results intended) and to examine its costs (both the directly measurable and those that are concealed as unintended and undesirable side-effects). If one of two measures which can achieve an intended result has more unintended, undesirable side-effects than the other, it ought to be rejected.

DIRECT ASSISTANCE

Measures of Type A, direct assistance to the poor, are, as a rule, the most immediately effective and involve the lowest cost—provided they are not discriminatory, and really go to the poor, not to others. This proviso is usually not satisfied in the case of *assistance in kind.* It is in the nature of housing programs, medical care programs, etc., that they are discriminatory and indiscriminate at the same time: discriminatory in the sense that they do not benefit all poor groups, and indiscriminate in the sense that they benefit many that are not poor and need no help. Some of the programs may degenerate into rackets.

Cash assistance can perhaps be more easily identified and controlled. But, if certain groups are politically powerful, they may attain favored positions at the expense of the rest, including the really poor. This is notorious in the case of assistance to particular industries, which always starts with appeals that the members of the industry are intolerably poor, but usually ends up with a rich flow of cash into well-lined pockets. As a prototype, we may refer to our farm program: it is true that many, perhaps most, of the 3,500,000 farmers in the United States are poor; but it is also true that 80 per cent of the direct and indirect assistance under that program goes to 1,000,000 farmers with an average income of almost $10,000 a year, and that only the remaining 20 per cent of the assistance goes to the 2,500,000 poorer farmers.

The only really efficient cash-assistance programs are the ones that help *only* the poor and help *all* the poor, regardless of industry and of occupation. Assistance for the poor farmer should be given, not because he is a farmer, but only because he is poor. For administrative reasons, the proposal of the "negative income tax" is probably the most efficient of all such programs. Just as we use the system of exemptions—$600 per person—to free families with low incomes from all income tax obligations, we may under the proposed system make persons whose income is farther below these exemptions eligible to receive payments from the Internal Revenue Service. They would receive checks from the Government just as those who have overpaid their income tax receive checks as refunds. Perhaps their asset holdings could be taken into account—because we may not wish that wealthy people whose annual income may be negative, counting losses from capital transactions, get a bonus—though the total amount of such negative tax payments to the wealthy may be negligible.

Indirect Assistance

Measures of Type B are ordinarily stupid or wicked, from the point of view of economic welfare, and are almost certainly wasteful. They cost the nation much more than they benefit those whom they favor and, since the beneficiaries include many nonpoor, the cost to the nation is a multiple of the benefit to the poor. Thus, if the producers and workers in any line of production, be it in agriculture or in the manufacturing of watch movements or bicycles, obtain an increase in their "earning power," this is achieved by making their products scarcer (more expensive) to domestic consumers and by using productive resources less efficiently than it would be possible. While virtually nothing good can be said about subsidization or protection to particular industries, the case for particular depressed geographic areas is not entirely open and shut. *Ex ante* some persuasive arguments in terms of deviations of social from private benefits and costs can be made for area development or rehabilitation—but *ex post* things usually look disappointing. Experience, on balance, has not been good.

ABOLISHING DISCRIMINATION

Type C measures would get high marks from this professor if their cost—in resources and in individual freedoms—is not excessive. Since the costs may be only temporary, but the benefits permanent, the net yield of a breakdown of discriminatory barriers may be very high. If the barriers can be removed by noncoercive measures, by using incentives rather than police force, even the temporary cost can be reduced. But one should also bear in mind that the cost of inaction or delayed action against discrimination may be high—indeed, terribly high—in resources, freedoms, and even in blood. Some well-meaning defenders of civil liberties in the battle for civil rights, and of personal freedoms in the battle for nondiscrimination, should note that it is wiser to hold one's nose and take distasteful medicine than to die in upholding the principle of nonintervention.

ABOLISHING RESTRAINTS ON JOB OPPORTUNITIES

In explaining my position regarding measures of Type D, I shall probably arouse the anger of many allies in the war against poverty, especially the noneconomists in the field of labor economics. For they often believe that restrictive laws and practices which set a floor under the wage rates of various categories of labor, especially under the pay for the lowest grades of labor, are measures against poverty. I submit that, on the contrary, the *abolition* of these restrictions would be among the effective measures in the war against poverty.

To explain this, I may resort to an analogy. Assume there are two types of coal of different caloric content; in a free market, high-calory coal will fetch a higher price, corresponding to the difference in technical efficiency. Assume now that, for reasons good or bad, a minimum price is fixed, raising the price for the poorer coal. The reduction of the price difference will undoubtedly reduce the demand for the low-grade coal, and some portion of the supply will remain unused. The chief beneficiaries will be the producers of the high-calory coal. Similarly, if there are two types of labor, wage differentials in a free labor market would reflect differences in productivity. If a minimum wage is fixed, raising the rate for the lower-grade labor, the wage differential is reduced, the demand for the low-grade labor decreases, and some portion of it remains unemployed. While those finding employment are paid better, the jobless earn nothing at all. Their potential product is lost to society and their potential earnings are lost to the poor.

Minimum wages, although demanded in the name of helping the poor, in effect create more unemployment and more poverty. Perhaps they can be regarded as examples of the notorious attitude of the well-to-do man who, facing a poor beggar at the door of his house, says to his butler: "He breaks my heart, throw him out!" In a more realistic interpretation, the minimum-wage constraint is an example of restraint of competition, since, in reducing the employability of low-grade workers, it shelters nonpoor workers against competition from poor workers.

My argument is not directed at legal minimum wages alone. Even if there were no such laws, and no trade union contracts either, there still might be minimum wages by social convention. Employers, ordinarily, prefer paying higher wages for higher-grade labor to employing low-grade labor at very low wages, because it is bad public relations to pay less than a "living wage." Businessmen do not want to be known as employers of labor at substandard pay. These inhibitions restrict employment of poor labor and thus contribute to unemployment and poverty. Society stands to gain by the disappearance of such inhibitions. If very low wages paid to poor labor leave these workers too poor, society can supplement their family earnings by means of a negative income tax. This is not a recommendation of subsidies paid to the employers of substandard labor, but only of income supplements paid to poor families. Subsidies would lead to inefficient uses of labor; moreover, where families include several wage earners, such subsidies might accrue to nonpoor families. Hence we conclude: income supplements to the poor—yes; subsidies to their employers—no.

The second item under D refers to regressive deductions from wages and regressive taxes on the employment of cheap labor. Social-security contributions, falling more heavily on low-paid labor than on well-paid labor, may be the unintended product of thoughtless legislators, but in any event they operate to reduce the earnings and the employment of poor workers. The abolition of such provisions in the laws would be a measure reducing poverty.

The third item under D is of greater significance. It refers to existing restrictions on the access to better-paid jobs, forcing many more workers to compete for jobs of lower grade than would be the case if more could be employed as skilled labor. The restrictions are of two sorts: (1) direct barriers through apprenticeship rules in various crafts, limited admission into trade unions, and similar exclusions, and (2) indirect barriers through wage contracts between unions and employers making labor costs so high that the amount of labor demanded is smaller than the amount of labor available.

Indirect barriers are rarely understood. Just as price-fixing businessmen often wrongly assume that the demand for their products is completely inelastic, so the wage-fixing trade-union officers believe that the number of jobs is "given," regardless of the cost of labor. This is a tragic error; in fact, practically every collective wage contract eliminates jobs. The workers thus excluded from better-paying employment are compelled to join less qualified workers in the market for jobs requiring lesser skills. If wage rates are similarly fixed for these jobs, increasing numbers of workers are pushed into markets for unskilled labor. The supply of labor in these markets is then far greater than it would be with unrestricted access to the better jobs.

It may be impossible to produce testable estimates of the number of jobs eliminated by restrictions of these sorts, but few trained economists will deny that the problem may be of serious magnitude. The responsibility for the reduction of job opportunities cannot even approximately be divided between a minimum wage setting an absolute floor for labor of any sort, and contractual wage rates for certain kinds of labor in particular industries. Given the latter, with the resulting reduction in the number of well-paying jobs, the minimum wage could be assigned most of the blame for unemployment. However, if none of the wages for higher grades of labor were fixed above competitive levels, and if, therefore, many more people could obtain better jobs and would not flood the market for low-grade labor, the employment-reducing effect of the minimum wage at the present level might be insignificant. A strong emphasis on the minimum wage as a cause of unemployment and poverty is justified only on the assumption that a successful attack on contractual wage fixing is probably out of the question.

A Digression on an Apparent Paradox

In my appraisal of various policies I endorsed the proposal of a negative income tax for the poor but condemned the adopted practice of setting minimum wages. The negative income tax, by providing "transfer incomes" to persons without earned incomes, would probably reduce the eagerness of some of these persons to seek or accept work. Is it not inconsistent to approve of a plan that would induce some people to remain idle, and to reject a widely approved device of preventing people from working for less than a "decent" rate of pay? Both these schemes reduce the total amount of work performed, and their different evaluation may look paradoxical.

The paradox is only apparent, for there is an essential difference between the two schemes. To offer a "social minimum" for no work is to increase the choices of some persons: the very lazy ones may prefer to enjoy leisure and collect the negative tax rather than work and earn an income. To forbid work for less than a "minimum wage" is to reduce the choices of some persons: the very unskilled ones might prefer to work for low wages rather than remain idle because payment of such wages is prohibited. In other words, the social minimum (the negative income tax) may increase voluntary leisure; the minimum wage increases involuntary idleness. Voluntary leisure is a "good," while forced idleness is an evil.

RAISING THE PRODUCTIVITY OF LABOR

Labor can be made more employable by lowering its price or by raising its productivity. There are essentially three ways of doing the latter: to give it better tools and facilities, to move it to places and occupations in which it can do better than where it is now, and to increase its physical and mental performance. The first of these types of measures involves investment in physical capital, the third, investment in "human capital." All investment, of course, is risky: the return is uncertain and it is easy to make mistakes.

The provision of complementary facilities in the form of highways, factories, and modern equipment by the government or with financial aid from the government is advocated especially for the development or rehabilitation of distress areas. We must keep in mind that capital is not abundant and greater allocations to one area imply smaller allocations to others. The only justification for such reshuffling is that the return, counting all benefits, is thereby increased. Advance calculations often contain serious fallacies and wrong estimates; and even where everything looks all right, the actual outcome is ordinarily far less favorable than what had been anticipated. This is not an argument against all regional investment programs, but a warning that many projects have been wasteful from their very conception and even more of them have been both wasteful and ineffective in their execution.

Whereas the record of programs of bringing productive facilities to areas of surplus labor has been discouraging, experience with programs of facilitating the movement of surplus labor to regions and occupations where it can be more efficiently employed has been good. Better information about job opportunities is a prerequisite for the improved use of labor, and the provision of loans or other assistance in moving may be necessary if the information is to be used to full advantage.

Investment in human capital in the form of improved skills may pay off handsomely if the right techniques are used. The proposed programs under this heading emphasize training, retraining, and general adult education. Some programs, providing specialized vocational training, have been quite ineffective because they trained people for nonexisting jobs. Other programs, for example, improving the reading and writing abilities of quasi-illiterates, have had very good results. By and large, the enthusiasm with which some local and national programs have been launched merits approval and ought not to be doused with excessive skepticism.

Raising the Productivity of Future Workers

Programs designed to raise the productivity of *present* members of the labor force who are unemployable at the minimum wage or whose earning capacity is too low to put them above the poverty line, are *remedial* strategies in the war on poverty. In contrast, programs designed to raise the productivity of *future* recruits to the labor force are *preventive.* Viewed as investment in human capital, these programs are more long-term in character, but their return is not for that matter more uncertain. The point is, rather, that the flow of income produced by retraining a person of age 40 or so is surely of shorter duration than the flow of income produced by improved education of the young. To raise the lifetime earnings of future members of the labor force is an opportunity for a social investment with a high yield.

This does not mean that all projects under this heading are equally promising. The most meritorious seem to be (1) family-planning assistance, (2) prenatal and postnatal care, and (3) schooling for children at ages 3 to 5.

The incidence of poverty is very high among large families, especially if the poverty line is redrawn to take account of nutritive adequacy. Since children in oversized families are more likely to be undernourished and undereducated, planned parenthood, in avoiding excessive numbers of neglected children, can reduce the percentage of substandard members in the labor force of the future.

Mental retardation is responsible for a large share of the number of those whose earning power is small or nil. Prenatal and postnatal care can do much to reduce the incidence of mental deficiency.

Adding a few years of schooling has been proposed by many as a measure for raising the productivity of the next generation. Many school reformers, however, propose to add the years at the wrong end, at ages 15 to 18 instead of 3 to 6. Schooling ought to be provided at the earliest age, when systematic mental stimulation can still do something to increase the capacity of the mind. Children thus prepared will be able to absorb much more of what they are taught later.

Programs to prevent dropouts from school are rather useless under the present system. Many of those who leave school at ages 15 or 16, insufficiently prepared for work, would not be much better prepared if forced or persuaded to stay in school for another two or three years. They will only be bored, resentful, hateful, rebellious against a society that keeps them against their will from a more active, more useful life. As Michael Harrington said yesterday, these dropouts know that school cannot do anything for them any more and they have enough sense to get out. It is a shame that so many virtuous educators and educationalists do not have enough sense to know how little they can help the would-be dropout by chaining him to the school bench. If schooling started at ages 3 or 4, there would be fewer wanting to quit school at age 14 or 15, and those who quit would be better prepared than if they stayed in school until 18 under the present system.

Acceleration and other improvements of school programs rank high in my list of promising measures. I said "acceleration and *other* improvements," because I contend that acceleration is *per se* one of the most potent improvements of education. Compression of the curriculum, requiring more concentrated learning, develops better working habits as well as better-trained minds. Perhaps I may refer you to my book on *The Production and Distribution of Knowledge in the United States,* in which I argued this case.

I am inclined to endorse the plans for "job corps" for dropouts and high-school graduates, and the plans to provide work experience for new entrants into the labor force. We do not know yet whether the hopes of the proponents will be fulfilled, at least in part, but again these are projects attractive to people inspired by a will to help others without taking excessive amounts of public funds. I am sympathetic with the enthusiasm that fills the job corps workers, and I want them to succeed.

All in all, I regard measures to raise the productivity of future recruits to the labor force as promising strategies in the war on poverty.

Increasing Aggregate Demand

Some very excellent economists argue that the most powerful policy against poverty is to create enough "effective demand" to secure "full employment" and a faster growth rate. Increased aggregate demand for goods and services is easily translated into demand for more labor of all sorts, and this means more employment as well as higher earnings of the employed.

Advocates of more spending by private business and consumers favor either a monetary policy of increasing the availability of credit or a fiscal policy of tax reduction. Advocates of more spending by government favor a fiscal policy of enlarged budgets. Opponents of the strategy of "spending one's way out of unemployment and poverty" are suspicious of a tendency to regard the creation of effective demand as a cure-all and fearful of possible inflationary effects, and sometimes also neurotically fearful of the increase in the public debt.

Real deficiencies in effective demand undoubtedly call for compensatory increases in spending. Such deficiencies may be viewed as absolute reductions in total spending or as reductions relative to the size of the labor force (or, alternatively, total population). It has become fashionable, however, to diagnose all lapses from full employment as demand deficiency and / or to prescribe demand creation as the therapy for every case of unemployment. Many of those who quarrel about whether, or to what extent, unemployment is due to "structural causes" or to "demand deficiency" overlook that structural unemployment may be cured by demand creation and that demand deficiency may be offset by structural adjustments. (The demand for labor, as for anything else, is elastic with respect to changes in both relative prices and aggregate income.) The more reasonable participants in the controversy, however, do not deny either the existence of "structural causes" of unemployment or the possibility of reducing unemployment through "structural adjustments," but they hold that reductions in wage rates cannot be arranged whereas increases in spending can be arranged quite easily. This is a straightforward policy recommendation without a cloak of pseudo-scientific analysis.

Some want to rely on demand creation as the sole strategy in the war on poverty. Professor Harry Johnson is a protagonist of this view:

> The key to the solution of the poverty problem . . . is not to try to educate and train the poor up to the point where someone will find them employable at a decent wage, but to raise demand so as to make labor scarce enough for it to be privately profitable to find a way of making the poor employable at a decent wage.
>
> But in the absence of a policy of raising the demand for labor to the stretching point, ad hoc policies for remedying poverty by piecemeal assaults on particular poverty-associated characteristics are likely to prove both ineffective and expensive.

This position is objectionable on several grounds:

1. Increases in the demand for labor "to the stretching point" will cause continuous increases in wage rates; employment will increase only as long as wage rates lag behind the increase in spending; but in advanced industrial countries this lag may become very short, zero, or even negative (in the sense that wages will rise faster than demand).

2. Even before the policy of monetary expansion becomes ineffective in reducing unemployment, political forces are likely to lead to its discontinuance, with the result that unemployment

will vary "cyclically" without being reduced in the long run.

3. The increase in consumer prices effected by the creation of monetary demand for goods and services will reduce the purchasing power of the dollar and make the low incomes of the poor still less adequate.

4. Even if the policy of creating effective demand were to succeed in more than temporary increases in the rate of employment and in continual increases in the real incomes of the employed, it still could not be the sole weapon in combating poverty. For it would do nothing to relieve the poverty of families with no member in the labor force—and this means 39 per cent of all poor families. (As a matter of fact, higher consumer prices would make them still poorer.)

On the fourth point, a qualification is called for regarding persons who are outside the labor force only because they have given up hope of finding employment, but would rejoin the labor force when jobs became easier to find. This possibility would not exist for the disabled, the aged, the women with small children, and hence the qualification may be relatively insignificant.

If I reject full-employment policy through demand creation as the sole anti-poverty measure, this should not stigmatize me as a "deflationist." I have no doubt that the fiscal and monetary policies of the United States were unduly restrictive at times and that more expansionary policies during these periods would have helped to reduce poverty.

No Single Strategy

The conclusion of my evaluation of policies is clear: the war on poverty cannot be won with a single strategy but must be fought on several fronts and with several strategies. Some of the policies adopted are actually harmful and ought to be abolished; some of the policies proposed but never tried look quite promising and ought to be adopted; and some of the policies initiated may prove useful and ought to be continued.

The war on poverty is of course not without cost, and all measures should be subjected to judicious cost-benefit analyses.

In such analyses a strict distinction must be made between the adoption of a new project *in lieu* of an existing one and the adoption of a new project *on top* of the existing ones. There may be a huge difference in the respective findings, since the substitution of a better project for a weak one may have a great payoff, whereas the addition of even an excellent project to all existing ones may run into the difficulties of rapidly increasing costs. Since among the existing programs there are some rather ineffectual ones with high costs and low benefits, new projects in lieu of others stand a chance for a high mark in even a very strict examination. Some of the programs proposed in the war on poverty may have a net yield for the nation of really spectacular magnitude *if* their adoption can be linked with the abolition of some of the existing programs of support and protection for particular groups.